IFIP Advances in Information and Communication Technology 651

IFIP – The International Federation for Information Processing

IFIP was founded in 1960 under the auspices of UNESCO, following the first World Computer Congress held in Paris the previous year. A federation for societies working in information processing, IFIP's aim is two-fold: to support information processing in the countries of its members and to encourage technology transfer to developing nations. As its mission statement clearly states:

> *IFIP is the global non-profit federation of societies of ICT professionals that aims at achieving a worldwide professional and socially responsible development and application of information and communication technologies.*

IFIP is a non-profit-making organization, run almost solely by 2500 volunteers. It operates through a number of technical committees and working groups, which organize events and publications. IFIP's events range from large international open conferences to working conferences and local seminars.

The flagship event is the IFIP World Computer Congress, at which both invited and contributed papers are presented. Contributed papers are rigorously refereed and the rejection rate is high.

As with the Congress, participation in the open conferences is open to all and papers may be invited or submitted. Again, submitted papers are stringently refereed.

The working conferences are structured differently. They are usually run by a working group and attendance is generally smaller and occasionally by invitation only. Their purpose is to create an atmosphere conducive to innovation and development. Refereeing is also rigorous and papers are subjected to extensive group discussion.

Publications arising from IFIP events vary. The papers presented at the IFIP World Computer Congress and at open conferences are published as conference proceedings, while the results of the working conferences are often published as collections of selected and edited papers.

IFIP distinguishes three types of institutional membership: Country Representative Members, Members at Large, and Associate Members. The type of organization that can apply for membership is a wide variety and includes national or international societies of individual computer scientists/ICT professionals, associations or federations of such societies, government institutions/government related organizations, national or international research institutes or consortia, universities, academies of sciences, companies, national or international associations or federations of companies.

More information about this series at https://link.springer.com/bookseries/6102

Erich J. Neuhold · Xavier Fernando ·
Joan Lu · Selwyn Piramuthu ·
Aravindan Chandrabose (Eds.)

Computer, Communication, and Signal Processing

6th IFIP TC 5 International Conference, ICCCSP 2022
Chennai, India, February 24–25, 2022
Revised Selected Papers

Editors
Erich J. Neuhold
University of Vienna
Vienna, Austria

Joan Lu
University of Huddersfield
Huddersfield, UK

Aravindan Chandrabose
SSN College of Engineering
Kalavakkam, India

Xavier Fernando
Ryerson University
Toronto, ON, Canada

Selwyn Piramuthu
University of Florida
Gainesville, FL, USA

ISSN 1868-4238 ISSN 1868-422X (electronic)
IFIP Advances in Information and Communication Technology
ISBN 978-3-031-11635-3 ISBN 978-3-031-11633-9 (eBook)
https://doi.org/10.1007/978-3-031-11633-9

This Springer imprint is published by the registered company Springer Nature Switzerland AG
The registered company address is: Gewerbestrasse 11, 6330 Cham, Switzerland

Preface

The Department of Information Technology is glad to present the proceedings of the IFIP 6th International Conference on Computer, Communication and Signal Processing (ICCCSP 2022) which was held at Sri Sivasubramaniya Nadar College of Engineering (SSN), Kalavakkam, India, during February 24–25, 2022. The conference was organized by the Department of Information Technology and was supported by the Machine Learning Research Group (MLRG) of SSN along with the Speech and Image Processing and Internet of Things (IoT) research groups of the department.

ICCCSP 2022 highlighted the rapidly developing technologies related to artificial intelligence (AI) and cyber security. The conference acted as a premier interdisciplinary platform for researchers, practitioners, and educators to present and discuss the most recent innovations, trends, concerns, and solutions adopted in these fields.

The conference received 111 paper submissions through the EasyChair conference management system from authors across India and various other countries, including the USA, Malaysia, Singapore, Dubai, Bangladesh, and Sri Lanka. With tremendous support from 100 experts in the fields of data science and cyber security the papers were scrutinized. Each submission was comprehensively reviewed by at least three reviewers, and their comments were communicated to the authors before the conference. The Program Committee accepted the top 25% of submissions, with contributions coming from globally recognized universities, such as the National University of Singapore, the University of Texas, and Oakland University, research labs at Accenture and Cognizant, national research labs such as the National Informatics Centre, India, and SAMEER-CEM, India, and other universities such as CEG and VIT. All 23 presented papers were again reviewed by the session chairs and their comments were communicated to the authors to allow for revisions prior to publication. The final submissions were checked by the Program Committee to ensure that all the comments had been addressed.

ICCCSP 2022 started with a series of three parallel workshops on February 23, 2022, on the topics of Text analysis and Information Extraction and Retrieval (TIER 2022), Microservices and Internet of Things (MIoT), and Trends in Deep Learning for Speech, Image, and Video Processing (SIVP). The workshops had international and national speakers from industry and academia to share their expertise with 120+ researchers and students across the country. TIER 2022 was the 6th workshop in this series conducted by the Machine Learning Research Group of SSN. It had 28 participants and the sessions were handled by M. Anand Kumar, NITK Suratkal, India, and Kamal Raj, Saama Technologies, India. A hands-on session on BERT models for Indian languages was delivered by D. Thenmozhi and B. Senthil Kumar of SSN. The MIoT workshop was conducted by the IoT research group of the Department of Information Technology, SSN, and had 28 participants. The sessions with demonstrations were presented by Sripaul C. Asokan, PayPal, USA, Nakeeran Annamalai, Chewy, Inc., USA, and R. Vinob Chander, SSN, India. The SIVP workshop was supported by the Speech and Image Processing research group of the Department of Information Technology, SSN. The workshop had 74 active participants who were engaged by Ashwin Shanmugam, Mitsubishi Electric Research Laboratories, USA, V. Masilamani, IIIT DM Kancheepuram, India, and Subham Tiwari, Tech Mahindra, India.

The conference was inaugurated on February 24, 2022, amidst the presence of Kala Vijayakumar, President of SSN Institutions, Bhavani Thuraisingham from the University of Texas at Dallas, as the guest of honour, and V. E. Annamalai, Principal of SSN Institutions, along with the Head of the Department of Information Technology, faculty members, participants of the conference, research scholars, and students of SSN. This was followed by the keynote lecture of Bhavani Thuraisingham from the University of Texas at Dallas, USA, who addressed "Integrating Cyber Security and Data Science/Machine Learning with Applications in the Internet of Transportation and Healthcare". The second keynote was delivered by Sethumadhavan from Amrita University, India, on "Crypto Vulnerabilities". On February 25, 2022, the second day of conference, Naveena Yanamala, an Associate Professor at Rutgers University and Adjunct Professor at Carnegie Mellon University, USA, delivered her keynote lecture on "Mirroring AI for IA - Intellect Augmentation that Enhances Human Lives".

The papers were presented under three tracks, namely, AI and ML, cyber security, and IoT. The sessions were chaired by eminent experts from NITK Surathkal, NIT Trichy, the cyber security industry, and Pondicherry Technological University, along with the domain experts from SSN research groups.

This volume is a collection of the 23 papers accepted for ICCCSP 2022 reflecting the revisions suggested during the presentation session. We hope that every research work showcases an insightful approach and solution for the problem discussed in the paper, amalgamating AI and cyber security. We sincerely thank the International Federation of Information Processing (IFIP) for accepting the conference proposal and supporting in various avenues. We extend our gratitude to Springer for publishing the proceedings and presenting these papers to the global research community.

We take this opportunity to thank and acknowledge the financial support provided by SSN Institutions. We also extend our appreciation to all the Program Committee members, reviewers, session chairs, Organizing Committee members, and the participants for their contributions towards the success of the conference.

June 2022

Aravindan Chandrabose
Erich J. Neuhold
Xavier Fernando
Joan Lu
Selwyn Piramuthu

Organization

General Chair

Aravindan Chandrabose	Sri Sivasubramaniya Nadar College of Engineering, India

Program Committee Chairs

Erich J. Neuhold	University of Vienna, Austria
Xavier Fernando	Ryerson Communications Lab, Canada
Joan Lu	University of Huddersfield, UK
Selwyn Piramuthu	University of Florida, USA

Steering Committee

G. Kulanthaivel	National Institute for Technical Teachers Training and Research, Chennai, India
V. Mahendran	Indian Institute of Technology, Tirupati, India
Chandrasekar Vuppalapati	San Jose State University, USA
Sheila Anand	Rajalakshmi Engineering College, India
Vijayalakshmi	Central University of Tamil Nadu, India
Saravanan Chandran	National Institute of Technology, Durgapur, India
S. Nickolas	National Institute of Technology, Tiruchirappalli, India
S. S. Sridhar	SRM Institute of Science and Technology, India
S. Bose	CEG, Anna University, India
Harish Ramani	Tevel Cyber Corps Private Limited, India
M. Saravanan	Ericsson Research, India
R. Srinivasan	Sri Sivasubramaniya Nadar College of Engineering, India
A. Shahina	Sri Sivasubramaniya Nadar College of Engineering, India

Program Committee

Danilo Pelusi	Teramo University, Italy
Michael S. Packianather	Cardiff University, UK
Xiao-Zhi Gao	University of Eastern Finland, Finland
Bhalaji N.	Sri Sivasubramaniya Nadar College of Engineering, India
Chithra S.	Sri Sivasubramaniya Nadar College of Engineering, India
Karthika S.	Sri Sivasubramaniya Nadar College of Engineering, India

Additional Reviewers

Amudha R.
Amutha B.
Annie Uthra
Arulkumar Venkatachalam
Arun S.
Ashok Kumar Mohan
Ashwinth Janarthanan
Asnath Victy Phamila Y.
Aswani Kumar Cherukuri
Balasubramanian Viswanathan
Balasundaram Prabavathy
Bharathi B.
Bharathi Varadharajulu
Bhuvana Jayaraman
Bose S.
Chandra Mouli P. V. S. S. R.
Chandrakala S.
Durga G.
Ganeshkumar S.
Gayathri K. S.
Geetha R.
Gulam Alsath
Harish Ramani
Hemalatha R.
Jino Hans W.
Joe Louis Paul I.
Kabilan Kadhirvelu
Kalaivani Kathirvelu
Karthikeyan Anbu
Kavitha Srinivasan
Kulandai Josephine Julina J.
Mahendran V.
Mahesh Veezhinathan
Malathy C.
Mohanavalli S.
Nagappan Govindarajan
Nagappan N.
Neelanarayanan Venkataraman
Neeymullah Khan A.
Nickolas Savarimuthu
Parthiban Natarajan
Poornima S.
Poovammal E.
Prakash M.
Prasanna J.
Priyadharsini Ravisankar
Pushpalatha M.
R. Vinob Chander
Rajavel Ramadoss
Rajeswari Sridhar
Rajkumar R.
Ramachandran B.
Sandanakaruppan Ammavasai
Sangeetha M.
Santhi Natarajan
Saranya S.
Sarath Chandran K. R.
Saravanakumar N. M.
Saravanan Chandran
Sasirekha S.
Selvakumar K.
Shahina A.
Shanmuga Priya T.
Sheeba J.
Sheela T.
Sivabalakrishnan M.
Sivakumar B.
Sivamuragan V.
Sofia Jennifer J.
Sree Sharmila T.
Sreedevi B.
Sridevi M.
Sridhar S.
Sridhar S. S.
Srinivasan R.
Sujaudeen N.
Sundharakumar K. B.
Suthanthira Devi P.
Swathika Rengasamy
Syed Ibrahim S. P.
Thanikachalam V.
Thenmozhi D.
Ushadevi G.
Uthayan K. R.

Vallidevi Krishnamurthy
Vasuki P.
Venkatesan S.
Venugopal Padmanabhan
Vijayakumar V.
Vijayalakshmi C.
Vishnuraja P.
Yugha Ramasamy

Sponsor

Contents

Artificial Intelligence and Machine Learning

Artificial Intelligence and Machine Learning

Malayalam Language Textual Inference Identification Through Attention over Embeddings

Sara Renjit[1(✉)] and Sumam Mary Idicula[2]

[1] Department of Computer Science, Cochin University of Science and Technology, Kochi, India
sararenjit.g@gmail.com

[2] Department of Computer Science, Muthoot Institute of Technology and Science, Ernakulam, India

Abstract. This work focus on natural language inference between two text fragments, which is a uni-directional relationship. Natural language inference is attempted for a language called Malayalam. The Malayalam language is a South Indian, low-resource language. NLI is a subtask in every language because of its importance in summarization, information retrieval, and many other applications. There are only a few attempts in NLI for the Malayalam language. In this work, the application of the attention mechanism helped to enhance the classification performance for binary and multiclass systems. A densenet with additive attention is implemented for softmax and sigmoid classification, increasing accuracy, recall, and F1-score.

Keywords: Natural language inference · Malayalam · Attention

1 Introduction

A directional relationship between sentence pairs is known as textual entailment. Natural language inference is another term used commonly now for recognizing textual entailment. Recognizing textual entailment is one of the two types of textual entailment, where the idea is to identify the entailments in text. Another type of textual entailment is generating textual entailment, where the entailed sentence is generated from a text.

Text (T) and hypothesis (H) are sentences or text fragments, where text T entails hypothesis H if the meaning of hypothesis can be inferred from the meaning of the text. Text contradicts with hypothesis if the meaning of text and hypothesis is opposite. The hypothesis is neutral with text if the meaning of the hypothesis cannot be inferred/ remains neutral with the meaning of the text.

Textual entailment has its definition in different senses. Most classically, it is defined as the text entails hypothesis, if the hypothesis is valid in all possible circumstances in which text is true. In a more applied sense, text entails a

Published by Springer Nature Switzerland AG 2022
E. J. Neuhold et al. (Eds.): ICCCSP 2022, IFIP AICT 651, pp. 3–11, 2022.
https://doi.org/10.1007/978-3-031-11633-9_1

hypothesis if the hypothesis is true when a human reads it. Mathematically, entailment is defined as the probability of the hypothesis being true with respect to text is greater than the likelihood of hypothesis as true [7].

NLI is a binary classification task identifying entailment and contradiction classes. It can also be a multiclass classification with entailment, neutral, and contradiction classes. Identifying these distinct classes for sentence pairs is vital for many language processing applications. In multi-document summarization, redundant sentences can be removed. In information retrieval, it helps in the faster retrieval of entailed sentences. In question answering systems, it helps in the efficient retrieval of answers for query input. NLI is also considered as an evaluation task for various sentence models and transformer models.

The contribution of this work is the application of the attention mechanism over a dense net with LASER sentence representation. We have obtained a performance improvement on the best so far results with additive attention applied. The subsequent sections include related works in Sect. 2. Dataset information is in Sect. 3. Section 4 details the proposed system, and Sect. 5 details the experimental evaluations. Section 6 discusses the results and their observations, and Sect. 7 concludes the work.

2 Background

Textual entailment started as a challenge in 2005 for the English language to develop systems that can identify similar meanings between text fragments. This challenge continued in the following years by the name RTE-1, RTE-2, RTE-3, RTE-4, RTE-5 with different sized datasets in the order of 1k sentence fragments. The approaches used with the RTE dataset classification are mainly cross pair similarity, word and phrase alignments, dependency tree-based transformation, logical inference, ontology-based learning, and machine learning algorithms like Support Vector Machines (SVM) [5].

Table 1. RTE challenges [6]

RTE	T-H pairs	Features
1	287	Mostly lexical systems
2	800	Question answering domain
3	800	Longer sentences
4	1000	3-way tasks
5	600	Unedited real world texts
6	15955	221 hypothesis
7	21,420	Paragraph long texts

Since the inception of the RTE challenge in 2005, there have been numerous attempts for RTE in English and other languages like French, German, and Italian. The evolution of RTE challenges is described in Table 1. Recognizing textual entailment is now known by the term natural language inference. Later in 2015, the Stanford Natural Language Inference dataset [3] was introduced, which is a large dataset of size 570k sentence pairs collected through Amazon mechanical trunk. With this dataset, deep learning techniques are also used for RTE tasks. Sum of words, RNN, and LSTM based embeddings are used to obtain the sentence representations for classification.

MNLI (Multi-genre natural language inference dataset) [13] and XNLI (cross-lingual natural language) [4] datasets are newer versions of NLI dataset. MNLI has sentences derived from multiple genres like face-to-face, letters, telephone, government, slate. XNLI is a cross-lingual dataset derived from MNLI by automatic translations to 15 languages.

With the XNLI dataset, identifying entailments in the text is attempted in other languages like French, German, Japanese, Italian, Spanish, Hindi, and low resource languages like Swahili and Urdu. Different approaches using LSTM (Long Short Term Memory networks), BiLSTMs, GRU, XLM-R, and transformers are used. [9] gives an overview of the deep learning approaches used for textual entailment with sentence encoding models, match encoding models, tree-based CNN models, and other hybrid models.

Some of the existing works for textual entailment approaches include generating inferences from texts using residual LSTM [8], recognizing entailments using word by word neural attention [11], using sentence embeddings and decomposable attention model for Japanese language [12]. Textual entailment in languages other than English is also attempted by automatic translation into English and using the best approaches for English language [10].

For the Malayalam language in the context of this work, there are very few works for entailment. The MaNLI (Malayalam Natural Language Inference) dataset is introduced, which are translated pairs from the SNLI dataset. In their work, language agnostic sentence representation (LASER) based embedding encodes the sentence pairs, which are then classified through a dense net with Softmax or sigmoid classifier. They have obtained an accuracy of 64% for multiclass and 77% for binary classification.

3 Dataset

In this work, the MaNLI (Malayalam Natural Language Inference) dataset is used, created through the human and google translations of text hypothesis pairs from the SNLI (Stanford Natural Language Inference) dataset. The linguistic corrections and semantic consistency are manually verified by linguists from the Thunchath Ezhuthachan Malayalam University, Kerala.

The dataset consists of 12k pairs of text hypothesis sentence pairs labeled as entailment, contradictory and neutral. The same dataset as binary classes has 7989 pairs of sentences with classes entailment and contradiction. The statistics of the dataset are given in Table 2.

A sample from the Malayalam language dataset and its English translations is in Figure 1 and Table 3 respectively.

Table 2. MaNLI dataset

Classes	No of sentence pairs
Entailment	4026
Contradiction	3963
Neutral	4011

Text	Hypothesis	Label
രണ്ട് ആളുകൾ സൈക്കിളിൽ മത്സര ഓട്ടം നടത്തുന്നു.	ആളുകൾ സൈക്കിളിൽ സഞ്ചരിക്കുന്നു.	entailment
രണ്ട് ആളുകൾ സൈക്കിളിൽ മത്സര ഓട്ടം നടത്തുന്നു.	ആളുകൾ തെരുവിൽ സൈക്കിളിൽ സഞ്ചരിക്കുന്നു.	neutral
രണ്ട് ആളുകൾ സൈക്കിളിൽ മത്സര ഓട്ടം നടത്തുന്നു.	കുറച്ച് ആളുകൾ മീൻ പിടിക്കുന്നു.	contradiction

Fig. 1. Sample from the MaNLI dataset

4 Proposed System

Natural language inference is regarded as a two-way (binary) and three-way (multiclass) classification task. The design of the system implemented is shown in Fig. 2. The input sentences, namely text, and hypothesis are embedded using LASER. LASER embedding based representations are fed to the dense net with relu activations, and then attention is applied and fed to the final dense layer with sigmoid/ softmax activations to obtain probability distributions to each class.

The proposed system for this classification consist of the following modules: **LASER embeddings for sentence representation**: Language agnostic sentence representations [1] are used for representing text and hypothesis pairs in a meaningful numerical format. It is an encoder-decoder architecture where the input words are encoded using byte pair encoding and trained on parallel corpora. Sentence embeddings are obtained by max-pooling over the BiLSTM layer. In the previous work, LASER representation showed higher performance as compared to other representations namely, Doc2Vec, mBERT and fastText. This work improves the LASER representation based classifier with the application of attention.

Dense Layers: The attention outputs are then passed through feed forward network consisting of multiple dense layers. Dense layers are deeply connected layers that apply the activation function on the summation of weighted input (WX) with bias (B),(WX+B), where W is the weight matrix, and X is the input.

Additive Attention: Additive attention [2] computes attention score using the tanh activation on a feed forward layer for attention alignment (Eq. 1).

Table 3. Sample dataset in English (SNLI [3])

Text	Hypothesis	Label
Two men on bicycles competing in a race	People are riding bikes	entailment
	Men are riding bicycles on the street	neutral
	A few people are catching fish	contradiction

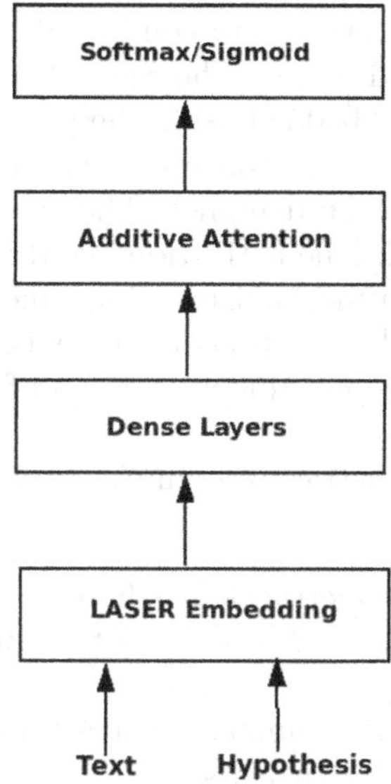

Fig. 2. System design

Softmax operation is applied to the attention score and attention weights are obtained (Eq. 2). These weights are probabilities that indicate the importance of words in a sequence. Finally context vector is derived as weighted sum of previous hidden representation (Eq. 3).

$$e_{t,i} = tanh(W[h_i; s_{t-1}]), \tag{1}$$

where $e_{t,i}$ is the attention score, h_i is the hidden representation and s_{t-1} is the previous state.

$$\alpha_{t,i} = softmax(e_{t,i}) \tag{2}$$

where $\alpha_{t,i}$ is the attention weight.

$$c_t = \sum_{i=1}^{T} \alpha_{t,i} h_i \tag{3}$$

where c_t is the context vector.

Softmax/Sigmoid: Softmax activation is used in the final dense layer to predict probability distribution for classification into three classes, namely entailment, contradiction, and neutral. Sigmoid activation is used to classify the input into two classes, entailment, and contradiction for binary classification.

5 Experiments and Evaluation

Experiments: The implementations are conducted in Google Colab and using Python3 with Tensorflow and Keras. The Spyder environment is also used for training. The sentences are embedded using the pretrained LASER model. Text and hypothesis representations are concatenated with their difference and dot product before it is input to the densenet. The dense layers have neuron configurations of 4096X512X384. The activations used in hidden layers is rectified leaky unit (ReLu). Attention mechanism is implemented using the dense layer with tanh activation followed by softmax of the output. This softmax output is then multiplied with the previous hidden state and fed to the final dense layer.

Evaluation: The evaluation metrics used in this classification are accuracy, precision, recall, and F1-score.

- Accuracy is defined as the metric that defines the performance of the model across all classes. Accuracy = No of correct predictions/Total no of predictions.
- Precision (P) is defined as the number of correct predictions for a class divided by the total predictions for that class.
- Recall (R) is the number of correct predictions for a class divided by all relevant samples for that class.
- F1-score (F1) measures the precision of the classifier. It is the harmonic mean of precision and recall.
- Support (S) is the number of the actual occurrence of each class in the dataset.

Table 4 shows the results for binary classification. Table 5 shows the results obtained for multiclass classification.

Table 4. Classification report for binary classification

Class	Precision	Recall	F1-score	Support
Contradiction	0.84	0.72	0.78	798
Entailment	0.76	0.86	0.81	800
Accuracy			0.79	1598
Macro average	0.80	0.79	0.79	1598
Weighted average	0.80	0.79	0.79	1598

Table 5. Classification report for multiclass classification

Class	Precision	Recall	F1-score	Support
Contradiction	0.65	0.63	0.64	1651
Entailment	0.71	0.68	0.70	1682
Neutral	0.59	0.63	0.61	1667
Accuracy			0.65	5000
Macro average	0.65	0.65	0.65	5000
Weighted average	0.65	0.65	0.65	5000

6 Results and Observations

Table 6 shows the comparison of weighted average precision, recall and F1-scores. An improvement in recall F1-measure is obtained with attention. Table 7 gives accuracy based comparison with the previous LASER based system. Attentive context vector in the final representation also helped in increasing accuracy measures.

Table 6. Weighted average precision, recall and F1-score comparison of LASER embedding based classification with and without attention

LASER model	Class	Precision	Recall	F1-score
Densenet	Binary	0.79	0.77	0.77
	Multiclass	0.65	0.64	0.64
Densenet + Attention	Binary	0.80	0.79	0.79
	Multiclass	0.65	0.65	0.65

Table 7. Accuracy of models with and without attention for binary and multiclass classification

Method	Binary	Multiclass
LASER+Densenet	0.77	0.64
LASER + Densenet + **Attention**	**0.79**	**0.65**

The application of attention mechanism better classifies the text hypothesis pairs with improved scores. This highlights that sentence representation is improved through attentive context vector representation.

The semantic content differs between sentence pairs, and generalizations are difficult in this type of dataset. Also, the dataset has a dynamic nature representing different factual information and inherit properties of the language such as inflectional nature, agglutination, word compounding, multiple words having similar meanings. These distinct properties make the dataset and its classification a challenging task, and hence these are few factors that affect the performance.

7 Conclusion

This work has been an attempt to improve the existing performance of textual entailment for Malayalam language using attention mechanism. Attentive sentence representations through multiple layers in the existing LASER based dense-net system gained an improvement in accuracy and other classification metrics. This is also an application and understanding of the performance of attention in NLI context for a Dravidian language like Malayalam. The semantic context variability and neutral category data are challenging elements in the dataset, on which attention has improved the performance.

References

1. Artetxe, M., Schwenk, H.: Massively multilingual sentence embeddings for zero-shot cross-lingual transfer and beyond. Trans. Assoc. Comput. Linguist. **7**, 597–610 (2019)
2. Bahdanau, D., Cho, K., Bengio, Y.: Neural machine translation by jointly learning to align and translate. arXiv preprint arXiv:1409.0473 (2014)
3. Bowman, S., Angeli, G., Potts, C., Manning, C.D.: A large annotated corpus for learning natural language inference. In: Proceedings of the 2015 Conference on Empirical Methods in Natural Language Processing, pp. 632–642 (2015)
4. Conneau, A., et al.: XNLI: evaluating cross-lingual sentence representations. In: Proceedings of the 2018 Conference on Empirical Methods in Natural Language Processing, pp. 2475–2485 (2018)
5. Dagan, I., Dolan, B., Magnini, B., Roth, D.: Recognizing textual entailment: rational, evaluation and approaches-erratum. Nat. Lang. Eng. **16**(1), 105–105 (2010)
6. Ghuge, S., Bhattacharya, A.: Survey in textual entailment. Center for Indian Language Technology, retrieved on April (2014)
7. Glickman, O., Dagan, I., Koppel, M.: A probabilistic lexical approach to textual entailment. In: IJCAI. vol. 5, pp. 1682–1683 (2005)
8. Guo, M., Zhang, Yu., Zhao, D., Liu, T.: Generating textual entailment using residual LSTMs. In: Sun, M., Wang, X., Chang, B., Xiong, D. (eds.) CCL/NLP-NABD -2017. LNCS (LNAI), vol. 10565, pp. 263–272. Springer, Cham (2017). https://doi.org/10.1007/978-3-319-69005-6_22
9. Mishra, A., Bhattacharyya, P.: Deep learning techniques in textual entailment. Survey Paper, Center For Indian Language Technology (2018)
10. Pakray, P., Neogi, S., Bandyopadhyay, S., Gelbukh, A.: Recognizing textual entailment in non-English text via automatic translation into English. In: Batyrshin, I., Mendoza, M.G. (eds.) MICAI 2012. LNCS (LNAI), vol. 7630, pp. 26–35. Springer, Heidelberg (2013). https://doi.org/10.1007/978-3-642-37798-3_3
11. Rocktäschel, T., Grefenstette, E., Hermann, K.M., Kočiskỳ, T., Blunsom, P.: Reasoning about entailment with neural attention. arXiv preprint arXiv:1509.06664 (2015)

12. Son, N.T., Phan, V.A., Nguyen, L.M.: Recognizing entailments in legal texts using sentence encoding-based and decomposable attention models. In: COLIEE@ ICAIL, pp. 31–42 (2017)
13. Williams, A., Nangia, N., Bowman, S.: A broad-coverage challenge corpus for sentence understanding through inference. In: Proceedings of the 2018 Conference of the North American Chapter of the Association for Computational Linguistics: Human Language Technologies, Volume 1 (Long Papers), pp. 1112–1122 (2018)

Early Prognosis of Preeclampsia Using Machine Learning

E. Sivaram[1(✉)], G. Vadivu[1], K. Sangeetha[1], and Vijayan Sugumaran[2]

[1] SRMIST, Kattankulathur, Chengalpet, Tamilnadu 603203, India
{se3033,vadivug,sangeetk}@srmist.edu.in
[2] Oakland University, Rochester, MI 48309, USA
sugumara@oakland.edu

Abstract. Preeclampsia is a type of hypertension condition that can be induced by a variety of circumstances during pregnancy. Typically, a diagnosis is made after 20 weeks of gestation. Several investigations employing machine learning techniques have been undertaken to diagnose preeclampsia. SVM, KNN, random forest, gradient boosting methods, and deep learning approaches are examples of these. These techniques can be implemented to detect preeclampsia earlier in an efficient way for preventing the complications caused. This paper demonstrates how hyperparameter tuning of Support vector classification of the various factors involved in the classification of preeclampsia helps in efficiently separating the patients who are prone to have preeclampsia. The selection of the hyperparameter is done through the Grid Search CV algorithm by iterative trialing of the different hyperparameters.

Keywords: Preeclampsia · SVM · Grid search · Hyperparameter

1 Introduction

One of the hypertensive outcomes of pregnancy is preeclampsia. Preeclampsia influences 3–5% of pregnant ladies around the world, remembering 5.4% for India. This can likewise be lethal for both the mother and the embryo [1]. Preeclampsia is related with vasospasm, pathologic vascular sores in various organ frameworks, expanded platelet initiation, and ensuing enactment of the coagulation framework in the miniature vasculature. After the twentieth seven day stretch of pregnancy, preeclampsia is progressively logical. Several studies have shown the ratio of the PlGF to sFLT-1 and Placental protein 13, soluble Endoglin, Triglycerides and Cystatin C as major biomarkers for the detection of the preeclampsia [1–4]. Also, many physiological and clinical parameters are also used in detection of the preeclampsia [5]. The proposed system is an application based on the hyperparameter tuning of which takes the above-mentioned data as input. This will help us in predicting and protecting the patient who are prone to preeclampsia earlier. Initially the patients are recruited in the first trimester of the pregnancy. The physiological data, blood count values, Thyroid level, medical history of the particular patient

Published by Springer Nature Switzerland AG 2022
E. J. Neuhold et al. (Eds.): ICCCSP 2022, IFIP AICT 651, pp. 12–19, 2022.
https://doi.org/10.1007/978-3-031-11633-9_2

and family along with regular activity data will be collected. With these data collected a statistical analysis will be conducted using and a comprehensive review on the factors for the preeclampsia will be discussed. The angiogenic factor that facilitates the growth of the placenta during the gestation is placental growth factor (PlGF) and its receptor Soluble fms-like tyrosine kinase 1 (s-FLT1) [6]. Other than these two biomarkers there are other biomarkers that will be taken as parameters, which are the Soluble endoglin (sENG) [7], placental protein 13 [2], Triglycerides and Cystatin C [8]. These markers are also expressed during the first trimester of the gestation, and the fluctuation in their values are caused in preeclampsia. The PlGF/sFLT-1 and sENG/PlGF are more accurate and sensitive. One of the most used algorithms is Support vector classifier with hyperparameter tuning will lead to have optimum selection of the parameter using Grid Search cross validation. This helps is to know how various kernels and their hyperparameter involves in the setting of boundaries with coverage of the data point. The Gamma, C, degree are the various hyperparameters. This hypermeter varies to different kernel that is considered for the SVC. This approach leads to define what kernel along with their hyperparameter that needs to tune to have good accuracy.

2 Related Literature Work

The studies that are intended to detect preeclampsia are mostly done after 20 weeks of the gestation and studies that use biomarkers like cystatin C and Placental protein are earlier in detection of preeclampsia patients had significantly greater levels of sFlt-1/PlGF than control women. Data suggest that the sFlt-1/PlGF ratio has a higher accuracy for distinguishing PE patients from non-PEs than it does for distinguishing severe or early onset forms of the disease [1]. Women with preeclampsia who experienced complications had a considerably greater PlGF/sFLT1 ratio than women with preeclampsia who did not develop issues [6]. Various serum markers were used to detect the preeclampsia, amongst them sFLT-1 /PlGF ratio was most promising in detecting the preeclampsia [4]. Associations between many first-trimester maternal factors and placental Doppler investigations that are connected to placental performance and serum PlGF levels to uncover significant relationships that should be considered in screening procedures When trophoblast cells were compared, they produced considerably more sEng, sFlt-1, and PlGF. compared to those from normal TCs without preeclampsia, which is more important and addresses the problem's core cause [9]. Placental Protein 13 (PP13) is ensnared in the pathophysiology of hindered placentation and the resulting improvement of early PE but estimating this placental protein at 11–13 weeks is unlikely to be viable in sickness screening. Maternal PP13 levels separating the principal trimester is a promising symptomatic procedure for foreseeing preeclampsia with great awareness and importance in the primary trimester [3]. The different variables of hypertension with Artificial neural network and other machine learning algorithms like SVM, decision tree and application for the equivalent [10]. The expectation of the preeclampsia by the random forest algorithm with 17 variables. It had the best AUROC in external validation. This minimal expense algorithm upgraded primer expectation to decide if pregnant ladies would be anticipated by models with high particularity and progressed indicators [11]. As a modelling procedure, the hidden Markov model was utilized. Knowledge is used to gain a better grasp of how an illness develops. The training method is hampered by prior knowledge of preeclampsia. Preeclampsia was classified, and the observations were categorized [12]. The usage of the elastic net algorithm, containing the informative model with most features for the prediction of preeclampsia [13]. The biomarkers are considered for the for producing the insights for preeclampsia and ANN used depicts varies features in preeclampsia [5].

3 Proposed Work

Studies have revealed that demographics and clinical indicators such as the total blood count are stronger predictors of preeclampsia. Placental growth factor, soluble fms like tyrosine kinase, soluble Endoglin, and other biomarkers were included in our study. Placental protein 13 showcases the novelty of the study [1–4, 7]. Once all the data are collected, the data will be pre-processed. After the pre-processing of the data, selection of the model is done in our case its Support vector classifier and this algorithm will be executed using scikit learn package. An incremental evaluation of all hyperparameters must then be performed to determine the ideal hyperparameter. That hyper parameter must be used to train the model. The trained model is then compared to the testing data to evaluate accuracy before the model is deployed. The support vector classifier is one of the most widely used machine learning techniques (SVC). This also applies to classification and regression problems. It also uses the kernel approach to adjust the data, and based on these modifications, the model finds the best fitting boundary or hyperplane for segregating preeclamptic patients from non-preeclamptic patients in our example.

The hyperplane can be circle, line, or sigmoidal plane, but it there with their margins to separate or to classify the different classes of data points. This transformation is called Kernel. This normally involves in every Support vector classification, but this produces generic results or classification. This model can be tuned by the introducing the hyperparameter to the model.

4 Tuning of Kernel Hyperparameter

The model first goes through a training phase where the system is trained with collected data which has undergone the pre-processing. This is where the system learns various patterns in the data that is fed into the system. In this supervised phase of the model, the output produced is compared with the actual or desired output for the pattern of the data that is given. The difference in the output value will be compared and iterative tuning of the hyperparameter will be done for the model to choose the best hyperparameters. This includes the tuning of C and Gamma function and the kernel of the Support vector classifier until the output produces lowest error possible with higher accuracy, more of the true positive and true false values compared to false positive and false negative values. Since different factors are used in the detection of the preeclampsia and various machine learning algorithm has parameters that can be tuned, called hyperparameter. It is necessary that it is to be notified before training the model. This approach helps in creating a more robust and accurate model and also creates the balance between the bias and variance preventing the model from the underfitting or overfitting.

The hyperparameters that are actually considered for the support vector classifier are C and Gamma. The SVC's major operation is to create a decision boundary which segregates different classes, binary in our study, need not be definitely a straight line. Since the real-world data is noisy and dirty, this might lead to the overfitting or underfitting of the model. The major concern to have great model are,

- To have wider decision boundary for classes.
- To minimize the false positive and false negative prediction.

to achieve this an obvious trade-off must be taken care, as a matter of fact that decision boundaries are sensitive to minor changes.

The trade-off could be controlled by C parameter, which implements the cost for each misclassified data point. Considering that C is small and the cost for the misclassified is low so that, the decision boundary has higher margin which is included. If the C is large, the tries to reduce the number of the misclassified values or the datapoints along with a narrowed margin. The cost involved is actually directly proportional to the distance between the decision boundaries.

In many cases, the dataset will not be linearly separable; however, employing the kernel function will make it so. This is also true in our case. As a result, the kernel was chosen, and it is far better suited for the classification process. It should also be more accurate in data point segregation than other kernels such as poly, linear, rbf, and so on [14]. The kernel function converts the input data points into the required output data points. In this case, we're interested in the polynomial kernel for the SVC.

The polynomial kernel doesn't only take in account the similarity of the vector in a particular dimension but also the cross dimension. This enables us to have the interaction between the features. The polynomial function is computed by the degree (d) of the polynomial kernel between two vectors in-turn describing the relationship between vectors [15, 16].

Formally, the Polynomial kernel is defined by the equation:

$$\mathrm{K}\,(\mathrm{x},\ \mathrm{y}) = (\gamma.\,\mathrm{x.y} + \mathrm{C})^{\mathrm{d}} \tag{1}$$

The x and y are input vectors and d is degree of polynomial function (Fig. 1).

The accuracy produced by the different hyperparameters is shown visuall. With the polynomial kernel, C value at 0.5 and gamma value 1, it will produce the good classification the data points.

This value is achieved by various iteration of the C, gamma, kernel and degree value, this is carried by the algorithm grid search cv. This works as follows:

- The selection of the machine learning that is to be tuned here, SVC.
- Deciding the parameters such as Kernel (poly, linear, rbf, sigmoid), gamma, C, (10^{-3} to 10^{3}) and the degree (1, 2, 3, 4, 5..).

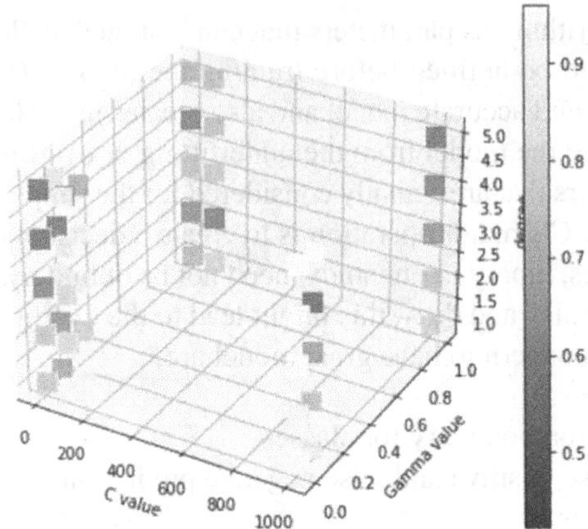

Fig. 1. Visualisation of the accuracy produced by various iteration

- From these parameters iterative application of the parameters is done.
- The scores produced from the iterations are compared to choose the best C and gamma value along with accuracy score.

After the training and test is done, the system is ready for the prediction, once the patients register and the describe demographical and clinical data are collected initially. With data model is created to predict what is the probability a particular patient is prone to have preeclampsia. The cut-off values will be set through the statistical analysis that will be done for the data collected. Once the prediction for the patient is above cut-off value then, the patient is marked as the preeclampsia prone patient.

5 Discussion and Results

Based on the above discussion, the prediction of the preeclampsia in the earlier stages can be done by incorporating various biomarkers which has their significance in the first trimester during the development of the placenta. This approach helps to address the root cause and the pathology of the preeclampsia. Since, considering the facts that Placental growth factor and soluble fms like trysine kinase 1, and other early biomarkers like the cystatin C and serum lipids has a significant weightage in the early prediction of the preeclampsia and the fluctuation of these biomarkers in first trimester helps determine the preeclampsia condition in the earlier stage. The hyperparameter tuning will provide us the insights in various data pattern and distinguishes minor difference between the preeclamptic people. Also, the C value is only one parameter that needs to be tuned for the linear model. However, considering the polynomial model, both the C and gamma values must be tuned to achieve good accuracy.

Table 1. Comparison of the accuracy for various kernel

C value	Degree	Gamma	Kernel
0.5	1	1	Poly
0.5	1	1	Rbf
0.5	1	1	Sigmoid

Table 1 shows the various values of the hyperparameters that produce good results. The polynomial kernel seems to produce the most accurate results compared to others. In future even if more data points are added for the further training purposes the polynomial kernel will be able produce more result compared to the linear kernel. Since the linear kernel includes only the C value and not the gamma and might be easily influence the margin compared to the Polynomial kernel. Also, the polynomial kernel is more likely to handle data points of larger dimensionalities, and hence better suited for our study (Fig. 2).

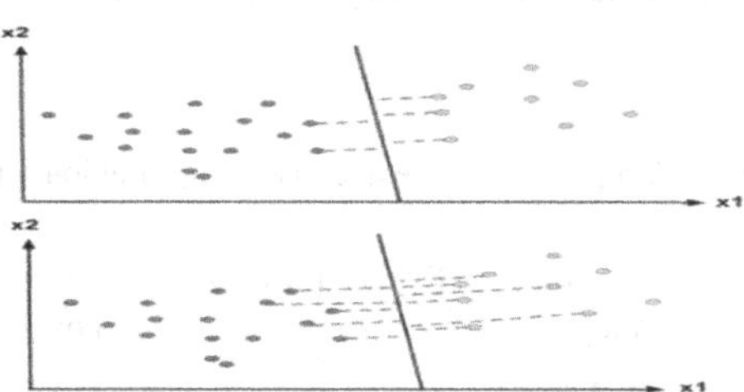

Fig. 2. Comparison of low and high gamma values

The lower gamma value has higher decision boundary taking many data points into account. Also, from the Table 1 parameter the degree is 1 and the gamma is 1 and change is seen only in the C value which makes both the linear and polynomial kernel to same.

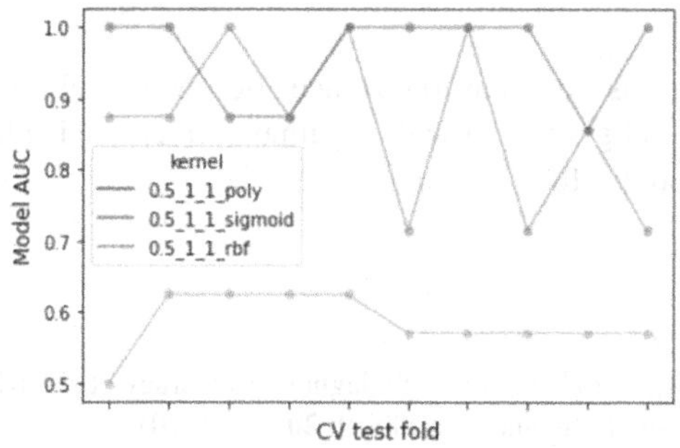

Fig. 3. Cross validation results of various SVM kernel

(See Fig. 3) depicts the 10-fold cross validation of the various kernels considered with stipulated amount of the data point at each fold and proves that the polynomial kernel is most suited for our dataset and produces a good classification of the datapoint this produces us the very lesser false positive and false negative datapoint.

Table 2. Correlation between the various SVM kernel

Kernel	Poly	Sigmoid	Rbf
Poly	1.000	−0.269	−0.331
Sigmoid	−0.269	1.000	0.358
Rbf	−0.331	0.358	1.000

The Table 2, explains that the correlation between the both the kernel poly and linear are more lesser considering our dataset and dimensionalities.

The tuning of the hyperparameters have given us a good accuracy compared to the SVC with without the hyperparameter tuning and previous study quoted in the related work (Table 3).

Table 3. Comparison of the accuracy with previous study

Accuracy of SVC w/o hyperparameter tuning	Accuracy of SVM in previous study	Accuracy of SVC with hyperparameter tuning
84.6%	89.2%	96.07%

From the above table is seen that the tuning of the hyperparameter helps in correctly predicting patients prone to preeclampsia. This model is also efficient even if the data points expand in the future.

6 Future Work

Further, the product of this study has to be Once after the model is ready for the deployment, application that is lightweight with minimalist interface is planned to develop so that the end user it more useful.

References

1. Nikuei, P., Rajaei, M., Roozbeh, N.E.A.: Diagnostic accuracy of sFlt1/PlGF ratio as a marker for preeclampsia. BMC Pregnancy Childbirth **20**, 80 (2020)
2. Akolekar, R., Syngelaki, A., Beta, J., Kocylowski, R., Nicolaides, K.H.: Maternal serum placental protein 13 at 11–13 weeks of gestation in preeclampsia, vol. 29, pp. 1103–1108 (2009)

3. Chafetz, I., et al.: First-trimester placental protein 13 screening for preeclampsia and intrauterine growth restriction. Am. J. Obstet. Gynecol. **197**(1) (2007)
4. Wang, J., Hu, H., Liu, X., et al.: Predictive values of multiple serum biomarkers in women with suspected preeclampsia: a prospective study. available at Research Square, vol. 3, no. PREPRINT (2020)
5. Nair, T.M.: Statistical and artificial neural network-based analysis to understand complexity and heterogeneity in preeclampsia. Comput. Biol. Chem. **75** (2018)
6. Pant, V., Yadav, B.K., Sharma, J.: A cross sectional study to assess the sFlt-1:PlGF ratio in pregnant women with and without preeclampsia. BMC Pregnancy Childbirth **19**, 266 (2019)
7. Leaños-Miranda, A., Navarro-Romero, C.S., Sillas-Pardo, L.J., Ramírez-Valenzuela, K.L., Isordia-Salas, I., Jiménez-Trejo, L.M.: Soluble endoglin as a marker for preeclampsia, its severity, and the occurrence of adverse outcomes. Hypertension **74**(4), 991–997 (2019)
8. Mukherjee, B., Sarangi, G.: Predictive significance of serum Cystatin-C and serum lipid in preeclampsia. Int. J. Clin. Obstet. Gynaecol. **2**, 24–28 (2018)
9. Gu, Y., Lewis, D.F., Wang, Y.: Placental productions and expressions of soluble endoglin, soluble fms-Like Tyrosine Kinase Receptor-1, and placental growth factor in normal and Preeclamptic Pregnancies. J. Clin. Endocrinol. Metabol. **93**(1), 260–266 (2008)
10. Tengnah, M.A.J., Sooklall, R., Nagowaha, S.D.: A predictive model for hypertension diagnosis using machine learning techniques. Telemedicine Technologies Big Data, Deep Learning, Robotics, Mobile and Remote Application for Global Healthcare, vol. 9, pp. 139–152 (2019)
11. Sufriyana, h., Wu, Y.-W., Su, E.C.-Y.: Artificial intelligence-assisted prediction of preeclampsia: development and external validation of a nationwide health insurance dataset of the BPJS Kesehatan in Indonesia. EBioMedicine **54** (2020)
12. Marin, I., Pavaloiu, B., Marian, C., Racovita, V., Goga, N.: Early Detection of Preeclampsia based on a Machine Learning Approach, E-Health and Bioengineering Conference (EHB), pp. 1–4. Iasi, Romania (2019)
13. Marić, I., et al.: Early prediction of preeclampsia via machine learning. Am. J. Obstet. Gynecol. MFM **2**(2) (2020)
14. van Rijn, J.N. Hutter, F.: Hyperparameter Importance Across Datasets, pp. 2367–2376. Association for Computing Machinery (2018)
15. Rojas-Domínguez, A., Padierna, L.C., Valadez, J.M.C., Puga-Soberanes, H.J., Fraire, H.J.: Optimal hyper-parameter tuning of SVM classifiers with application to medical diagnosis. IEEE Access **6**, 7164–7176 (2018)
16. Duarte, E., Wainer, J.: Empirical comparison of cross-validation and internal metrics for tuning SVM hyperparameters, vol. 88, pp. 6–11 (2017)

Predicting Students' Satisfaction Towards Online Courses Using Aspect-Based Sentiment Analysis

J. Melba Rosalind[1(✉)] and S. Suguna[2]

[1] Madurai Kamaraj University, Madurai, Tamilnadu 625021, India
melbarosalind@ldc.edu.in
[2] Sri Meenaskhi Govt. Arts College for Women (A), Madurai, Tamilnadu 625002, India

Abstract. In recent times, quality of teaching and students' participation is monitored in most of the universities and colleges to improve academic performance. Outcome-based education system also requires experiential learning. Student opinion is one of the powerful mechanisms to evaluate academic activity and quality in education system. It helps to decide on corrective measures towards various entities of teaching and learning process. Many research studies have been carried out in classifying the sentiment polarities of opinions. In educational domain, very limited study is carried out in fetching the key aspects or entities from the students' review. Mining the opinions in a deeper level to fetch the specific aspects confined to the topic will bring productive results. In this paper, aspect-based sentiment analysis is carried out at sentence level to find the students' satisfaction with reference to the online courses using machine learning algorithm. The proposed system has attained improved accuracy than the existing model. From this study, the specific aspects are obtained using both unsupervised and semi-supervised LDA algorithms. Students' satisfaction with specific aspects of the online courses also examined.

Keywords: Aspects · Sentiment analysis · Machine learning · Course reviews · LDA · Education

1 Introduction

Generally, every human [8] prefer to refer the opinion of friends and family before purchasing a product. Researchers and companies tend to use the conventional methods of polling and surveys for collecting information. Common sentiment analyzer that defines [2] the overall sentiment towards the product or service is not enough to describe the entire context of the review. Hence for efficient and fine-grained analysis of user feedback the demand of Aspect-based Sentiment Analysis arises, which would facilitate service providers and product manufacturers to detect the context specific aspects that requires improvement. The Aspect Category Detection process consists of finding every entity E and attribute A pair E#A towards which an opinion is stated in the given review.

Published by Springer Nature Switzerland AG 2022
E. J. Neuhold et al. (Eds.): ICCCSP 2022, IFIP AICT 651, pp. 20–35, 2022.
https://doi.org/10.1007/978-3-031-11633-9_3

In review summarization procedure, aspect extraction is considered as a significant task [10] to gain a full view about the evaluation of the products or services from the review comments. Sentiment analysis on subjectivity is an essential indicator for developing products and services according to customer's preferences and to satisfy customers in the areas where negative feedback is earned [14].

In this paper, our aim is to suggest a model that facilitates online course providers achieve greater insights and an extensive view of their course takers' requirements. Therefore, the proposed model inspects the course reviews data and improves the course providers' service perspectives. Aspect-based sentiment analysis (ABSA) model is helpful to extract the sentiments thoroughly, from the reviews of electronic products on specific brands. Other relevant sources are discussion forums where people give reviews and share their experiences in using the product [11]. ABSA is widely applied to gain useful insights. Very little number of researches is carried out in analyzing the sentiments at aspect level in education domain. In teaching learning process, students' feedback is an effective [7] tool that gives valuable insights. Handling opinions of students expressed in reviews is a quite laborious and tiresome task. This task may be feasible for small scale courses that involve less amount of students' feedback; it is impractical for large-scale online courses providers like MOOCs. In the teaching–learning process, classifying opinionated texts [5] at document level or at sentence level is helpful but it does not suggest required points for further enhancement. Aspect-Based Sentiment Analysis is quite new field of study [13] and extensive research is must to attain a higher level. Simple sentiment polarity analysis on a particular domain is not sufficient to meet the needs of people and organizations. We should have more understanding on what aspects are presented when the student gives opinion about the teachers. Aspect-based SA is valuable from both user and enterprise point [8] of view. The unsupervised dependency-based methods do not require any [6] human labeled data. Opinions have targets and there exists explicit syntactic relations between opinion words (e.g., "good") and target aspects (e.g., "screen").

In this paper, the specific aspects of the feedback reviews are fetched. It facilitates to acquire discernment on particular entity about the online course which would be helpful to take corrective decisions in course designing. Aspect-Based Sentiment Analysis (or even Text/Opinion Mining in general) on any review may serve well [13] for applying future methodologies to the problem. In document-level sentiment analysis, the mining gives opinion about whole reviews [5]. The overall framework of this paper relies on aspect-level sentiment analysis and focuses on classifying sentiment and polarity expressed in relation to a given aspect associated to the reviews given for the online courses offered by Coursera. The open dataset available in Kaggle repository is taken for research.

The rest of this paper is arranged as follows. Section 2 gives a brief overview of ABSA. Section 3 presents the related work carried out in ABSA. In Sect. 4, objectives and limitation of the research study is presented. System framework is presented in Sect. 5. In Sect. 6, methodology of the study and implication of results are explained. Finally, in Sect. 7, the conclusion is portrayed.

2 Overview of Aspect-Based Sentiment Analysis

Aspect term extraction is an effective method to trace out aspect terms in reviews. Aspects can be categorized as explicit or implicit. Explicit aspects are clearly stated in the review itself; the implicit aspect term is not present in the text [8] but it is implied by another term. Identifying relevant aspects of an entity is very significant [12] to discover the specific areas of improvement. Detecting explicit aspects can be done at ease but implicit aspects detection is cumbersome, without human involvement [10]. Aspect grouping deals with hierarchical alignment of aspects [8]. Aspect weight rating aims to find the importance of each aspect for each entity; this is vital to companies to discover the key aspects of their products from the customers' viewpoint. In aspect-based recommendation, the goal is to produce suggestions for other users based on the aspects examined in existing reviews. Aspect summarization gives an overview of total polarity of aspect groups for each entity.

Aspect extraction and Topics modeling are constantly used [14] in text mining literature which extracts bunch of text features related to a specific topic based on the frequency of words within the sentence. Here one topic can be viewed as a set of words having a similar meaning. Topic model covers the feature that one document can bring on several topics. LDA model differs from Seeded-LDA where it allows user to pre-define topics with keywords to carry out context-based analysis of textual data. In the LDA selection model, lots of contextually important words [10] can be missed. Both methods are implemented to distinguish the efficiency in topic categorization. In topic analysis model, topic coherence is useful measure to evaluate the topics extraction. Coherence value decides the quality [10] of the topics by calculating the semantic similarity of the words representing the topics. While using the LDA model, this measure provides an idea of deciding the topics.

3 Related Work in ABSA

Several research papers have been committed to sentiment analysis study. In this section, the literature review of aspect-based sentiment analysis on different domains is carried out which is the focal point of the study. Aspect-based Sentiment Analysis on employer branding domain [1] is carried out for giant companies Amazon, Apple and Google using Glassdoor platform. After preprocessing the reviews using Stanford POS tagger the nouns are extracted and then the keywords are categorized into some of the predefined categories. The keywords in each aspect are verified and each document that holds the keyword is assigned a sentimental score. Performance results are compared for all five aspects where 'career opportunities' aspect has high recall value (92%, 96%, and 94.11%) for all three companies.

The study on Amazon's review data aims at recognizing key smartness dimensions that notably influence the satisfaction of smart speaker users [3] using Latent Dirichlet Allocation (LDA). Initially they identified the smartness elements of smart speakers using actual users' review data and users' star ratings. Feature importance is extracted using SVM, NN, RF and XGBoost algorithms to compare the influences of the topics and find relatively more essential topics. Importance ranking is also done accordingly.

An integrated lexicon and rule-based aspect-based sentiment analysis approach is proposed to extract the aspects of government mobile apps [4] and classify the related implicit and explicit sentiments. Sentiment classification is also done for these aspects. This hybrid method outperformed the lexicon baseline and other rules combinations with a score of 0.81. Two semi supervised models namely, seeded LDA and Newsmap is compared in topic modeling on debate transcripts. The seed words and topics are correlated and compared. The result shows that Newsmap outperformed [9] Seeded LDA model since Newsmap executes multilingual geographical classification of news articles. Knowledge-based seed words and frequency-based seed words are fetched using both models. In this literature, performance measure of teaching evaluation and course evaluation using aspect-based sentiment analysis [5] is done. Concept ontology is applied to eradicate irrelevant terms. Both single and multi-word explicit and implicit aspects are found [11] using Association Rule Mining and finally sentiment classification is done using support vector machine (SVM). In this proposed work, aspect-based sentiment analysis on students' reviews to predict students' satisfaction towards online course is accomplished.

4 Objectives of the Study

This paper includes following notable research contributions:

1. Construction of tagged academic domain dataset using LDA/seeded LDA, consisting of 2397 instances. Each course review is tagged in one of nine aspects including course, content, learning, teaching, instructor, lab/practical, charge/fee, career/job, and grade/test.
2. Building a hybrid model for aspect extraction and sentiment classification using customized lexicon and machine learning classifier.
3. Predicting students' satisfaction of online courses in different aspects based on aspect-based sentiment analysis.

4.1 Limitations of Research

- The study focuses on explicit aspect terms detection and classification alone.
- For sentiment scoring, lexicon-based approach and machine learning approach is used.

5 System Framework

The proposed hybrid model is given in Fig. 1. The text reviews are fed into the system for analysis in the first step. Later, the fine-grained text pre-processing methods are employed on the dataset. It involves removal of stop words, numbers, punctuation marks and white spaces. Then it is transformed into lowercase. Afterwards, the reviews are converted into individual sentences. The sentences were transformed into document feature matrix (DFM). Stanford NLP parser was used to detect meaningful features. From the DFM, the aspects were detected with the help of LDA methods. In order to enhance the detection of sentiment words our own customized lexicon is used and polarity is calculated. Finally, the results are predicted using aspect-based sentiment analysis model using machine learning algorithm.

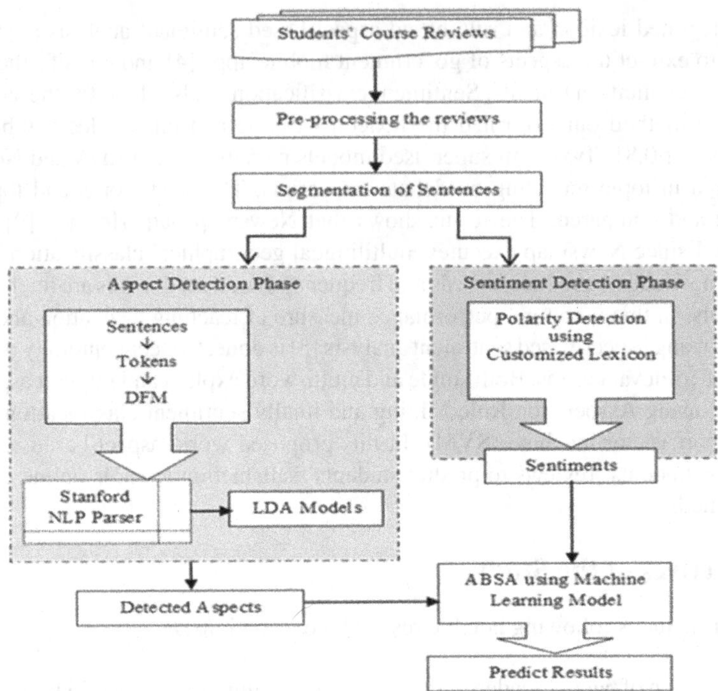

Fig. 1. Proposed hybrid model

6 Methodology and Results

Nowadays, plenty of work is accomplished in sentiment analysis in various domains. It includes hotel reviews, movie reviews, news headlines, online shopping, and online courses. Among these, very few datasets are properly labeled. Real time datasets in education domain are less available with sentiment labels. Apart from sentiment computation, if these datasets give additional inputs on different aspects or entities of educational characteristic it will be productive. This would be possible only through Aspect Based Sentiment Analysis. For the study, the real Coursera dataset available in Kaggle repository is collected through web scraping. Totally 1100 course reviews were randomly chosen from different courses. These reviews are again segmented into sentences for ABSA progression.

Initially in preprocessing, reviews are chopped into sentences which come around 2397. The sentences are converted into same case, punctuation, numbers are removed. After preprocessing the reviews, the text is converted into tokens to derive document features. These features are further tagged with POS tagger. In the proposed model, Stanford NLP parser is used for POS tagging. Since nouns and adjectives mostly contribute towards topic modeling, so the data limited to only terms with these kinds of tags. Different forms of terms are analyzed and classified under different aspects using LDA and seeded LDA algorithm.

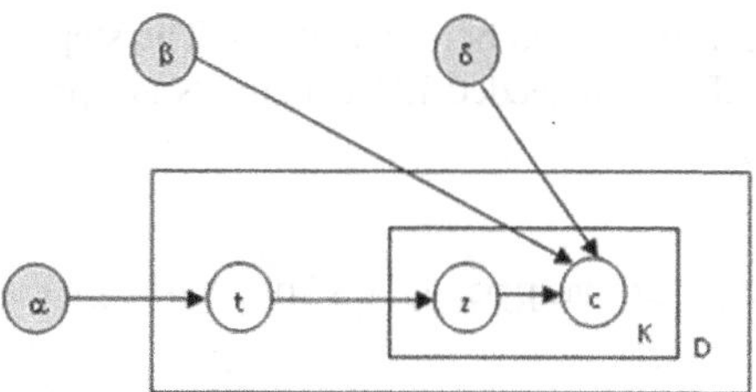

Fig. 2. Proposed plate model for topic modeling

LDA is applied to locate topic with the help of semantic information in unstructured text data [10]. Figure 2 represents the proposed model in plate notation with the modified parameter of δcn where it has topics z and set of K words c with the parameters α and β, the joint distribution of a topic t in document D. Here, δcn denotes a pair wise score of the top n words in a topic. LDA places its own seed words under the topics based on the text features z_n.

The probability of estimating the relevant topic or aspect from the set of topics and words for the given features is given in Eqs. (1) and (2)

$$p(t, z, c|\alpha, \beta) = p(t|\alpha)\prod\nolimits_{n=1}^{K} p(z_n|t)p(\delta c_n|z_n, \beta) \tag{1}$$

where,

$$\delta c_n = \sum\nolimits_{i<j} \text{score}(c_i, c_j) \tag{2}$$

By using seeded LDA, most frequent seed words are introduced occurring in the feature vectors based on topics suggested. The factors that do not fall under the above category are considered as NA. The quality of topic is evaluated using coherence measures. The Hellinger distance is also calculated to find the closely related topics (Fig. 3). In the proposed model, coherence and prevalence score calculation is also carried out to find the best topics/aspects. It is given in Fig. 4.

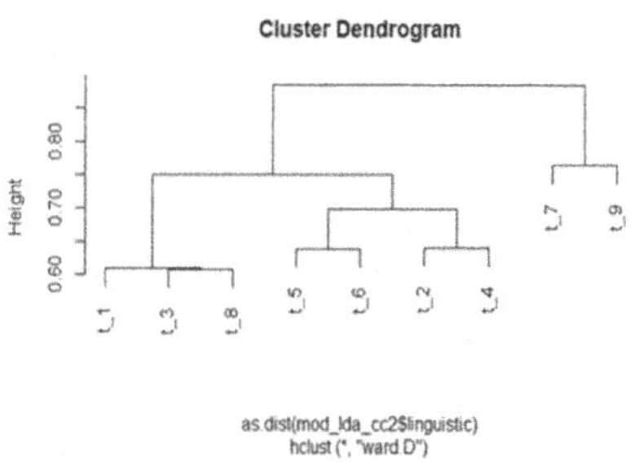

Fig. 3. Hellinger distance measure

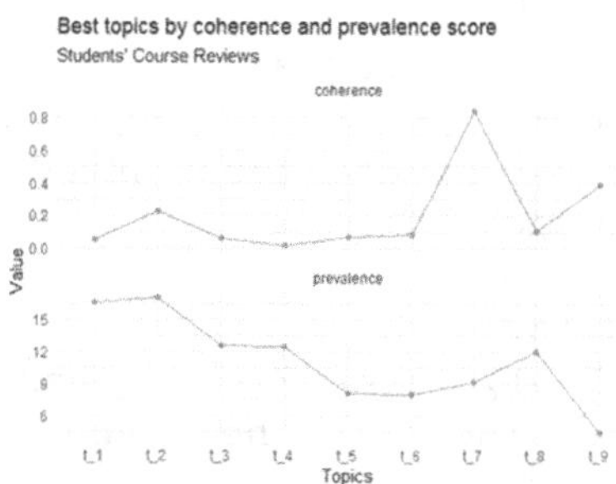

Fig. 4. Coherence vs. prevalence

For this analysis, 1100 course reviews are fetched initially afterwards the reviews were divided into individual sentences with the count of 2397. Few sentences that do not have aspect words were also ignored before analysis. The steps involved for extracting the aspects using both LDA and seeded LDA methods are presented in Algorithm 1a and Algorithm 1b.

```
Algorithm 1a: Aspect mapping using unsupervised algorithm

Input: CR - Course Review sentences, A - Course Aspects
Output: Aspect-based sentences
Start
R ← ~ CR
|F | ←NLP Parser (R)
|T| ← execute LDA (F)
for every T∈F
A →  T
end for
for each A scan F
if F∈T, fetch F and classify
otherwise skip the F and assign Ø
end if
end for
End
```

```
Algorithm 1b: Aspect mapping using semi supervised
algorithm
Input: CR - Course Review sentences, FM - Document- Fea-
ture Matrix, SD - Dictionary of seeded terms, SA - Course
Aspects relevant to seeded terms
Output: Aspect-based sentences

Start
R ← CR9
|F | ← NLP Parser (R)
FM ← F
|ST |← execute seededLDA ∀ SD_i ∈ SD in FM
for each ST
SA →  ST
end for
if F∈ST, fetch F and classify
otherwise skip the F and assign Ø
End if
End
```

The Table 1 shows the sample review dataset representation with its resultant aspects and sentiment labels derived using ABSA. The actual reviews are segmented into sentences to add more clarity in terms of fetching the specific aspects and its related sentiment values.

Table 1. Sample dataset representation with identified aspects

Review	Sentences extracted	Aspects Identified using LDA methods	Sentiment Score obtained
Professors need to undergo a presentation and Instruction Design skills. They were talking a lot and everything was going over my head, the reason was there were not visual prompt for the examples, specifically in the last week.	professors need to undergo a presentation and instruction design skills	Teaching	-1
	they were talking a lot and everything was going over my head, the reason was there were not visual prompt for the examples, specifically in the last week.	Instructor	-1

The following Table 2 shows the sentiment polarity count at review and sentence level aspects. Few sentences were ignored in sentence level since they do not comprise any aspects in the given domain. They are under NA category. Aspect-based sentiment polarity is estimated both at review level and sentence level. Among both models, sentence level reveals more clarity in detecting the polarity. It exhibits positive polarity towards 4 aspects.

Table 2. Aspect-specific sentiment count

Aspect	Positive	Negative	Neutral	Overall aspect sentiment	Positive	Negative	Overall aspect sentiment
	Sentence-based classification				Review-based classification		
Career/Job	62	90	44	Negative	51	47	**Positive**
Charge/Fee	55	99	44	Negative	25	73	Negative
Content	71	138	68	Negative	16	84	Negative
Course	275	138	74	**Positive**	96	26	**Positive**
Instructor	71	91	32	Negative	31	46	Negative
Lab	98	70	61	**Positive**	37	57	Negative
Learning	126	67	32	**Positive**	33	55	Negative
Teaching	95	83	41	**Positive**	27	59	Negative
Test/grade	32	119	36	Negative	30	58	Negative

Most frequent words are also fetched to understand the context of reviews which is given in Fig. 5. When the reviews are examined using the Bing lexicon, the results achieve elevated ratio of positive sentiment than the negative sentiment in the reviews. It is depicted in Fig. 6. The sentiment of reviews with specific aspects is also analyzed using proposed customized lexicon.

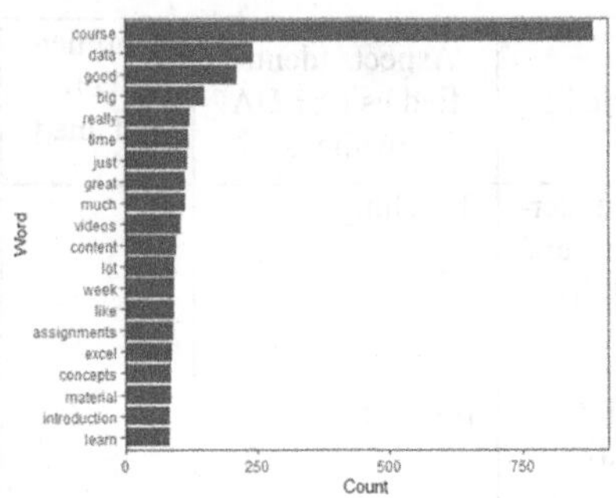

Fig. 5. Word frequency

Fig. 6. Bing sentiment

The polarity of various aspects expressed in the sentence is calculated using customized sentiment lexicon (CSL) developed by us and it is shown in Fig. 7. It yields positive polarity for grade/test, instructor, job, learning aspects. For content, course, fee, instructor and teaching it yields negative polarity. The emotions about the course participants are also analyzed using nrc sentiment lexicon and presented in Fig. 8.

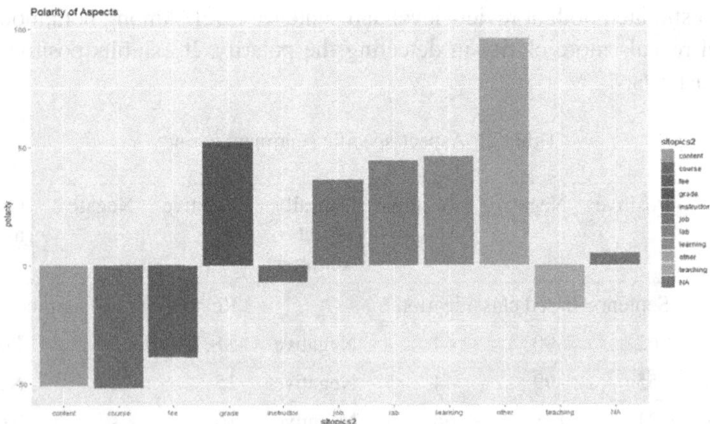

Fig. 7. Polarity of aspects identified using proposed customized lexicon

For few aspects, visualization is presented to find their emotions. Though most of them expresses positive note on emotions still it reveals mixed feelings of students in teaching, learning, test, and course content aspects.

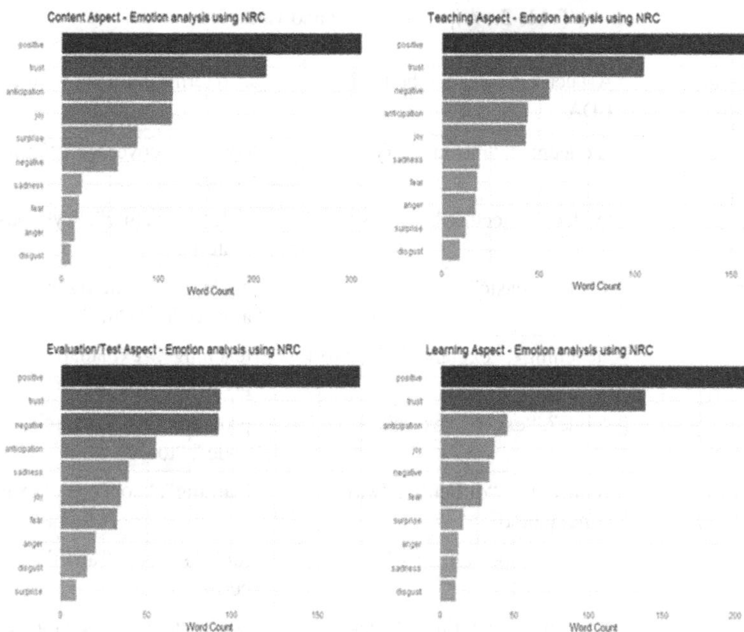

Fig. 8. Emotion analysis using nrc lexicon

After evaluating the optimal number of topics, correlation between two variables word and topic is computed using the phi value for both models. It is depicted as heat map representation in Fig. 9a. and Fig. 9b. Based on visualization of results, it is understood that sentence-based aspect extraction gives more subtle identification of sentiments in aspect-based sentiment analysis. The aspects were fetched using both unsupervised (LDA) and semi-supervised (seeded LDA) model and their efficiency in classifying the aspects are also measured. Seeded LDA covers even implicit aspect words that are relevant to the topic categorization. The detected aspect and its associated feature entities are presented in Table 3. Based on the aspect extraction process, it is indicated that seeded LDA procedure is more accurate than traditional LDA to detect the relevant and related aspect terms. Sentences are tagged with the aspects for further study.

Table 3. Aspect category and variables

Aspect category	Aspect variables fetched using LDA	Seed terms defined in seededLDA
Course	"concepts", "introductory"	"course", "coverage", "rating", "complex"
Content	"videos", "lecture", "slides"	"video", "lecture", "syllabus", "material"
Instructor	"stuff", "basic"	"professor", "intelligent", "approach", "stuff"
Teaching	"teaching", "explanation", "work"	"teaching", "explanation", "presentation", "understand"
Lab	"code", "excel", "exercises"	"programming", "exercises", "code", "tools"
Learning	"concepts", "difficult", "way", "understand"	"learning", "concept", "example"
Job	"skills", "specialization"	"job", "skills", "career", "certificate"
Fee	"money", "material", "weeks"	"cost", "money", "charge", "price"
Grade	"stars", "certificate", project	"test", "practice", "assignment", "quiz"

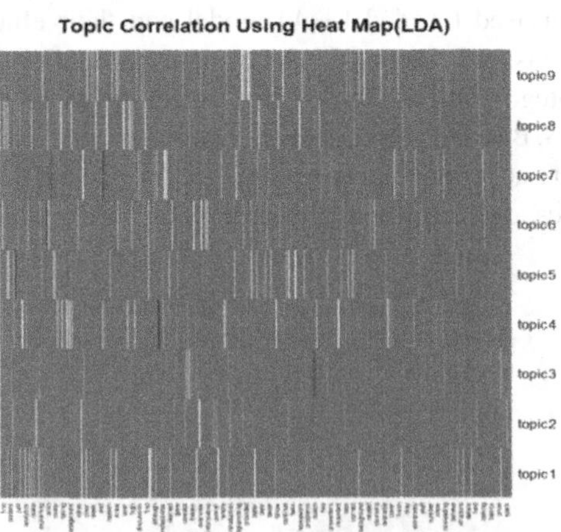

Fig. 9a. LDA results for sentence-based aspect categorization

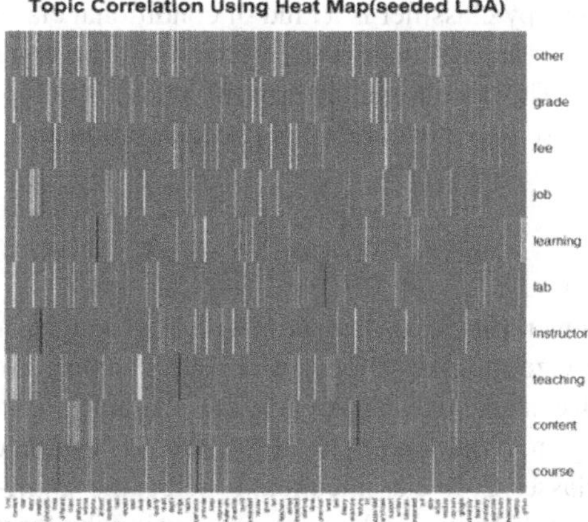

Fig. 9b. seededLDA results for sentence-based aspect categorization

Maximum entropy (MaxEnt) classifier is trained and tested, for estimating the classification accuracy in terms of sentence level aspect-based sentiment classification using hybrid approach. The proposed hybrid aspect-based sentiment classification is done based on the following Algorithm 2.

```
Algorithm 2: Hybrid aspect-based sentiment classifica-
tion algorithm

Input: Aspect-labeled course review sentences, and A
collection of aspect categories (SA_1, SA_2,…, SA_i)
Output: Predicted results
Start
Step 1: SL ← Aspect-labeled course review sentences
Step 2: For each SL
Step 3: SL_e ← Compute sentiment using CSL
Step 4: Segment the SL_e into train and test set
Step 5: Train and test with machine learning model
Step 6: Classify SL_e
Step 7: end
Step 8: for each SA
Step 9: Compute overall sentiment weight
Step10: Print the predicted results
End
```

Since maximum entropy classifier is a kind of conditional classifier, the probability of each label is computed using conditional probability. The equation for calculation is given in formula (3). The conditional probability p(c|x) is computed with respect to exponential value of the series of feature weight vectors product (w * f) for labels l with respect to Z topics.

$$\mathrm{p(c|x)} = \frac{1}{\mathrm{Z}}\mathrm{exp}\sum\nolimits_{\mathrm{i}} \mathrm{w_i} * \mathrm{f_i} \tag{3}$$

Basically, maximum entropy classifier starts with least weights and optimizes to find the weights that maximize the likelihood of the data. For that, the target value y is a random variable which can take on C different values matching to the classes' c1, c2...., cC. The feature belongs to a particular class or aspect c is estimated using probability distribution over the classes C. In classification, to select the single-best class, the class that has the maximum probability can be considered using the formula (4).

$$\hat{c} = argmaxP(c|x), where\ c \in C \tag{4}$$

The Fig. 10 portrays the accuracy obtained in various aspects. It is a kind of exponential classifier that helps to identify the feature that maximizes the likelihood of the data with respect to the topic it belongs. Aspect Sentiment classification is implemented for test set after training MaxEnt classifier model. The proposed model has achieved improved accuracy results in sentiment classification as 88% for positive, 93.5% for negative and 60.5% for neutral. It is presented in Fig. 11.

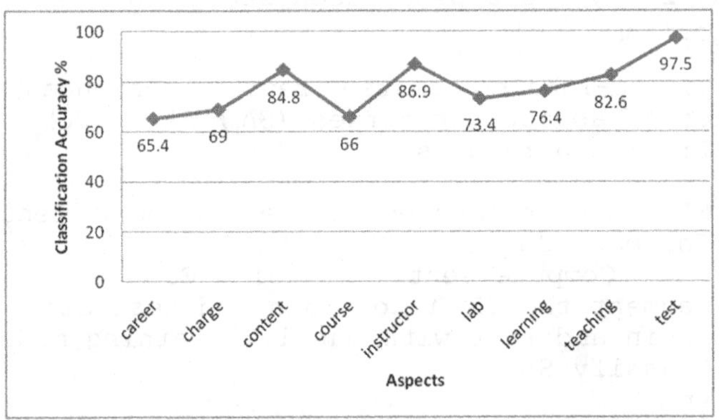

Fig. 10. Aspect classification accuracy of MaxEnt classifier

From the results of sentence level ABSA, it is inferred that sentence level ABSA gives better results than the review level ABSA. And seeded LDA covers most of the domain specific aspects than the LDA model.

6.1 Comparison with Baseline Model

Aspect-based hybrid sentiment classification analysis is carried out using Stanford Twitter Sentiment (STS), [11] Hate Crime Twitter Sentiment (HCTS) and Sanders Twitter

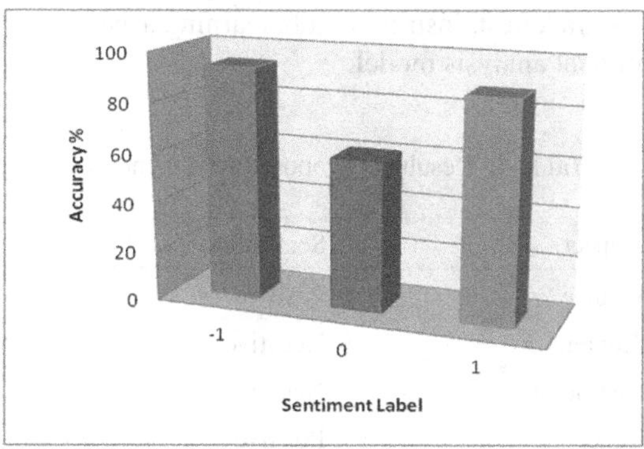

Fig. 11. Sentiment classification using MaxEnt model

Corpus (STC) datasets. Different classification algorithms namely SVM, Random Forest (RF) and Naïve Bayes (NB) are trained along with principal component analysis (PCA) feature selection and Sentiwordnet. Out of these model, SVM classifier attained accuracy % as 76.55, 71.62 and 74.24 respectively for the datasets in aspect-based classification. While comparing with the existing model our proposed hybrid model on course review dataset with the combination of customized sentiment lexicon along with seeded LDA method and Maximum entropy classifier has obtained enhanced accuracy as 80.67% for aspect-based sentiment classification of unigram features. It is shown in Fig. 12. Since ME classifier learns also by non-independent features it helps to trace the uncovered feature vectors in the document. This rationale improves the classification performance of the proposed model than other baseline methods.

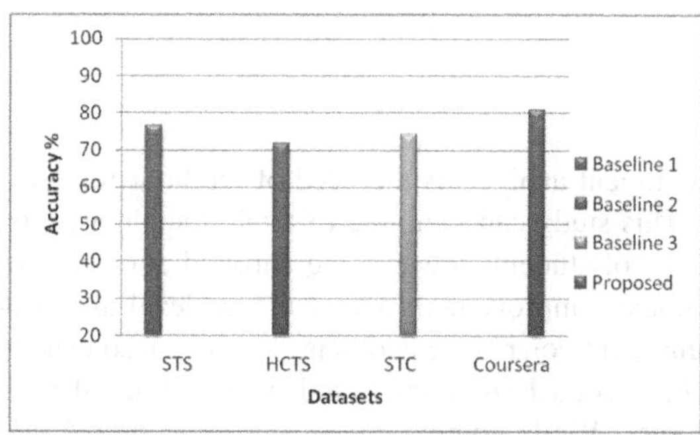

Fig. 12. Comparison of sentiment classification accuracy with other models

6.2 Predicted Results of the Proposed Hybrid Model

According to the proposed hybrid aspect-based sentiment analysis held using the dataset; nine different aspects are considered to trace out the issues in various courses undertaken by the students. As per the results shown in Table 4, on the whole students are satisfied in few aspects such as grade/test, instructor, job, learning aspects based on the sentence level aspect and sentiment analysis model.

Table 4. Results of proposed ABSA model

Aspect	Sentiment
Course	Positive
Content	Negative
Instructor	Negative
Teaching	Positive
Lab	Positive
Learning	Positive
Job	Negative
Fee	Negative
Grade	Negative

As per the proposed model, in few aspects, certain expectations of students are not met out to some extent and predicted as negative. This aspect-based sentiment analysis on course reviews helps us to find the aspects on which the students are really satisfied. It is also helpful to locate the area where the course providers need to give more attention. Few aspects also exhibit good quality feedback about the course. Accuracy of the proposed model is also compared with baseline model and shows significant improvement over the model for the aspect sentiment classification using maximum entropy.

7 Conclusion

The aspect-based sentiment analysis is the need of the hour for various online course providers platform. This study can facilitate to fetch notable aspects of feedback, the emotion and sentiment of students towards the enrolled course. The proposed hybrid model exhibits significant improvement over sentence-level aspect detection than the review level. The sentiment polarity detection is also enhanced using the proposed customized lexicon. The seeded LDA contributed well to trace the contextual features under the aspects/topics. While comparing with existing model the proposed model shows improved accuracy in aspect-based sentiment classification and topic modeling using maximum entropy. Students' satisfaction on various explicit aspects is computed through the proposed model. This would be very essential to enhance the quality of courses offered online. The proposed study will also assist to make corrective decisions based on the results achieved and can improve the quality of services by estimating the students' satisfaction level.

For future studies, implicit aspects can also be investigated through word embedding and linguistic analysis methods.

References

1. Dina, N.Z., Juniarta, N.: Aspect based sentiment analysis of employee's review experience. J. Inf. Syst. Eng. Bus. Intell. **6**(1), 79 (2020). https://doi.org/10.20473/jisebi.6.1.79-88
2. Guha, S., et al.: SIEL: aspect based sentiment analysis in reviews. In: Proceedings of the 9th International Workshop on Semantic Evaluation, pp. 759–766. Denver, Colorado, Association for Computational Linguistics (2015)
3. Park, W., et al.: Extracting principal smartness dimensions of smart speakers using topic modeling and sentiment analysis, 2375-9356/20. IEEE (2020). https://doi.org/10.1109/BigComp48618.2020.00-60
4. Alqaryouti, O., Siyam, N., Monem, A.A., Shaalan, K.: Aspect-based sentiment analysis using smart government review data. Appl. Comput. Inf. (2019). https://doi.org/10.1016/j.aci.2019.11.003
5. Chauhan, G.S., Agrawal, P., Meena, Y.K.: Aspect-based sentiment analysis of students' feedback to improve teaching–learning process. In: Satapathy, S.C., Joshi, A. (eds.) Information and Communication Technology for Intelligent Systems. SIST, vol. 107, pp. 259–266. Springer, Singapore (2019). https://doi.org/10.1007/978-981-13-1747-7_25
6. Liu, Q., Liu, B., Zhang, Y., Kim, D.S., Gao, Z.: Improving opinion aspect extraction using semantic similarity and aspect associations. In: Proceedings of the Thirtieth AAAI Conference on Artificial Intelligence (AAAI-16), pp. 2986–2992. Association for the Advancement of Artificial Intelligence (2016)
7. Kastrati, Z., Imran, A.S., Kurti, A.: Weakly supervised framework for aspect-based sentiment analysis on students' reviews of MOOCs, IEEE Access (2020). https://doi.org/10.1109/ACCESS.2020.3000739
8. Mowlaei, M.E., Abadeh, M.S., Keshavarz, H.: Aspect-based sentiment analysis using adaptive aspect-based lexicons. Elsevier Ltd. (2020). https://doi.org/10.1016/j.eswa.2020.113234 0957-4174/
9. Watanabe, K., Zhou, Y.: Theory-driven analysis of large corpora: semi supervised topic classification of the UN speeches. Soc. Sci. Comput. Rev. 1–21 (2020). https://doi.org/10.1177/0894439320907027. SAGE
10. Das, S.Y., Murakami, R., Chakraborty, B.: Development of a two-step LDA based aspect extraction technique for review summarization. Int. J. Appl. Sci. Eng. 1–18 (2020). https://doi.org/10.6703/IJASE.202103_18(1).003
11. Zainuddin, N., Selamat, A., Ibrahim, R.: Hybrid sentiment classification on twitter aspect-based sentiment analysis. Appl. Intell. **48**(5), 1218–1232 (2017). https://doi.org/10.1007/s10489-017-1098-6
12. Sindhu, I., Daudpota, S.M., Badar, K., Bakhtyar, M., Baber, J., Nurunnabi, M.: Aspect-based opinion mining on student's feedback for faculty teaching performance evaluation. IEEE Access **7**, 108729–108741 (2019). https://doi.org/10.1109/ACCESS.2019.2928872
13. Hajrizi, R., Nuçi, K.P.: Aspect-Based Sentiment Analysis in Education Domain. arXiv:2010.01429 [cs.CL] (2020)
14. Soon-Hong, K., Byong-Kook, Y.: Topics and sentiment analysis based on reviews of omni-channel retailing. J. Distrib. Sci. 25–35 (2021). https://doi.org/10.15722/jds.19.4.202104.25

A Survey on DL Based Frameworks for COVID-19 Radiological Diagnosis

J. Kishan, G. Kalaichelvi, R. Surendiran, and Bhadru Amgothu(✉)

SAMEER – Centre for ElectroMagnetics, Meity, GoI, Chennai, India
amgothubhadru.sameer@nic.in

Abstract. The ongoing Coronavirus disease (COVID-19) pandemic still necessitates emphasis on diagnosis and management of the outbreaks due to the emergence of new variants. This paper is an extensive survey on the implementation of Deep Learning (DL) models used for diagnosing COVID-19 from chest imaging, enriched with quantitative measures and regulatory aspects. The authors have searched, collated and categorised various models and techniques that reported different architectures with respect to COVID-19 diagnosis in the literature. This survey also briefs about quantifying metrics and the reported results are enumerated, also regulatory frameworks for public use of Artificial Intelligence (AI) in medical devices are comprehended.

Keywords: AI · DL · CNN · GAN · LSTM · Medical devices

1 Introduction

COVID-19 pandemic had devastating effects affecting over 247,968,227 cases (as of 5th Nov '21) and 5,020,204 deaths as per World Health Organisation [1], leading to large ramifications in public health management. Though the search for prevention and treatment have shown fruits, the concern of new outbreaks due to variants intensifies further research.

When bioindicators like Reverse Transcription-Polymerase Chain Reaction (RT-PCR) and other methods such as serologic tests and viral throat swab testing, is primarily used for diagnosing, for confirmed or suspected COVID-19 cases, chest imaging is used to decide on the severity of the infection and further treatment plan [2]. However, limitation on X-rays and Computed Tomography (CT) imaging is the requirement of a human expert for diagnosis. This could cause a bottleneck in the smooth process of COVID treatment management. AI, specifically DL, can relieve this bottleneck.

This paper summarises research of various AI and Deep Learning (DL) implementations published during the period 2019–2021 on chest imaging namely X-ray & CT and lung cough pattern. Regulatory aspects with respect to the marketing and wide scale distribution of AI software as medical devices is also covered by this survey.

Published by Springer Nature Switzerland AG 2022
E. J. Neuhold et al. (Eds.): ICCCSP 2022, IFIP AICT 651, pp. 36–45, 2022.
https://doi.org/10.1007/978-3-031-11633-9_4

1.1 Deep Learning on Healthcare Use Cases

DL with its comprehensive feature extraction and self-learning ability is obviously a proven candidate for diagnosing COVID. As the application of DL technologies offer rapid and accurate results, a lot of research focus has been drawn towards its implementation on studying radiological images.

Multiple studies have shown the effectiveness and accuracy equaling human potential savings of human error and time [3]. Computer Vision (CV) and DL have extensive literature for diagnosis [4], such as various tumor detection [5, 6], diabetic retinopathy, skin laceration [7]. Several studies have reported about the accuracy of ML models for diagnosis from imaging versus human experts for comparison, particularly as reported [8], CV19-Net showed an Area Under Curve of 0.94 versus 0.85 achieved by radiologists.

2 Organisation of This Work

The following Fig. 1(a) represents the layout of the contents provided in this survey.

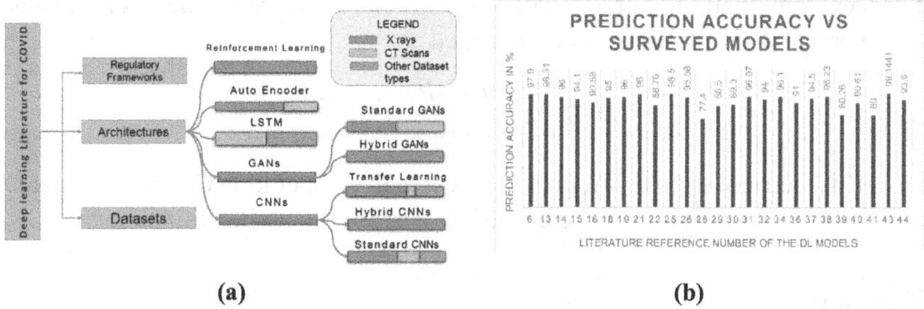

Fig. 1. (**a**) Organization of the survey (**b**) Prediction of models referenced

During the survey it was observed that the prediction accuracy is reported predominantly in order of 90% as diagrammatically presented in the Fig. 1(b) with their respective reference numbers along the X-axis.

The following section discusses the methodology to quantify with the corresponding metrics. Then sparse primary datasets & secondary datasets in use are discussed. Subsequently the literature on Deep Neural Network (DNN) on COVID-19 diagnosis are sorted based on the architectures and finally the regulatory frameworks are outlined.

3 Methodology and Metrics

This survey was done in phases, starting with identifying published journals and articles about the implementation of AI/ML models regarding pneumonia and the covid-19 diagnosis from reputed repositories like 1) IEEE 2) ScienceDirect 3) PubMed and 4) Scopus. Then the identified papers were evaluated based on the criteria like citations, model metrics and summarised with respect to quantitative parameters as described in [7, 8]. And finally the publications were sorted and summarised based on models like Convolutional Neural Networks(CNN), Generative Adversarial Neural (GAN) Networks, Transfer Learning, Long short Term Memory (LSTM), Reinforcement learning and Auto Encoders.

The metrics used in the literature to evaluate the performance of models are listed below.

- **Classification Accuracy:** Number of times predictions that the model correctly predicted, obtained by dividing Number of correct predictions to total predictions.
- **Precision:** It's fraction of samples to total samples, "It can be stated as

$$\frac{\textit{True Positives}}{\textit{True Positives} + \textit{False Positives}}\text{''} \tag{1}$$

- **Recall:** Denotes how sensitive the model is to correct predictions. Recall and TPR are the same

$$\frac{\text{True Positives}}{\text{True Positives} + \text{False Negatives}} \tag{2}$$

- **F1 score:** Combination of precision and recall, The F1 score reaches its best value at 1 and worst at 0. The F1 score is represented as:

$$\text{F1} = 2 * \left(\frac{(precision * recall)}{(precision + recall)}\right) \tag{3}$$

- **AUC:** This metric stands for "Area under the Receiver Operating Characteristic (ROC) Curve". AUC provides a measure of metrics across all classification thresholds.

4 Datasets

The performance of the model heavily depends on the quality of the dataset it is trained on [9]. Neural networks are non-linear models that work on by figuring out the non-linear relationship between variables and hence they can be said to have low bias and high variation. Thus, we can reliably generalise a need for a good balanced dataset for ensuring that models for real life solutions. However many real-life datasets are smaller and often constrained, especially in Medical field. Among the papers and studies reported, the significant sources of the dataset are as follows.

'Italian Society of Medical and Interventional Radiology (SIRM) COVID-19 Database' has 1525 X-ray images and is being reported in plenty [10]. Open sources datasets are listed in GitHub like that of Joseph Paul Cohen et al. named as Novel CoronaVirus 2019 Dataset and open source Datasets are listed in the Kaggle. The studies have used both primary datasets i.e. data collected during the research and approved by ethics board and secondary datasets which are collated from open sources and repositories.

An similar Indian datasets is not found however there are some publications where the chest xrays samples augmented with existing for testing their models are published. The xrays found in the datasets are primarily in jpeg format and resized to smaller size for the purpose. This is potential gap where dataset focused on Indian datasets can be done.

5 Deep Neural Networks Architectures

5.1 Convolutional Neural Networks (CNNs)

A CNN is a DL neural network configured for processing structured arrays of data, such as images. CNNs have a proven record for image classification, which is significant, as some studies have shown that they equal performance to human experts [11]. CNN has been extensively studied for medical diagnosis because of their advantage over linear ML methods as they can effectively extract features and make predictions from complex data and multi-dimensional data like images [12]. Many studies have implemented various types of CNN with basic layers and combinations of popular layers architectures.

Chest X-Rays

Mohit mishra et al. has reported two stage networks that classifies the input X-ray into pneumonia and COVID-19. The F1 score is reported as 96.5% for stage 1 and 98.31% for stage 2. Further to that, precision and sensitivity are quantified as 96.04% & 97% respectively for non-pneumonic class and 100%, 96.74% respectively for Covid positive and 97.74%, 100% for covid-19 negative [13]. While in MdGulzar Hussain et al. results showed that the CNN model of three layers reported the highest precision, recall, and F1-score of 96%, 94%, and 96% respectively, compared to one layer gave the accuracy of 95% and four layer CNNs 94% [14]. In have implemented COVID-GATNet for combining dense blocks and the attention mechanism for reduced parameters and increased performance. Results claimed the "best-case accuracy of 94.1%, and the F-1 score with 95.2%" for COVID-GATNet as compared to COVID-Net model of 93.3%, and the F-1 score of 94.8% [15].

CT Scans

Harsh Sharma et al. had evaluated the performance of a CNN network with and without dropout layer along with data augmentation techniques. They have reported a maximum accuracy of 90.6% and in the authors did a test of using various image pre-processing techniques. The observations reported for covid-19 diagnosis with accuracy of 97.2% using CNN versus 98.5% for Support Vector Machine (SVM) [17].

Other Diagnostic Imaging

Other sources like acoustics data of cough and breath sounds to train CNN, have studied the feasibility of using lung sounds and spectrograms for lung disease classification, to train on normalised and pre-processed sound recordings and spectrograms on 128x128 CNN model, Peak accuracy of 95% is reported [18].

5.2 Hybrid CNN

Hybrid CNNs are developed by taking advantage of CNN's layered structure. Phat Nguyen Kieu et al. have implemented a hybrid CNN for diagnosis of abnormalities from chest X-rays by using two 2-D 64 × 128 CNN's for left and right lung X-ray and a 128 × 128 CNN and then devising a method called fusion method for making a prediction of the abnormality reported with 96% accuracy [19].

5.3 Transfer Learning

For effective classification, there is a need for abundant data to enable effective learning for classification. However, in many situations, availability of data is constrained. Transfer learning provides a way to deal with this limitation. Transfer learning is the use of learning already learnt on one problem to solve a related problem.

Chest X-rays

In ResNet-50, Inception V3 and DenseNet121 models trained on the dataset of 112,120 images of chest X-rays are compared and densenet121 is reported for the best performance [20]. Another study reported CheXNet to outperform eight different CNN models. However with a bigger dataset, Densenet gave 2% more accuracy in [21]. The work has reported inception models the best with 98% accuracy against Visual Geometry Group (VGG)16, VGG19 and a basic CNN in [22]. The study has depicted an improved technique using knowledge transfer and distillation with Densenet -121 and lightweight squeezenet [23]. Additionally, an Xception for CXR classification and preprocessing like data augmentation and pixel intensity normalization were done to give 87% accuracy with AUC scores in ranges of 0.50–0.80 in [24]. D. Haritha et al. have achieved 98.5% accuracy with InceptionV1 training on 1824 Chest X-rays [25].

CT Scans

The CT and X Ray images are rotated, zoomed, horizontally flipped and shifted towards balancing the unbalanced dataset and Densenet-121 and Inception V3 are shown to produce a performance increase by 12% [26].

Ultrasounds

TLum et al. have shown an improvement of 4% and 10% of the POCVID-NET [28] which reported 85% precision and 90% recall for COVID-19, using attention mechanisms [27]. Similar attempts are also made by Julia Diaz-Escobar et al. with transfer learning on ultrasound samples and reported that Inception v3 has reported best accuracy of 89.3% [29].

5.4 Transfer Learning with Preprocessing

Md. Mehedi Hasan et al. had trained deep convolutional GAN for augmentation of synthetic images to supplement the dataset for the model to perform better. Then transfer learning was used with CNN by utilising VGG16 as the base model for image classification. The model achieved 94.5% accuracy on the validation set [30].

Ishan Mathew Nedumkunnel et al. had implemented a CNN using transfer learning on pre-processed image dataset through Segmentation using a U-NET model. Out of DensetNet201, EfficientNetB7 and VGG-16, DenseNet201 had performed the best [31].

5.5 Data Augmentations and Feature Extraction Spatial Domain and Frequency Domain

As real world data is limited, Data augmentation is used to diversify the training set by applying random real-like transformation, further feature extraction is done in frequency domain like Fast Fourier transform and Wavelet transform, and spatial domain like Grey level Difference Method (GLDM), Grey level Co-occurrence matrix (GLCM). Abolfazl Zargari Khuzani et al. have designed a CNN model where feature extraction is done is both spatial domain, i.e. GLDM, GLCM and also in frequency domain i.e. FFT and Wavelet. They tested the obtained dataset using a three layer model and the results with F1 scores of 0.98 for covid and 0.94 for pneumonia in [32]. Vladimir GROZA et al. had developed a robust method for covid detection with higher accuracy, They developed a semantic segmentation network on pneumothorax region using an ensemble of linknets with a backbone from se-resnext50, se-resnext101, SENet154, pre-processes image augmentation at localised regions when required instead of global random augmentation. They have shown a very good performance with an F1 of 0.8821 [33].

6 Generative Adversarial Networks (GANs)

Generative adversarial Networks, or GAN, are DL models, commonly used for generating the images. In general, a GAN is composed of "generator (G) networks and discriminator (D) networks". A generator model generates new artificial samples from an existing distribution of samples, and the discriminator is responsible for classifying whether samples are real or fake (generated).

6.1 Standard GANs

GANs can extract features from data and generate synthetic data that augment the limited dataset. Standard GANs consist of two neural networks as explained above working in tandem.

For X-rays

Zhaohui Liang et al. had implemented Conditional GAN for Image Dataset augmentation and improved the distribution of the classes for better training of the model, as in the case of many medical datasets which tend to be highly imbalanced. The result reported an improvement from 96.1% to 97.8% and also with an increase in F1 scores, precision and recall [34].

For CT Scans

Martin Jammes-Floreani et al. tried to reduce the difficulties in implementation of CT scan pneumonia classification due to reduced image quality or resolution. The authors have utilized GAN for image enhancement using ESRGAN and TomoGAN adapted from SRGAN (Super Resolution GAN) [35].

6.2 Hybrid GANs

The popularity of GANs in computer vision has led us to looking for more avenues and ways to improve the GANs' performance and hence there are attempts to use a combination of convolutional neural networks and GANs and Vedant Bhag et al had also implemented the GAN as a mechanism of improving the quality of the dataset which can be used in turn to improve the performance of the model classifying for pneumonia detection using x-ray. They have used the Progressive GAN (ProGAN) for high-quality synthetic images generation. The DCNN AlexNet when applied on the augmented data set D2, produced an accuracy of 91%, while the accuracy was 79.5% when applied on the original dataset D1 [36]. Devansh Srivastava et al. trained Deep convolutional GAN for augmentation of synthetic images to oversample the dataset for the model to perform better [37].

7 Long Short Term Memory Networks (LSTMs)

In a recurrent network, in addition to normal connection, a CNN has units that are self-connected or with previous layer units. This acts as a memory component and helps the network to 'remember'. The LSTM unit is a more complex form of the recurrent unit. It uses a gating unit to switch to choose between 'forget' or 'remember'. This also helps for LSTM to back propagate or in other words 'learn'.

A two-stage method to fully utilise cross-slice features of volumetric data by using a CNN and context aware Bi-LSTM, learned the dataset of 801 patients and shown an increased performance by 1–2% [38]. The cough recordings were analysed and diagnosing the underlying disease is implemented in [39]. LSTM is used over the preprocessed audio recordings with feature extraction of Mel-frequency cepstrum coefficients (MFCCs) in [40].

8 Auto Encoders for both CT and X-rays

Autoencoders are unsupervised neural networks which try to map the input data representation to output which results in a compressed version of the data thus effectively reducing the number of parameters required, it is used for image compression, denoising and generation.

A context based data extraction system is used with respect to diagnosing images and used for infecting source locating and spread monitoring using COVID-CHEST-XRay IEEE8023 dataset containing 760 images in [41]. An image retrieval system using Transfer learning and Denoising Auto encoder claims a precision of 0.436 in [42].

9 Reinforcement Learning

Reinforcement learning is a technique of AI like supervised and unsupervised learning, where a model is set up in an environment where it is tasked with taking decisions. Instead of using learning labels like the supervised the reward system is in place where the model is rewarded for the favourable decision and the objective is to maximise the rewards obtained. Few papers have implemented the technique for diagnosis, An adapted version of Gaining–Sharing Knowledge (GSK) optimization algorithm using the Opposition-Based learning (OBL) and Cauchy mutation operators is reported in [43] to provide comparable gains. A swap learning methodology called salp swarm algorithm is reported with 98% accuracy and lowest running time in [44].

10 Regulatory Framework

Industry regulators like International Medical Device Forum (IMDRF) have been consulted by the government regulators like the Federal Drug Administration (FDA) and European Medicine Agency (EMA) for development of a framework for regulating the marketing and introduction of AI software for categorising the devices and the action needed based on the risk present [45].

FDA has proposed a framework in January 2021 open for feedback and suggestions and proposed an action plan to increase transparency to users of AI/ML based devices. The EU have framework which deals with how medical device are classified based on risk, and which in turn denotes the testing and validation for testing and codified the requirements the medical devices manufacturer must demonstrate [46].

In India, The Ministry of Electronics and Information Technology formed a committee which has submitted a report to aid in the process of drafting an AI policy for India including healthcare.

11 Challenges and Future Research Directions

As promising as it sounds, the benefits offered by DL methods are not without caveats. The availability of dataset is a primary concern, especially with respect to Indian context. Though the datasets are widely available, the quality of datasets are to be evaluated. Many factors such as distribution, outlier identification, data cleaning and statistical evaluation should be emphasized for more holistic results. Accuracy is one of the heavily used metrics for citing the model's performance. However, accuracy may not give a whole picture of the real time performance of the model. Other metrics such as F1 score, AOC etc. can be employed to ensure that the models are more versatile for real life scenario. As in the case of healthcare domain, any innovation using DL methods should be strictly evaluated before public use. Many countries have already began work in framing protocols for the above purpose, creation of a common standard will aid in more assurance of public trust during real time implementation. Cross validation as with human evaluators can be employed as a benchmarking metric, though the cost and legal factors have also to be considered.

12 Conclusion

This paper surveys DL techniques implemented as a means of providing tools for rapid diagnosis and access to treatment for managing COVID-19 pandemic along with listing out available regulatory structures present. This DL based development is largely supported by the ease of access of literature, open datasets and tools. At SAMEER design and implementation, efforts are focusing on advanced statistical techniques, towards building optimized and reliable DL models for healthcare and industrial use cases.

References

1. WHO Coronavirus (COVID-19) Dashboard. https://covid19.who.int/
2. Ahuja, A.S.: The impact of artificial intelligence in medicine on the future role of the physician, PeerJ (2019)
3. Litjens, G., et al.: A survey on DL in medical image analysis, vol. 42, pp 60–68. Science Direct (2017)
4. Cheng, J.Z., Ni, Y.H., et al.: Computer-aided diagnosis with DLArchitecture: applications to breast lesions in US images and pulmonary nodules in CT scans. Sci. Rep. **6**, 24454 (2016). https://doi.org/10.1038/srep24454
5. Lakshmanaprabu, S.K., et al.: Optimal DL model for classification of lung cancer on CT images. Future Generation Computer Systems, vol. 92, pp. 374-382, Science Direct (2018). https://doi.org/10.1016/j.future.2018.10.009
6. Sadre, R., Sundaram, B., Majumdar, S., et al.: Validating DL inference during chest X-ray classification for COVID-19 screening. Sci. Rep. **11**, 16075 (2021)
7. Classification: ROC Curve and AUC. https://developers.google.com/machine-learning/crash-course/classification/roc-and-auc
8. ScikitDocumentation website. https://scikit-learn.org/
9. Althnian, A., AlSaeed, D., Al-Baity, H., et al.: Impact of dataset size on classification performance: an empirical evaluation in the medical domain. Appl. Sci. **11**, 796 (2021)
10. SISOMAI Radiology, COVID-19 Database (2020). https://www.sirm.org/category/senza-categoria/covid-19/
11. Rawat, W., Wang, Z.: Deep convolutional neural networks for image classification: a comprehensive review. NIH **29**, 2352–2449 (2017). https://doi.org/10.1162/NECO_a_00990
12. Akay, M.F.: Support vector machines combined with feature selection for breast cancer diagnosis, Elsevier, Expert Systems with Applications, vol. 36, pp 3240–3247, ScienceDirect (2009)
13. Mishra, M., Parashar, V., Shimpi, R.: Development and evaluation of an AI System for early detection of Covid-19 pneumonia using X-ray (Student Consortium). In: 2020 IEEE Sixth International Conference on Multimedia Big Data (BigMM), pp. 292–296 (2020)
14. Hussain, M.G., Shiren, Y.: Recognition of COVID-19 disease utilizing X-ray imaging of the chest using CNN. 2021(iCCECE), pp. 71–76 (2021)
15. Li, J., Zhang, D., Liu, Q., Bu, R., Wei, Q.: COVID-GATNet: a DL framework for screening of COVID-19 from chest X-ray images. 2020 IEEE 6th (ICCC) (2020)
16. Sharma, H., Jain, J.S., Bansal, P., Gupta, S.: Feature extraction and classification of chest X-ray images using CNN to detect pneumonia. 2020 10th (Confluence) (2020)
17. Sebdani, A.M., Mostafavi, A.: Medical image processing and DL to diagnose COVID-19 with CT images. 2021 5th (IPRIA), pp. 1–6 (2021)
18. Tariq, Z., Shah, S.K., Lee, Y.: Multimodal lung disease classification using deep convolutional neural network. 2020 (BIBM), pp. 2530–2537 (2020)
19. Kieu, P.N., et al.: Applying Multi-CNNs model for detecting abnormal problem on chest x-ray images. 2018 (KSE), pp. 300–305 (2018)
20. Irfan, A., et al.: Classifying pneumonia among chest X-rays using transfer learning. 2020 42nd (EMBC), 2020, pp. 2186–2189. https://doi.org/10.1109/EMBC44109.2020.9175594
21. Chowdhury, M.E.H., et al.: Can AI help in screening viral and COVID-19 pneumonia? IEEE Access **8**, 132665–132676 (2020). https://doi.org/10.1109/ACCESS.2020.3010287
22. Labhane, G., et al.: Detection of pediatric pneumonia from chest X-ray images using CNN and transfer learning. 2020 3rd(ICETCE), pp. 85–92 (2020)
23. Li, X., Li, C., Zhu, D.: COVID-MobileXpert: on-device COVID-19 patient triage and follow-up using chest X-rays. 2020 IEEE (BIBM), pp. 1063–1067 (2020)

24. Mondal, S., Agarwal, K., Rashid, M.: DL Approach for Automatic Classification of X-Ray Images using Convolutional Neural Network, (ICIIP), pp. 326–331 (2019)
25. Haritha, D., Swaroop, N., Mounika, M.: Prediction of COVID-19 cases using CNN with X-rays. 2020 5th, pp. 1–6. https://doi.org/10.1109/ICCCS49678.2020.9276753
26. Berrimi, M., Hamdi, S., Cherif, R.Y., Moussaoui, A., Oussalah, M., Chabane, M.: COVID-19 detection from Xray and CT scans using transfer learning. In: 2021 International Conference of Women in Data Science at Taif University (WiDSTaif), pp. 1–6 (2021). https://doi.org/10.1109/WiDSTaif52235.2021.9430229
27. Lum, T., Mahdavi, M., et al.: Covid-19 diagnosis by point of care lung ultrasound: a novel DL artificial intelligence method. Can. J. Cardiol. **37**(10) (2021)
28. Born, J., et al.: Accelerating detection of lung pathologies with explainable ultrasound image analysis. Appl. Sci. **11**, 672 (2021). https://doi.org/10.3390/app11020672
29. Diaz-Escobar, J., Ordóñez-Guillén, N.E.: Deep-learning based detection of COVID-19 using lung ultrasound imagery. PLOS ONE **16**(8), e0255886 (2021). https://doi.org/10.1371/journal.pone.0255886
30. Hasan, M.M., et al.: A Combined approach using image processing and DL to detect pneumonia from chest X-ray image. 2019 3rd ICECT, pp. 89–92 (2019)
31. Nedumkunnel, I.M., et al.: Explainable deep neural models for COVID-19 prediction from chest X-rays with region of interest visualization. 2021 2ndICSCCC (2021)
32. Khuzani, A.Z., et al.: COVID-classifier: an automated machine learning model to assist in the diagnosis of COVID-19 infection in chest x-ray images (2019)
33. Groza, V., Kuzin, A.: Pneumothorax segmentation with effective conditioned post-processing in chest X-ray. 2020 IEEE 17th ISBI Workshops, pp. 1–4 (2020)
34. Liang, Z., Huang, J.X., Li, J., Chan, S.: Enhancing automated COVID-19 cChest X-ray diagnosis by image-to-image GAN translation. 2020 BIBM, pp. 1068–1071 (2020)
35. Jammes-Floreani, M., et al.: Enhanced-Quality Gan (EQ-GAN) on Lung CT scans: toward truth and potential hallucinations. 2021 IEEE (ISBI), pp. 20–23 (2021)
36. Bhagat, V., Bhaumik, S.: Data augmentation using generative adversarial networks for pneumonia classification in chest Xrays. 2019 Fifth ICIIP, pp. 574–579 (2019)
37. Srivastav, D., Bajpai, A., Srivastava, P.: Improved classification for pneumonia detection using transfer learning with GAN based synthetic image augmentation. 2021 11th (Confluence), pp. 433–437 (2021). https://doi.org/10.1109/Confluence51648.2021.9377062
38. Cao, J., et al.: Exploiting deep cross-slice features from CT images for multi-class pneumonia classification. 2021 IEEE (ICIP), pp. 205–209 (2021)
39. Khriji, L., et al.: COVID-19 Recognition based on patient's coughing and breathing patterns analysis: DL approach. 2021 29th (FRUCT), pp. 185–191 (2021)
40. Sharan, R.V., et al.: Automatic croup diagnosis using cough sound recognition. IEEE Trans. Biomed. Eng. **66**(2), 485–495 (2019)
41. Benyelles, F.Z., et al.: Content based COVID-19 chest X-ray and CT images retrieval framework using stacked auto-encoders. 2020 2ndIHSH, pp. 119–124 (2021)
42. Layode, O.F., Rahman, M.: A chest X-ray image retrieval system for COVID-19 detection using deep transfer learning and denoising auto encoder 2020 (CSCI) (2020)
43. Jalali, S.M.J., et al.: An oppositional-Cauchy based GSK evolutionary algorithm with a novel deep ensemble reinforcement learning strategy for COVID-19 diagnosis. Appl. Soft Comput. **111** (2021)
44. Ahmadian, S., et al.: A novel deep neuroevolution-based image classification method to diagnose coronavirus disease (COVID-19). Comput. Biol. Med. **139** (2021)
45. Larson, D.B., et al.: Regulatory Frameworks for Development and Evaluation of AI–Based Diagnostic Imaging Algorithms: Summary and Recommendations (2020)
46. Regulation (EU) 2017/745 of the European Parliament and of the Council of 5 April 2017 on medical devices. http://data.europa.eu/eli/reg/2017/745/oj

Impact of Chronic Lung Disease Using Deep Learning: A Survey

N. Vignesh Kumaran(✉) and D. M. D. Preethi

Department of Computer Science and Engineering, PSNA College of Engineering and Technology, Dindigul, India

vigneshkumaran707@gmail.com, dmdpreeth@gmail.com

Abstract. Artificial intelligence has developed in recent years. It is mostly enviable to discover the facility of contemporaneous state-of-the-art techniques and to examine lung nodule features in terms of a large population. Now a days lung plays a major role all over the world in early prevention in disease identification. The latest progress of deep learning sustains the recognition and categorization of medical images of respiratory problems. There are varieties of lung diseases to be analyzed to select the high mortality rate among them. In this paper, we have provided a comprehensive study of several lung ailments, in particular lung cancer, pneumonia, and COVID-19/SARS, Chronic Obstructive Pulmonary Disease. Existing deep learning methodology used to diagnose lung diseases are clearly explained and it will be helpful for the lung disease identify the system.

Keywords: Artificial intelligence · Lung disease · Deep learning

1 Introduction

The living cells and extracellular substances are arranged into tissues, organs, and structures that make up a human's physical substance. Humans have five vital organs that must work properly in order for them to live [1]. The brain, lungs, heart, liver, kidneys are among these organs. The brain serves as a command centre, receiving and transmitting signals to other organs via the neurological system and producing hormones [2]. The human heart is in control of pumping blood around bodies [3]. The function of the kidneys is to eliminate waste and excess fluid from circulation [4]. The liver has to detoxify toxic substances from the body [5]. The lungs are in control of extracting oxygen from the air while breathing and transporting it to our bloodstream and delivered to our cells and Carbon dioxide is also removed by the lungs [6]. A coronavirus illness has begun to spread over the world, posing a serious threat to public health and the illness has been categorized as a pandemic, by March 2021, there were 118.7 million individuals on the globe, with 2.6 million fatalities confirmed [7]. As per the World Health Organization's most early stats, more than two hundred sixty-seven million individuals had been infected as of December 10th, 2021, with close to 5,285,888 fatalities [8].

Published by Springer Nature Switzerland AG 2022
E. J. Neuhold et al. (Eds.): ICCCSP 2022, IFIP AICT 651, pp. 46–59, 2022.
https://doi.org/10.1007/978-3-031-11633-9_5

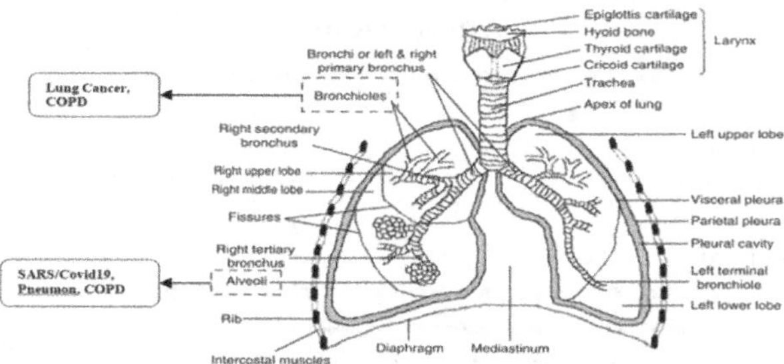

Fig. 1. Lung respiratory system anatomy [source: https://pharmacyimages.blogspot.com]

The basic tasks of the lungs are to inhale oxygen and expel carbon dioxide. On either side of the chest, the lungs are set of two soft air-filled organs thorax. The Lungs inhale, air enters through the nose and travels by way of the trachea (windpipe) [9]. Alveoli are small air sacs located near the end of the bronchioles. During breathing diaphragm muscle that moves up and down in the chest, forcing air in and out of the lung [10]. The basic tasks of the lungs are to take in oxygen and expel carbon dioxide. Lung Structure is shown in Fig. 1 Lung Respiratory System Anatomy.

2 Review of Lung Disease

Lung diseases generally called respiratory diseases are disorders that affect the lungs, bronchi, and other elements of the respiratory system. Chronic Obstructive Pulmonary Disease (COPD) is a chronic illness that makes it difficult to breathe and a symptom of this disease was having trouble blowing air out from the lung [11]. It has two types of COPD, Emphysema and chronic bronchitis which are both caused by smoking; lung alveoli (air sacs) get damaged [11]. Asthma indicia of the lung muscles tighten and irritability, Airway blockage, Inflammation are illuminated [12]. Acute bronchitis causes nagging cough and mucus and the manifestation of this disease was infected of the lung's large airways (bronchi) [13]. Recognition by checking the oxygen levels in the blood, lung function test, Blood tests, chest X-ray is expounded [14]. Pneumonia causes difficulty to get enough oxygen into the blood while breathing. A sign of this disease was streptococcus pneumonia (bacteria) [15]. Diagnosis along with CT scan, X-ray of the chest, arterial blood gas test, sputum test, blood testing and pulse oximetry test is illustrated [16]. Pulmonary fibrosis disease causes shortness of breath [17]. Different types of crucial diseases that affect the lung are shown in Fig. 2 Lung Disease Infection Rate.

Sarcoidosis disease causes inflammation in small regions of the lung. It is a sign of this disease was granulomas are abnormal lumps or nodules made up of inflammatory tissues. Blood tests, pulmonary function tests, HRCT scans, and upper body X-rays are all used to identify the condition discussed [18]. A thin membrane that borders the interior of the chest wall and the surface of the lungs is known as the pleura on X-rays, pleural effusions look white. Chest X-ray was used to make the identification [19]. Recognition by BMI Calculation, Skin fold callipers physical test is described [20].

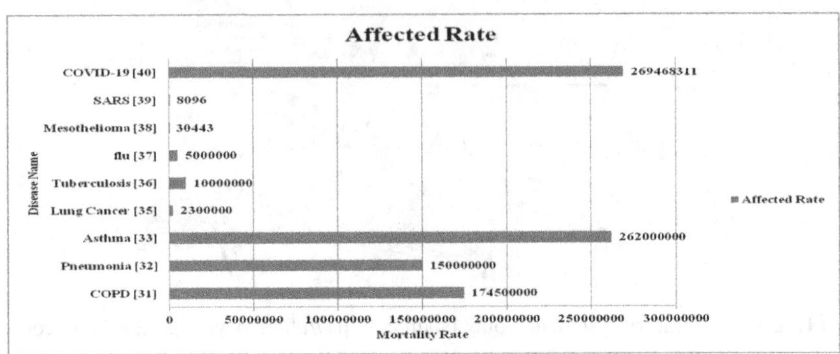

Fig. 2. Lung disease infection rate

Blood tests, chest film, CAT scans, and electrocardiograms are utilized to make recognition are illuminated [21]. Bronchiectasis lung disease causes coughing with large amounts of mucus. Blood tests, Roentgen rays test, pulmonary function tests and CAT scans and are used to make recognition is specified [22]. It symptom of this disease was cysts form throughout the lungs (gas). Blood tests, chest film scans, bronchoscopy test, pulmonary function tests, and thoracoscopy are used to make detection [23].Recognition by way of blood tests, DNA test, and sweat test is expounded [24]. Blood tests, chest X-rays, CT scans, and pulmonary function tests are used to make identification and it is amply elucidated [25]. Lung cancer disease causes cancer may affect almost any part of the lung. It looks like soft, pinkish grey walls of the bronchi or bronchioles (lung airways) or alveoli were the first to show signs of this illness (air sacs). Spiral or helical low-dose CT scanning is used to diagnose by early stages of lung cancer are illuminated [26]. Identification along with Blood tests, chest X-ray, Skin test, Acid-fast bacillus (AFB) tests [27]. Acute respiratory distress syndrome (ARDS), which causes breathing issues. The symptom of this disease was Fluid building up in the lung, limiting oxygen from reaching organs [28]. The symptom of this disease was fungus Coccidioides infection when inhaled. Recognition by way of Blood tests, chest X-ray, CT scan, a skin test is illustrated [29].

Histoplasmosis disease, which causes cough. The symptom of this disease was breathing in histoplasma capsulatum, a soil-borne fungus and a case of the flu disease [30]. Blood tests, CAT scans test, pulmonary function tests, chest roentgen rays test and lung biopsies are all used to make a recognition were explained [31]. Quick antigen testing, immune fluorescence tests, and rapid molecular assays reverse transcription-polymerase chain reaction test are all used to identify flu is elucidated [32].

These are the lung diseases affected. Lung Disease Death Rate is shown in Fig. 3 Perceive COVID-19, COPD, Pneumonia, Lung Cancer because of a higher fatality rate.

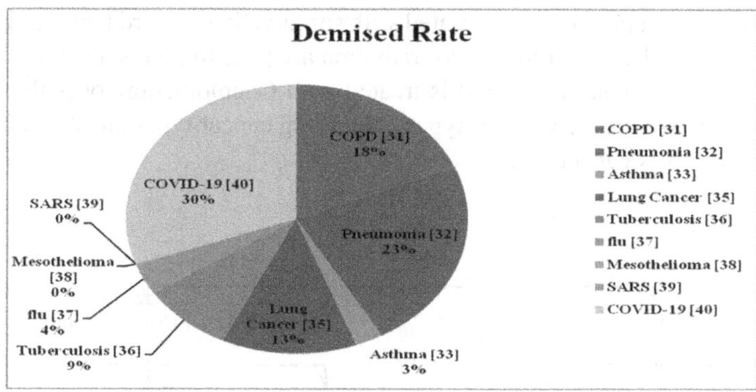

Fig. 3. Lung disease demised rate

Mesothelioma is a type of cancer cell, which invades and damages nearby tissues. Blood tests, fluid and tissue sample testing, chest X-ray, paracentesis, CT scan, and thoracentesis are all used to make a spotting tumor cell and it is clearly exemplified [33]. Pertussis disease causes coughing. It's a contagious infection of the bronchi (airways). Diagnosis by way of Blood tests, chest X-ray is expounded [34]. Pulmonary hypertension disease caused by High blood pressure and the indication of this illness was high blood pressure in the arteries [35]. Blood tests, CAT scans, upper body X-rays scan, and pulmonary function tests are used to make recognition was discussed [36].

Severe acute respiratory syndrome (SARS) disease causes a virus that infects body cells and uses them to replicate itself [28]. The SARS-CoV-2/COVID-19 disease can cause pneumonia, both lungs are affected and fill with fluid, making breathing difficult [37]. SARS-CoV-2/COVID-19 disease's symptoms immediately affect the lungs and destroy the alveoli (tiny air sacs). Pneumothorax disease, which causes coughing. Diagnosis by way of EKG to assess the heart functioning, arterial blood gas and pulse oximetry test to detect oxygen in the blood is illustrated [38].

3 Lung Disease Analysis

Due to Lung diseases bronchioles, alveoli are affected due to region, drug history, working environment, genetic predisposition and age. Let us discuss major causes of diseases such as Lung Cancer, Covid-19/SARS, Pneumonia, and Chronic Obstructive Pulmonary Disease. Lung Cancer detection methods and merits & demerits are illustrated in Sect. 3.1. Covid-19/SARS analyses are given in Sect. 3.2. Pneumonia analysis is given in Sect. 3.3. Chronic Obstructive Pulmonary Disease analysis is given in Sect. 3.4.

3.1 Lung Cancer

Lung cancer cells grow out of control and form a tumor, damaging healthy lung tissue in the meantime [39]. Sudden shortness of breath, continual chest pain, and vision issues, to mention a few symptoms, can occur at any time [40]. Stages first (single tumor) and second (spread to lymph nodes) are treated with surgery. Stages third (spread chest wall, lymph nodes) and Chemotherapy and/or radiation are used to treat stage four. The final fifth stage (Spread beyond the chest) is treated with Chemotherapy or palliative care. Lung cancer has two different major types [41]. Lung cancer types are shown in Fig. 4. [Source: https://www.cancer.org/].

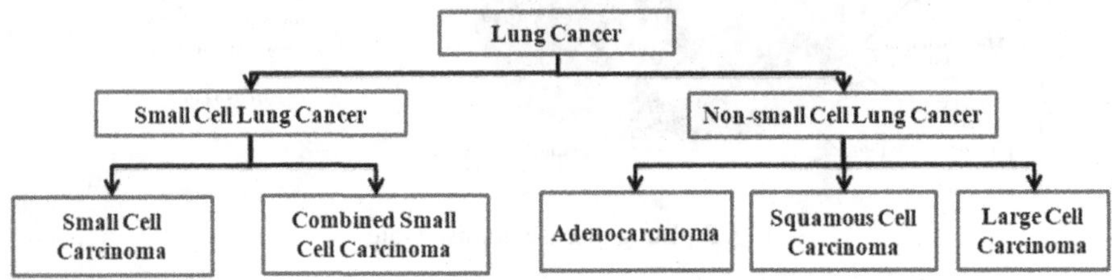

Fig. 4. Lung cancer types

- **Small cell lung cancer**
  It is also known as Oat cell lung cancer. It is estimated that 10% to 15% of all lung cancers are caused by this SCLC. Nearly 70% of those with SCLC will already have cancer that has spread by the time they are diagnosed. It can be treated with chemotherapy and radiation therapy [41].
  Small cell carcinoma
  It is most commonly found in the bronchi (breathing tubes) and spreads rapidly throughout the body, forming huge tumor and spreading metastasizing.
  Combined small cell carcinoma
  It is a combination of small cell and squamous cell carcinomas, with or without adenocarcinoma.
- **Non Small cell lung cancer**
  It is estimated that 80% to 85% of all lung cancers are caused by this NSCLC [42].
  Adenocarcinoma
  It's more typically seen in the outer regions of the lung. It's also more likely to be discovered before proceeding it spreads.
  Squamous cell carcinoma
  Squamous cells are flatter cells that line around the interior of the lung airways. It is generally located near an air tube in the middle of the lung (bronchus). Frequently seen near a primary airway bronchus in the middle area of the lungs and it is connected to a history of smoking.
  Large cell (undifferentiated) carcinoma
  It can develop in any region of the lungs. It has a proclivity for spreading and growing rapidly, increasing the difficulty of treatment.

Apart from common Lung cancer, there are some rare categories which are Pancoast Cancer, Carcinoid cancer. Table 1 is shown below discussing the lung cancer identification and it is methods with data set label and Performance Measure.

Table 1. Lung Cancer with their working methods

Author/Year	Methodology/Performance	Limitation
Surendar P, 2021 [40]	Classification using DNN-ASCCS Neural-Network with accuracy 99.17%	Difficulty in the discovery of early lung tumor classification
Ying Su, 2020 [43]	R-CNN algorithm can identify lung nodules with accuracy 91.2%	Lack of accuracy
Anushikha Singh, 2021 [44]	Deep neural network techniques are used for classification with accuracy 98%, specificity 99.71%, jaccard index 95.21%, dice coefficient restnet18 95.28%	New investigation is difficult
Stojan Trajanovski, 2021 [45]	DNN algorithm is used to assess cancer risk with Sensitivity-93%, specificity -81%, Area Under the Curve of 94%	Smaller database is only allowed
M. Ibrahim, 2021 [7]	Diagnosed using a VGG19 + CNN deep learning model with Accuracy-98.05%, Recall-98.05%,Precision-98.43%, Specificity-99.5%	Only pre-trained model is implemented

3.2 Covid-19/SARS

It starts from the Lung area only. Affects only lungs area damages the alveoli (tiny air sacs). It affected the Lungs mostly. The virus causes damage to the alveolus and capillary walls and linings. As a result of the damaged lung, plasma protein debris gathers on the alveolus wall and thickens the lining. Furthermore, a lack of oxygen reaching the body's interior organs generates a deficit and hinders organ function [46]. The air sacs are damaged, a fluid inflow ensues and it is mostly composed of inflammatory cells and protein, and this fluid build-up triggers pneumonia [47]. Table 2 shows Covid-19/SARS studies and their algorithm techniques.

Table 2. Covid-19/SARS with their working methods

Author/Year	Methodology/Performance	Limitation
Shayan Hassantaba, 2020 [48]	COVID-19 is evaluated using a ResNet with SVM model with 95.38% Accuracy, 97.29% Sensitivity	Smaller dataset is tried
Seda Arslan Tuncer, 2021 [49]	Scat-NET architecture with SVM Classification Layer with accuracy 92.4%	It requires more precision
Kabid Hassan Shibly, 2020 [50]	Faster R–CNN with Accuracy-97.36%, Specificity-95.48%, Sensitivity-97.65%	Robustness is less
Md. Zabirul Islam, 2020 [51]	Convolutional Neural Network model with Accuracy-99.4%, Specificity 99.2%, Sensitivity-99.3%	Algorithm complexity is high

3.3 Pneumonia

Pneumonia is a lung illness that affects the airways. It leads to inflammation of the alveoli in one or both lungs and alveoli filled with fluid or purulent substance. Different kinds of pneumonia [52] are shown in Fig. 5 [source: https://www.healthline.com/].

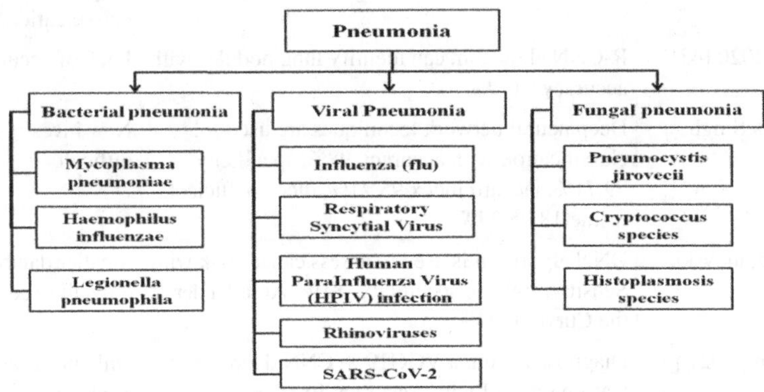

Fig. 5. Pneumonia types

Pneumonia can be categorized according to the part of the lungs it affects.

- **Bacterial pneumonia**
  Streptococcus pneumonia is the most prevalent cause of bacterial pneumonia.
  Mycoplasma pneumonia
  Mycoplasma pneumonia is a highly infectious respiratory illness spread via contact with respiratory secretions.
  Haemophilus influenza
  Haemophilus influenza is a Gram-negative coccobacillus that infects children's upper respiratory tracts through nasal secretions.
  Legionella pneumophila
  Legionnaires' disease is a particularly severe type of pneumonia, It is a lung infection.
- **Viral pneumonia**
  Pneumonia is frequently caused by respiratory viruses.
  Influenza (flu)
  Influenza is an infection that affects the nasal, windpipe, and lungs, among other parts of the respiratory system.
  Respiratory Syncytial Virus
  Respiratory Syncytial Virus is among the most common viruses that cause lung and airway infections in infants and small children.
  Human Parainfluenza Virus (HPIV)
  Babies, small children, the elderly, and anyone with weakened immune systems are all at risk and the most prevalent victims of the Human Parainfluenza Virus, however, anybody can become infected.
  Rhinoviruses

The common cold is an upper respiratory illness. Inhaling virus particles from an affected people's cough, sneeze, talk, or unwanted particles from when they wipe their nose spreads the common cold.
SARS-CoV-2
The SARS-CoV-2 virus can infect both the lungs and fluid fills them making breathing difficult. The symptoms of this illness strike the lungs first, destroying the alveoli (tiny air sacs).

- **Fungal pneumonia**
Fungal pneumonia can be caused by fungi found in soil or bird droppings. Immune-compromised individuals are more susceptible to pneumonia in the long run.
Pneumocystis jirovecii
Pneumocystis Carinii Pneumonia (PCP), is a kind of pneumonia caused by Pneumocystis Carinii, also known as Pneumocystis jirovecii.
Cryptococcus species
Cryptococcosis is an infectious illness caused by pathogenic encapsulated yeasts of the genus Cryptococcus; it can appear in a variety of ways.
Histoplasmosis species
Histoplasmosis is a bacterial illness that affects the lungs. Inhaling Histoplasma capsulatum fungus spores causes it. Apart from common pneumonia, there are some rare categories which are bronchi pneumonia, lobar pneumonia. Table 3 describes the methodology used in Pneumonia disease analysis.

Table 3. Pneumonia with their working methods

Author/Year	Methodology/Performance	Limitation
Adhiyaman Manickam, 2021 [16]	Segmented and classified using the U-Net architecture with ResNet50-Accuracy-93.06%, InceptionV3-Accuracy-92.97% and InceptionResNetV2-Accuracy-92.40%	It is validated with pre trained model
Helena Liz, 2021 [53]	Combines XAI Techniques and CNN Model with Area Under the Curve (AUC) = 0.92	It is incorporated into a particular dataset

3.4 Chronic Obstructive Pulmonary Disease (COPD)

Chronic Obstructive Pulmonary Disease (COPD) is a protracted lung illness that makes breathing difficult [54]. Emphysema and chronic bronchitis are the two most common conditions that cause COPD and two issues are generally present at the same time in COPD patients [55], and their severity varies is shown in Fig. 6 [Source: https://www.medicalnewstoday.com/articles/copd-types] and Table 4 summarizes the techniques used in studies of COPD.

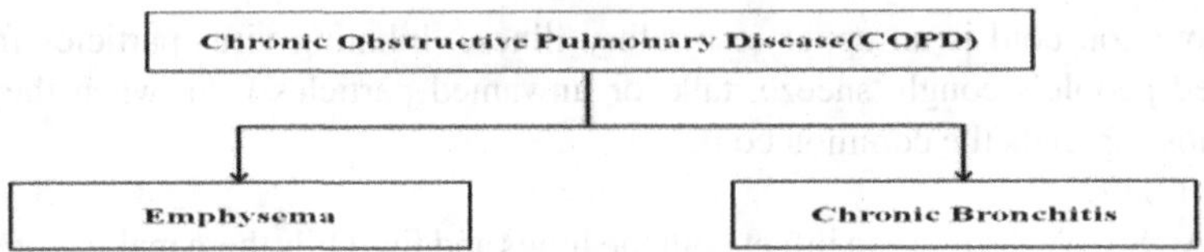

Fig. 6. Chronic obstructive pulmonary disease

Emphysema is a lung condition in toxic tobacco that damages the alveoli at the end of the lung bronchioles tiniest air channels. Chronic bronchitis is characterized by a daily cough as well as mucous production (sputum). Table 4 Represent the Chronic Obstructive Pulmonary Disease (COPD) recognition.

Table 4. COPD with their working method

Author/Year	Methodology/Performance	Limitation
Gokhan Altanc, 2020 [54]	Deep Learning techniques with Hilbert-Huang with Accuracy 93.67%, Sensitivity 91%, Specificity 96.33%	Complexity is high
Ran DU, 2020 [55]	Multi-view CNN based Classification with Accuracy 88.6%	Accuracy is less

The high lung disease demise rate is shown in Fig. 7 four major diseases that affect the lungs most in a current scenario. Commonly affected regions are the lung area and It is similar symptoms are Breathing Issues, Persistent cough.

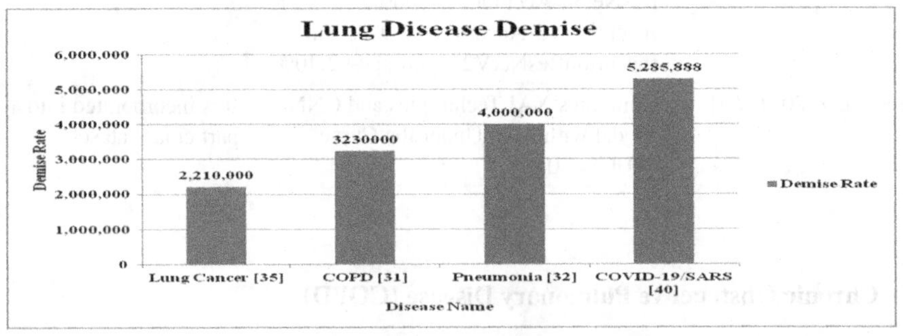

Fig. 7. Lung disease demise rate

4 Summary

Based on the literature carryout in the above sections four major diseases lung cancer, COPD, Pneumonia, COVID-19/SARS has been identified that cause major impact on lung. Research will be extended to improve the consequences faced due to above diseases. Here few dataset also represented in Table 5 to validate the disease in future.

Table 5. Dataset for lung diseases

Disease	Dataset
Lung Cancer	The Lung Image Database Consortium and Image Database Resource Initiative (LIDCIDRI) [40, 43]
	Japanese Society of Radiological Technology (JSRT) dataset, MC dataset, Shenzhen dataset, Indian hospital private dataset [44]
	National Lung Screening Trial (NLST), Lahey Hospital and Medical Center (LHMC), Kaggle competition data, the University of Chicago data [45]
	COVID19-GIT hub public data collection, the Radiological Society of North America (RSNA), the Italian Society of Medical and Interventional Radiology (SIRM), and Radiopaedia [7]
COVID-19/SARS	Github public access dataset: Name: Fig. 1 COVID-19 Chest X-ray Dataset Initiative [48]
	Private data Elazig City Hospital between 01.10.2020 and 01.01.2021 [49]
	COVID chest X-Ray dataset curated by Dr. Joseph Cohen, a postdoctoral fellow at the University of Montreal, RSNA pneumonia detection challenge Kaggle dataset [50]
	GitHub Public Dataset, Radiopaedia, The Cancer Imaging Archive (TCIA), and the Italian Society of Radiology (SIRM) [51]
Pneumonia	MIMIC-CXR dataset (X-ray images), LUNA16 and LIDC-IDRI datasets (CT images) [16]
	X-ray pediatric-pneumonia (XrPP) dataset provided by BenGurion University (Israel) [53]
COPD	RespiratoryDatabase@TR is a multi-media respiratory database and provides an equipped potentiality of analyzing COPD for digital signal processing [54]
	Central Hospital Affiliated to Shenyang Medical College during the period of 2016–2020 [55]

5 Conclusion

Lung diseases are one of the most widespread therapeutic situations in the world. Respiratory diseases are the primary source of disease and illness in the world. Sixty five million people suffer from lung diseases and three million expire from it each year, making it the third foremost reason for demise worldwide. This study shows the extensive survey of prospective lung diseases and the detailed view of lung cancer, COPD, Pneumonia, COVID-19/SARS. The lung diseases listed above cannot be completely healed but recognition at an early stage can assist professionals in treating it effectively and inhibit the patient's prominent lung disease. Further research is required into an impending snag for lung disease and it is useful for medical diagnosis.

References

1. Human Organs and Organ Systems Homepage. https://bio.libretexts.org/Bookshelves/Human_Biology/Book%3A_Human_Biology_(Wakim_and_Grewal)/10%3A_Introduction_to_the_Human_Body/10.4%3A_Human_Organs_and_Organ_Systems
2. Çetin, G., Akkulak, G., Özdemir, S.: Locate the Internal organs in the human body: a survey in Turkey. Procedia Soc. Behav. Sci. **116**, 2819–2824 (2014). https://doi.org/10.1016/j.sbspro.2014.01.663
3. Meng, Y.: A machine learning approach to classifying self-reported health status in a cohort of patients with heart disease using activity tracker data. IEEE J. Biomed. Heal. Inf. **24**(3), 878–884 (2020). https://doi.org/10.1109/JBHI.2019.2922178
4. Hussain, M.A., Hamarneh, G., Garbi, R.: Cascaded regression neural nets for kidney localization and segmentation-free volume estimation. IEEE Trans. Med. Imaging **40**(6), 1555–1567 (2021). https://doi.org/10.1109/TMI.2021.3060465
5. Ibragimov, B., Toesca, D.A.S., Yuan, Y., Koong, A.C., Chang, D.T., Xing, L.: Neural networks for deep radiotherapy dose analysis and prediction of liver SBRT outcomes. IEEE J. Biomed. Health Inf. **23**(5), 1821–1833 (2019). https://doi.org/10.1109/JBHI.2019.2904078
6. Alves, S.S.A., de Souza, E., Reboucas, S.A., de Oliveira, F., Braga, A.M., Filho, P.P.R.: Lung diseases classification by analysis of lung tissue densities. IEEE Latin America Trans. **18**(09), 1329–1336 (2020). https://doi.org/10.1109/TLA.2020.9381790
7. Ibrahim, D.M., Elshennawy, N.M., Sarhan, A.M.: Deep-chest: multi-classification deep learning model for diagnosing COVID-19, pneumonia, and lung cancer chest diseases. Comput. Biol. Med. **132**, 104348 (2021). https://doi.org/10.1016/j.compbiomed.2021.104348
8. WHO Coronavirus (COVID-19) Dashboard Homepage. https://covid19.who.int/. Accessed 27 Dec 2021
9. How Lungs Work | American Lung Association Homepage. https://www.lung.org/lung-health-diseases/how-lungs-work. Accessed 27 Dec 2021
10. Lung Anatomy, Function, and Homepage. https://www.healthline.com/human-body-maps/lung. Accessed 10 Dec 2021
11. Dobric, A., et al.: Novel pharmacological strategies to treat cognitive dysfunction in chronic obstructive pulmonary disease. Pharmacol. Ther. A., 108017 (2021). https://doi.org/10.1016/J.PHARMTHERA.2021.108017
12. Tomita, K., et al.: Deep learning facilitates the diagnosis of adult asthma. Allergol. Int. **68**(4), 456–461 (2019). https://doi.org/10.1016/J.ALIT.2019.04.010
13. Yu, G., et al.: Identification of pediatric respiratory diseases using a fine-grained diagnosis system. J. Biomed. Inform. **117**, 103754 (2021). https://doi.org/10.1016/J.JBI.2021.103754
14. Jefferson, N., Fitzgerald, K.: Antibiotic stewardship for treatment of acute bronchitis in retail health. J. Nurse Practit. **16**(8), 608–611 (2020). https://doi.org/10.1016/j.nurpra.2020.05.005
15. Stokes, K., et al.: A machine learning model for supporting symptom-based referral and diagnosis of bronchitis and pneumonia in limited resource settings. Biocybern. Biomed. Eng. **41**(4), 1288–1302 (2021). https://doi.org/10.1016/J.BBE.2021.09.002

16. Manickam, A., JJiang, Y., Zhou, A., Soundrapandiyan, R., Samuel, D.: Automated pneumonia detection on chest X-ray images: a deep learning approach with different optimizers and transfer learning architectures. Measurement **184**, 109953 (2021). https://doi.org/10.1016/j.measurement.2021.109953
17. Kim, G.H.J., Shi, Y., Yu, W., Wong, W.K.: A study design for statistical learning technique to predict radiological progression with an application of idiopathic pulmonary fibrosis using chest CT images. Contemp. Clin. Trials **104**, 106333 (2021). https://doi.org/10.1016/J.CCT.2021.106333
18. Togo, R., et al.: Cardiac sarcoidosis classification with deep convolutional neural network-based features using polar maps. Comput. Biol. Med. **104**, 81–86 (2019). https://doi.org/10.1016/J.COMPBIOMED.2018.11.008
19. Tsai, C.H., et al.: Automatic deep learning-based pleural effusion classification in lung ultrasound images for respiratory pathology diagnosis. Phys. Medica **83**, 38–45 (2021). https://doi.org/10.1016/J.EJMP.2021.02.023
20. Piper, A.J.: Obesity Hypoventilation Syndrome. In: Modulation of Sleep by Obesity, Diabetes, Age, and Diet, pp. 91–100. Elsevier (2015). https://doi.org/10.1016/B978-0-12-420168-2.00011-9
21. Schmuelling, L.: Deep learning-based automated detection of pulmonary embolism on CT pulmonary angiograms: no significant effects on report communication times and patient turnaround in the emergency department nine months after technical implementation. Eur. J. Radiol. **141**, 109816 (2021). https://doi.org/10.1016/j.ejrad.2021.109816
22. JWu, J.: Refining diagnostic criteria for paediatric bronchiectasis using low-dose CT scan. Respir. Med. **187**, 106547 (2021). https://doi.org/10.1016/j.rmed.2021.106547
23. Crivelli, P.: Role of thoracic imaging in the management of lymphangioleiomyomatosis. Respir. Med. **157**, 14–20 (2019). https://doi.org/10.1016/j.rmed.2019.08.013
24. Zucker, E.J.: Deep learning to automate Brasfield chest radiographic scoring for cystic fibrosis. J. Cystic Fibrosis **19**(1), 131–138 (2020). https://doi.org/10.1016/j.jcf.2019.04.016
25. Agarwala, S.: Deep learning for screening of interstitial lung disease patterns in high-resolution CT images. Clin. Radiol. **75**(6), 481.e1-481.e8 (2020). https://doi.org/10.1016/j.crad.2020.01.010
26. Doppalapudi, S., Qiu, R.G., Badr, Y.: Lung cancer survival period prediction and understanding: deep learning approaches. Int. J. Med. Inf. **148**, 104371 (2021). https://doi.org/10.1016/j.ijmedinf.2020.104371
27. Sathitratanacheewin, S., Sunanta, P., Pongpirul, K.: Deep learning for automated classification of tuberculosis-related chest X-Ray: dataset distribution shift limits diagnostic performance generalizability. Heliyon **6**(8), e04614 (2020). https://doi.org/10.1016/j.heliyon.2020.e04614
28. Reamaroon, N., Sjoding, M.W., Gryak, J., Athey, B.D., Najarian, K., Derksen, H.: Automated detection of acute respiratory distress syndrome from chest X-Rays using Directionality Measure and deep learning features. Comput. Biol. Med. **134**, 104463 (2021). https://doi.org/10.1016/j.compbiomed.2021.104463
29. Ott, J.: Detecting pulmonary Coccidioidomycosis with deep convolutional neural networks. Mach Learn Appl **5**, 100040 (2021). https://doi.org/10.1016/j.mlwa.2021.100040
30. Miller, J.: A structured program maximizes benefit of lung cancer screening in an area of endemic histoplasmosis. Ann. Thoracic Surg. **114**(1), 241–247 (2022). https://doi.org/10.1016/j.athoracsur.2021.06.070
31. Aliboni, L.: Quantitative CT analysis in chronic hypersensitivity pneumonitis: a convolutional neural network approach. Acad. Radiol. **29**, S31–S40 (2022). https://doi.org/10.1016/j.acra.2020.10.009
32. Zan, A., et al.: DeepFlu: a deep learning approach for forecasting symptomatic influenza a infection based on pre-exposure gene expression. Comput. Methods Programs Biomed. **213**, 106495 (2022). https://doi.org/10.1016/J.CMPB.2021.106495

33. Galateau Salle, F., et al.: Comprehensive molecular and pathologic evaluation of transitional mesothelioma assisted by deep learning approach: a multi-institutional study of the international mesothelioma panel from the MESOPATH reference center. J. Thorac. Oncol. **15**(6), 1037–1053 (2020). https://doi.org/10.1016/J.JTHO.2020.01.025
34. Sharan, R.V., Berkovsky, S., Navarro, D.F., Xiong, H., Jaffe, A.: Detecting pertussis in the pediatric population using respiratory sound events and CNN. Biomed Sig Process Control **68**, 102722 (2021). https://doi.org/10.1016/j.bspc.2021.102722
35. Jimenez-del-Toro, O.: A lung graph model for the radiological assessment of chronic thromboembolic pulmonary hypertension in CT. Comput. Biol. Med. **125**, 103962 (2020). https://doi.org/10.1016/j.compbiomed.2020.103962
36. Long, K.: Probability-based Mask R-CNN for pulmonary embolism detection. Neurocomputing **422**, 345–353 (2021). https://doi.org/10.1016/J.NEUCOM.2020.10.022
37. Sharma, A., Tiwari, S., Deb, M.K., Marty, J.L.: Severe acute respiratory syndrome coronavirus-2 (SARS-CoV-2): a global pandemic and treatment strategies. Int. J. Antimicrob. Agents **56**(2), 106054 (2020). https://doi.org/10.1016/j.ijantimicag.2020.106054
38. Li, X.: Deep learning-enabled system for rapid pneumothorax screening on chest CT. Eur. J. Radiol. **120**, 108692 (2019). https://doi.org/10.1016/j.ejrad.2019.108692
39. Jiang, J., et al.: Multiple resolution residually connected feature streams for automatic lung tumor segmentation from CT images. IEEE Trans. Med. Imaging **38**(1), 134–144 (2019). https://doi.org/10.1109/TMI.2018.2857800
40. Surendar, P.: Diagnosis of lung cancer using hybrid deep neural network with adaptive sine cosine crow search algorithm, Elsevier. Accessed Dec 06 2021. https://www.sciencedirect.com/science/article/pii/S1877750321000636
41. Guo, Y.: Histological subtypes classification of lung cancers on CT images using 3D Deep learning and radiomics. Acad. Radiol. **28**(9), e258–e266 (2021) https://doi.org/10.1016/J.ACRA.2020.06.010
42. Tortora, M.: Deep reinforcement learning for fractionated radiotherapy in non-small cell lung carcinoma. Artif. Intell. Med. **119**, p. 102137 (2021). https://doi.org/10.1016/J.ARTMED.2021.102137
43. Su, Y.: Lung nodule detection based on faster R-CNN framework. Elsevier. Accessed 6 Dec 2021. https://www.sciencedirect.com/science/article/pii/S0169260720316990
44. Singh, A., Lall, B., Panigrahi, B.: Deep LF-Net: Semantic lung segmentation from Indian chest radiographs including severely unhealthy images. Elsevier. Accessed 6 Dec 2021. https://www.sciencedirect.com/science/article/pii/S1746809421002639
45. Trajanovski, S.: Towards radiologist-level cancer risk assessment in CT lung screening using deep learning. Elsevier (2019). Accessed 06 Dec 2021. https://www.sciencedirect.com/science/article/pii/S0895611121000318
46. Xu, X.: A deep learning system to screen novel coronavirus disease 2019 pneumonia. Engineering **6**(10), 1122–1129 (2020). https://doi.org/10.1016/J.ENG.2020.04.010
47. Jiang, H., Tang, S., Liu, W., Zhang, Y.: Deep learning for COVID-19 chest CT (computed tomography) image analysis: a lesson from lung cancer. Comput. Struct. Biotechnol. J. **19**, 1391–1399 (2021). https://doi.org/10.1016/J.CSBJ.2021.02.016
48. Hassantabar, S., Ahmadi, M., Sharifi, A.: Diagnosis and detection of infected tissue of COVID-19 patients based on lung x-ray image using convolutional neural network approaches. Chaos, Solitons Fractals **140** (2020). https://doi.org/10.1016/J.CHAOS.2020.110170
49. Tuncer, S.A., Ayyıldız, H., Kalaycı, M., Tuncer, T.: Scat-NET: COVID-19 diagnosis with a CNN model using scattergram images. Comput. Biol. Med. **135**, 104579 (2021). https://doi.org/10.1016/J.COMPBIOMED.2021.104579
50. Shibly, K.H., Dey, S.K., Islam, M.T.U., Rahman, M.M.: COVID faster R–CNN: a novel framework to Diagnose Novel Coronavirus Disease (COVID-19) in X-Ray images. Inf. Med. Unlocked **20**, 100405 (2020). https://doi.org/10.1016/J.IMU.2020.100405

51. Islam, M.Z., Islam, M.M., Asraf, A.: A combined deep CNN-LSTM network for the detection of novel coronavirus (COVID-19) using X-ray images. Inf. Med. Unlocked **20**, 100412 (2020). https://doi.org/10.1016/J.IMU.2020.100412
52. Manickam, A., Jiang, J., Zhou, Y., Sagar, A., Soundrapandiyan, R., Dinesh Jackson Samuel, R.: Automated pneumonia detection on chest X-ray images: a deep learning approach with different optimizers and transfer learning architectures. Measurement **184**, 109953 (2021). https://doi.org/10.1016/J.MEASUREMENT.2021.109953
53. Liz, H., Sánchez-Montañés, M., Tagarro, A., Domínguez-Rodríguez, S., Dagan, R., Camacho, D.: Ensembles of Convolutional Neural Network models for pediatric pneumonia diagnosis. Futur. Gener. Comput. Syst. **122**, 220–233 (2021). https://doi.org/10.1016/J.FUTURE.2021.04.007
54. Altan, G., Kutlu, Y., Allahverdi, N.: Deep learning on computerized analysis of chronic obstructive pulmonary disease. IEEE J. Biomed. Heal. Inf. **24**(5), 1344–1350 (2020). https://doi.org/10.1109/JBHI.2019.2931395
55. Du, R.: Identification of COPD from multi-view snapshots of 3D Lung Airway Tree via Deep CNN. IEEE Access **8**, 38907–38919 (2020). https://doi.org/10.1109/ACCESS.2020.2974617

Detection and Classification of Paddy Leaf Diseases Using Deep Learning (CNN)

S. Maheswaran[1(✉)], S. Sathesh[1], P. Rithika[1], I. Mohammed Shafiq[1], S. Nandita[1], and R. D. Gomathi[2]

[1] Department of Electronics and Communication Engineering, Kongu Engineering College, Perundurai, Erode 638060, Tamil Nadu, India
mmaheswaraneie@gmail.com, sathesh808@gmail.com, {rithikap.20ece, mohammedshafiqi.20ece,nanditas.20ece}@kongu.edu

[2] Department of English, Kongu Engineering College, Perundurai, Erode 638060, Tamil Nadu, India
gomathimaheswaran6@gmail.com

Abstract. India has a huge population and the major source of food supply is from agriculture. Agricultural lands are getting destroyed mostly due to crop diseases, pests and plant diseases. Nowadays it increased fiercely. Plant pathogens are fungi, bacteria, virus or nematodes that damage plant parts such as leaf, panicle, node, stem and roots. So In agriculture, one of the latest researches is detection and classification of crop diseases using images of leaves from plants. The detection of plant diseases by using the image processing methods can help the farmers to protect the agricultural field from getting destroyed or affected. Paddy is a staple crop for much of the world's population. In this research we discuss classification and detection of paddy Leaf diseases using convolutional neural network. We captured paddy leaf images from the field for normal, sheath rot, rice blast, bacterial leaf blight, rice blast, brown spot, rymv and rice tungro for processing the image. In pre-processing, background exclusion is done based on the hue value to extract the non-diseased and diseased part. Feature Extraction is executed by applying Convolutional Neural Network. The proposed system achieved a high accuracy.

Keywords: Crop diseases · Leaves · Pre-processing · Feature extraction · Deep learning model · Convolutional Neural Network

1 Introduction

India is mainly an agriculture country. India is the world's second (2nd) largest producer of sugarcane, rice, cotton and wheat. Agriculture is an important sector of the Indian economy and many people livelihood depend on agriculture. It's the source of our food supply. Industries like small-scale and cottage industries directly depend on raw material from agriculture. It is also associated with foreign trade. Many crops are cultivated in India due to pests and pathogens, most of them are destroyed. Farmers are the backbone of India. Due to yield loss they suffer a lot in terms of production and money. The main

Published by Springer Nature Switzerland AG 2022
E. J. Neuhold et al. (Eds.): ICCCSP 2022, IFIP AICT 651, pp. 60–74, 2022.
https://doi.org/10.1007/978-3-031-11633-9_6

thing is the producer wants to identify the disease at an earlier stage for preventing the widespread of disease to the whole plant. Only early diagnosis of disease will prevent severe loss. Paddy is the primary source of energy for over half of the world's people. Due to this crop, India is one of the leading producers. It is a staple crop. It contains fibre, vitamins, manganese and protein. By-products of paddy are used in many ways. Paddy is affected by various causes. Major causes are fungi, pests, viruses and bacteria. Every year farmers lose nearly 40% of production due to crop disease. Farmers are unable to diagnosis and give preventive measures to control the disease. Like pesticides and insecticides there are various measures available to maintain the crop healthier. But prior recognition of disease and control of the spread of disease is essential. If the plant is affected with disease it shows some specific symptoms which are unique for that disease. These symptoms are known as features of that disease. Using these features, we can identify the disease. Identification of disease through the human eye will not produce more accuracy. It requires expert knowledge and it is expensive and time consuming. So, we approach one of the deep learning methods CNN to detect paddy crop disease from plant images. We take six major paddy crop disease for research they are Pyricularia grisea (P.oryzae) and Xanthomonas oryzae caused blast disease and bacterial leaf blight to paddy crop respectively, Helminthosporium Oryzae and Sarocladium Oryzae caused brown spot and sheath rot respectively, Sobemovirus and Rice tungro bacilliform virus (RTBV) and Rice tungro spherical virus (RTSV) caused rice yellow mottle virus and rice tungro respectively.

Nowadays deep learning has a major role play in recognition of image and speech. In deep learning, the algorithms are inspired from the neurons of the human which is in brain and act as neural networks. Convolutional Neural Network (CNN) is a class of deep neural networks. It is mainly used for processing and recognition of image. One of the advantages of CNN is it predicts the features of an input image automatically without involvement of humans. We develop the model using one of the deep learning methods CNN to detect the crop disease. For that the steps are prepare a dataset, pre-processing, convolution, Relu, pooling and classification.

2 Problem Statement

In agriculture, loss in yield is due to many problems one of the main reasons is crop disease. This crop disease is caused by bacteria, fungi, viruses and pests. Farmers required lot of money for maintenance of yield. If we do not properly diagnosis the disease and causing agent, it leads to further loss in crop, money and time. Proper diagnosis is very important. Paddy is an important staple food crop for nearly 62% of India's population. Undiagnosed paddy crop diseases will lead to severe damage to the cultivation and production of crops. To overcome this issue, in this research we used deep learning (CNN) method. Deep learning is a network capable of adapting itself to new data. Deep learning is developed from composed algorithms of machine learning that enable software to train models to perform specific tasks. They recognise image and speech using neural networks. To overcome the disadvantages of conventional methods we approach a deep learning method. Using deep learning we can easily detect plant diseases. Identifying symptoms for crop disease and knowing the way to control plant diseases is very important. So from this paper, we will give the idea of disease identification using images of leaf. We use image processing and deep learning to overcome this problem. We designed and trained the model using features extracted from CNN. In this system feature extraction is executed by CNN. This paper mainly points out six most common paddy diseases such as blast, sheath rot, bacterial blight, rice tungro, brown spot and rymv. For extracting a feature first we prepare a dataset. Then split that into two, one for testing and another one for training. The images are pre-processed to remove background and reduce the dimension. Feature extraction is carried out by the three layers of conventional neural network namely input, output and hidden layer. These images are fed into the CNN as input. CNN performs convolution and pooling operations and generates a feature map. Finally the output layer classifies the image and shows which disease affected the plant. The proposed system is a model of recognizing the leaf images by deep learning method.

2.1 Paddy Leaf Diseases

Blast

Caused by: Pyricularia grisea (P. oryzae)

Symptoms: At first stage, spots, dots or grey-brown lesions appear on the leaf. Next stage, these lesions become spindle or oval shaped. It has a grey with brown or grey centre. After the lesions become enlarged and affect the leaf.

Effects: This fungus affects all aboveground parts (node, neck, and leaf collar) of paddy. It can kill the plants at seedling stage. If it is severely infected it leads to yield losses (Fig. 1).

Fig. 1. Blast disease

Bacterial Leaf Blight

Caused by: Xanthomonas oryzae.

Symptoms: Initially it appears as water-soaked or yellowish stripes in leaf edges. At severe stages in the leaves greyish white lesions appears and after sometimes it changes to yellowing. If it is severely affected, leaves tend to dry quickly.

Effects: This disease causes yellowing of plants. It leads to yield loss from 20 to more than 70% (Fig. 2).

Fig. 2. Bacterial blight disease

Brown Spot

Caused by: Helminthosporium Oryzae.

Symptoms: It occurs at all stages and affects different parts of the plant. Initially, it begins as small brown spots on leaves at the tillering stage. At a later stage it forms circular or oval brown spots and it kills the entire leaf. When the seed was affected, it leads to discoloration on the grains.

Effects: It affects the spikelet, panicle branches, leaf sheath, glumes, leaves, and coleoptile. Also it affects the rice grains (Fig. 3).

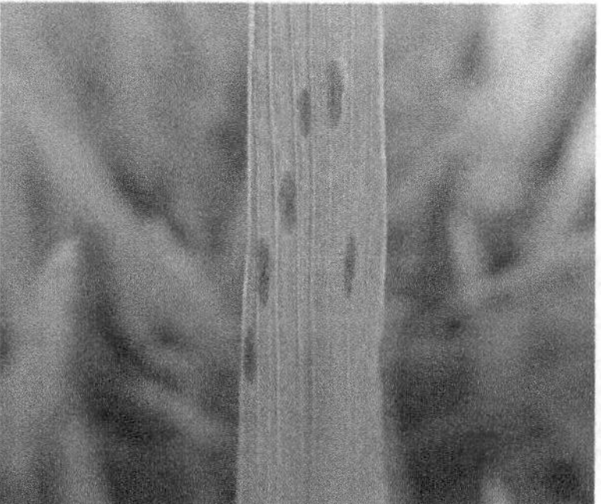

Fig. 3. Brown spot

Sheath Rot

Caused by: Sarocladium Oryzae.

Symptoms: It starts with rotting on the upper sheath of the spikelet that encloses the panicles. It looks like irregular spots with grey midpoint and reddish brown border. These spots become enlarged and often coalesce and it covers most of the leaf sheath. At drastic stage it affects the parts of the grains to persist in the cloak.

Effects: The outer surface of the infected leaflets had a whitish powdery layer. The affected grains became sterile, shrivelled and discoloured (Fig. 4).

Fig. 4. Sheath rot

Rice Yellow Mottle Virus (RYMV)

Caused by: Sobemovirus.

Symptoms: Its characteristics are a general stunting of the plant, an overall yellowing in appearance. After infection, leaves formed are mottled and twisted. At a severe stage, the whole plant will appear yellowish green.

Effects: The infected plants have stunted growth, sterile spikelet and eventually die (Fig. 5).

Fig. 5. RYMV

Rice Tungro

Caused by: Rice tungro spherical virus (RTSV) and Rice tungro bacilliform virus (RTBV).

Symptoms: This disease is spreaded from grasshoppers. It changes the leaf colour into orange yellow colour. It affects plants in all stages of growth.

Effects: It causes leaf discoloration, stunted growth and reduction in tiller numbers. It causes half of the yield losses (Fig. 6).

Fig. 6. Rice tungro

3 Literature Review

In [1], they used histogram to detect paddy leaf. They used image processing methods like enhancement, pre-process, augmentation and then transformed into histogram. Using histogram they extract the difference between the intensity among the original paddy leaf and disease affected leaf. In [2], they used threshold values for identify the symptoms due to rice blast disease. They use the image processing techniques for their research. By using Multi level thresholding, blast disease is split into three stages for identification. In [3], rice diseases are detected from two classifier's Bayes and SVM. The implemented steps are collected images from the plants, it is pre-processed, that result is segmented and feature extracted. Finally, classification is based on classifiers. In [4], detection of crop disease using image processing. In acquisition images are collected and the dataset is prepared and using pre-processing the background is removed. Using segmentation method the Feature extraction is done and finally classification of leaf disease.

In [5], using colour and shape features diseases are detected. After pre-processing, histogram is plotted then segmentation of image, extraction of feature and finally classification. In [6], for recognition of paddy leaf disease they used optimised deep neural networks. They followed image processing methods such as acquisition of image, pre-processing of image, segmentation, extracting features and identification. In feature extraction they used JOA and then classification.

Even though many methods have achieved better results for recognition and classification of plant disease, they have some problems [7–13]. In segmentation, if the image has another leaf or plant it will not consider it. Like histogram, threshold values many methods rely on hand-crafted features they require expensive work and depend on expert knowledge. So we proposed CNN in this research. The better way for leaf disease detection is convolutional neural network [14–18]. This method doesn't require segmentation and hand-crafted features. Compared to many methods CNN provides better accuracy [19–21].

4 Proposed Methodology

Plants are destroyed by various causes. They are crop disease, temperature, climate, insufficient food, sunlight, pests and disease caused by bacteria and fungi. So we proposed the CNN algorithm to diagnosis the disease in plants. From this system, we can achieve high accuracy. The presented system is advanced with three stages they are acquisition of image, pre-processing and extracting features based on CNN. The dataset is prepared by images captured from paddy fields. Then the dataset is divided into two groups for testing and training. In pre-processing background is removed from the images in the dataset and dimensions are reduced. Then feature extraction is carried out by CNN which has a convolutional layer for convolution, Rectified linear unit for non-linearity, pooling layer for decrease the dimensions and fully connected layer for classification. Using this we trained the model. Then it classifies the images of paddy leaves (Figs. 7 and 8).

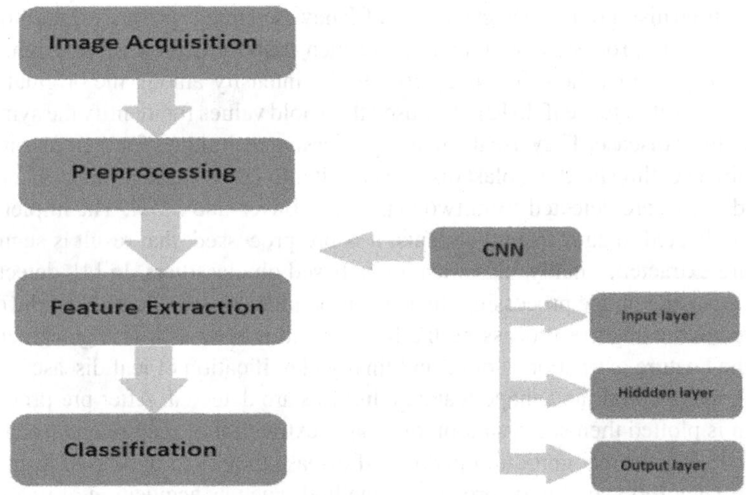

Fig. 7. Basic workflow

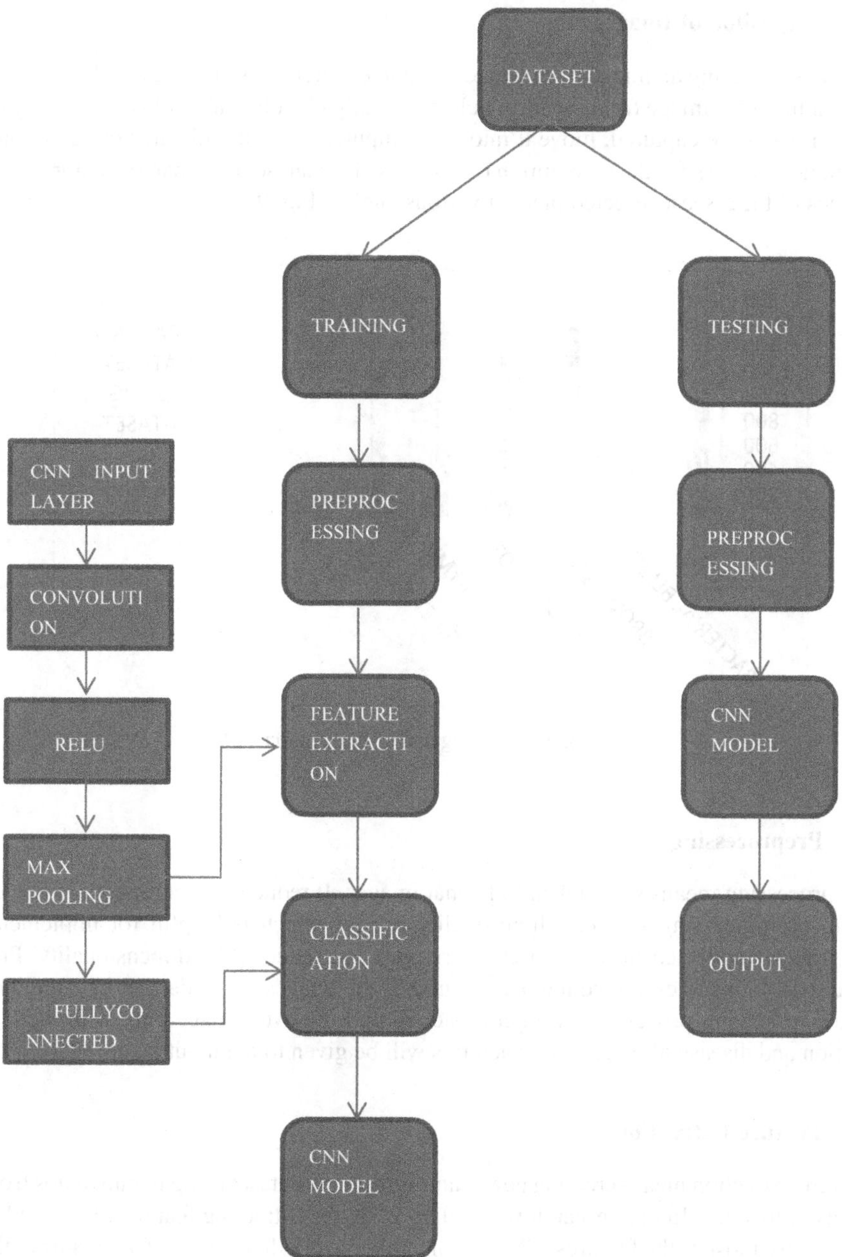

Fig. 8. Workflow block diagram

4.1 Acquisiton of Images

It means retrieving an image from whatever source which is used for research purposes. We captured the image from the farm field of a paddy plant in real world circumstances. After images are captured, move it into the computer. Then it will carry out an implementation process for the recognition of diseases. The dataset is prepared by storing the images of the disease affected plant at various angles (Fig. 9).

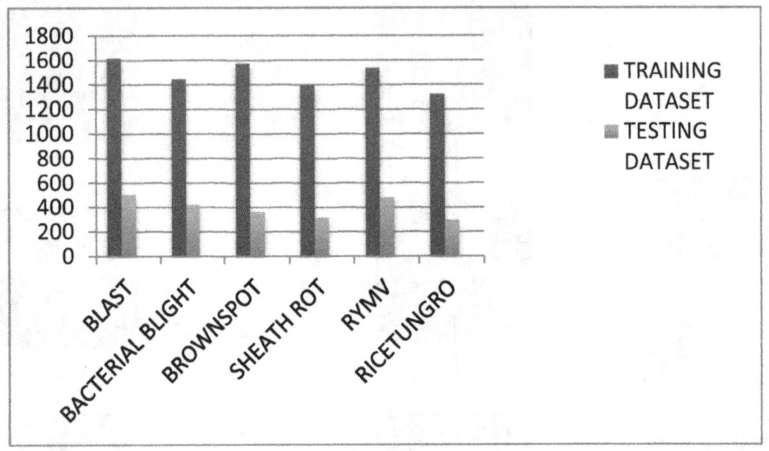

Fig. 9. Training and testing dataset

4.2 Preprocessing

Pre-processing means steps taken to format images. It reduces the computation power. From pre-processing we get a high quality images which is helpful for implementing. Images collected in the dataset are resized and reduced the dimensionality. Preprocessing aims to eliminate the background of the images in the dataset by using hue values. After pre-processing, we get a background removed image only with the leaf portion and disease affected part. Then this will be given to the input layer in CNN.

4.3 Feature Extraction

Feature extraction means creating new features from the dataset using feature maps from the existing ones. In this research we applied CNN for extracting features. It is used to summarise most of the features. CNN is a neural network that extracts features from the images which are given as input. Then it classifies the images based on their extracted features.

4.4 Convolutional Neural Network

ConvNet is a deep learning method shown in Fig. 10. Uses of CNN are recognition and processing of image and to process pixel data. CNN is a location invariant. It has the ability to develop an internal representation of a two dimensional image. Using CNN it is fast to implement. A CNN consists of three layers. First an input layer, where we give input data. Second hidden layer, which processes feature extraction and it has three layers. Third an output layer processes classification and produces output.

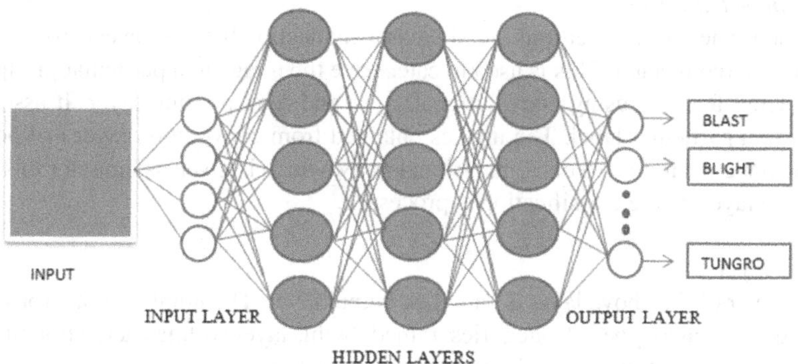

Fig. 10. Layers of convolutional neural network

Input Layer

The images of the disease affected leaves and normal paddy leaves which want to be trained are given as an input to input layer of ConvNet. It takes the grey scaled images for implementation. It accepts the pixel data of the image as input in order of arrays.

Hidden Layers

Convolutional Layer

Convolutional layer carry out convolution operation on input images. Filters are feature detectors by using these filters (like corner, edge, diagonal etc.,) we generate a feature map. The input images are convoluted with filters. It is known as kernels. This is mainly used for extracting features from images which was given.

Rectified Linear Unit

Rectified linear unit is called the activation function. In CNN we use Relu to increase the non-linearity of the images. Usually images are nonlinear so we use this Relu. It speeds up and is faster to compute. There are different types of activation functions available; here we used the Relu activation function. In this layer if the input has positive value it takes the same as output. Or else it replaces the negative value with zero. From this we get a sort out feature map for further implementation.

Pooling Layer

Pooling layer is used to decrease the image dimensions. Two methods of pooling, they are average and max. In max pooling, it considers the maximum value of the pixel data. It reduces the size as much as possible. Max pooling along with convolution helps with position invariant detection. In another method average pooling it considers the average of the pixel data. Most max pooling is used. After pooling it generates a new feature map. Benefits of pooling layers are reduced dimensions and computation power. So the model is tolerant towards variations and distortions.

Fully Connected Layer

It has a dense network of neurons and there is a connection between every two neurons. They are interconnected. This is used to categorize the image to a particular group after we extracted features using convolutional layer and max pooling layer. It associates features to a particular label. The images obtained from convolution layer and pooling layer are flattened to form a one dimensional array, which is given as input for this layer. This is the layer where classification is processed.

Output Layer

The last layer of the above layer is called an output layer. The number of neurons in the final layer is equal to types of categories trained. In this layer softmax activation function is used for classification. It classifies the paddy leaf diseases.

4.5 Experimental Result

We have obtained results from the training model. For six paddy leaf disease we obtained recall and precision in percentage whereas, average precision is obtained by sum of recall and precision divided by two. Mean average precision is the mean of average precision of six diseases. In this research the mean average precision is 95.06% (Table 1).

Table 1. Disease detection result

Diseases	Recall (%)	Precision (%)	Average precision (%)
Blast	98.2	96.43	97.31
Bacterial blight	99.5	95.6	97.55
Brownspot	85.3	93.2	89.25
Sheathrot	100	100	100
RYMV	93.55	99.12	96.3
Ricetungro	82.1	97.8	89.95

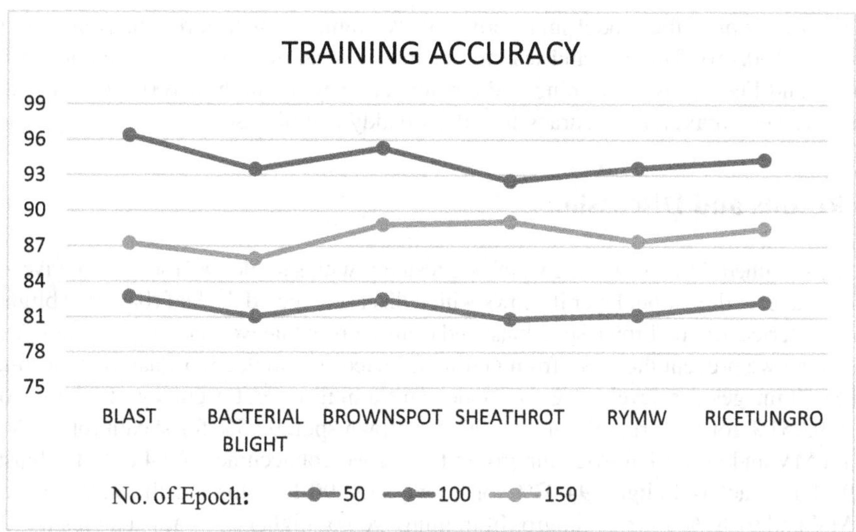

Fig. 11. Training accuracy vs. no. of epoch

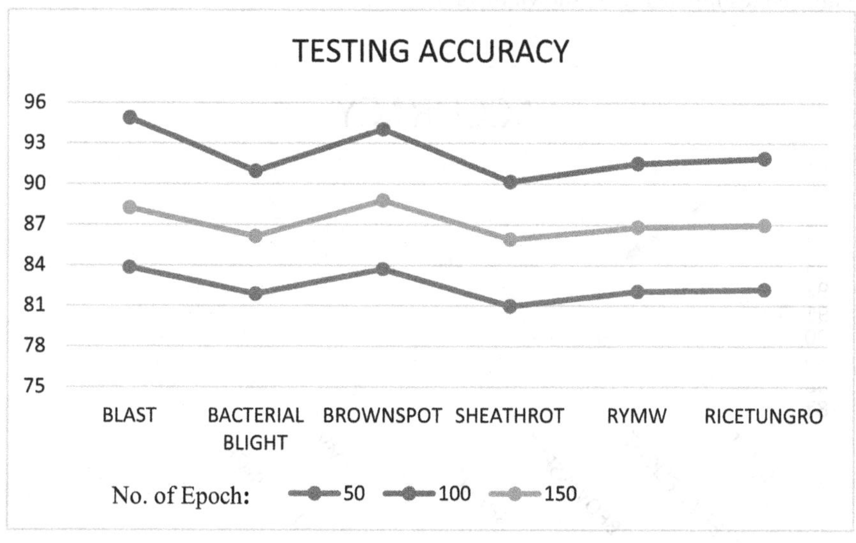

Fig. 12. Testing accuracy vs. no. of epoch

For developing the model more efficient we trained it with three different no. of epoch 50,100,150. Training and testing accuracy for no.of epoch is plotted above in Fig. 11 and Fig. 12. Both training and testing accuracy are high in 100 epoch. In 100 epoch we get a maximum accuracy for all six paddy leaf diseases.

5 Results and Discussions

After we trained the model using CNN, we tested it with samples we took. If we give an input image, at the output layer it shows which disease affected the leaf (bacterial blight, sheath rot, rice tungro, brown spot, blast and rymv). From that we can easily diagnose the disease so we prevent the plant from getting affected. We took 2385 images for testing and 8910 images for developing the model. In training we got accuracy of 96.38%for blast, 93.51% for bacterial blight, 95.29% for brown spot, 92.5% for sheath rot, 93.6% for RYMV and 94.32% for rice tungro. In testing we got accuracy of 94.88% for blast, 90.94% for bacterial blight, 94.03% for brown spot, 90.15% for sheath rot, 91.5% for RYMV and 91.89% for rice tungro. In training we got higher accuracy than testing. If we increase the samples for training and testing we will get more accuracy. Using this data we plot a graph for training and testing accuracy shown in Fig. 13. Accuracy of training and testing dataset is shown in Table 2.

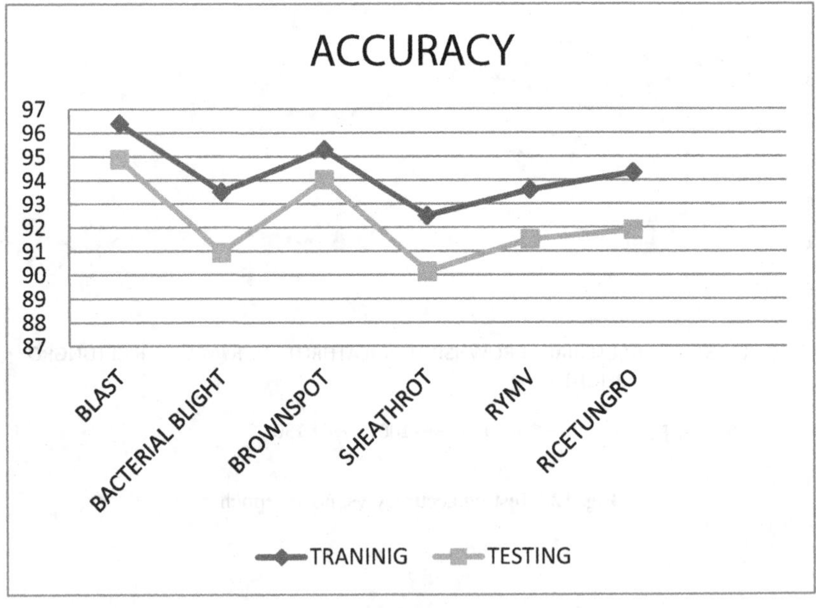

Fig. 13. Training and testing accuracy

Table 2. Accuracy of training and testing dataset

Accuracy	Traninig	Testing
Blast	96.38	94.88
Bacterial blight	93.51	90.94
Brownspot	95.29	94.03
Sheathrot	92.5	90.15
RYMV	93.6	91.5
Ricetungro	94.32	91.89

6 Conclusion

In agriculture, loss of crops mostly occurs due to plant diseases. After the disease gets into a severe stage, we identify the disease. So it leads to severe loss. Plant disease reduces the production and quality of food. It also causes loss in money. We proposed the CNN method because more accuracy can be achieved. For this issue we developed a model using CNN which can recognize and classify the image. For training we took 8910 images and testing 2385 images. In the output, it shows out of six which disease affected the plant. The results can be made more accurate by taking more convolutional layers and hidden neurons. From this we can predict the disease at an early stage. We can prevent crop losses due to plant disease.

References

1. Mukherjee, M., Pal, T., Samanta, D.: Damaged paddy leaf detection using image processing. J. Global Res. Comput. Sci. **3**(10), 07–10 (2012)
2. Bakar, M.A., Abdullah, A., Rahim, N.A., Yazid, H., Misman, S., Masnan, M.: Rice leaf blast disease detection using multi-level colour image thresholding. J. Telecommun. Electron. Comput. Eng. **10**(1–15), 1–6 (2018)
3. Phadikar, S., Sil, J., Das, A.K.: Classification of rice leaf diseases based on morphological changes. Int. J. Inf. Electron. Eng. **2**(3), 460–463 (2012)
4. Khirade, S.D., Patil, A.: Plant disease detection using image processing. 2015 International Conference on Computing Communication Control and Automation. IEEE (2015)
5. Suman, T., Dhruvakumar, T.: Classification of paddy leaf diseases using shape and color features. IJEEE. **7**(01), 239–250 (2015)
6. Ramesh, S., Vydeki, D.: Recognition and classification of paddy leaf diseases using Optimized Deep Neural network with Jaya algorithm. Inf. Process. Agric. **7**(2), 249–260 (2020)
7. Saradhambal, G., Dhivya, R., Latha, S., Rajesh, R.: Plant disease detection and its solution using image classification. Int. J. Pure Appl. Math. **119**(14), 879–884 (2018)
8. Ahmed, K., Shahidi, T.R., Alam, S.M.I., Momen, S.: Rice leaf disease detection using machine learning techniques. In: 2019 International Conference on Sustainable Technologies for Industry 40 (STI). IEEE (2019)
9. Devaraj, A., Rathan, K., Jaahnavi, S., Indira, K.: Identification of plant disease using image processing technique. In: 2019 International Conference on Communication and Signal Processing (ICCSP). IEEE (2019)

10. Al Bashish, D., Braik, M., Bani-Ahmad, S.: Detection and classification of leaf diseases using K-means-based segmentation and. Inf. Technol. J. **10**(2), 267–275 (2011)
11. Maheswaran, S., Sathesh, S., Priyadharshini, P., Vivek, B.: Identification of artificially ripened fruits using smart phones. In: International Conference on Intelligent Computing and Control 2017 (I2C2) (2017)
12. Amara, J., Bouaziz, B., Algergawy, A.: A deep learning-based approach for banana leaf diseases classification. Datenbanksysteme für Business, Technologie und Web (BTW 2017)-Workshopband (2017)
13. Hari, S.S., Sivakumar, M., Renuga, P., Suriya, S.: Detection of plant disease by leaf image using convolutional neural network. In: 2019 International Conference on Vision Towards Emerging Trends in Communication and Networking (ViTECoN). IEEE (2019)
14. Dhaygude, S.B., Kumbhar, N.P.: Agricultural plant leaf disease detection using image processing. Int. J. Adv. Res. Electric. Electron. Instrum. Eng. **2**(1), 599–602 (2013)
15. Al-Hiary, H., Bani-Ahmad, S., Reyalat, M., Braik, M., Alrahamneh, Z.: Fast and accurate detection and classification of plant diseases. Int. J. Comput. Appl.. **17**(1), 31–38 (2011)
16. Pratapagiri, S., Gangula, R., Ravi, G., Srinivasulu, B., Sowjanya, B., Thirupathi, L.: Early detection of plant leaf disease using convolutional neural networks. In: 2021 3rd International Conference on Electronics Representation and Algorithm (ICERA). IEEE (2021)
17. Ferentinos, K.P.: Deep learning models for plant disease detection and diagnosis. Comput. Electron. Agric. **145**, 311–318 (2018)
18. Sathesh, S., Pradheep, V.A., Maheswaran, S., Premkumar, P., Gokul, N.S., Sriram, P.: Computer vision based real time tracking system to identify overtaking vehicles for safety precaution using single board computer. J. Adv. Res. Dyn. Control Syst. **12**(07-Special Issue), 1551–1561 (2020)
19. Arivazhagan, S., Shebiah, R.N., Ananthi, S., Varthini, S.V.: Detection of unhealthy region of plant leaves and classification of plant leaf diseases using texture features. Agric. Eng. Int. CIGR J. **15**(1), 211–217 (2013)
20. Maheswaran, S., Sathesh, S., Saran, G., Vivek, B.: Automated coconut tree climber. In: International Conference on Intelligent Computing and Control 2017 (I2C2) (2017)
21. Khamparia, A., Saini, G., Gupta, D., Khanna, A., Tiwari, S., de Albuquerque, V.H.C.: Seasonal crops disease prediction and classification using deep convolutional encoder network. Circuits Syst. Sig. Process **39**(2), 818–836 (2020)

Converting Nebulous Ideas to Reality – A Deep Learning Tool for Conditional Synthesis of Character Designs

Lilian Guo(✉) and Anand Bhojan

National University of Singapore, 21 Lower Kent Ridge Rd, Singapore 119077, Singapore
e0201602@u.nus.edu.sg, banand@comp.nus.edu.sg

Abstract. Characters are essential elements of games and are critical to their success. At the same time, designing good characters can be time and labor intensive, especially when developing games with thousands of characters. In such cases, procedural generation may be used to expedite the process. However, characters generated by traditional procedural generation techniques often rely on a limited pool of premade assets and may lack novelty. This work explores deep learning for the conditional generation of creative character designs with artist input. It proposes a framework which receives artists' inputs in the form of blurred character silhouettes and converts these into high resolution character designs using Generative Adversarial Networks. In addition, the paper presents a demo Graphical User Interface and user study evaluating the tool's effectiveness.

Keywords: Generative Adversarial Networks · Game development · Creativity · Character design

1 Introduction

1.1 Character Design in Games and Multimedia

Characters are essential elements of productions like games, films, and books. The visual appearances of characters can affect players' perception of the gameplay narrative [1] and their ability to project themselves onto virtual avatars, and are thus important to the success of a game. However, designing good characters can be time and labor-intensive.

This is particularly true for role-playing games (RPGs), where the player assumes roles of characters in a fictional setting. In many RPGs, character designs are not only needed for the player's own avatar but also the various interactable non-playable characters which the player encounters in their gaming adventure. Another example is the trading card game, a type of collectible card game which lets players assemble decks strategically from an often large pool of character cards. Many character designers have to be involved to develop games of such genres – this is evident in titles like Magic: The Gathering, which contained more than 22,000 character cards as of March 2020 [2]. Developing a good character design involves many stages, including researching on

Published by Springer Nature Switzerland AG 2022
E. J. Neuhold et al. (Eds.): ICCCSP 2022, IFIP AICT 651, pp. 75–89, 2022.
https://doi.org/10.1007/978-3-031-11633-9_7

the character's background, sketching the characters, rendering the best sketches, and deciding on a final design [3]. This can amount to a lot of work for character concept artists.

Currently, artists may search for references online or look at examples of their past work to gather inspiration for new character designs. The first approach is time-consuming, and furthermore, artists have to be careful not to refer too closely to designs which do not belong to themselves for fear of copyright infringement. The second approach is limited when it comes to discovering new sources of inspiration. Moreover, neither approach attempts to generate novel character designs—they can only assist the artist in gathering inspiration, and the designs ultimately originate from the artist's own imagination.

The limitations of these approaches, together with the large number of character designs some games require, point to procedural generation as a solution to speed up designers' workflows.

1.2 Generating Creative Character Designs

Procedural generation refers to creating assets algorithmically as opposed to manually. This can be assisted, where content is generated with human guidance, or non-assisted, where the algorithm produces results with little to no human intervention. In game development, procedural generation is often used to generate terrain such as roads, rivers, cities and vegetation [4]. There also exist 3D character creator software such as Autodesk's Character Generator, Reallusion's Character Creator 3 and the open-sourced MakeHuman [5]. These applications allow users to combine selections of premade body parts, clothing and textures to produce a new character. However, designs created by such applications are limited by the number of combinations allowed by existing assets, and characters may be spotted using the same premade hairstyle or accessory. As such, it is hard to describe these forms of procedural generation as being creative or capable of novelty, and their usage is limited to less important characters who do not need to have distinctive design flairs.

In the domain of 2D concept art, computer applications like Adobe Photoshop have traditionally only been tools for realizing human creativity. They enable artists to visualize their designs more rapidly and at potentially lower cost than painting on a physical canvas, but it is ultimately the artist's own creativity which decides what is being rendered to screen.

Unlike the above-mentioned tools and character generation techniques, advances in deep learning have made it possible for artificial intelligence to come much closer to being true agents of creativity. State-of-the-art neural networks can generate high-quality, previously unseen images matching or surpassing those produced by human creators. With deep learning, it is possible to rapidly generate new character designs which may inspire artists or serve as a base for their final concept art. This method of procedural generation hopes to assist artists by making their design workflow less cumbersome and more efficient, allowing them to refer directly to generated designs and reducing the need to gather inspiration from various online sources.

1.3 A Deep Generative Tool for 2D Character Designs

In this work, we propose and study the use of deep generative frameworks like pix2pixHD and StyleGAN2 for assisting artists in producing character designs. The availability of a reference image which closely matches the final design can help to reduce much of the time spent on ideating, and generated images which are of adequate quality may only require minimal post-processing to be used in production. Furthermore, basing a final design off a computer-generated image avoids any potential copyright issues associated with reference to designs drawn by human artists.

Our work focuses on methods which allow artists to control the model's output in order to finetune results to match their desired aesthetic, instead of generating completely random designs. The main contributions of this work are as follows: (1) We propose a method to convert character artists' nebulous ideas in the form of blurred silhouettes to coherent character designs in high resolution. (2) We conduct experiments on two different datasets to compare the effectiveness of different generative frameworks for realizing the proposed method. (3) We develop a demo GUI application which enables artists to paint nebulous, blurred forms of their intended design on a drawing canvas and generate a high-resolution output image conditioned on the blurred input.

2 Related Works

2.1 Image Generation Using Deep Learning

A Generative Adversarial Network (GAN) [6] is a class of deep learning network architectures comprising a generator and a discriminator which contest against each other in a zero-sum game. For instance, in an image generation task, the generator attempts to synthesize a realistic image while the discriminator attempts to detect flaws which point to the synthesized image being fake.

GANs have proven to be highly competent at image synthesis tasks. Unconditional GANs are capable of producing random novel images belonging to classes within the dataset. On the other hand, a conditional GAN (cGAN) is a subtype of GAN which receives input from the user and conditions the synthesized output image on the user input. While cGANs may appear more suited to the task of generating character designs in a manner that is controlled by the artist, it is also possible to do the same by manipulating the latent space of an unconditional GAN.

Existing works on conditional image synthesis can be broadly classified into two categories: firstly, involving direct image-to-image translation using a cGAN; and secondly, involving a prior step of training an unconditional GAN model before introducing other means of finetuning the output to the user's desired look.

2.2 cGAN Image-to-Image Translation

Image-to-image translation involves changing an image's domain. For instance, given a sketch of an object and a photograph of the same object, the goal of image-to-image translation is to translate the sketch to the photograph or vice versa. To attain this goal, the neural network learns a mapping from the image's input domain to its output domain.

pix2pix is an image-to-image translation framework [7] which performs domain translation using a cGAN trained on image pairs of both domains. The original pix2pix produced images with obvious artefacts when the resolution was raised to 512 × 512 and above. This was corrected by pix2pixHD [8], which improves results on resolutions as high as 2048 × 1024. Other notable image-to-image translation works include BicycleGAN [9] and SPADE [10].

2.3 Controlling Outputs of Unconditional GANs

The second common method for conditional image generation relies on first training an unconditional model, and then guiding the synthesis of output images by discovering latent space controls or other means.

StyleGAN [11] is known for being able to synthesize high resolution images of subject matter like faces, animals, and cars. The architecture of StyleGAN encourages the automatic, unsupervised separation of high-level attributes, enabling intuitive control of the synthesized results by modifying latent space vectors. Additionally, "style mixing", which refers to applying different styles to the content of an image, can be performed by manipulating the W latent space. A later work, StyleGAN2 [12], proposed changes in model architecture and training methods to address the common artefacts found in images generated by StyleGAN, and in doing so redefined the state-of-the-art in unconditional image synthesis.

As StyleGAN2 is an unconditional GAN, the model is unable to directly condition the output to the user's needs. However, this can be done with the help of Pixel2Style2Pixel (psp) [13]. Building upon StyleGAN and StyleGAN2, the authors of psp introduce an encoder network which can be trained to embed real images into an extended W+ latent space. By feeding the artist's input image into the psp encoder and leveraging an existing StyleGAN generator for image synthesis, image-to-image translation can be accomplished. This approach also facilitates multi-modal synthesis via style-mixing and is capable of yielding high quality outputs without local pixel-to-pixel correspondence.

Finally, the problem of identifying latent space controls has been explored by works like SeFa [14] and GANspace [15]. The former proposes a closed-form approach for unsupervised latent semantic factorization in GANs. The latter proposes applying Principal Component Analysis in the latent space or feature space to identify important latent directions. Both works contribute to discovering interpretable GAN controls and includes results from experiments conducted on notable frameworks like BigGAN [16], StyleGAN and StyleGAN2. These controls enable the targeted manipulation of attributes such as viewpoint, aging, lighting and time of day in the GAN's synthesized outputs.

2.4 Applications in Art and Design

GANs have been popularized by sites like thispersondoesnotexist.com, which displays photorealistic portraits of people generated by StyleGAN2. Many variations of this site have sprung up and employ unconditional GANs for generating images of subject matter such as cats and bedrooms. While these can be interesting and useful for niche purposes like populating a site with mock data, they are unlikely to be helpful to designers as the images synthesized are completely random.

The rest of this section will focus on applications which are able to respond to inputs from designers and attempt to integrate deep learning into an art or design workflow. In particular, both ArtBreeder [17] and Google Chimera Painter [18] provide an interface for users to submit input to the model, which conditions its synthesized output on the given inputs.

ArtBreeder is a deep learning based collaborative web application which allows users to upload, generate and modify images from various categories. Its character design category was the main source of inspiration for this work. Currently, users can modify ("breed") character design images by adjusting a list of sliders loosely corresponding to character attributes such as "Female", "Clothing", and "Armor". Other features include morphing two images while varying the contribution of content and style influence from each image, and generating random images resembling the input image. ArtBreeder can be a powerful tool for character designers. However, the platform still contains limitations – such as the input slider controls not feeling intuitive to designers – which this work hopes to address. This is explored in the user study in Sect. 5.3 and is one of the considerations when designing the GUI demo.

Another related work is Google Chimera Painter, a web application which converts segmentation maps of fantastical creatures into fully fleshed out renderings. The model was trained on input pairs comprising images of 3D creature models and their corresponding artist-labelled segmentation maps indicating the various creature body parts. In the interactive demonstration, users are able to paint on a canvas and control the generated output by adding strokes of colors corresponding to different creature body parts. A major limitation of this method is that training requires a large and high quality dataset of images paired with accurate segmentation maps, which is costly to produce. Furthermore, artists do not have control over the final output colors because segmentations may not correspond to the RGB color of the corresponding regions in the generated output. This work aims to address these limitations by proposing a method which greatly simplifies creation of the training dataset, and also enables control over the generated colors.

3 Data Collection

3.1 Overview

To the best of our knowledge, there is no existing public dataset for full-body character designs apart from an anime style dataset [19], which is limited to a specific art style. Hence, we decided to build a new character designs dataset to compare the models' performance on different styles of character designs and to evaluate the transferability of the approach to different styles. Compared to the anime style dataset, the new dataset is more challenging as the poses, lighting conditions and general contents of the designs are more diverse.

To build the character designs dataset, images were first downloaded in bulk from web browser DuckDuckGo [20] image search results. The results were fetched using 20 different keywords related to common fictional genres for character designs, such as "warrior character design", "archer character design", and "elf character design". Images were filtered for portrait dimensions to increase the probability of them depicting single full body characters.

3.2 Data Cleaning

A list of requirements was curated to increase consistency across images in the dataset. Characters should be humanoid and be shown in full body. In addition, each image should only contain one character in a straightforward pose. The art style should also avoid being too "cartoonish", i.e. rendered with flat colors and lacking detailed shading. This is done to distinguish the new dataset from the anime style public dataset and to ensure consistency in the art style. After downloading, images were manually inspected to ensure that they conform to the requirements, and the non-conforming images were discarded. Duplicates were also removed by computing the MD5 hash of each image and discarding the ones with hash collisions. After filtering, the dataset contains 5119 images of full-body character designs.

To further improve the dataset quality, we initially used a pre-trained segmentation model [21] to identify background regions and color them white. This was ineffective as many images lacked a clear distinction between foreground and background. Hence, all images were re-processed using another method which applies a strong Gaussian blur to backgrounds instead of coloring them white. Thereafter, images were resized to a standard 512×512 dimension while preserving aspect ratio, and the empty areas padded with blurred, repeated sections of the image. This method produced more coherent-looking results even if large sections were segmented wrongly. For instance, body parts which were mistakenly identified as background are now blurred instead of being completely blanked out. Samples of the dataset are shown in Fig. 1.

Fig. 1. Examples from our new dataset. Original (unprocessed) images from Pinterest, Artstation, DeviantArt.

4 Experiments

4.1 Overview and Training Details

In our experiments, we compared the results from using pix2pixHD to perform domain translation directly and using the psp framework together with a StyleGAN2 generator for image-to-image translation. This was done on both a public dataset of anime style character designs [19] and on our own collected data. Training was conducted on two Titan Xp GPUs at a standard size of 512×512 pixels.

4.2 Input Domain Selection

When approaching the problem of generating character designs as an image to image translation task, an important question is what input domain would be most suitable. In order to maximize the usefulness of the tool for character designers, we try to fulfil the following criteria in our selection of the input domain: (1) The input domain allows for a balance between artist control and the neural network's ability to generate creative and realistic outputs. (2) When using the tool, it is easy for artists to modify the input domain. (3) There exists an easy, automated way to produce training data in the form of input output image pairs.

For instance, if the input domain very closely matches the output, (1) may not be satisfied because the network may be trained to simply reproduce the input rather than generating a novel interpretation. (2) is also unsatisfied because significant effort is required to edit a fully rendered character design.

Using the above criteria, we decide to apply a simple Gaussian blur transformation to the output images in our training dataset to obtain the corresponding input pairs. After training, a blurred input image can be passed to the psp encoder and StyleGAN2 generator to obtain a high-resolution result. Artist control exists to a rather high degree as the image encoded by the network will be similar in both pose and color to the input. Users can also tweak the input easily by painting blurred blobs of color without having to worry about details. Moreover, it is convenient to produce training image pairs – the blur transformation can be easily applied to any new dataset in a completely automated process. This is not true for some input domains like sketches or segmentation maps, which usually require extensive manual labelling to produce.

4.3 Results

pix2pixHD models were trained to convert blurred images of character designs into their high-resolution versions. This was done with batch size 8 for 165 epochs, producing results such as in Fig. 2, selected randomly from the test set.

Next, we trained StyleGAN2 models to generate unconditional samples of character designs. This was done using batch size 4 over 400,000 iterations. Sample outputs are shown in Fig. 3.

Fig. 2. Examples randomly selected from the test set of pix2pixHD model trained on image pairs from anime-style dataset (top rows) and new dataset (bottom row).

Fig. 3. Example character designs produced by StyleGAN2 models trained on anime-style dataset (top row) and new dataset (bottom row).

Finally, we trained a psp encoder which accepts blurred images and encodes them into the W+ latent space. This was done using batch size 2 for 500,000 iterations. Together with the StyleGAN2 generator, this framework performs domain translation from a blurred image into a high resolution image (Fig. 4). Style mixing can be used to generate varied outputs from a single input image, as shown in Fig. 5.

Fig. 4. Examples randomly selected from the test set of psp model trained on image pairs from anime-style dataset (top rows) and the new dataset (bottom row). For each pair, the left image is the input and the right image is the generated output.

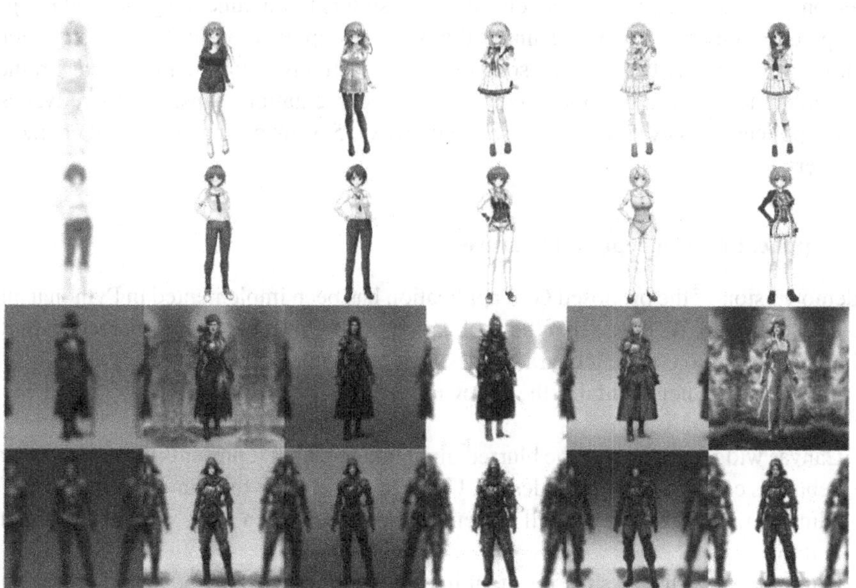

Fig. 5. Examples of style-mixing on outputs of psp model from Fig. 4. The leftmost column shows the input image, and the remaining columns show random style-mixed examples.

Comparing the results from both frameworks, we observed that pix2pixHD produces outputs with more local pixelwise correspondence to the input but tends to produce undesirable artefacts on details such as the eyes. While psp outputs do not match the input as closely, they often possess more convincing details. Furthermore, psp has the advantage of being able to easily synthesize varied outputs using a single input by performing style mixing on the StyleGAN2 generator. Hence, we eventually chose to use psp for our final application.

5 GUI Application

5.1 Methods Evaluation

In Sect. 2, we described two approaches for conditional image synthesis: the first involving direct image-to-image translation using a conditional GAN, and the second involving training an unconditional GAN followed by making adjustments in the latent space to produce outputs of desired styles. Section 3 elaborated on the model training conducted to evaluate different frameworks for both approaches, and it was decided that psp would be more suitable for the final application.

Section 2.4 reviewed existing applications which integrate deep learning into an art or design workflow, namely ArtBreeder and Google Chimera Painter, and mentioned some of their current limitations. The GUI application proposed in the following section shall attempt to address these limitations. In particular, it distinguishes itself from ArtBreeder by introducing a more intuitive form of control for the artist, allowing them to directly draw on a canvas as opposed to solely adjusting sliders to finetune the generated image. Compared to Google Chimera Painter, the proposed application offers the artist more control over generated colors. It also allows users to freely color the input image rather than having to block in regions of color to form segmentation maps. The effectiveness of the application is evaluated in a user study (Sect. 5.3) involving artists and character designers.

5.2 Application Concept and Features

A demo version of the proposed GUI application has been implemented in Python using the Tkinter library. As the goal of the application is to help artists transform their initially nebulous ideas into coherent character designs, it is named ‘Lucid’.

In summary, Lucid contains the following features (refer to Fig. 6):

1. Canvas widget – Displays the blurred input image which represents the artist’s initial nebulous conception of their design. Users can freely edit the canvas using the app’s painting tools. This image will be sent to the model when users click the Generate button.
2. Output label – Displays the resultant image generated by the model. The output can be refreshed anytime by clicking the Generate button.
3. Artist painting tools – Buttons on the left side panel serve as basic painting tools for artists to modify the canvas. They include an airbrush, eyedropper (color picker),

Fig. 6. Screenshot of our demo GUI. A video demo is included here.

and color chooser (RGB color selection), as well as a slider to control the brush size. There are also buttons for clearing and resetting the canvas to the originally imported image.

4. File utilities – Users can choose to either start drawing on a blank canvas or to import an image into the program using the Import Canvas function in the file menu. New users can also use the Randomize button to load a random image from a directory of example images. After importing, the app automatically blurs the image to fit the model's input domain. The menu options also support saving the canvas and generated output for future reference.
5. Checkpoint switcher – Lucid allows different StyleGAN2 checkpoints to be loaded via a menu option. There are currently two pretrained generators available: an anime style model trained on the public dataset and a semi-realistic model trained on the newly assembled character designs dataset.
6. Style randomizer – This injects random vectors into the latent space of the generated image to produce variants with different styles.
7. Style-mix gallery – A collection of thumbnails displays the variants generated by the style randomizer. Users can hover over a thumbnail to preview the image on the output label, or click on the thumbnail to set it as the current output.

The sample workflow for a character designer is as follows: The designer opens the app and either starts drawing on the blank canvas or imports an existing design they are inspired by. The canvas now contains their initial nebulous conception of the design. The user can then click on the Generate button and evaluate the image synthesized by StyleGAN2 on the output label (example shown in Fig. 6). If they are not satisfied, they can continue making adjustments to the canvas using the airbrush tool and click Generate to refresh the output. The style-mixer can also be used to produce variants of the current design. Once the user is satisfied with the design, they can save it for future reference using the file utilities.

5.3 User Study

To assess the usefulness of the GUI application, we conducted a user study involving a survey sent to messaging groups interested in art and design. Participation in the survey was voluntary. As the app can currently only be run locally, the questions are based on videos, images, and descriptions of the interface. The survey had a total of 27 respondents, 15 of whom indicated they draw or design characters "often" or "all the time".

The main objectives of the user study are to determine how helpful the application is to artists and character designers, compare it with existing platforms like ArtBreeder and Google Chimera Painter, as well as gather feedback for improvements.

In general, the responses were very positive, with 77.8% stating they would use the proposed application for generating ideas or references for character design. A few options were provided for justification, and the main options selected were "It can potentially speed up my workflow", "The ability to control the output generated by drawing on the canvas is useful for ensuring the design doesn't stray too far from my intention", and "It is easier to select and modify AI generated ideas than to generate them myself". Of the 22.2% who would not use the application, the main reasons given involve the generated outputs being of insufficient quality or too generic for specific design intentions.

The next section of the survey asked respondents to compare existing platforms to the proposed application. Links to the platforms were provided and respondents were given the option to try them if they had not done so before. Of the 9 respondents who have used ArtBreeder, 100% felt that the proposed application's method of drawing on a canvas directly was more intuitive than the slider modifiers provided by ArtBreeder. The reasons given include it being "simpler to draw a vague idea" as opposed to choosing from Artbreeder options, which can be "a little confusing". Respondents also felt that the canvas interface made the deep learning assisted workflow more closely resemble the natural process of drawing.

Subsequently, respondents were asked to compare the application with Google Chimera Painter based on visual and text descriptions of the web app, as well as a link to the demo page. 59.3% of respondents felt that drawing the blurred form of a character, as proposed by this project, was more intuitive than drawing segmentation maps in Google Chimera Painter. Those who preferred this project's method stated that it had a "simple user experience", required "less knowledge on how elements interact with each other", and "allows more control over the colors". On the other hand, those who preferred Google Chimera Painter answered that segmentation maps provided better control over details of the design.

In summary, the surveyed target users expressed significant interest in using the application to enhance their existing design workflows. 100% of respondents indicated that they would like to try out an interactive web demo if it was made available. Compared with existing platforms like ArtBreeder and Google Chimera Painter, the majority of respondents felt that this proposed method was more intuitive. One of the main reasons provided for not choosing to use the application relate to the quality and distinctiveness of the model output, which we believe can be further improved with a larger training dataset.

6 Conclusion and Future Work

6.1 Summary

Conditional synthesis of full body character designs in varied poses and clothing is a challenging task, but one with promising applications in game development and other media industries. This work has proposed a method for helping artists transform the nebulous ideas they may have at the start of a design process into coherently rendered designs. It has also showcased an interactive demo providing artist friendly features for engaging in the proposed workflow, which uses StyleGAN2 and the psp framework to convert blurred images into high resolution character designs of varying styles. The user study indicates that most of the respondents surveyed would like to use this application and find the proposed user experience more intuitive than existing platforms. Additionally, we have assembled a rare new dataset of full body character designs and will make it available for future research on related topics.

6.2 Limitations

While a majority of respondents in the user study felt that the proposed user experience (drawing the blurred form of a character on a canvas) was more intuitive than adjusting slider controls or drawing segmentation maps, there was still a significant minority who felt the opposite and pointed out problems about the input method. In particular, a few respondents felt that drawing the blurred form of a character was difficult and preferred blocking in silhouettes such as in Google Chimera Painter. To address this issue, future works can explore alternative input domains and may take into consideration the criteria suggested in Sect. 4.2.

Some respondents also felt that the input method did not allow the artist to specify sufficient details and gave the model too much freedom for interpretation. This may sound ironic as the purpose of the application is to help transform vague ideas into more coherent designs, and having the artist draw more details in the input seems to defeat the point of using the application. However, it is possible that the respondents were seeking ways to guide the model towards more specific design intentions without having to specify details directly on the canvas, or to inform the model to preserve certain details which they already have in mind while exercising creativity on other aspects of the design. The former can be addressed by introducing features such as slider controls in the style of platforms like ArtBreeder, which would allow artists to fine-tune specific attributes of the generated output. The latter is more challenging as it requires a way of segregating important details from other more flexible attributes. For instance, if the artist requires a red bow decal to be present in the final design, the framework will have to somehow relay this information to the neural network. It may be possible to do so by selectively varying the strength of the blur filter on different parts of the input image, such that important details are sharper and thus emphasized.

6.3 Recommendations for Future Work

Apart from addressing the limitations raised above, future work may focus on making the proposed interface more accessible to users by developing it as a web application.

Thereafter, a larger scale user study can be conducted to gather more representative opinions on the effectiveness of this tool.

In addition, extensions to this work can examine ways to expand the character designs dataset and improve data quality. This can enhance StyleGAN2's generation as well as prevent overfitting.

References

1. Pradantyo, R., Birk, M.V., Bateman, S.: How the visual design of video game antagonists affects perception of morality. Front. Comput. Sci. **3** (2021)
2. Magic: The Gathering. https://magic.wizards.com/en. Accessed 21 Nov 2021
3. Filho, J., Machado, L., Chiccha, N., Franco, A., Maia, J.: Character design: a new process and its application in a trading card game. In: Proceedings of SBGames. São Paulo (2016)
4. Freiknecht, J., Effelsberg, W.: A survey on the procedural generation of virtual worlds. Multimodal Technol. Interact. **1**(4), 27 (2017)
5. MakeHuman. https://windows.softwsp.com/makehuman/. Accessed 21 Nov 2021
6. Goodfellow, I., et al.: Generative Adversarial Nets. Advances in Neural Information Processing Systems, pp. 2672–2680 (2014)
7. Isola, P., Zhu, J., Zhou, T., Efros, A.A.: Image-to-image translation with conditional adversarial networks. In: Proceedings of the IEEE conference on Computer Vision and Pattern Recognition (2017)
8. Wang, T., Liu, M., Zhu, J., Tao, A., Kautz, J., Catanzaro, B.: High-resolution image synthesis and semantic manipulation with conditional GANs. In: Proceedings of the IEEE conference on Computer Vision and Pattern Recognition (2018)
9. Zhu, J., et al.: Toward multimodal image-to-image translation. In: Proceedings of the IEEE Conference on Computer Vision and Pattern Recognition (2017)
10. Park, T., Liu, M., Wang, T., Zhu, J.: semantic image synthesis with spatially-adaptive normalization. In: Proceedings of the IEEE conference on Computer Vision and Pattern Recognition (2019)
11. Karras, T., Laine, S., Aila, T.: A style-based generator architecture for generative adversarial networks. In Proceedings of the IEEE Conference on Computer Vision and Pattern Recognition (2019)
12. Karras, T., Laine, S., Aittala, M., Hellsten, J., Lehtinen, J., Aila, T.: Analyzing and Improving the Image Quality of StyleGAN. arXiv:1912.04958 [cs.CV] (2019)
13. Elad, R., et al.: Encoding in style: a StyleGAN encoder for image to image translation. In: Proceedings of the IEEE conference on Computer Vision and Pattern Recognition, pp. 2287–2296 (2021)
14. Shen, Y., Zhou, B.: Closed-form factorization of latent semantics in GANs. In: Proceedings of the IEEE Conference on Computer Vision and Pattern Recognition (2021)
15. Härkönen, E., Hertzmann, A., Lehtinen, J., Paris, S.: GANSpace: discovering interpretable GAN controls. arXiv:2004.02546 [cs.CV] (2020)
16. Brock, A., Donahue, J., Simonyan, K.: Large scale GAN training for high fidelity natural image synthesis. arXiv:1809.11096 [cs.CV] (2018)
17. This Person Does Not Exist. https://thispersondoesnotexist.com/. Accessed 21 Nov 2021
18. Simon, J.: ArtBreeder. https://www.artbreeder.com/. Accessed 21 Nov 2021
19. Toor, A.S., Bertsch, F.: Using GANs to create fantastical creatures. Google AI Blog. https://ai.googleblog.com/2020/11/using-gans-to-create-fantastical.html/. Accessed 21 Nov 2021
20. DuckDuckGo. https://duckduckgo.com/. Accessed 21 Nov 2021

21. Zepeng, L.: Generating Full-Body Standing Figures of Anime Characters and Its Style Transfer by GAN. Graduate School of Fundamental Science and Engineering, Waseda University, Thesis (2020)
22. Breheret, A.: Github repository. https://github.com/abreheret/PixelAnnotationTool. Accessed 21 Nov 2021

Long-Text-to-Video-GAN

Ayman Talkani(✉) and Anand Bhojan

School of Computing, National University of Singapore, COM1, 13, Computing Dr, Singapore 117417, Singapore
t0920909@u.nus.edu

Abstract. While there have been several works regarding the task of video generation from short text [1–3], which tend to focus more on the continuity of the generated images or frames, there has been very little attention drawn towards the task of story visualization [4], which attempts to generate dynamic scenes and characters described in a large amount of detail in a multi-para input text. We therefore propose our own novel take on this task which attempts to compile these dynamic scenes into a larger video, while also improving the scores of the current state of the art models in story visualization and video generation respectively. We intend to do this by making use of semantic disentangling connections [5] in between our generators in order to maintain global consistency between consecutive images, as well as ensuring similarity between the video re-description and the input text, thus leading to a higher image quality. Once these images are generated, we make use of a depth-aware video interpolation framework [6] in order to generate the remaining non-existing frames of the video in between the generated images. We then evaluate our model on the CLEVR-SV and Pororo-SV datasets for the story visualization task, and the UCF-101 dataset to measure the accuracy of the video generated. This way, we intend to outperform existing state-of-the-art models significantly.

Keywords: Generating adversarial networks · Text-to-video

1 Introduction

Recently, there has been an explosive influx of research on generating models. These include GANs [7] and VAEs [8], which are currently the best performing models in this area. These models have been utilized in many tasks from the generation of new unseen images or text, to generating multiple output images from the given input text. While producing sequences of images from natural language is a daunting task by itself, very little work has been done in order to generate coherent sequences of images for multi-paragraph sentences as input [4], and virtually no work has attempted the generation of video from this long text. We thus propose our own take on a Story visualization GAN which attempts to successfully achieve the above task as shown in Fig. 1. In order to attain this

E. J. Neuhold et al. (Eds.): ICCCSP 2022, IFIP AICT 651, pp. 90–97, 2022.
https://doi.org/10.1007/978-3-031-11633-9_8

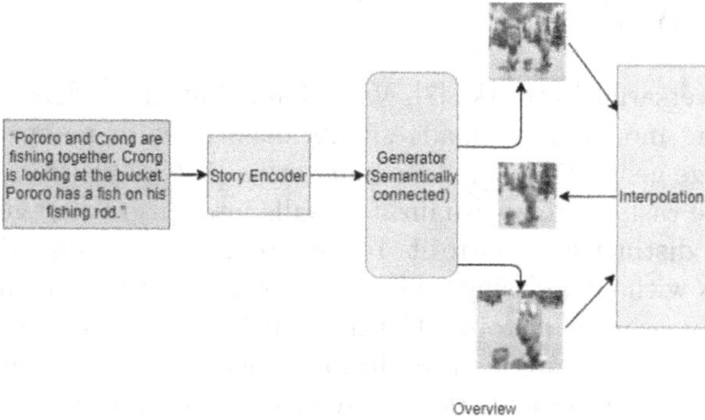

Fig. 1. Overview of model with example

result, we must ensure that the images generated consistently and coherently depict the whole story described in the input. This task is highly related to text-to-image generation, a topic that has been extensively researched [5]. However, one of the most conspicuous flaws with these types of models is their inherent lack of consistency. As human descriptions are highly subjective and diverse in their expressions, we frequently attain different images for the same input text. [5] attempts to fix this problem by making use the SD-GAN, which makes use of a Siamese structure along with a contrastive loss in order to distill semantic commons from texts for a more consistent output with similar text. Inspired by this approach, we propose a novel GAN that generates sequential images by making use of a context encoder in order to generate sequential images of the different visual scenes, while ensuring that the images maintain semantic consistency. Once we have attained the relevant scenes, we make use of a depth-aware video interpolation [6] method in order to develop additional frames, thus creating a longer and more dynamic video from the input text.

We summarize our contributions as follows:

(1) We propose a novel GAN architecture for the story visualization task that makes use of semantic connections in order to output a cohesive output from our input.
(2) With the use of our novel GAN that makes use of Attention networks [9] and Video captioning in order to ensure similarity between this generated caption and the input text, we attempt to attain a higher visual quality that the current state-of-the-art models.
(3) We propose a novel task where we convert the sequence of images from a multi-paragraph text into a long video involving dynamic scene changes. We experiment on the CLEVR-SV and Pororo-SV datasets in hopes of out-performing current state of the art models in story visualization, and the UCF-101 dataset in order to test the accuracy of our video generation. We further add annotations to the CUB dataset in order to test our model on similar text in order to test it's inter-class and intra-class variability, similar to [5].

2 Related Work

Generative Adversarial Networks [7], Variational Auto-Encoders [8] and several other generating models have made significant strides in many tasks, including text-to-image generation [5], video-generation [1–4], style transfer and many more tasks. The task of story visualization falls into this task of generating networks, but has distinct aspects to it. It aims to generate sequential images for dynamic scenes without focusing on continuous frames between the images.

One of the most relevant topics to this topic is text-to image generating networks [5] which can generate high resolution images through the use of cascaded generators [10], Attention-networks [9], Re-descriptions [11] and so on. The task of story visualization [4] also attempts to understand longer and more complex input text. For example, this has been explored in dialogue-to-image generation, where the input is a complete dialogue session rather than a single sentence [12]. In our particular model, we prioritize output consistency [5]. We will further modify this SD-GAN in order to attain a higher video quality.

Another important task related to story visualization is video generating networks, especially that of text-to video [1–4] or image to video generators. Models in this domain tend to be focused on a smooth motion transition across successive video frames. A trajectory, skeleton or simple landmark is used in existing work, to help model the motion feature [13–15]. In the task of story visualization however, the whole story sets the static features and each input sentence encodes dynamic features. While conditional video generation has only one input, the story visualization task has sequential, evolving inputs; and while images in this task aim to visualize a story through discrete and often with different scene views, we will attempt to make these frames continuous with the help of interpolation.

We will also be making use of video frame interpolation in order to attain a smooth transition between the dynamic scene changes based on the input text. While there have been several implementations in this field [16,17], we will be making use of [6], which makes use of depth estimation and optical flow in order to attain a relatively high performance. While existing research aims to increase the frame rate of video, we intend to utilize this model in order to generate more sequential images between our key images, thus leading to smoother video generation.

Inspired by [11], we also attempt to make use of re-descriptions for our outputs in order to compare it with the input text. However, as the output is a video in this case, we cannot make use of standard image captioning. We will thus make use of recent advancements in video captioning, particularly multi modal dense video captioning [18] in order to achieve this task.

3 Our Method

In this section, we go over the basic pipeline utilized in this model. We make use of advancements in text-to-image GANs [5,9–11] in order to significantly

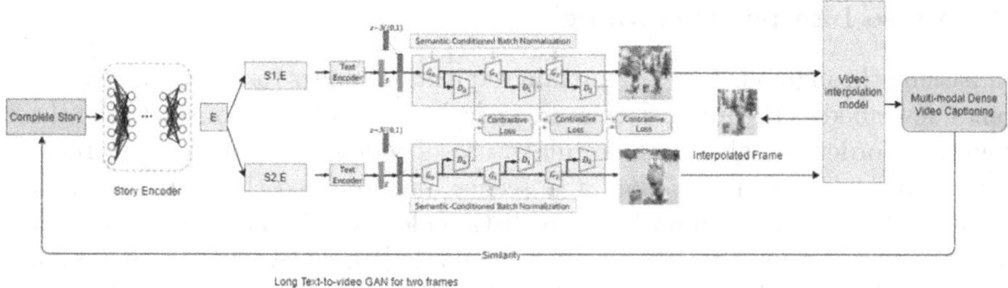

Fig. 2. Long-text-to-video-GAN. Note that the discriminators here refer to both the image and story discriminator as described in [4]

enhance the quality of the video produced. We further make use of multi-modal dense video-captioning [18] along with the comparison of the text used in the STREAM module from [11] in order to attain a higher video quality. We also add semantic connections similar to [5] in the current state-of-the-art models in order to implicitly disentangle semantics from the text description. This way, we can make sure that the sequentially generated images remain semantically consistent for similar text throughout the generating process. While this text-to-image GAN can help the model visualize the different dynamic scenes used in the story visualization task [1], it does not generate enough frames for a smooth transition between these scenes due to a lack of semantic consistency between their images, leading to drastic changes between the scenes. We attempt to ameliorate this effect with the help of the semantic connections from [5], along with video interpolation [6,16,17]. Through this pipeline, we are able to attain a smooth video from the given text, while also ensuring it's cohesiveness. We will then train this model in the CLEVRSV and Pororo-SV datasets for the story visualization task, and the UCF-101 dataset for the video generation task, and compare the results with state of the art models in terms of quality, overall relevance and consistency (Fig. 2).

3.1 Long-Text-to-Video-GAN

Our text to video GAN is motivated by the image re-descriptions utilized in [11] so as to guide the multistage cascaded generator [9] to produce more accurate images with relatively scarce data. We will also make use of the contrastive loss from [5] in order to maintain semantic consistency between the generated scenes. These semantic connections between the discriminators ensure image consistency throughout the generation process. This way, we can produce high quality sequential images that are relevant in both global, as well as sentence levels. We will then make use of multi-modal dense video captioning in order to achieve our novel task of long-text to video interpolation.

3.2 Video Interpolation Model

On passing through our GAN, we attain sequential images for the many dynamic scenes described in the input. However, we lack smooth transitions between these images. In order to solve this, we make use of video interpolation in order to interpolate in between the generated scenes and increase the frame-rate, thus leading to a much more smooth and realistic video. While there are many different kinds of video interpolating models available [16,17], we will be making use of the depth based frame interpolation [6] as it is the current state of-the-art, making use of optical flows and depth maps in order to achieve this result.

3.3 Objective Functions

We shall train our Generator, Discriminator and text re-description on the loss functions described in the basic architecture of [11]. However, we will be making use of multi-modal dense video captioning in this loss instead of the standard image-captioning model used in [11]. We will also be adding the contrastive loss from [5] in order to ensure inter-class diversity and intra-class similarity. The loss for our generator will thus look like this:

$$L_g = L_{mg} + \lambda * L_{stream} - E_z * [D_w[I_i]] + L_{contr} \tag{1}$$

where the last term is Wasserstein loss, L_{mg} is the generator loss without the image captioning part and I_i is the generated image from the distribution pi in the i_{th} stage.The first term of L_{mg} is the visual realism adversarial loss, which is used to distinguish whether the image is visually real or fake, while the second term is the text-image paired semantic consistency adversarial loss, which is used to determine whether the underlying image and sentence semantics are consistent. L_{stream} refers to the loss from our text-similarity score from [11] and lambda is a loss weight to handle the importance of adversarial loss and the text-semantic reconstruction loss.

Finally, in order to train our model for the story visualization task, we will be making use of the CLEVR-SV and Pororo-SV datasets for the story visualization task, and the UCF-101 dataset for the text-to-video task, as these are used by the current state of the art models. By making use of our superior generators, as well as video interpolation, we hope to surpass it's performance in visual quality, as well as relevance and consistence.

4 Experiments

While this project is still a work in progress, we have made some progress regarding this task that we would like to document here. As mentioned earlier, we intend to test our model out on both the story-visualization task, as well as the video-synthesis task. For now, we have prioritized working on the story visualization task as we primarily need to generate sequential images that are similar

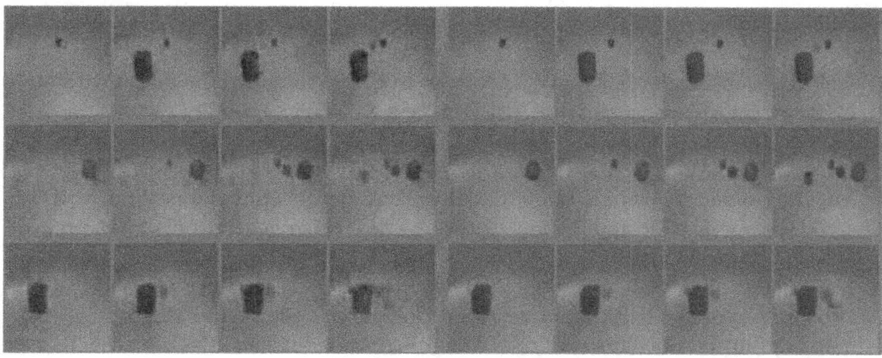

Fig. 3. Story visualization task on CLEVR dataset. Our generated images take the first five columns on the left, and ground truth takes the next five columns on the right

to each other, as this will make it an easier task to interpolate between the sequential images and generate a dynamic video from it.

While we would ideally like to use the modified PororoSV dataset from [4], we had been unable to attain this dataset until very recently. For our initial experiments, we were limited to the use of the modified CLEVR dataset as it was publicly available, and had aimed to generate sequential images from relatively long input text.

By utilizing a contrastive loss between our discriminators similar to [5], we have been able to produce consecutive images that are very similar to each other. We have added these results in Fig. 3 as shown.

5 Conclusion and Future Work

While the sequential images generated by our GAN are similar, the CLEVR dataset is not particularly dynamic in general. Therefore, we must test our architecture on a more challenging and dynamic dataset with diverse sequential images in order to truly test our model. As we have recently attained the Pororo-SV dataset from the authors of [4], we can now test our model out on this dynamic dataset instead, and aim to generate similar sequential images that are still able to outperform [4] in this task.

Once we are able to generate similar sequential images, we can then use video interpolating models like [6] in order to generate a dynamic video from multi-paragraph text as input. We will then attempt to further improve video quality by making use of video captioning models like [18] to improve image quality similar to [11].

Acknowledgment. This work is supported by the Singapore Ministry of Education Academic Research grant T1 251RES1812, "Dynamic Hybrid Real-time Rendering with Hardware Accelerated Ray-tracing and Rasterization for Interactive Applications". Special thanks to the 'National Supercomputing Centre (NSCC) Singapore', for providing the computational resources required for training our architecture.

References

1. Kim, D., Joo, D., Kim, J.: TiVGAN: text to image to video generation with step-by-step evolutionary generator. IEEE Access **8**, 153113–153122 (2020)
2. Li, Y., Min, M.R., Shen, D., Carlson, D.E., Carin, L.: Video generation from text. In: AAAI, vol. 2, p. 5 (2018)
3. Yu, H., Huang, Y., Pi, L., Wang, L.: Recurrent deconvolutional generative adversarial networks with application to text guided video generation. arXiv preprint arXiv:2008.05856 (2020)
4. Li, Y., et al.: StoryGAN: a sequential conditional GAN for story visualization. In: Proceedings of the IEEE Conference on Computer Vision and Pattern
5. Yin, G., Liu, B., Sheng, L., Yu, N., Wang, X., Shao, J.: Semantics disentangling for text-to-image generation. In: Proceedings of the IEEE Conference on Computer Vision and Pattern Recognition, pp. 2327–2336 (2019)
6. Bao, W., Lai, W.-S., Ma, C., Zhang, X., Gao, Z., Yang, M.-H.: Depth-aware video frame interpolation. In: Proceedings of the IEEE Conference on Computer Vision and Pattern Recognition, pp. 3703–3712 (2019)
7. Goodfellow, I.: NIPS 2016 tutorial: Generative adversarial networks. arXiv preprint arXiv:1701.00160 (2016)
8. Pu, Y., et al.: Variational autoencoder for deep learning of images, labels and captions. In: Advances in Neural Information Processing Systems, pp. 2352–2360 (2016)
9. Xu, T., et al.: AttnGAN: fine-grained text to image generation with attentional generative adversarial networks. In: Proceedings of the IEEE Conference on Computer Vision and Pattern Recognition, pp. 1316–1324 (2018)
10. Zhang, H., et al.: StackGAN: text to photo-realistic image synthesis with stacked generative adversarial networks. In: Proceedings of the IEEE International Conference on Computer Vision, pp. 5907–5915 (2017)
11. Qiao, T., Zhang, J., Xu, D., Tao, D.: MirrorGAN: learning text-to-image generation by redescription. In: Proceedings of the IEEE Conference on Computer Vision and Pattern Recognition, pp. 1505–1514 (2019)
12. Sharma, S., Suhubdy, D., Michalski, V., Kahou, S.E., Bengio, Y.: ChatPainter: improving text to image generation using dialogue. arXiv preprint arXiv:1802.08216 (2018)
13. Hao, Z., Huang, X., Belongie, S.: Controllable video generation with sparse trajectories. In: Proceedings of the IEEE Conference on Computer Vision and Pattern Recognition, pp. 7854–7863 (2018)
14. Wang, W., Alameda-Pineda, X., Xu, D., Fua, P., Ricci, E., Sebe, N.: Every smile is unique: landmark-guided diverse smile generation. In: Proceedings of the IEEE Conference on Computer Vision and Pattern Recognition, pp. 7083–7092 (2018)
15. Rebuffi, S.-A., Bilen, H., Vedaldi, A.: Efficient parametrization of multi-domain deep neural networks. In: Proceedings of the IEEE Conference on Computer Vision and Pattern Recognition, pp. 8119–8127 (2018)
16. Niklaus, S., Liu, F.: Context-aware synthesis for video frame interpolation. In: Proceedings of the IEEE Conference on Computer Vision and Pattern Recognition, pp. 1701–1710 (2018)

17. Revaud, J., Weinzaepfel, P., Harchaoui, Z., Schmid, C.: EpicFlow: edge-preserving interpolation of correspondences for optical flow. In: Proceedings of the IEEE conference on computer vision and pattern recognition, pp. 1164–1172 (2015)
18. Iashin, V., Rahtu, E.: Multi-modal dense video captioning. In: Proceedings of the IEEE/CVF Conference on Computer Vision and Pattern Recognition Workshops, pp. 958–959 (2020)

Intelligent System for Diagnosis of Herbs Disease Using Deep Learning

Rabindra Kumar Singh[1(✉)], B. V. A. N. S. Prabhakar Rao[1], M. Sivabalakrishnan[1], and M. Shiny Pidugu[2]

[1] School of Computer Science and Engineering, Vellore Institute of Technology, Chennai, India
mail2rksingh@gmail.com

[2] Cognizant Technology Solutions, Hyderabad, India

Abstract. The agricultural production of the country is severely affected when herbs and crops are attacked by disease. The usual methods adopted by farmers or even agriculture experts are to make several observation to the herbs with naked eye in order to identifying and detecting the disease, and make an approximate decision for herbs treatment. This method happens to be always a time consuming and inaccurate that leads to be expensive. Now we have advanced technology such as automatic detection using deep learning, which produce results accurate and fast. This paper aims to present an approach to develop a model to detect herbs disease progress, depending on the leaf images classification, using deep convolutional network. With the advent of computer vision, it has been noticed that the precision herbal protection were improvised and therefore the computer vision applications have gained more popularity even in precision agriculture field. Here, Novel training techniques are proposed which actually enables faster and less complex implementations in order to herb dieses detection. All the necessary key steps required in order to implement disease detection model has been described in this paper. These key steps ranges from collection of images to building database, evaluated by experts in the field of agriculture with the assistance of deep CNN training are described. The described technique is nothing but intelligent system development in order to classifying herb infections by means of deep convolutional neural networks. This model were trained and tweaked in order to suit the database of herb's leaves images, that were congregated self-sufficient for diverse plant diseases. The growth and novelty of this developed model dwell in its simplicity. Healthy leaves and background images match other classes, allowing the model to use CNN to distinguish between diseased leaves and healthy leaves.

Keywords: Herb leaf disease detection · Convolutional Neural Network · Deep learning · Computer vision · ResNet

1 Introduction

Viruses, bacteria, oomycetes, fungus, nematodes, and parasitic plants are among the pathogens that cause herb diseases. Plant diseases can be an issue for any plant system,

Published by Springer Nature Switzerland AG 2022
E. J. Neuhold et al. (Eds.): ICCCSP 2022, IFIP AICT 651, pp. 98–115, 2022.
https://doi.org/10.1007/978-3-031-11633-9_9

but those affecting agricultural systems can have a particularly detrimental impact on human livelihoods and health. For example, the late blight of potatoes, a disease caused by Phytophthora infestans – a fungus-like oomycete pathogen, was first discovered in the early 1840s in Ireland. After the epidemic outbreak, approximately one million people lost their life from starvation, and approximately two 2 million immigrated to other countries to escape starvation. This example points to the tremendous human impacts that major agricultural disease outbreaks can cause. More common are less massive outbreaks that result in loss of yield, detrimental effects on economies, and particularly devastating effects on small farm holders or subsistence farmers.

Most traditional strategies in herb disease monitoring and tracking depend on visual inspection. In some cases, disease detection is aided by microscopic observation at the molecular level. These approaches tend to be accurate but are limited in the spatial extent to which they can be applied and can be biased by the previous experiences of the person making the visual inspections. These methods are likewise costly and not practical for the broad agricultural community. What is required is an accurate and affordable plant disease diagnosis system that will help farmers, especially smallholder farmers, to detect herb diseases at early stages, across extensive fields, and with the ability to be deployed many times throughout a growing season.

A major consideration for agriculture in the coming decades is the need to provide an early warning and forecast for effective prevention and control of herb disease. A primary factor in this effort could be herb disease detection, which would prevent significant economic losses and enhance smallholder agriculture's resilience. The development of accurate and affordable herb disease diagnosis systems is, therefore, an urgent priority.

Since the victory of the ImageNet Large Scale Visual Recognition, continuous advancements in deep learning have been accomplished, fueled by current breakthroughs in computer vision and machine learning systems. For some herb disease recognition challenges, it has been shown that the deep learning methodology can generate more accurate results than the classical approach. These initial studies merit further research and extension to different diseases, cropping systems, and geographic contexts. As well, much less progress has been made in the more complicated problem of diagnosing disease severity level and in differentiating the type of disease that is occurring – critical for adequately managing or mitigating a disease outbreak situation.

Machine learning algorithms are used in research to detect plant disease. Traditional machine learning techniques were utilised by some, while deep learning models were used by others. Support Vector Machine approach was proposed to detect and classify plant diseases in [3], the dataset used was small and thus the accuracy achieved was average. The authors in [1] proposed a CNN based Learning Vector Quantization algorithm, in which they classified the tomato related diseases. A dataset of 500 images that were divided into training and testing images of 400 and 100 images respectively. Totally 5 classes including one healthy class were available in classification result.

Three matrices of R, G, and B channels were used as inputs to the CNN model, and the output was fed to a neural network known as Learning Vector Quantization (LVQ). Due to its great efficacy in image processing, deep learning models, particularly CNN, have been frequently deployed. In [2] the authors compared different classifiers such as logistic regression, KNN, SVM, and CNN to identify and classify plant leaf diseases. The dataset comprised of about 20,000 images and total of 19 classes. They applied different classifiers separately and recorded the accuracy obtained in each case. The CNN classifier performed the best and the other classifiers gave below average performance. Thus verifying the power of CNN in image classification. In [4] the authors used deep learning approach to classify banana leaf disease. They classified the disease in two classes: banana sigatoka and banana speckle. The Computer Vision technology is not just limited to leaf disease detection, it can also diagnose fruits as described in [5] where the authors used grab cut segmentation to segment the image of pomegranate and identify the diseased part of the fruit. There are many pre-trained models are available in which better performance achieved even with less data. In literature many methods have been used as a pre-trained model. One such methodology is cited in [7] in which a comparison between SqueezeNet and AlexNet has been done. SqueezeNet was found to have an accuracy of 94.3%, whereas AlexNet had 95.6%.

Deep convolutional neural network have headed to numerous discoveries in the field of image categorization. The network depth is important and nearly all prominent picture classification methods use models that are extremely deep. The performance of the Residual Network (ResNet50) for identifying and classifying plant diseases is addressed in this research. The use of Residual Network is because of a great deal of success in computer vision field. Working with ResNet is primarily motivated by the need to provide alternatives to traditional connections while also generating residual connections. The use of ResNet is to solve the problem at hand has been well known, as studied in previous research. Although this study reported superhuman findings, one of the primary issues addressed in this study is that the model can be fooled by the resemblance between different leaf diseases, causing it to make inaccurate predictions.

ResNet50 [18], which has 50 layers, is used to see if Residual Networks produce superior plant disease classification results. ResNet50 was successfully applied on a dataset including 20,000 photos for the trials.

The following are the research contributions of this paper:

- To detect diseases in herb leaf photos.
- To classify the detected disease into different classes.
- To demonstrate that residual networks (ResNet) may be used to classify plant diseases.
- Understanding the role of ResNets in increasing disease detection and classification scores.

The remaining part of the paper is sub-divided in the following sections: Section 2 covers the basic method of disease identification and classification. In Sect. 3, CNN is discussed. The ResNet, which is the suggested model, is described in length in Sect. 4. The outcomes of the experiments are presented in Sect. 5. Section 6 is devoted to the paper's conclusion. Section 7 discusses potential future projects.

2 Classification and Detection of Plant Diseases

It comprises of the following steps:
2.1 Acquisition of Image

2.2 Image Pre-processing
2.3 Feature Extraction
2.4 Classification

2.1 Acquisition of Image

The dataset consists of 20000 photos separated into 15 different classes and covers three crops. This information comes from the Plant Village dataset (Figs. 1 and 2).

Fig. 1. Leaf image samples for PlantVillage dataset

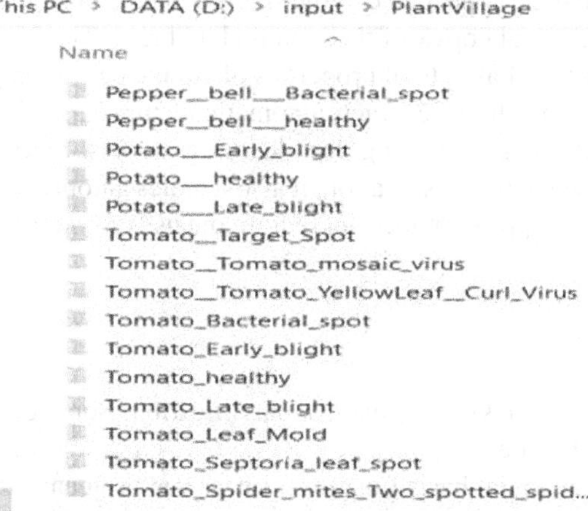

Fig. 2. Category path for the PlantVillage dataset

2.2 Image Pre-processing

It is carried out in order to convert the data into a format that will allow the feature extraction method and future steps to function properly. This process involves data augmentation and normalisation.

1. Data Augmentation: It is a common regularization system, which delivers a concrete solution to the problem of overfitting. In this system image is rotated to 90° and the probability of the image getting rotated is 0.75. This used to improve the learning speed of the model.
2. Data Normalization: Normalization is performed so that all pixel values have the same mean and standard deviation. This speeds up the learning of the model.

2.3 Feature Extraction

Relevant features are extracted first to solve the classification problem at hand. Color, texture and shape of images are known as features. Structures that discover diseases with the help of leaf images emphasis better on the texture feature. Examples of methods that can be used include gray-level co-occurrence matrices, autocorrelation, Gabor transforms, and 2D Gabor functions. Grey level co-occurrence matrix (GLCM) is a statistical technique that describes the image texture by calculating how often pairs of pixels with certain values and in a definite spatial relationship appear in an image.

Autocorrelation represents the degree of correlation over a continuous period between a particular time series and previous versions. The Gabor transform is a type of short-time Fourier transform used to calculate the phase component of the local part of the signal over time and the appearance of the sine wave. The Gabor function can model simple neurons in the visual cortex of the mammalian brain. The 2D Gabor function is used to simulate the space-based total properties of simple cells (receptive fields) in the visual cortex. In addition to high accuracy, automatic feature extraction has proven to be one of the greatest advantages of using deep learning models. Since the deep learning model ResNet50 is used with classification, it also handles automatic feature extraction. Therefore, the proposed approach does not require the use of separate feature extraction methods.

2.4 Classification

There are more than one picks to be had for classification. Some of the classifiers that may be used on this step are:

Logistic regression, radial basis functions, linear vector quantization, ANN, classification tree, support vector machine, CNN, KNN, etc. ResNet50-the proposed method uses the CNN architecture for classification purposes.

3 Convolutional Neural Network

The way human brain works inspired the development of a classification algorithms that belong under the deep learning umbrella. It entails teaching ANN how to make predictions. ANN stands for "a network of neurons structured in a multilayer form." The output of previous layer develops the input for the following layer. Because deep learning models extract features automatically during training, there is no need for a separate approach for the extraction feature step of the fundamental process outlined previously. The first layer of ANN acquire low level features (such as edges), and as they get deeper, they learn higher-level characteristics (such as whole objects).

CNN is a form of ANN, which is specifically designed for image processing. CNN has been proved in studies to be capable of providing excellent accuracy in image processing jobs. Because single neuron in a layer of an ANN receives input from previous layer's neurons, learning a large number of parameters for image-based tasks becomes a difficulty. In compared to ANN, CNN is preferred for image- related jobs since it involves less parameters. This reduction can be attributed to parameter sharing. To extract all the activations in the output volume from an input volume of activations, similar parameters (called filters in CNN nomenclature) are utilised. Parameter sharing is the term for this. A Convolutional Network's purpose is to reduce the size of an image without losing important elements that aid in issue solving. Figure 3 shows the general architecture of CNN. There are four sorts of layers in a CNN architecture:

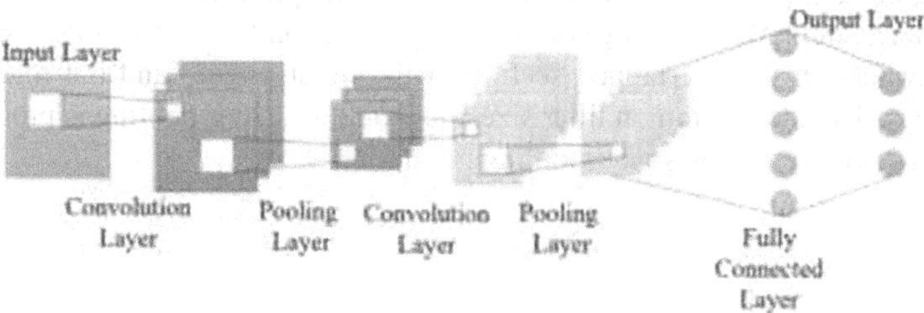

Fig. 3. CNN architecture

3.1 Convolutional Layer

Convolutional layer was given the term CNN. The image size is lowered by using a number of convolutional processes. A filter is set in the upper left corner of the image and then moved along the width of the image by a stride value towards the right. After covering the entire width, the filter bounces down by the same stride value and starts over from the left to complete the coverage. This technique is repeated until the entire image has been explored. In a single step, the sum of product of comparable values in the coinciding region of the image and filter is evaluated. From the input matrix, a new matrix (or volume) is created (or volume). Figure 4 demonstrates convolution applied to a 5×5 image in a convolutional layer with a 3×3 filter.

Fig. 4. Convolutional operator applied to 5 × 5 input and 3 × 3 filter

3.2 Pooling Layer

Functions this layer include shrinking image and extracting most important elements. A filter is positioned as it was done in convolutional layer and moved to the end. A function is applied in this layer as single step. This function can be either a max-function that determines the maximum of all the values in the overlapping section of the input image and the filter (called Max-pooling) or an average function that determines the average of all the values in the overlapped section of the input picture and the filter (called avg-pooling). The most common filter size and stride is 2. Avg-pooling is preferable to max-pooling. Figure 5 shows max-pooling.

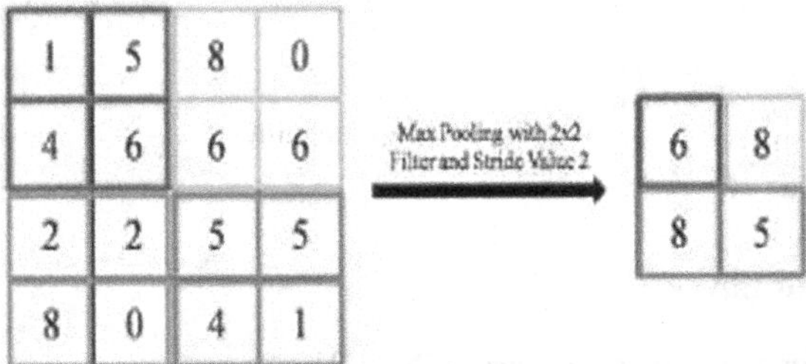

Fig. 5. .

3.3 Fully Connected Layer (FC)

A matrix is the outcome of a series of convolutional + pooling layers. This is flattened, and then an ANN-like series of completely connected layers is used. In a layer, a single neuron receives information from all neurons in the previous layer. FC Layers are only utilised after a series of convolutional plus pooling layers has decreased the size of the image to the point where the fully connected layers don't have a huge number of parameters to learn.

3.4 Activation Layer

Each element of the input matrix is given an activation function. As a result, the input and output dimensions for this layer are the same. Linear hypothesis functions can only be approached with the help of linear activation functions. The usage of non-linear activation functions is frequent. For complicated situations, there is usually a non-linear relationship between input and output. The ReLU function is commonly utilized because it allows for faster learning.

4 Proposed Model: ResNet Networks

Previous research has revealed the critical role of network depth. The accuracy of a neural network should theoretically improve as more layers are added. In truth, it proves to be a misunderstanding. When the network's depth is increased, the accuracy tends to become saturated and subsequently decline quickly. This is referred to as the degrading issue. Surprisingly, overfitting is not the root of the problem.

This well-known degradation problem is caused by the phenomenon of vanishing/exploding gradients in deep neural networks. Due to repeated multiplication during the backpropagation stage, the gradients in the vanishing gradient problem become endlessly small, resulting in negligible parameter updates. Exploding gradients is a problem when gradients build up and cause unusually high parameter updates during training, preventing the model from learning from the data. This was handled before the discovery of residual networks by the use of normalised initialization and intermediary normalisation layers.

Residual network (ResNet) is a CNN design with a residual block as its main building block. A residual block is shown in Fig. 6.

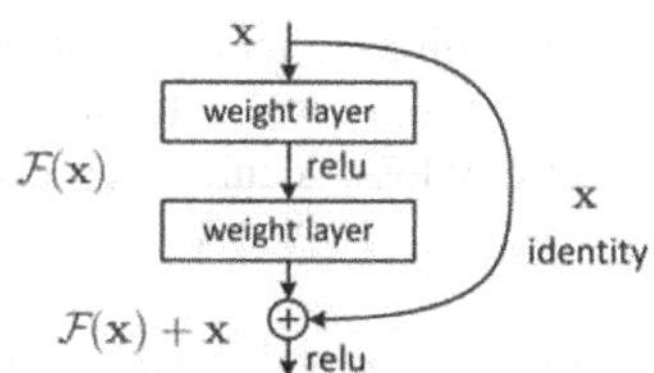

Fig. 6. Residual block

By utilizing skip connections, a residual block tackles the degradation issue. Shortcut connections are those that leap one or more levels (also known as skip connections). If the ordered connection's coefficient converges to zero during the training period, the residual shortcut ensures network integrity. It has been proposed that the layers learn the residual function F(x) instead of the hypothesis function H(x) = F(x) + x. This is owing to the ease with which the residual function can be optimised. To demonstrate that a deeper network does not have a higher training error than its shallow version, the researchers created a deep network by concatenating a residual block at the end of a shallow network and then demonstrated that the residual block functions as an identity mapping.

5 Experiments and Analysis

5.1 Training

The dataset used in this thesis was divided into training and validation datasets by 80% and 20%, respectively, as it has shown the best performance in Table 1. The validation data is used for evaluating the performance after each epoch and did not involve in the training process. Before the training, each pixel of images was firstly normalized dividing by 224, and For all models, the input size was fixed at 224 × 224 by default, and the batch size was set to 32, which is the highest accuracy performance based on the experimental result as shown in Table 2. In order to expedite the training process, the CNN models ResNet50 and VGG16 were utilised in conjunction with the transfer learning strategy, and these pre-trained models were previously trained on the ImageNet dataset.

To shorten the training time and lower the computation cost, all layers in the pre-trained model were frozen during transfer learning. The last fully connected layer of all pre-trained models was taken for the fined-tuning purpose, and a dense layer with 1024 neurons was appended before transmitting to the 15 neurons in the output layer.

In the last layer, Softmax was employed as the activation function, and the categorical cross entropy was used for computing the loss function, which showed no significant difference to sparse categorical cross-entropy demonstrated in Table 3. SGD was utilised as the optimization method throughout the training, with the learning rate and momentum set at 0.001 and 0.9, respectively.

5.2 Evaluation Metrics

Choosing appropriate evaluation metrics is as important as choosing the learning algorithm, especially when the dataset is unbalanced. In this section, we will explain some differences in the statistics that we collected and shed some light on why they can be important to the study. The statistics that were collected after each epoch of training include time per epoch, cross-entropy loss, accuracy, precision, recall, and Area under the Curve (AUC).

1) *Accuracy:* Accuracy is the most widely used and the simplest indicator for evaluating the number of correct predictions that had been made over the data, but we must ask ourselves several questions: Does accuracy always perform well in evaluating the performance of a model? and when might accuracy not be an appropriate metric to use? In short speaking, accuracy might not be a good indicator for an unbalanced dataset. For example, if we have an unbalanced dataset that contains 999 negative samples and 1 positive sample in the dataset, as a result, the accuracy for this model will be 99.9%.

   However, the result is not fairly evaluated for the positive categories whereas the dataset only contains one positive sample, and the result can be misleading and can be costly. The percentage of correct predictions is the definition of accuracy as defined below:

$$\text{Accuracy} = \frac{\text{\# of corrected prediction}}{\textit{Total Samples}}$$

As in the previous example, accuracy cannot explain well for an unbalanced dataset, and other evaluation metrics should take into consideration, such as precision, recall or F1 score.

2) *Precision:* Precision is defined as the fraction of true positives examples among the total retrieved positive instances(a true positive(TP) + false positive(FP)). The range of precision is between 0 and 1, and can be calculated as below equation:

$$\text{Precision} = \frac{TP}{TP + FP} = \frac{TP}{Total\ Predicted\ Positive}$$

As the formula suggested, the precision metric evaluates the number of true positive prediction within total predicted positive samples and only need to take into consideration if false positive (or Type I error rate) is significant to the study [28].

3) *Recall:* The recall is defined as the proposition of TP examples amount the total true positive (TP + false negative(FN)) and is also known as sensitivity or True Positive Rate (TPR). The range of recall is also between 0 and 1, and can be calculated as following equation:

$$\text{Recall} = \frac{TP}{TP + FN} = \frac{TP}{Total\ Actual\ Positive}$$

As the formula suggested, the recall should be taken into consideration if the FN is significant to the study.

4) *F1 Score:* A weighted harmonic mean of recall and precision is used to get the F1 score and had been widely used for many machine learning algorithms. The equation is defined below:

$$\text{F1} = 2 * \frac{Precision\ * \text{Recall}}{Precision\ + \text{Recall}}$$

5) *AUC:* The area under the curve(AUC) is a popular metric for evaluating how good our model performed in distinguishing between classes, and sometimes it is also known as (Area Under the Receiver Operating Characteristics) AUROC. Each recall and precision will have a corresponding instance of AUC, The AUC has values ranged between 0 and 1. The higher the AUC, the better the separation capacity of the model in distinguishing between classes. Ideally, if AUC is 1, the model can perfectly distinguish between positive and negative samples; on the other hand, if the AUC is 0, the model has no separability. Overall, accuracy is commonly used for the balanced dataset. For an unbalanced dataset, if the false positive is more significant than the false negative, we should use recall as an indicator, otherwise, precision should be used. In the case that both false positives and false negatives are important to us, we should consider the F1 score for the evaluation purpose, and the AUC curve is a valuable tool to visualize the model's separability on a skewed dataset [27].

6) *Intersection over union:* IoU is an accuracy evaluation metric that is commonly used in image object detection tasks. Unlike the traditional classification or object recognition tasks, the accuracy was measured based on the number of predicted results matched to the ground-truth labels. It is hard to expect two bounding boxes will align exactly in the same coordination x-y axis. The IoU calculated the accuracy by dividing the anticipated bounding box by the ground-truth bounding box. Specifically, it

measures the proportion of intersected area between two bounding boxes over the area of their union. The more overlapping between two bounding boxes indicates a better predicted result. This can be expressed as the equation below:

$$\text{IoU} = \frac{\text{area}(\text{Bp} \cap \text{Bgt})}{\text{area}(\text{Bp} \cup \text{Bgt})}$$

where Bgt is the ground truth bounding box and Bp is the predicted bounding box for detection.

5.3 TRAIN/TEST Dataset

In deep learning development, we could not initially come up with the optimal configuration parameters. Therefore, applying deep learning is a very repetitive process where we must follow the development circle from generating the idea, training the model, evaluating the performance, and over and over again. Therefore, one thing that can expedite the speed of the development process is to improve the efficiency in going through that cycle and setting up the appropriate partition ratio of the dataset in terms of training, validation, and testing. The development dataset is also known as a held-out validation set or development set, but for brevity, we commonly just call it the "dev set" or "valid set". A valid set is what we use to compare different models' performance and see which one performs the best during the development stage. Once we have the final model that we want to evaluate, the test set will be used to produce an unbiased estimation of the unseen data. In many applications of the machine learning algorithm, we often start with the 60/20/20 train-dev-test split, or 70/30 train-test split (if you do not need an explicit dev set).

However, in the modern deep learning application, or the big data era, we might have a million examples in total, and taking up 20% of the dataset for testing can be excessive. Since the goal of the dev set is for comparing the performance of a different algorithm, sometimes even just 1% of the dev set and 1% of the test set can suffice that purpose.

5.4 Division of Training and Validation Sets

The size of training data is an important factor in deciding the quality of generalization ability of a model. In this paper, I conducted 12 sets of experiments on 2 DNN architectures (ResNet50 and VGG16) and 6 various ratios of the train validation split to show the accuracy after 3 epochs of training. The result in Table 1 show that there exists a clear trend that, as the size of the training dataset increased, the training accuracy for the model tends to increase. However, we also noticed that the performance of ResNet50 does get degraded as the train to valid set ratio exceeds 80/20.

Therefore, it was concluded that the 80/20 train-valid set split ratio is a good balance point to have a reliable model performance.

5.5 Batch Size

The traditional SGD takes one example at a time and was trained sequentially. As the dataset grows and the availability of GPUs resource, the mini-batch SGD become more

Table 1. Accuracy score across various experiment configurations after 3 epochs of training

Train-Validation split\NN model	ResNet50	VGG16
Train 20%, Valid 80%	0.8856	0.7456
Train 40%, Valid 60%	0.8974	0.7745
Train 50%, Valid 50%	0.9147	0.7954
Train 60%, Valid 40%	0.9248	0.8147
Train 80%, Valid 20%	0.9326	0.8756
Train 90%, Valid 10%	0.9321	0.8614

and more popular in training large scale dataset in a parallel and distributed fashion, where a subset of data is used to perform forward, and backward-propagation independently amount processors and synchronize the update through the global all reduce operation(a type of MPI communication). However, there is trade-off between the batch size, training speed, and the convergence rate.

On the one extreme case, if the mini-batch size is too small (e.g., use single sample for weight update), we can have faster convergence to an approximate solution, but we might face the problem of I/O communication overhead and the model is not guaranteed to converge to the global optima; on the other hand, if the mini-batch size is too large (e.g., use the entire dataset to perform weight update), the model can guarantee to converge to the global optima of the objective function. However, the convergence rate can be reduced dramatically and can take much longer for a single weight update. To determine the best batch size to use for this thesis, I conducted seven set of experiments for discovering the best mini-batch size to use. All the experiments were trained on ResNet50 neural network with 80/20 train-validation split ratio, and the result is listed in Table 2:

Table 2. Training accuracy on various batch size after first epoch

Batch size	Valid accuracy	Train accuracy	Time/Epoch
32	0.8521	0.9144	587
64	0.8112	0.9127	612
128	0.7645	0.8196	619
256	0.7154	0.7988	634
512	0.6455	0.7122	654
1024	0.4789	0.6523	694
2048	0.3312	0.4345	688

From the result, it was observed that the training accuracy increased as we reduce the mini-batch size, but there is no significant impact on the training time per epoch.

As suggested in a paper, the mini-batch size b should not be larger than the T/b iteration, where T represents the total number of steps for one epoch. Therefore, 32 can be an appropriate balance-point for this study, and all the following experiments were performed with a batch size of 32.

5.6 Loss Function

As there are 15 classes in the dataset, two common categorical loss functions were selected for determining the top loss function in this study: Categorical Cross- Entropy (CCE) and Sparse Categorical Cross-Entropy (SCCE). CCE is a loss function that most used in multi-class classification, and the formula has defined below:

$$\text{generalized cross-entropy} = \sum_{i}^{C} \log(f_i(x_i;\theta))$$

where y_i and $f_i(x_i,\theta)$ are the one-hot encoded label and DNN scores for each *class* in C(as the activation function is always applied to the score function before computing the loss, the notation $f()$ is used to refer to that activation function). The CCE applied the one-hot encoding to compute the target score. For example, considering applying neuron network to train a model with 5 categories. The label can be represented as [0, 0, 1, 0, 0], and the predicted score can be [.2, .3, .5, .1, .1].

SCCE is similar to CCE except the integer encoding is used to replace the one hot encoding. For comparing two loss functions, 6 sets of experiments were conducted, and the result in our situation, Table 3 indicates that there are no significant differences between two-loss functions. CCE was chosen for the rest of the studies because it retains all of the information (it can measure both top-1 and top-5 error) and because it was suggested in a paper that it is more robust in overcoming noisy labels.

Table 3. Loss function comparison between CCE and SCCE

Loss function\Evaluation metrics	Time/Epoch (sec)	Accuracy after 1st epoch	Accuracy after 25 epochs
Categorical Cross Entropy (CCE)	670	0.4908	0.9654
Sparse Categorical Cross Entropy (SCCE)	630	0.4881	0.9613

5.7 CNN Model Performance Evaluation

The major goal of our research is to diagnose herb leaves, and as part of that, I'm comparing the performance of two existing state-of-the-art CNN models and evaluating the success of the best deep learning architecture in the context of plant leaf disease diagnosis. As previously stated, the transfer learning strategy was employed to train all of the deep learning models employed in this work. As seen in Table 4, after 30 epochs of training, the ResNet50 model achieved the best performance with 96.26% and 96.30% on the training and validation dataset, respectively, and this result outperformed VGG16 by a large amount. Therefore, ResNet50 is a good candidate to be considered for heavily loaded backend application.

As seen in Table 5, we provide other information about the two models (e.g., Input size, total parameter, trainable parameter, throughput, and training accuracy after 30 epochs), and it reveals the relationship between the model complexity, training speed, and accuracy. We observed that the ResNet50 model has higher classification accuracy (96.30%) than VGG1, which suggest that the ResNet50 model could produce high performance in the mobile device application as well.

As seen in Fig. 7 and Fig. 8, there is no obvious sign of overfitting in the model that we choose. The ResNet50 model shows the best performance in terms of the training and validation accuracy. In Fig. 7, we see that the ResNet50 can achieve above 94% accuracy by less than 10 epochs of training, in contrast to VGG16 models that were struggling to reach the 90% accuracy even after 10 epochs of training, and the progression line for both accuracy and loss tends to fluctuate more violently. Thus, we believe that the ResNet50 model offers the fastest learning efficiency in our study and, therefore, is the most suitable model to be used in plant leave disease recognition.

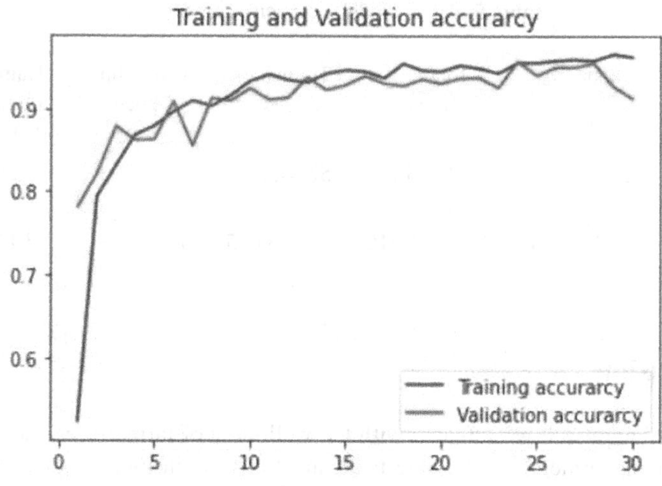

Fig. 7. ResNet50 accuracy and validation accuracy

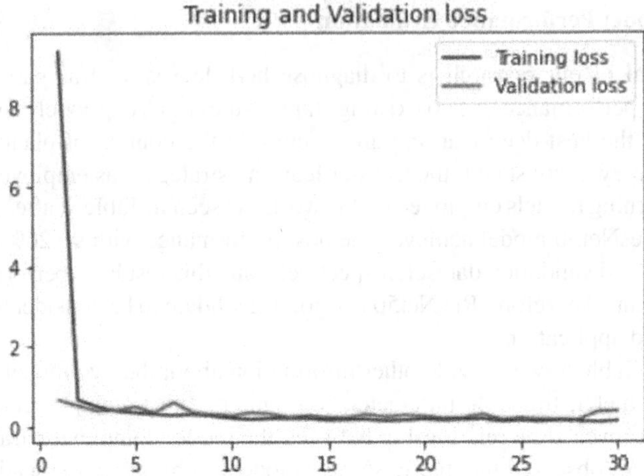

Fig. 8. ResNet50 loss and validation loss

Table 4. DNN models' performance comparison after 30 epochs of training

Model	Train accuracy %	Validation accuracy %	Training loss	Validation loss
ResNet50	96.26	96.30	0.1370	0.17030
VGG16	93.11	93.67	0.1869	0.22714

Table 5. DNN models' capacity comparison

DNN model	Input size	Total parameters	Trainable parameter	Throughput (s/epoch)	Train accuracy after 30 epochs (%)
ResNet50	224 × 224 × 3	74,976,143	52,443,151	580	96.26
VGG16	224 × 224 × 3	40,938,319	33,303,055	3000	93.11

6 Conclusion

The proposed approach was created with the wellbeing of farmers and the agricultural sector in mind. Farmers will be able to identify disease in their crops and apply the appropriate sort and amount of pesticides in their fields with the help of such systems. This will not only reduce the excess use of pesticides in the filed but will also help in increasing the yield of the farms.

Deep learning algorithms are undergoing extensive research. To diagnose the herbs in this thesis, I used CNN and its network designs ResNet50 and VGG16. The created technology can detect illness in herbs with a 96% accuracy rate. Only if we have a thorough understanding of the disease can we apply the right cure to improve the plant's health. Python is used in the suggested system. The accuracy and speed of processing can be improved by using Google's GPU.

In our study, ResNet50 deep learning architecture was tested to be the most suitable CNN model in applying to the image-based plant leaf disease recognition on our dataset. Throughout the study, I have conducted a comprehensive literature review on the past related research on the field of deep-learning-based herb disease detection and provided a series of empirical experiments in applying the techniques, including tuning the performance by varying train-valid set split ratio, pre-trained CNN models, loss functions, and batch size. All the experiments conducted in the study were trained on the googles Colab platform with the help of their GPUs. The result of this study showed that the ResNet50 neural network architecture outperformed the VGG16 architecture. Specifically, we demonstrated in the experimental section that the ResNet50 can achieve accuracy of 96.30% in training and 96.26% in validation over 5-h training and VGG16 can achieve a accuracy of around 93% by over 12 h of training, which suggest that the ResNet50 model is suitable for both lightweight mobile applications and backend workstation purpose development within the context of plant leaf disease recognition.

7 Future Work

Plant disease poses the main threat to the agricultural development of the world, and especially critical to the smallholder farmers in many developing countries. Therefore, affordable and accurate automatic plant disease detection can be valuable tools to provide early warning and forecast that mitigating the efforts to control disease propagation. The application of the deep learning approach has been growing quickly in the field of plant disease diagnosis. The result of deep learning approaches reported in many works of literature so far had shown a promising future. However, the deep learning approach is not omnipotent. There are some shortcomings and challenges that I have not mentioned in the thesis, such as its lack of adaptively to the ever changing environment, poor interpretability of the model, and the demand for a large volume of the dataset. Therefore, one important goal that our future work will be aligned on is the development of robust image detection that only requires a small set of image samples.

There can be other enhancements to the proposed model, one enhancement which can be very useful to the farmers is an alerting mechanism. The system as soon as detects a disease will alert the farmers using buzzer and LEDs so that the spread of the disease can be stopped. The alerting mechanism should only be triggered when a plant has a disease, if it is healthy then no alert is needed. After alerting the farmers, the system should tell the farmers the type and amount of pesticides needed to control the spread of the disease. This will not only reduce the excess use of pesticides in the field but will also help in increasing the yield of the farms.

References

1. Sardogan, M., Tuncer, A., Ozen, Y.: Plant leaf disease detection and classification based on CNN with LVQ algorithm. In: 3rd International Conference on Computer Science and Engineering (2018)
2. Sharma, P., Hans, P., Gupta, S.C.: Classification of plant leaf diseases using machine learning and image preprocessing techniques. In: 10th International Conference on Cloud Computing, Data Science &Engineering (2020)
3. Elangovan, K., Nalini, S.: Plant Disease Classification Using Image Segmentation and SVM Techniques, International Journal of Computational Intelligence Research ISSN 0973-1873, vol.13, no.7, pp. 1821–1828 (2017)
4. Amara, J., Bouaziz, B., Algergawy, A.: A deep learning-based approach for banana leaf diseases classification, Proceedings of the Datenbanksysteme für Business, Technologie und Web (BTW 2017) - Workshopband (2017)
5. Sharath, D.M., Akhilesh, S., Kumar, A., Rohan, M.G. Prathap, C.: Image based plant disease detection in pomegranate plant for bacterial blight. International Conference on Communication and Signal Processing (2019)
6. Saradhambal, G., Dhivya, R., Latha, S., Rajesh, R.: Plant disease detection and its solution using image classification. Int. J. Pure Appl. Math. **119**(14) (2018)
7. Durmuú, H., Güneú, E.O., Mürvet KÕrcÕ,: Disease Detection on the Leaves of the Tomato Plants by Using Deep Learning. Department of Electronics and Communication Engineering Istanbul Technical University, Electrical and Electronics Engineering Faculty, Maslak, Istanbul, Turkey (2017)
8. Belkin, M., Hsu, D., Mitra, P.: Overfitting or perfect fitting? Risk bounds for classification and regression rules that interpolate (2018)
9. Yosinski, J., Clune, J., Bengio, Y., Lipson, H.: How transferable are features in deep neural networks? (2014)
10. Mishkin, D., Sergievskiy, N., Matas, J.: Systematic evaluation of CNN advances on the ImageNet (2016)
11. Maas, A.L., Hannun, A.Y., Ng, A.Y.: Rectifier Nonlinearities Improve Neural Network Acoustic Models. ICML (2013)
12. Ferri, C., Hernández-Orallo, J., Modroiu, R.: An experimental comparison of performance measures for classification. Pattern Recogn. Lett. **30**, 27–38 (2009)
13. Everingham, M., Van Gool, L., Williams, C.K.I., Winn, J., Zisserman, A.: The pascal visual object classes (VOC) challenge. Int. J. Comput. Vis. **88**(2), 303–338 (2010)
14. Dryden, N., Maruyama, N., Moon, T., Benson, T., Snir, M., Van Essen, B.: Channel and filter parallelism for large-scale CNN training. In: SC 2019: Proceedings of the International Conference for High Performance Computing, Networking, Storage and Analysis, pp. 1–20 (2019)
15. Geetharamani, G., Arun Pandian, J.: Identification of plant leaf diseases using a nine- layer deep convolutional neural network. Comput. Electr. Eng. **76**, 323–338 (2019)
16. Géron, A.: Hands-On Machine Learning with Scikit-Learn, Keras, and TensorFlow. O'Reilly Media, Sebastopol, CA (2019)
17. Goodfellow, I., Bengio, Y., Courville, A.: Deep Learning. MIT Press, Cambridge, MA (2017)
18. He, K., Zhang, X., Ren, S., Sun, J.: Deep Residual Learning for Image Recognition. IEEE Conference on Computer Vision and Pattern Recognition CVPR, pp. 770–778 (2016)
19. Keskar, N.S., Mudigere, D., Nocedal, J., Smelyanskiy, M., Tang, P.T.P.: On Large-Batch Training for Deep Learning: Generalization Gap and Sharp. ICLR (2017)
20. Li, M., Zhang, T., Chen, Y., Smola, A.J.: Efficient mini-batch training for stochastic optimization. In: KDD 2014: Proceedings of the 20th ACM SIGKDD International Conference on Knowledge Discovery and Data Mining, pp. 661–670 (2014)

21. Pantazi, X.E., Moshou, D., Tamouridou, A.A., Kasderidis, S.: Leaf disease recognition in vine plants based on local binary patterns and one class support vector machines. In: Iliadis, L., Maglogiannis, I. (eds.) Artificial Intelligence Applications and Innovations. IFIPAICT, vol. 475. Springer, Cham (2016). https://doi.org/10.1007/978-3-319-44944-9_27
22. Kawasaki, Y., Uga, H., Kagiwada, S., Iyatomi, H.: Basic study of automated diagnosis of viral plant diseases using convolutional neural networks. In: Bebis, G., et al. (eds.) ISVC 2015. LNCS, vol. 9475, pp. 638–645. Springer, Cham (2015). https://doi.org/10.1007/978-3-319-27863-6_59
23. Zoph, B., Vasudevan, V., Shlens, J., Le, Q.V.: Learning Transferable Architectures for Scalable Image Recognition. Arxiv (2017)
24. Zoph, B., Le, Q.V.: Neural architecture search with reinforcement learning. Arxiv (2016)
25. Zhang, Z., Sabuncu, M.R.: Generalized Cross Entropy Loss for Training Deep Neural Networks with Noisy Labels. Arxiv (2018)
26. Szegedy, C., Vanhoucke, V., Ioffe, S., Shlens, J., Wojna, Z.: Rethinking the Inception Architecture for Computer Vision (2016)
27. Koushik, C., Madhav, A.V.S., Singh, R.K.: An efficient approach to microarray data classification using elastic net feature selection, SVM and RF. Journal of Physics: Conference Series, vol. 1911, no. 1. IOP Publishing (2021)
28. Singh, R.K., Sivabalakrishnan, M.J.P.C.S.: Feature selection of gene expression data for cancer classification: a review. Procedia Comput. Sci. **50**, 52–57 (2015)

Fashion Image Classification Using Deep Convolution Neural Network

M. S. Saranya(✉) and P. Geetha

Anna University, Chennai, India
saranyasivaraman5@gmail.com, geethap@cs.annauniv.edu

Abstract. We present an analysis of optimal Convolution Neural Network (CNN) for fashion data classification by altering the layers of CNN in this paper. The suggested system employs three deep convolution layers, max pooling layers, and two fully connected layers, as well as dropout layers. While modified layers enhance the test accuracy of Adam optimizer when compared to start-of-art-models. The objective of this work is to address the multi class classification problem and to evaluate the performance of CNN's Adam and RMSProp optimizer. The experiment was carried out using the Fashion-MNIST benchmark dataset. The suggested method has a test accuracy of 92.68%, compared to 91.86% in CNN using the softmax function and 92.22% in CNN utilizing batch normalization.

Keywords: Fashion MNIST · ADAM optimizer · Deep Convolution Neural Network · Image classification

1 Introduction

Object Classification is one of the most prominent applications in computer vision [14]. The fundamental goal of object classification would be feature extraction from photos and categorize them into appropriate classes using any of the available classifiers or classification techniques. Object categorization is a critical issue in a variety of computer vision applications, including image retrieval, autonomous driving, and monitoring. Yan Zhang et al. [1] advocated using stacked sparse auto-encoders (SAE) for obtaining beneficial properties of halftone pictures and furthermore developed an efficient patches extraction method for halftone images in one of their previous research. Anselmo Ferreira et al. [2] have used ad-hoc Convolution Neural Network approaches to classify granite under different resolutions and this was the first approach to compare with texture descriptors.

The fashion-MNIST images were determined by Han Xiao et al. [3] is grayscale images of 28 * 28 with 70,000 fashion products from 10 class labels. The very first 60,000 photographs are being used for training, while the final 10,000 images were used for testing. The original MNIST dataset is still outstanding for machine learning approaches that could benefit from a direct drop-in change. For the fashion-MNIST pictures data set categorization, several studies were presented.

Emmanuel Dufourq et al. [4] have proposed Evolutionary Deep Networks (EDEN) which is an efficient neuro-evolutionary algorithm to address the increasing complexity.

Published by Springer Nature Switzerland AG 2022
E. J. Neuhold et al. (Eds.): ICCCSP 2022, IFIP AICT 651, pp. 116–127, 2022.
https://doi.org/10.1007/978-3-031-11633-9_10

Alexander Schindler et al. [17] have analyzed five different CNN for fashion image classification to improve the e-commerce applications. Shuning Shen et al. [5] have used Long Short-Term memory network for fashion image classification on Fashion-MNIST benchmark dataset which obtained accuracy of 88.26%. Greeshma K V et al. [6] have explored Hyper-Parameter Optimization (HPO) methods and regularization techniques with deep neural networks for apparel image classification. To characterize the fashion articles in the fashion-MNIST dataset, the authors created three convolutional neural networks. On the benchmark dataset, the method achieves fantastic results.

EnsNet is a new model suggested by Daiki Hirata et al. [7] which is made up of one base CNN and several Fully Connected SubNetworks (FCSNs). Since deep learning necessitates a large amount of data, the insufficiency of photo testing can be exacerbated by various techniques like as rotation, cropping, shifting, and flipping. Kota Hara et al. [8] have proposed a pose-dependent prior model for automatic selection of human body joints and used deep convolution neural network for cloth detection. They have conducted experiments on Fashionista and PaperDoll datasets for image classification.

The rest of the paper is organized as follows: Sect. 2 begins with a comprehensive examination of relevant literature. Section 3 provides an outline of the suggested methodology. Section 4 describes the experimental setting as well as the results of four model performance evaluations using the fashion MNIST dataset. Section 5 describes the conclusion and future work.

2 Related Works

Mustafa Amer Obaid et al. [16] have discussed the fashion image classification using pre-convoluted neural networks. They have conducted experiments on Fashion MNIST. They have achieved 94% accuracy in using pre-convoluted neural networks. The Hierarchical Convolutional Neural Networks model for the fashion and apparel categorization task was presented by Seo Yian et al. [17]. The model achieved better classification results by using VGGNet. They tested their hypothesis on the Fashion MNIST dataset. EnsNET is a new model presented by Daiki Hirata et al. [7] which is made up of one base CNN and many Fully Connected SubNetworks (FCSN). For fashion image categorization, Greeshma K V et al. [18] have classified the fashion products using Histogram of Oriented Gradients (HOG) features with multiclass Support Vector Machine (SVM) classifier. They have conducted experiments on the Fashion MNIST dataset.

Mohammed Kayed et al. [19] have applied CNN LeNet-5 architecture for the classification of garments. They tested their hypothesis on the Fashion MNIST dataset. The accuracy of the CNN LeNet-5 architecture was 98%. For the fashion-MNIST picture categorization, Khatereh Meshkini et al. [20] have employed different CNN activation functions. They tested their hypothesis on the Fashion MNIST dataset. Zhang et al. [21] investigated LeNet-5, AlexNet, VGG-16, and ResNet, four CNN models. These are utilised in the categorising of fashion images. ResNet has the highest validation accuracy of the four models. They tested their hypothesis on the Fashion MNIST dataset.

3 Proposed System

General system architecture of CNN [9] is shown in Fig. 1. Modified CNN architecture of proposed system is shown in Fig. 2. Input image has been preprocessed using resizing and normalization. Then CNN framework is employed for fashion image classification task.

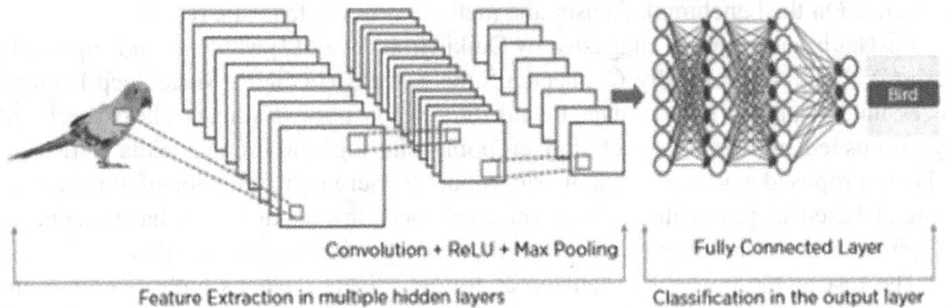

Fig. 1. General system architecture of convolution neural network

3.1 Model Definition

The convolution operations in between two-dimensional picture $\mathrm{I_n}$ and also a two-dimensional kernel k is,

$$S(x, y) = (k * \mathrm{I_n})(x, y) = \sum\nolimits_{\alpha} \sum\nolimits_{\beta} \mathrm{I_n}(\alpha, \beta) k(x - \alpha, y - \beta) \tag{1}$$

The equation becomes with a kernel size of 3 × 3

$$S(x, y) = (k * \mathrm{I_n})(x, y) = \sum\nolimits_{\alpha=1}^{3} \sum\nolimits_{\beta=1}^{3} \mathrm{I_n}(\alpha, \beta) k(x - \alpha, y - \beta) \tag{2}$$

ReLU is one of the activation functions in CNN. The output is $f(x) = \max(0, x)$. ReLU is computed using

$$f(x) = \begin{cases} x, \textit{if } x > 0 \\ 0, \textit{if } x < 0 \end{cases} \tag{3}$$

The pooling layer also known to as the down sampling operation that reduces the dimensionality of the feature map. The parameter used in the max pooling layer is pool size which specifies the 2 × 2 filter.

The flattening layer is used to convert two-dimensional arrays into one-dimensional array of input so that the flattened input will be given to the final classification layer that is the fully connected layer.

The dropout layer randomly dropping some connections produces several thinned network architecture and one representative network is selected with small weights.

The fully connected layer is used for classification and it is mostly used at the end of the network. Finally, the classification task is performed to generate the output of 10 classes probabilities.

Softmax activation function was used in the neural network for multi-class classification of fashion images.

$$\text{Softmax} f(X_i) = \frac{exp^{X_i}}{\sum_{j=1}^{n} exp^{X_j}} \tag{4}$$

In general, it is the ratio of the exponential of a specific input value to the sum of exponential values of all input values.

3.2 Output Shapes

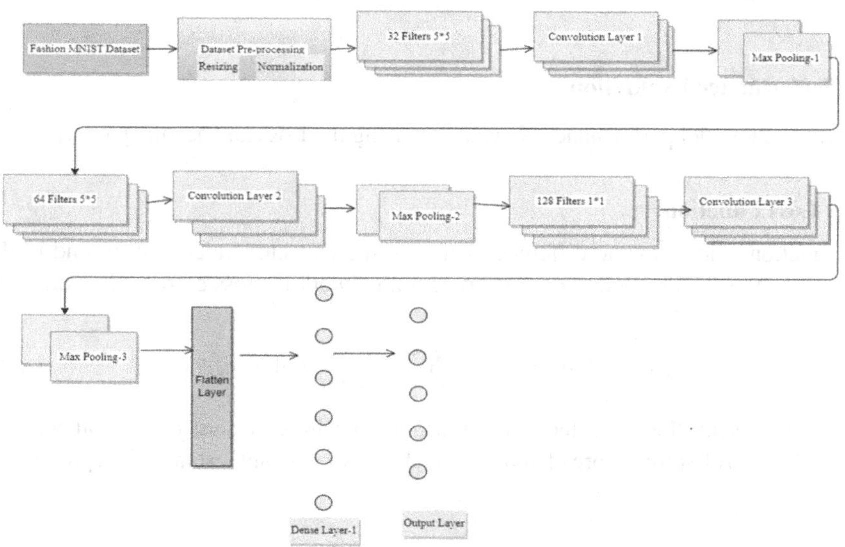

Fig. 2. CNN architecture of proposed system

The suggested CNN model comprises of three convolution layers with 32, 64, and 128 filters, respectively. 5 * 5 kernel sizes are used in Layers 1 and 2, whereas 3 * 3 kernel sizes are used in Layer 3. In ReLU Activation, all three layers are enabled. Following layer 1 and layer 2, the max pooling is handled as 2 * 2 kernel sizes, while layer 3 is applied as 1 * 1 kernel sizes. There is a 0.5% dropout after layer 1 and 2 are applied; this dropout is obtained from layers 1 and 2 to minimize overfitting. Finally, the fully connected neural network is used for classification task, which is then assessed by the softmax activation function to generate the output of 10 classes probabilities (Table 1).

Table 1. Fashion image classification using CNN

Layer	Kernel size	Activation	Output shape	Parameter
Conv2d	5 × 5	ReLU	(None, 24, 24, 32)	812
MP2d	2 × 2	-	(None, 12, 12, 32)	0
Conv2d_1	5 × 5	ReLU	(None, 8, 8, 64)	51264
MP2d_1	2 × 2	-	(None, 4, 4, 64)	0
Conv2d_2	1 × 1	ReLU	(None, 4, 4, 128)	8320
MP2d_2	2 × 2	-	(None, 2, 2, 64)	0
Flatten_1	-	-	(None, 512)	0
Dense_1		ReLU	(None, 10)	5130
Dropout_1	-	-	(None, 10)	0
Dense_2		ReLU	(None, 10)	110
Dropout_2	-	-	(None, 10)	0
Fully connected	-	Softmax	(None, 10)	110

3.3 Performance Evaluation

The proposed model performance is evaluated using the Loss and accuracy metrics.

3.3.1 Loss Function

Loss function calculates the difference between the expected value and ground truth value. Widely used loss function for deep neural network is cross entropy. It is defined as

$$Cross - Entrophy = -\sum_{i=1}^{n}\sum_{j=1}^{m} t_{i,j}\log(p_{i.j}) \tag{5}$$

where $t_{i,j}$ represents the true value that is, If instance i belongs to class j, it is 1; otherwise, it is 0.and The probability score of anticipated class j for relevant instance i is represented by $p_{i.j}$.

3.3.2 Accuracy

Accuracy is a common statistic for evaluating model performance. Accuracy metrics are used to determine how effectively the classifier predicts the output classes and to measure the classification model's efficacy. Accuracy is usually inversely related to error. It is defined as

$$Accuracy = \frac{\mu + \gamma}{\mu + \gamma + \vartheta + \varphi} \tag{6}$$

Here, μ, $\boldsymbol{\varphi}$ denotes the true occurrence for number of true and false predictions respectively and $\boldsymbol{\vartheta}$, $\boldsymbol{\gamma}$ denotes the false occurrence for the number of true and false predictions respectively.

4 Experiments and Discussion

4.1 Dataset

In this paper, experiments were carried out using the Fashion MNIST dataset of zalando's article [10–13]. Dataset information is shown in Table 2. The Fashion MNIST dataset contains images from a training dataset of 60,000 samples as well as a test set of 10,000 samples. The size of the grayscale images is 28 × 28 pixels associated with a 10 class labels.

Table 2. Dataset information

Name	Explanation	#Example	Size
train-image-idx3-ubyte.gz	Training sample images	60,000	25 MBytes
train-labels-idx1-ubyte.gz	Training class labels	60,000	140 Bytes
t10k-images-idx3-ubyte.gz	Testing sample images	10,000	4.2 MBytes
t10k-labels-idx1-ubyte.gz	Testing class labels	10,000	92 Bytes

Labels

As indicated in Table 3, each training and testing sample is labelled with one of the class labels.

Table 3. Class labels in benchmark fashion MNIST dataset

Class Label	Explanation	Samples
0	T-Shirt/Top	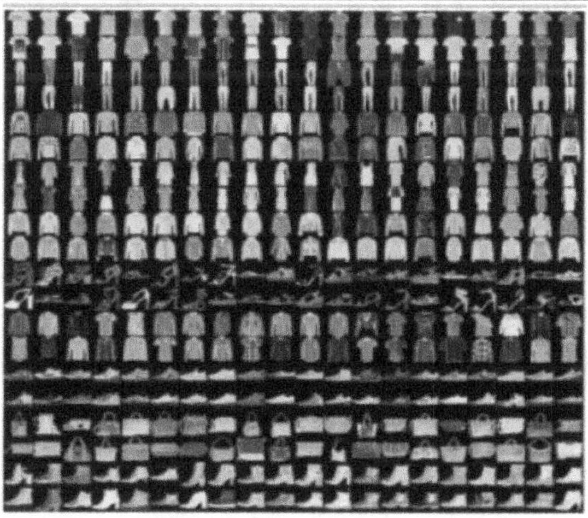
1	Trouser	
2	Pullover	
3	Dress	
4	Coat	
5	Sandals	
6	Bag	
7	Shirt	
8	Sneaker	
9	Ankle boots	

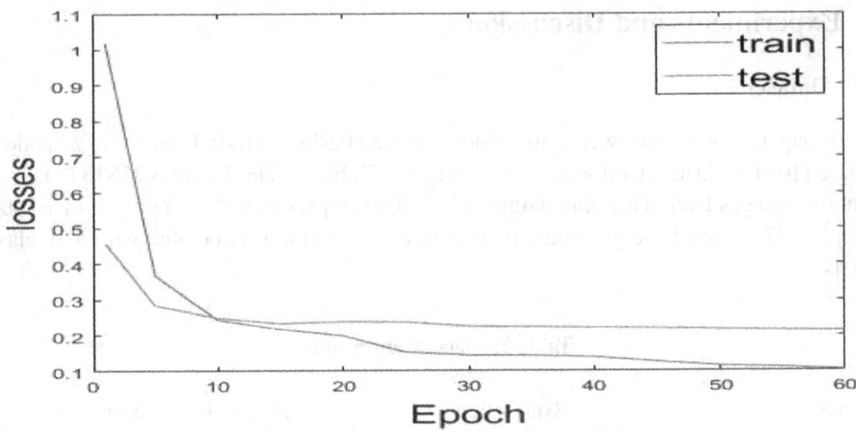

Fig. 3. Loss in ADAM model per epoch

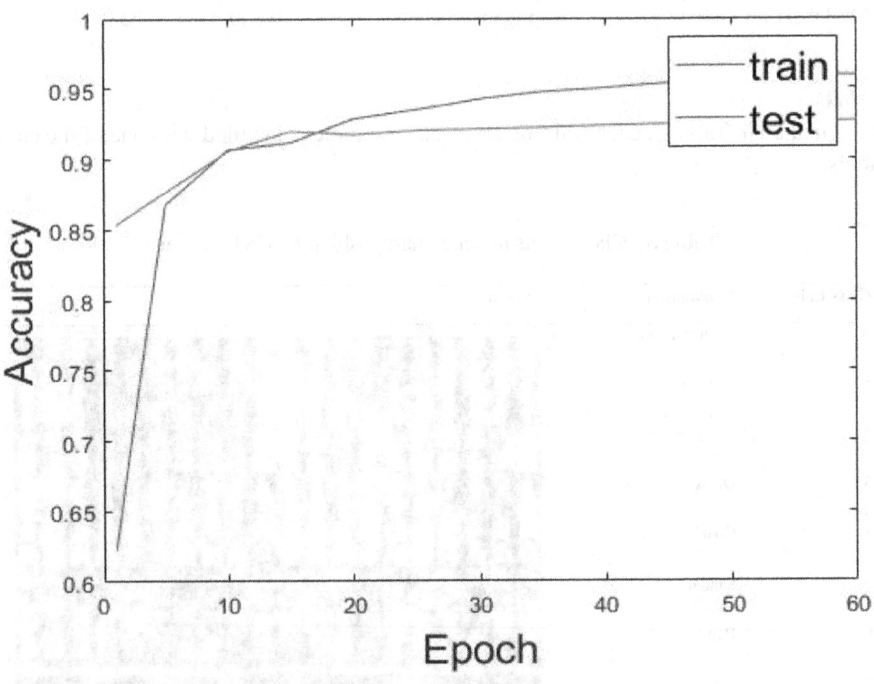

Fig. 4. Accuracy in ADAM model per epoch

4.2 Results

Figure 3 depicts the training and testing losses of the ADAM optimizer model each epoch. Figure 4 depicts the ADAM optimizer model's training and testing accuracy per epoch. Figure 5 depicts the training and testing losses of the RMSProp optimizer model each epoch. Figure 6 depicts the RMSProp optimizer model's training and testing accuracy per epoch. Table 4 compares the classification results of the Fashion MNIST dataset to those found in the literature. Table 5 displays the loss and accuracy on the Adam model per epoch. Table 6 displays the loss and accuracy on the RMSProp model per epoch.

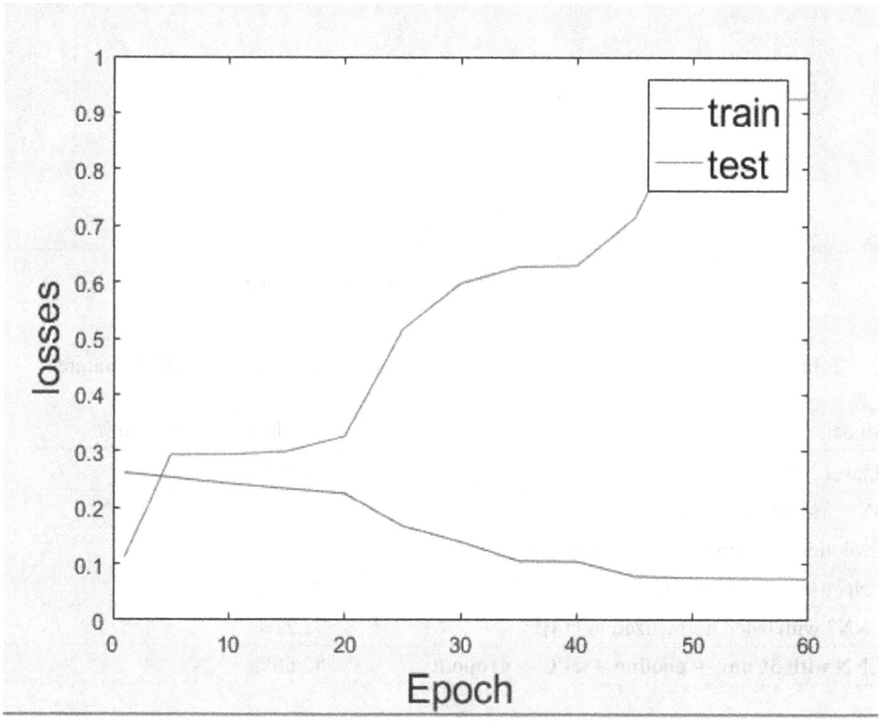

Fig. 5. Loss in RMSProp model per epoch

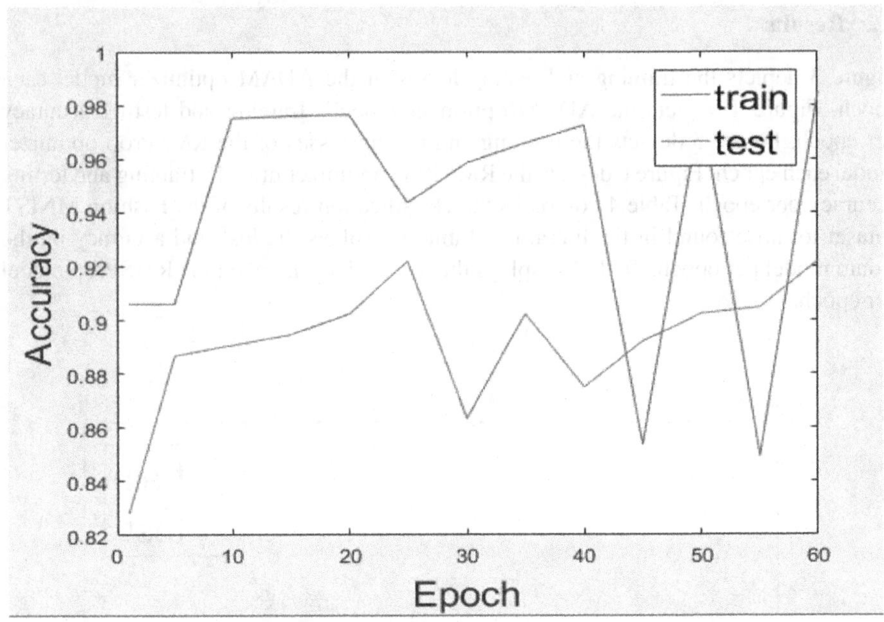

Fig. 6. Loss in RMSProp model per epoch

Table 4. Fashion MNIST dataset classification outcomes comparison with literatures

Model	Validation accuracy in %
3 layer NN [15]	87.23%
SVC with rbf kernel [3]	89.70%
Evolutionary deep learning framework [4]	90.60%
CNN using softmax [14]	91.86%
CNN2 with batch normalization [14]	92.22%
CNN with 3Conv + pooling + 2FC + dropout	**92.68%**

Table 5. Loss and accuracy on Adam model per epoch

Epoch	ADAM optimizer			
	Training		Testing	
	Loss	Acc	Loss	Acc
1	1.0178	0.6224	0.4563	0.8532
5	0.3675	0.8675	0.2846	0.8764
10	0.2436	0.9067	0.2489	0.9056
15	0.2176	0.9117	0.2340	0.9198
20	0.1983	0.9285	0.2386	0.9173
25	0.1528	0.9349	0.2373	0.9202
30	0.1437	0.9423	0.2254	0.9213
35	0.1428	0.9475	0.2232	0.9223
40	0.1386	0.9502	0.2214	0.9237
45	0.1256	0.9537	0.2198	0.9247
50	0.1143	0.9558	0.2164	0.9253
55	0.1105	0.9589	0.2142	0.9263
60	0.1031	0.9592	0.2126	0.9268

Table 6. Loss and accuracy on RMSProp model per epoch

Epoch	RMSProp optimizer			
	Training		Testing	
	Loss	Acc	Loss	Acc
1	0.2614	0.9060	0.1113	0.8281
5	0.2535	0.9060	0.2939	0.8867
10	0.2426	0.9751	0.2942	0.8906
15	0.2332	0.9760	0.2992	0.8945
20	0.2252	0.9764	0.3264	0.9023
25	0.1669	0.9436	0.5165	0.9219
30	0.1392	0.9584	0.5974	0.8633
35	0.1053	0.9658	0.6272	0.9023
40	0.1043	0.9724	0.6292	0.8750
45	0.0782	0.8536	0.7156	0.8920
50	0.0757	0.9794	0.9224	0.9023
55	0.0748	0.8493	0.9248	0.9047
60	0.0740	0.9846	0.9257	0.9219

5 Conclusion

In this paper, proposed system uses three convolution neural network layers. In the suggested approach, the regular CNN's convolution layer is enhanced by expanding the number of layers to three layers with max pooling for fashion image classification. In the future, we will try to use the new benchmark clothing dataset to decide classification algorithms and alternative convolution architectures. Other CNN models can be used to apply the suggested technique in the future, and the work has been expanded to incorporate real-world online clothing imagery.

References

1. Zhang, Y., Zhang, E., Chen, W.: Deep neural network for halftone image classification based on sparse auto-encoder. Eng. Appl. Artif. Intell. **50**, 245–255 (2016). https://doi.org/10.1016/j.engappai.2016.01.032
2. Ferreira, A., Giraldi, G.: Convolutional neural network approaches to granite tiles classification. Expert Syst. Appl. **84**, 1–11 (2017). https://doi.org/10.1016/j.eswa.2017.04.053
3. Xiao, H., Rasul, K., Vollgraf, R.: Fashion-mnist: a novel image dataset for benchmarking machine learning algorithms. arXiv preprint arXiv:1708.07747 (2017)
4. Dufourq, E., Bassett, B.A.: Eden: Evolutionary deep networks for efficient machine learning. In: Pattern Recognition Association of South Africa and Robotics and Mechatronics (PRASA-RobMech), pp. 110–115. IEEE (2017). https://doi.org/10.1109/RoboMech.2017.8261132
5. Shen, S.: Image classification of Fashion-MNIST dataset using long short-term memory networks. Research School of Computer Science (2018)
6. Greeshma, K.V., Sreekumar, K.: Hyperparameter optimization and regularization on Fashion-MNIST classification. Int. J. Recent Technol. Eng. (IJRTE). **8**(2), 3713–3719 (2019). https://doi.org/10.35940/ijrte.B3092.078219
7. Hirata, D., Takahashi, N.: Ensemble learning in CNN augmented with fully connected subnetworks. arXiv preprint arXiv:2003.08562 (2020)
8. Hara, K., Jagadeesh, V., Piramuthu, R.: Fashion apparel detection: the role of deep convolutional neural network and pose-dependent priors. In: 2016 IEEE Winter Conference on Applications of Computer Vision (WACV), pp. 1–9. IEEE (2016). https://doi.org/10.1109/WACV.2016.7477611
9. Sewak, M., Sahay, S.K., Rathore, H.: An overview of deep learning architecture of deep neural networks and autoencoders. J. Comput. Theor. Nanosci. **17**(1), 182–188 (2020). https://doi.org/10.1166/jctn.2020.8648
10. Leithardt, V.: Classifying garments from fashion-MNIST dataset through CNNs. Adv. Sci. Technol. Eng. Syst. J. **6**(1), 989–994 (2021). https://doi.org/10.25046/aj0601109
11. Teow, M.Y.: Experimenting deep convolutional visual feature learning using compositional subspace representation and fashion-MNIST. In: 2nd International Conference on Artificial Intelligence in Engineering and Technology (IICAIET), pp. 1–6. IEEE (2020). https://doi.org/10.1109/IICAIET49801.2020.9257819
12. Pathak, A.R., Pandey, M., Rautaray, S.: Application of deep learning for object detection. Proc. Comput. Sci. **132**, 1706–1717 (2018). https://doi.org/10.1016/j.procs.2018.05.144
13. Gnatushenko, V., Dorosh, N., Fenenko, T.: Fashion MNIST image recognition by deep learning methods. Appl. Ques. Math. Model. **4**(1), 78–85 (2021)
14. Bhatnagar, S., Ghosal, D., Kolekar, M.H.: Classification of fashion article images using convolutional neural networks. In: Fourth International Conference on Image Information Processing (ICIIP), pp. 1–6. IEEE (2017). https://doi.org/10.1109/ICIIP.2017.8313740

15. Zhang, K.: LSTM: An Image Classification Model Based on Fashion-MNIST Dataset (2017)
16. Obaid, M.A., Jasim, W.M.: Pre-convoluted neural networks for fashion classification. Bull. Elect. Eng. Inform. **10**(2), 750–758 (2021). https://doi.org/10.11591/eei.v10i2.2750
17. Seo, Y., Shin, K.S.: Hierarchical convolutional neural networks for fashion image classification. Expert Syst. Appl. **116**, 328–339 (2019). https://doi.org/10.1016/j.eswa.2018.09.022
18. Greeshma, K.V., Sreekumar, K.: Fashion-MNIST classification based on HOG feature descriptor using SVM. Int. J. Innov. Technol. Explor. Eng. **8**(5), 960–962 (2019). https://doi.org/10.35940/ijrte.B3092.078219
19. Kayed, M., Anter, A., Mohamed, H.: Classification of garments from fashion mnist dataset using cnn lenet-5 architecture. In: 2020 International Conference on Innovative Trends in Communication and Computer Engineering (ITCE), pp. 238–243 (2020). https://doi.org/10.1109/ITCE48509.2020.9047776
20. Meshkini, K., Platos, J., Ghassemain, H.: An analysis of convolutional neural network for fashion images classification (Fashion-MNIST). In: Kovalev, S., Tarassov, V., Snasel, V., Sukhanov, A. (eds.) Proceedings of the Fourth International Scientific Conference "Intelligent Information Technologies for Industry" (IITI'19). AISC, vol. 1156, pp. 85–95. Springer, Cham (2020). https://doi.org/10.1007/978-3-030-50097-9_10
21. A MNIST-like fashion product database. https://github.com/zalandoresearch/fashion-mnist

Performance Analysis of Adaptive Variable Exponent Based Total Variation Image Regularization Algorithm

V. Kamalaveni[1](✉), S. Veni[1], and K. A. Narayanankuttty[2]

[1] Department of Electronics and Communication Engineering, Amrita School of Engineering, Amrita Vishwa Vidyapeetham, Coimbatore, India
vvkamalaveni@gmail.com, s_veni@cb.amrita.edu

[2] Amrita School of Engineering, Amrita Vishwa Vidyapeetham, Coimbatore, India

Abstract. In this paper, a new adaptive variable exponent based total variation image regularization algorithm is proposed. In the proposed algorithm a regularizing term based on variable exponent is used. The model adaptively switches between TV-ROF model and Tikhonov model. At the edges the model behaves like a ROF model preserving edges effectively. In the inner region the model behaves like a Tikhonov model which enables strong smoothing. The weight of the fidelity term is also adaptive. The weight is large at edges and small in the constant flat area. In this paper the performance of proposed adaptive variable exponent based total variation model is compared with TV-ROF model and Tikhonov model. The performance of the proposed model is compared with other classical diffusion algorithms such as perona-malik model and self-snake model. In addition the proposed model is also compared with nonlocal means filter. The performance of the proposed algorithm is validated by denoising rician noise corrupted brain magnetic resonance images as well as denoising salt and pepper noise corrupted standard images.

Keywords: Total variation · Adaptive model · Tikhonov model · TV-ROF model · Variable exponent

1 Introduction and Related Work

Images are often corrupted by noise during acquisition and transmission and so image denoising becomes one of the most essential tasks in image processing applications. The objective of image denoising is to remove noise in the image by protecting edges and fine-scale details. During past two decades mathematical techniques such as partial differential equation (PDE) models and variational models have been used for image denoising [1]. Most popularly used variational model is total variation regularization also known as TV-ROF model. While total variation based regularization can able to minimize noise and also regularize the edges, it has some undesirable properties. The undesirable properties are as follows. Loss of contrast, Loss of Geometry, Loss of Texture

Published by Springer Nature Switzerland AG 2022
E. J. Neuhold et al. (Eds.): ICCCSP 2022, IFIP AICT 651, pp. 128–150, 2022.
https://doi.org/10.1007/978-3-031-11633-9_11

and Staircase Effect- this refers to the concept that the denoised image may have blocky regions that is piecewise constant regions [2, 3].

To overcome the drawbacks associated with total variation regularization different variational regularization models have been proposed. Among several variational models two models used for contrasting purposes are Tikhonov model and TV-ROF model. Tikhonov model is used for smoothing flat region and TV-ROF model is used for edge preservation. The TV-ROF model can remove noise properly and produce sharper edges. But it introduces staircase effect in the constant uniform areas or flat regions [4, 5]. Considering the drawbacks of TV-ROF model many improvements have been suggested by different researchers. To overcome the loss of contrast and texture an iterative regularization method for ROF model was proposed by Osher et al. [6] Another improvement to ROF model is squared L2 norm in the fidelity term is replaced by L1 norm [7, 8, 17, 19].Yet another improvement is spatially varying fidelity term was used to preserve texture and contrast [9–11].

The tikhonov regularization can minimize staircase effect but it blurs the edges. To bring a balance between tikhonov model and TV-ROF model that is to avoid staircase effect and protect edges and fine details, we introduce new adaptive variable exponent based total variation model which behaves like TV-ROF model at edges and behaves like Tikhonov model in the inner region. In this work the brain magnetic resonance (MR) images corrupted by rician noise are taken for experimental analysis. In the proposed adaptive total variation model both regularization term and fidelity term are adaptive which eliminates staircasing effect [12, 13].

The paper is written as follows. Section 2 explains in detail the proposed adaptive variable exponent based total variation model, its partial differential equation solution (PDE) and the numerical implementation of PDE. In Sect. 3 performance of proposed model is analysed in depth and compared with other models. Finally Sect. 4 concludes the paper.

2 Materials and Methods

2.1 Proposed Adaptive Variable Exponent Based Total Variation Model

The proposed adaptive local feature driven variable exponent based total variation regularization model is described by the Eq. 1. The local feature of an image that is whether the pixel belongs to an edge or flat inner region is determined using an edge stopping function c(|∇u|) [14]. The edge stopping function described by Eq. 4 is used in the proposed model. The flowchart in Fig. 1 describes steps of proposed algorithm.

$$\min_u\{E(u)\} = \min_u \int_\Omega \left(|\nabla u|^{\alpha}(|\nabla u|) + \frac{1}{2}\beta(|\nabla u|)(u-u_0)^2 \right) dxdy \tag{1}$$

In the above mentioned model

$$\alpha(|\nabla u|) = 1 + c(|\nabla u|) \tag{2}$$

$$\beta(|\nabla u|) = \rho(1 + c(|\nabla u|)) \tag{3}$$

$$c(|\nabla u|) = \exp\left(-\left(\frac{|\nabla u|}{k}\right)^2\right) \tag{4}$$

In the Eq. 1 E(u) is the energy functional, |∇u| is the magnitude of image gradient, α(|∇u|) is the variable exponent, u is the observed image, u_0 is the original noisy image and β(|∇u|) is the regularization parameter [15]. In Eq. 1 the first term in the integration is regularizing term and second term is the fidelity term. In Eq. 2 and Eq. 3 c(|∇u|) is the edge stopping function. In the Eq. 4 k is the gradient threshold parameter. k decides which are the gradients to be considered as edges. The property of edge stopping function is that it has zero or insignificant value for higher image gradient magnitudes and it has value one wherever image gradient is zero [14, 17, 18]. The edge stopping function has value in the range from 0 to 1 for different image gradients. In this model the regularising term whose exponent is a variable that is function α(|∇u|) dependent on the image gradient. At image edges the value of the exponent is 1 since value of c(|∇u|) is zero. The regularising term is total variation which is the sum of image gradients across the entire image domain. So the model becomes Rudin-Osher-Fatemi model at edges [20–22] which is more efficient in preserving edges [16, 19]. In noisy inner region where the gradient value is low, so the value of c(|∇u|) becomes one. The exponent becomes the value two since value of c(|∇u|) is one. Here square of the gradient is used as regularising term that is l_2 norm so the model becomes the tikhonov model in the inner region which enables strong image smoothing in the flat inner region [16, 19].

The regularization parameter [23, 31, 32] β(|∇u|) is selected adaptively based on the local feature of an image. At the object boundaries the value of the edge function becomes zero that is where image gradient is high. The value of the regularization parameter β(|∇u|) becomes equal to constant parameter ρ. The parameter ρ can be set to value 0.2 which enables better edge preservation [16]. In the inner region of an image the value of edge function c(|∇u|) becomes a value exactly one or value closer to 1. So the value of the regularization parameter β(|∇u|) becomes much smaller than 0.2 and this causes strong smoothing in the flat inner region. If c(|∇u|) is 0.999 and the parameter ρ is 0.2 then β(|∇u|) becomes 0.0002 which enables strong smoothing. This is proved in our previous work [16].

2.2 Partial Differential Equation Solution of Proposed Adaptive Variational Model

The proposed model is solved using the steepest descent method [4, 24, 25] and the following partial differential Eq. 5 is obtained as solution of the proposed model.

$$\frac{\partial u}{\partial t} = \nabla(g(|\nabla u|)\nabla u) + \beta(|\nabla u|)(u_0 = u) \tag{5}$$

Here u = u_0 the original noisy image at time t = t_0 and the diffusivity function g(|∇u|) is given below.

$$g(|\nabla u|) = \phi'(|\nabla u|)/|\nabla u| \tag{6}$$

$$\phi(|\nabla u|) = |\nabla u|^{\alpha(|\nabla u|)} \tag{7}$$

The orthogonal decomposition [26–28] of Eq. 5 is given in Eq. 8.

$$\frac{\partial u}{\partial t} = c_\xi u_{\xi\xi} + c_\eta u_{\eta\eta} + \beta(|\nabla u|)(u - u_o) \tag{8}$$

$$c_\xi = g(|\nabla u|) \tag{9}$$

$$c_\eta = g'(|\nabla u|)|\nabla u| + g(|\nabla u|) \tag{10}$$

$$\frac{\partial u}{\partial t} = \phi''(|\nabla u|)u_{\eta\eta} + g(|\nabla u|)u_{\xi\xi} + \beta(|\nabla u|)(u_0 - u) \tag{11}$$

The first term in the Eq. 11 describes the amount of diffusion along the normal direction of an image edge and second term describes the amount of diffusion along the edge direction. In our model

$$\phi''(|\nabla u|) = \alpha(|\nabla u|)(\alpha(|\nabla u|) - 1)|\nabla u|^{\alpha(|\nabla u|)-2} \tag{12}$$

$$g(|\nabla u|) = \alpha(|\nabla u|)|\nabla u|^{\alpha(|\nabla u|)-2} \tag{13}$$

$$u_{\eta\eta} = \frac{1}{(u_x^2 + u_y^2)}\left(u_{yy}u_y^2 + u_{xx}u_x^2 + 2u_x u_y u_{xy}\right) \tag{14}$$

$$u_{\xi\xi} = \frac{1}{(u_x^2 + u_y^2)}\left(u_{xx}u_y^2 + u_{yy}u_x^2 - 2u_x u_y u_{xy}\right) \tag{15}$$

The Eq. 14 describes directional second derivative along gradient direction and Eq. 15 describes directional second derivative along edge direction. In this model ϕ'' is positive for image gradients corresponding to inner regions or flat regions. This enables a forward diffusion [29] in the flat inner region thus preventing staircasing effect in the flat region.

The proposed model described by Eq. 11 can be implemented by means of numerical iterative algorithm given in Eq. 16. In Eq. 16 n denotes number of iterations.

$$u_{i,j}^{n+1} = u_{i,j}^n + \Delta t\phi''(|\nabla u|)_{i,j}^n(u_{\eta\eta})_{i,j}^n + \Delta t g(|\nabla|)_{i,j}^n(u_{\xi\xi})_{i,j}^n + \Delta t\beta(|\nabla u|)_{i,j}^n\left(u_{i,j}^n - (u_o)_{i,j}^n\right) \tag{16}$$

3 Experimental Results and Performance Analysis of Proposed Model

Brain MR images of different modalities that is T1, T2, Protein density (PD) weighted from Brain Web database are taken for validation of proposed algorithm. We compared the performance of proposed algorithm with classical partial differential equation based algorithms namely self-snake diffusion, perona-malik diffusion, non local means algorithm proposed by antoni buades [30], tikhonov model and total-variation ROF model. Rican noise corrupted brain MR images having noise levels 10% and 15% are denoised

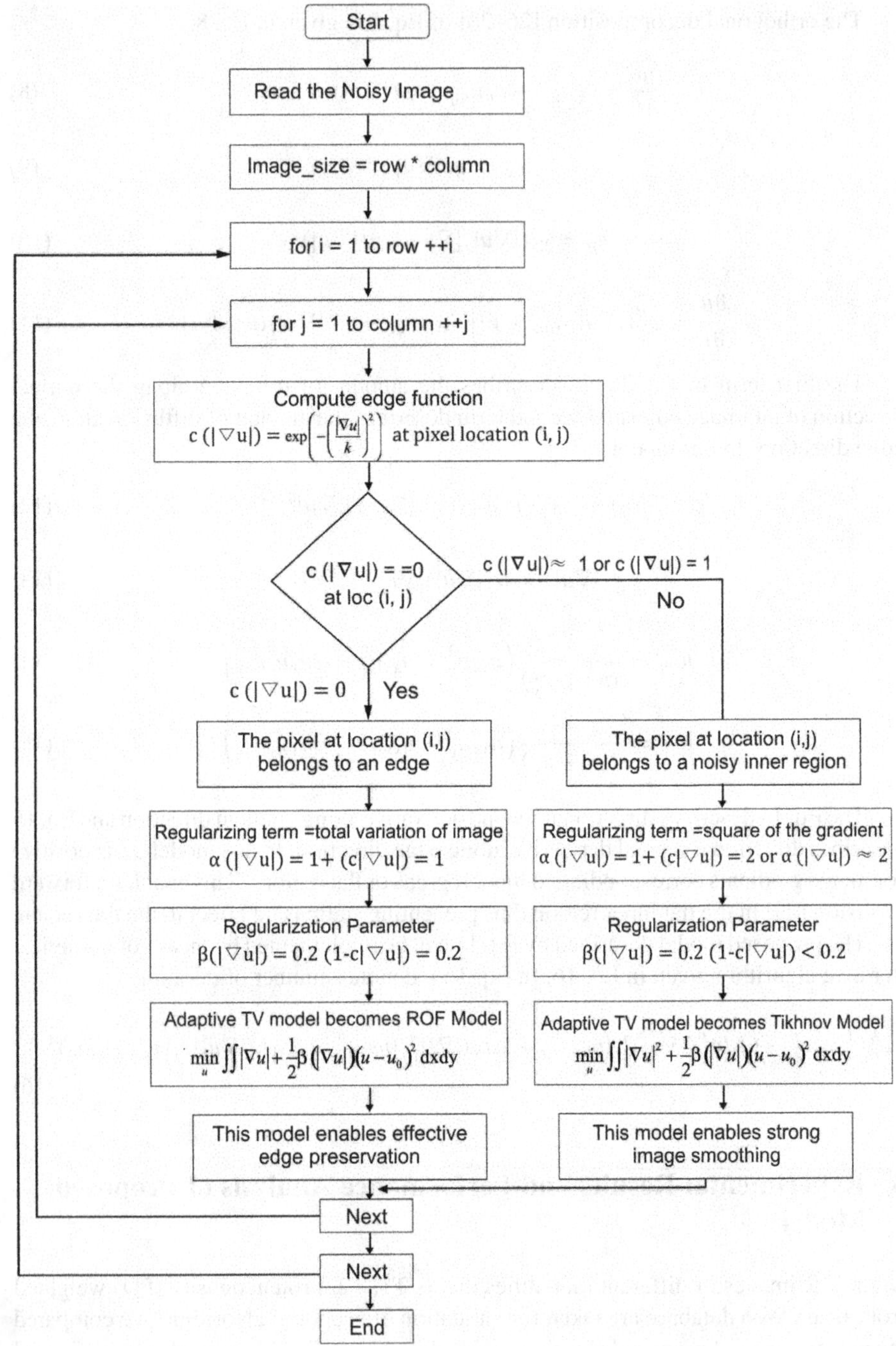

Fig. 1. Flowchart of proposed adaptive variable exponent based image regularization algorithm

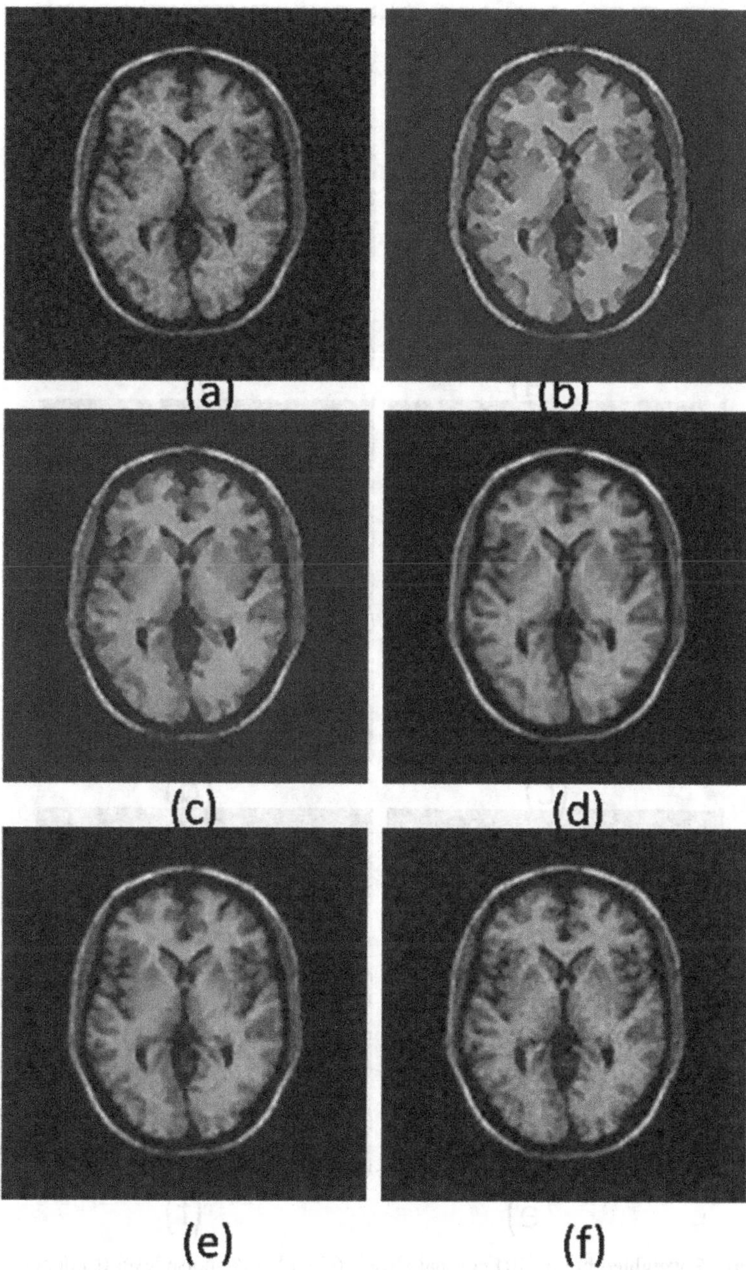

Fig. 2. (a) T1-weighted brain MRI slice −55 with 15% noise level (b) denoised image by self-snake model (c) denoised image by perona-malik model (d) denoised image by non-local means algorithm (e) denoised image by TV-ROF (f) denoised image by proposed algorithm.

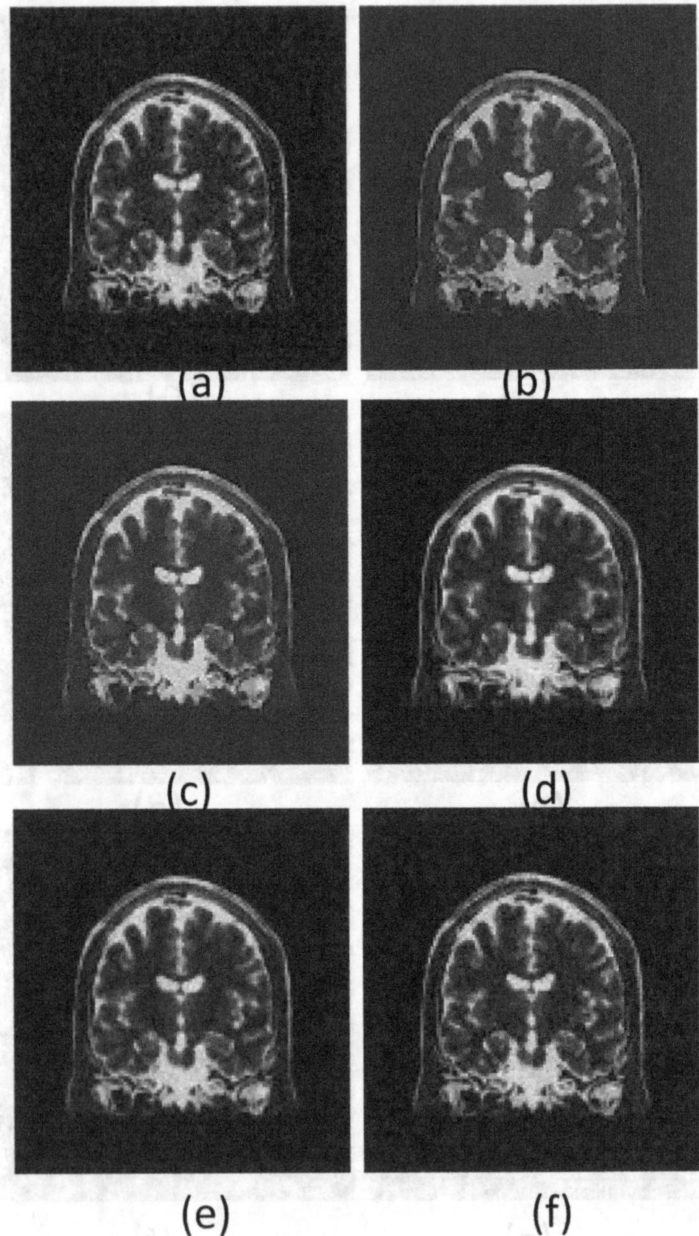

Fig. 3. (a) T2-weighted brain MRI coronal slice −67 with 15% noise level (b) denoised image by self-snake model (c) denoised image by perona-malik model (d) denoised image by non-local means algorithm (e) denoised image by TV-ROF (f) denoised image by proposed algorithm.

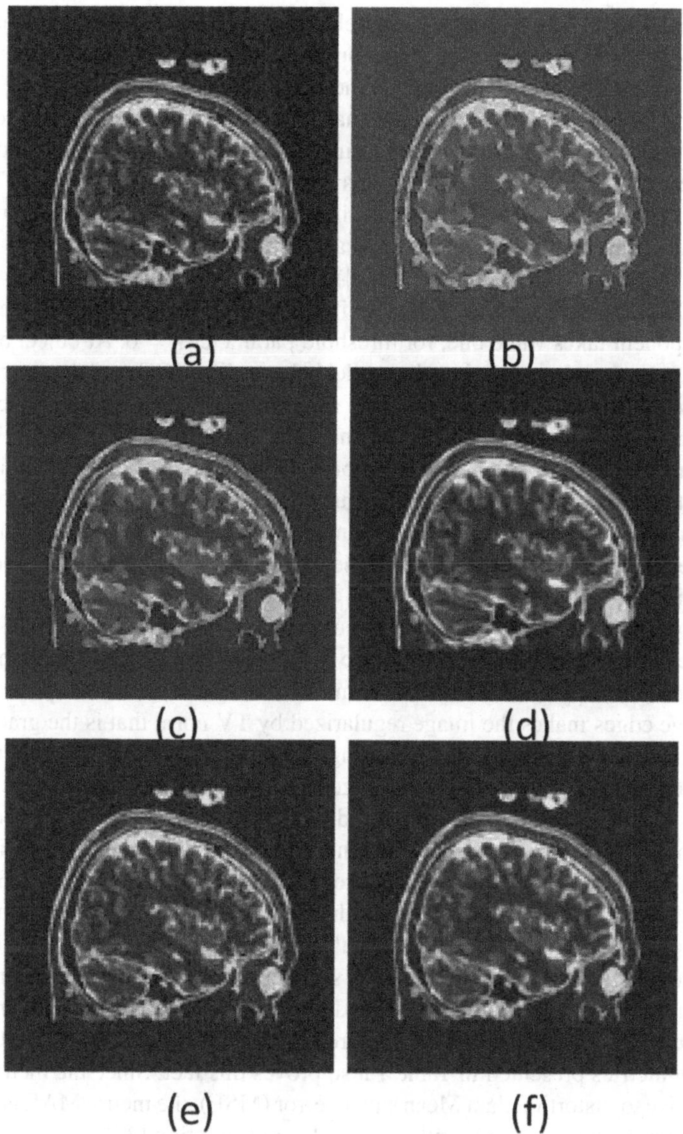

Fig. 4. (a) T2-weighted brain MRI sagittal slice −84 with 15% noise level (b) denoised image by self-snake model (c) denoised image by perona-malik model (d) denoised image by non-local means algorithm (e) denoised image by TV-ROF (f) denoised image by proposed algorithm.

using proposed algorithm as well as other classical methods for experimental purpose. The visual quality of processed images of proposed algorithm shows that the algorithm proposed outperforms other conventional methods.

The new method is able to produce sharper edges whereas other methods reveal loss of texture, loss of contrast and staircasing. The comparison between visual quality of processed images of different algorithms are shown in Figs. 2, 3 and 4. The quality metrics are computed to evaluate the denoising performance of different algorithms and the values are presented in Tables 1, 2, 3, 4 and 5.

The value of variable exponent $\alpha(|\nabla u|)$ for different values of image gradient is shown in the graph given in Fig. 7. Higher image gradients from value 12 onwards the variable exponent takes value one, for threshold parameter $k = 6$. At object boundaries the variable exponent becomes 1 so the model behaves like ROF model preserves edges, contrast and texture very effectively. The value of regularization parameter $\beta(|\nabla u|)$ for different values of image gradient is shown in the graph in Fig. 8. Higher image gradients from 12 onwards the regularization parameter takes value 0.2 that is at edges the model takes value 0.2, this value of regularization parameter well preserves edges, object boundaries and texture. The lower image gradients that is gradient value from 1 to 12 the regularisation parameter takes lesser value which enables strong smoothing in the flat region.

The experimental results prove that the adaptive version of the proposed model enables the preservation of important image features such as edges, corner and textures also concurrently suppresses noise. In the model setting the variable exponent $\alpha(|\nabla u|)$ to 1 at image edges makes the image regularized by TV norm that is the gradient of an image this enables edge recovery and setting the variable exponent $\alpha(|\nabla u|)$ to 2 in the flat ramp region makes the image regularized by square of the gradient this promotes strong noise removal. When $\alpha(|\nabla u|)$ is used as constant with value 1 then the model is TV-ROF model preserves edges well. When $\alpha(|\nabla u|)$ is used as a constant with value 2 then the model is Tikhonov model enbles strong smoothing. In Figs. 5–6 we could notice that when adaptively changing $\alpha(|\nabla u|)$ produces better quality image rather using fixed value of 1 or 2. Adaptively changing $\alpha(|\nabla u|)$ produces denoised images having higher values of peak signal to noise ratio (PSNR), structural similarity index measure (SSIM), feature similarity index measure (FSIM) and lower value of Mean average error (MAE) compared to constant 2 and 1 that is compared to Tikhonov model and TV-ROF model. The quality metrics presented in Table 1 also proves this fact. Since the metric MAE is more sensitive to distortion than Mean square error (MSE), the metric MAE is computed to measure how efficient the algorithm is in edge preservation [33].

Quantitative analysis also confirms that adaptive regularization model is superior since it produces higher values of quality metrics. Table 2 shows the proposed method generates higher SSIM values in comparison with other models, which means that denoised image is highly similar to the original image. Table 3 shows the value of PSNR

Table 1. Performance comparison for variable exponent adaptive model, constant exponent – 1 ROF model, constant exponent –2 Tikhonov model for rician noise corrupted brain magnetic resonance images.

Modality	Slice/Noise level	Variable exponent-$\alpha(.)$	SSIM	FSIM	PSNR	MAE
T1-weighted	Transverse-55 (10%)	Constant-2 (Tikhonov)	0.7184	0.8296	16.6563	24.2551
	Transverse-55 (10%)	Constant-1 (TV-ROF)	0.8620	0.9497	32.8754	4.3333
	Transverse-55 (10%)	Adaptive model	0.9127	0.9815	35.1619	3.2415
	Transverse-55 (15%)	Constant-2 (Tikhnov)	0.6024	0.8035	16.1997	26.4457
	Transverse-55 (15%)	Constant-1 (TV-ROF)	0.8462	0.9508	31.3885	5.0586
	Transverse-55 (15%)	Adaptive model	0.9202	0.9804	33.5143	3.7520
T2-weighted	Sagittal-84 (10%)	Constant-2 (Tikhonov)	0.6647	0.7554	20.2204	14.9718
	Sagittal-84 (10%)	Constant-1 (TV-ROF)	0.8585	0.9546	30.9716	4.9697
	Sagittal-84 (10%)	Adaptive model	0.9124	0.9818	32.1781	4.5780
PD-weighted	Transverse-64 (15%)	Constant-2 (Tikhonov)	0.5444	0.7471	19.9165	17.9889
	Transverse-64 (15%)	Constant-1 (TV-ROF)	0.7967	0.9114	23.2581	13.0546
	Transverse-64 (15%)	Adaptive model	0.9008	0.9658	24.2840	11.7736

quality metric for different brain MR images of different modality. The proposed algorithm performs best since it achieves maximum PSNR values for most of the brain MR images compared to conventional methods. This finding agrees with the visual quality of images generated by the proposed algorithm.

Table 2. SSIM comparison for perona-malik model, self-snake model, nonlocal means, TV-ROF model and proposed model for rician noise corrupted brain magnetic resonance images.

Modality	Slice/Noise level	Sel-snake	Perona-Malik	Nonlocal means	TV-ROF	Proposed model
T1-weighted	Transverse-55 (10%)	0.6038	0.6697	0.8655	0.8620	0.9127
	Transverse-55 (15%)	0.5982	0.6475	0.8735	0.8462	0.9202
T1-weighted	Transverse-69 (10%)	0.5977	0.6533	0.8579	0.8421	0.9025
	Transverse-69 (15%)	0.5739	0.6040	0.8362	0.8219	0.9019
T2-weighted	Coronal-67 (10%)	0.6289	0.6487	0.8305	0.8310	0.8950
	Coronal-67 (15%)	0.5919	0.6300	0.8441	0.8021	0.8852
T2-weighted	Sagittal-84 (10%)	0.5567	0.6719	0.8550	0.8525	0.9124
	Sagittal-84 (15%)	0.5444	0.6605	0.8541	0.8331	0.9012
PD-weighted	Transverse-64 (10%)	0.5515	0.5884	0.8372	0.8308	0.8969
	Transverse-64 (15%)	0.5264	0.5403	0.8371	0.7967	0.9008
PD-weighted	Sagittal-64 (10%)	0.4996	0.5798	0.8468	0.7610	0.8952
	Sagittal-64 (15%)	0.4808	0.5616	0.8441	0.8003	0.8768

The images processed by the proposed algorithm are sharper and have clear and thicker edges also there is no contrast loss. In addition there is no blocking or staircasing effect and texture of image is also preserved. Table 4 shows that the proposed algorithm can able to attain a visually enhanced image compared to other methods which is proved from the higher values of FSIM quality metric. An important thing we notice from Table 5 is that mean absolute error is very minimum for the images produced by the proposed algorithm compared to other conventional diffusion methods.

Table 3. PSNR comparison for perona-malik model, self-snake model, nonlocal means, TV-ROF model and proposed model for rician noise corrupted brain magnetic resonance images.

Modality	Slice/Noise level	Self-snake	Perona-Malik	Nonlocal means	TV-ROF	Proposed model
T1-weighted	Transverse-55 (10%)	18.9073	22.2435	30.3852	32.8754	35.1619
	Transverse-55 (15%)	19.7320	23.2769	28.6867	31.3885	33.5143
T1-weighted	Transverse-69 (10%)	20.5831	22.9230	30.8812	33.3433	34.4658
	Transverse-69 (15%)	20.2350	22.4040	26.8884	30.4625	30.4869
T2-weighted	Coronal-67 (10%)	21.2482	22.1694	25.9446	29.0323	29.7941
	Coronal-67 (15%)	20.8966	22.4176	25.1335	26.3274	26.8026
T2-weighted	Sagittal-84 (10%)	16.5027	22.1631	26.8262	30.9716	32.1781
	Sagittal-84 (15%)	16.7555	23.2785	25.2645	28.4651	28.0697
PD-weighted	Transverse-64 (10%)	17.4738	20.2082	25.9456	27.9979	28.5296
	Transverse-64 (15%)	17.5916	19.3665	22.9762	23.2581	24.2840
PD-weighted	Sagittal-64 (10%)	14.5507	19.0951	23.2714	25.6401	26.6356
	Sagittal-64 (15%)	15.1156	19.6809	21.1692	23.1255	20.4818

The TV-ROF model's performance comes next to our proposed method. Visually these two methods produces nearly same quality images. However, the experimental results proves that the proposed method performs best for most of the images except brain MR image slice PD-weighted sagittal-64 having rician noise level 15%. For this image the proposed method achieves lesser PSNR value and higher MAE compare to TV-ROF model. For all other MR image slices proposed algorithm achieves higher values for PSNR, SSIM and FSIM. The proposed algorithm generates lesser mean absolute error compared to all other methods for most of the images. This could be noticed in

Table 4. FSIM comparison for perona-malik model, self-snake model, nonlocal means, TV-ROF model and proposed model for rician noise corrupted brain magnetic resonance images.

Modality	Slice/Noise level	Self-snake	Perona-Malik	Nonlocal means	TV-ROF	Proposed model
T1-weighted	Transverse-55 (10%)	0.8565	0.8621	0.9436	0.9497	0.9815
	Transverse-55 (15%)	0.8358	0.8308	0.9389	0.9508	0.9804
T1-weighted	Transverse-69 (10%)	0.8390	0.8554	0.9316	0.9391	0.9772
	Transverse-69 (15%)	0.8229	0.8111	0.9314	0.9384	0.9763
T2-weighted	Coronal-67 (10%)	0.8453	0.8596	0.9273	0.9405	0.9763
	Coronal-67 (15%)	0.8164	0.8364	0.9234	0.9355	0.9745
T2-weighted	Sagittal-84 (10%)	0.8440	0.8787	0.9376	0.9546	0.9818
	Sagittal-84 (15%)	0.8189	0.8498	0.9332	0.9524	0.9775
PD-weighted	Transverse-64 (10%)	0.8081	0.8162	0.9158	0.9167	0.9677
	Transverse-64 (15%)	0.7673	0.7645	0.9152	0.9114	0.9658
PD-weighted	Sagittal-64 (10%)	0.7786	0.8023	0.9178	0.9073	0.9673
	Sagittal-64 (15%)	0.7418	0.7621	0.9169	0.9107	0.9544

Tables 2, 3, 4 and 5. The performance of conventional self-snake diffusion algorithm is worst among all. Next lower performance algorithm is conventional perona-malik diffusion. Performance of non-local means algorithm takes third place.

Table 5. MAE comparison for perona-malik model, self-snake model, nonlocal means, TV-ROF model and proposed model for rician noise corrupted brain magnetic resonance images.

Modality	Slice/Noise level	Self-snake	Perona-Malik	Nonlocal means	TV-ROF	Proposed model
T1-weighted	Transverse-55 (10%)	26.7403	17.8043	5.7336	4.3333	3.2415
	Transverse-55 (15%)	23.6213	15.0556	7.0900	5.0586	3.7520
T1-weighted	Transverse-69 (10%)	21.6645	16.4206	5.4028	4.0323	3.6584
	Transverse-69 (15%)	22.1466	16.8208	8.7500	5.7304	5.8004
T2-weighted	Coronal-67 (10%)	19.6359	17.6339	8.3136	6.1917	5.7506
	Coronal-67 (15%)	19.2307	14.3109	9.4163	8.5844	8.3494
T2-weighted	Sagittal-84 (10%)	35.4803	17.6224	7.5367	4.9697	4.5780
	Sagittal-84 (15%)	34.0533	14.3241	9.3645	6.8341	7.3172
PD-weighted	Transverse-64 (10%)	32.3348	22.9958	9.6304	7.6477	7.5582
	Transverse-64 (15%)	31.2467	24.8262	13.7285	13.0546	11.7736
PD-weighted	Sagittal-64 (10%)	44.6690	26.5114	13.1873	12.0372	9.2879
	Sagittal-64 (15%)	42.3315	23.1104	16.9389	13.6376	18.4209

The proposed algorithm is found to be very efficient in removing salt and pepper noise also. The salt and pepper noise corrupted standard images are denoised using proposed algorithm as well as other diffusion algorithms such as self-snake model, perona-malik model, non-local means algorithm and TV-ROF model. The visual quality of denoised images produced by various algorithms are compared in Fig. 7 and Fig. 8. For salt and pepper noise corrupted standard images also the visual quality of denoised image produced by the proposed algorithm is found to be of best quality compared to other algorithms. The quality metrics such as PSNR, MAE, SSIM and FSIM are computed

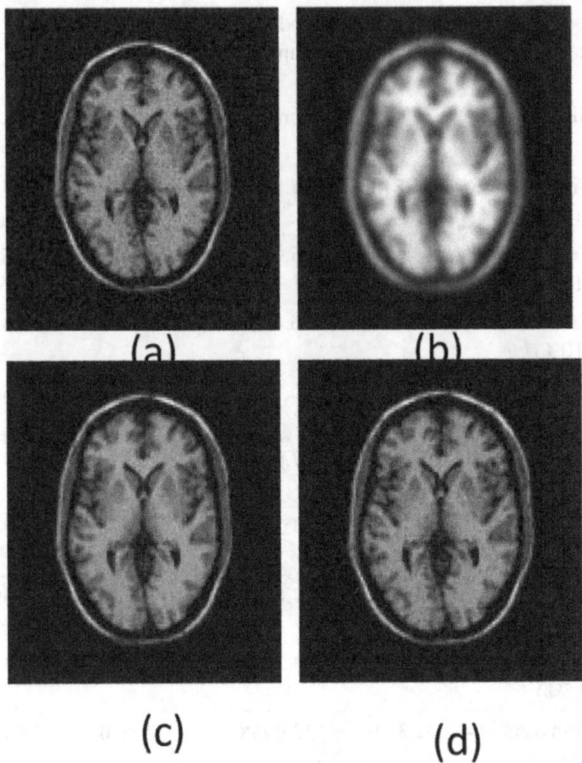

Fig. 5. (a) T1-weighted transverse-55 MRI slice with 10% rician noise level (b) denoised image using $\alpha = 2$ (Tikhonov)) (c) denoised image using $\alpha = 1$ (TV-ROF). (d) denoised image using adaptive $\alpha(|\nabla u|)$

for denoised images produced by various algorithms for salt and pepper noise corrupted standard images. The quality metrics are presented in the Tables 6, 7, 8 and 9. The proposed algorithm generates highest quality metric values for PSNR, FSIM and SSIM compared to other models for salt and pepper noise corrupted standard images also. The proposed algorithm produces lowest mean average error (MAE) compared to other diffusion algorithms.

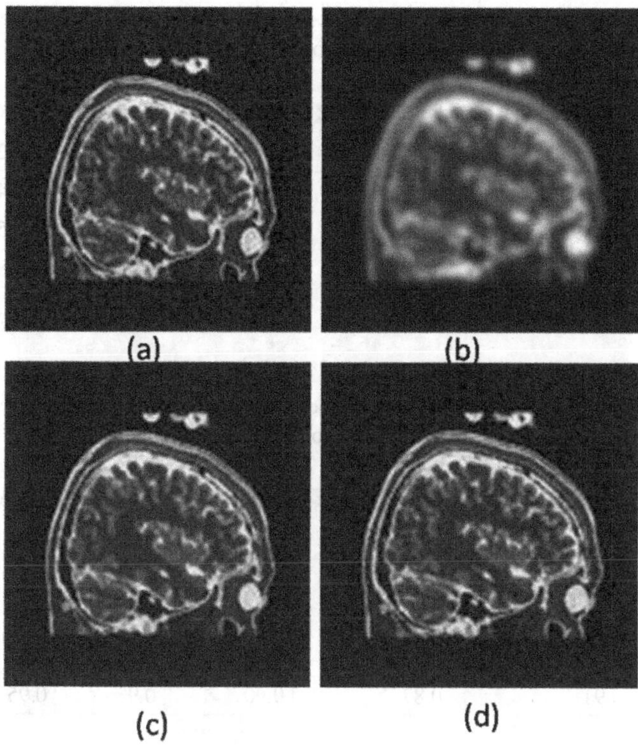

Fig. 6. (a) T2-weighted sagittal slice 84 10% rician noise level (b) denoised image using $\alpha = 2$ (Tikhonov) (c) denoised image using $\alpha = 1$ (TV-ROF) (d) denoised image using adaptive $\alpha(|\nabla u|)$.

Table 6. SSIM comparison for perona-malik model, self-snake model, nonlocal means, TV-ROF model and proposed model for salt and pepper noise corrupted standard images.

Image	Nonlocal means	Perona-Malik	Self-snake	TV-ROF	Proposed model
Cameraman	0.79	0.63	0.70	0.82	0.87
Lena	0.82	0.73	0.80	0.85	0.90
Wheel	0.84	0.71	0.77	0.85	0.89
Liftingbody	0.74	0.65	0.71	0.75	0.82
Coins	0.80	0.70	0.77	0.80	0.86

Table 7. PSNR comparison for perona-malik model, self-snake model, nonlocal means, TV-ROF model and proposed model for salt and pepper noise corrupted standard images.

Image	Nonlocal means	Perona-Malik	Self-snake	TV-ROF	Proposed model
Cameraman	26.51	21.59	22.41	27.71	28.42
Lena	27.49	25.17	26.40	28.55	30.04
Wheel	25.79	18.50	18.83	22.11	28.05
Liftingbody	27.46	24.51	25.15	27.36	28.48
Coins	27.04	21.33	23.87	26.56	28.31

Table 8. FSIM comparison for perona-malik model, self-snake model, nonlocal means, TV-ROF model and proposed model for salt and pepper noise corrupted standard images.

Image	Nonlocal means	Perona-Malik	Self-snake	TV-ROF	Proposed model
Cameraman	0.91	0.84	0.88	0.93	0.97
Lena	0.93	0.88	0.91	0.95	0.96
Wheel	0.97	0.90	0.91	0.96	0.98
Liftingbody	0.92	0.87	0.89	0.91	0.94
Coins	0.91	0.87	0.90	0.93	0.95

Table 9. MAE comparison for perona-malik model, self-snake model, nonlocal means, TV-ROF model and proposed model for salt and pepper noise corrupted standard images.

Image	Nonlocal means	Perona-Malik	Self-snake	TV-ROF	Proposed model
Cameraman	4.18	13.39	11.91	3.11	1.91
Lena	4.17	6.05	5.49	2.96	1.69
Wheel	5.06	25.70	25.36	16.15	2.47
Liftingbody	2.96	7.66	6.822	3.15	2.01
Coins	2.85	15.01	9.26	3.20	1.55

Fig. 7. (a) cameraman image with salt and pepper noise with density 0.01 (b) denoised image by self-snake model (c) denoised image by perona-malik model (d) denoised image by non-local means algorithm (e) denoised image by TV-ROF (f) denoised image by proposed algorithm.

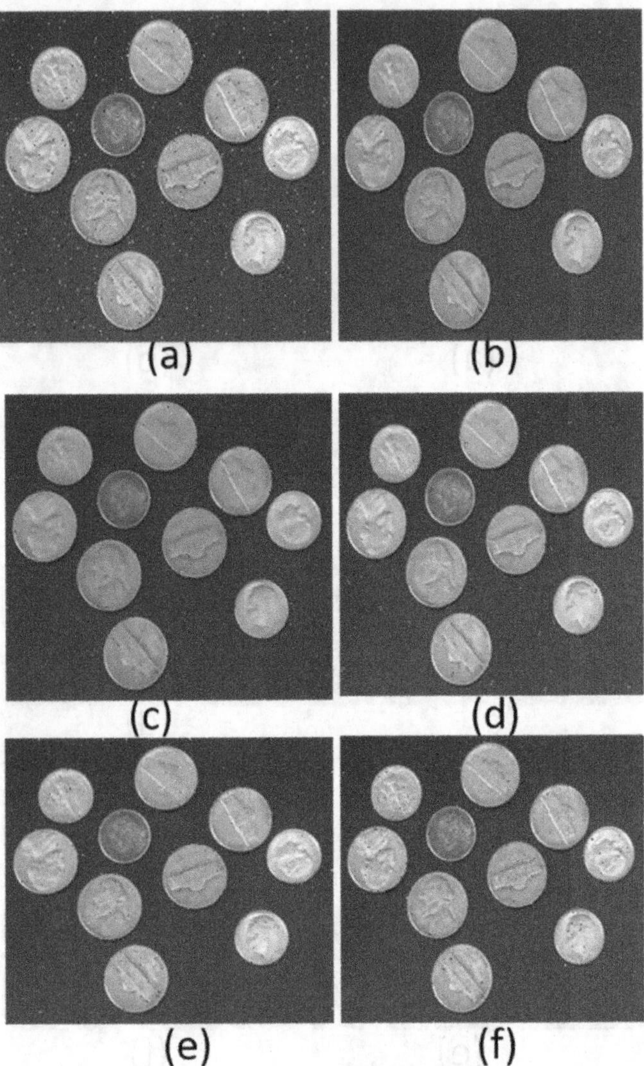

Fig. 8. (a) coins image with salt and pepper noise with density 0.01 (b) denoised image by self-snake model (c) denoised image by perona-malik model (d) denoised image by non-local means algorithm (e) denoised image by TV-ROF (f) denoised image by proposed algorithm.

4 Conclusions

To overcome the drawbacks of conventional total variation regularization model such as TV-ROF model and Tikhonov model the adaptive variable exponent based total variation regularization model is proposed which uses a variable exponent based on an edge stopping function in the regularization term and the weight of the fidelity term is also adaptive. The performance of proposed adaptive total variation regularization algorithm is analyzed by denoising rician noise corrupted brain MR images for varying noise levels and also by denoising salt and pepper noise corrupted standard images. The performance is evaluated in terms of MAE, PSNR, FSIM and SSIM for rician noise. Experimental results show that the proposed algorithm performs best compared with other methods such as classical perona-malik filter, self-snake filter, total variation- ROF model, Tikhonov model and nonlocal means filter both qualitatively as well as quantitatively. The research work can be extended in the direction using different numerical algorithms for solving the functional such as duality based splitting method and alternating minimization method (Figs. 9 and 10).

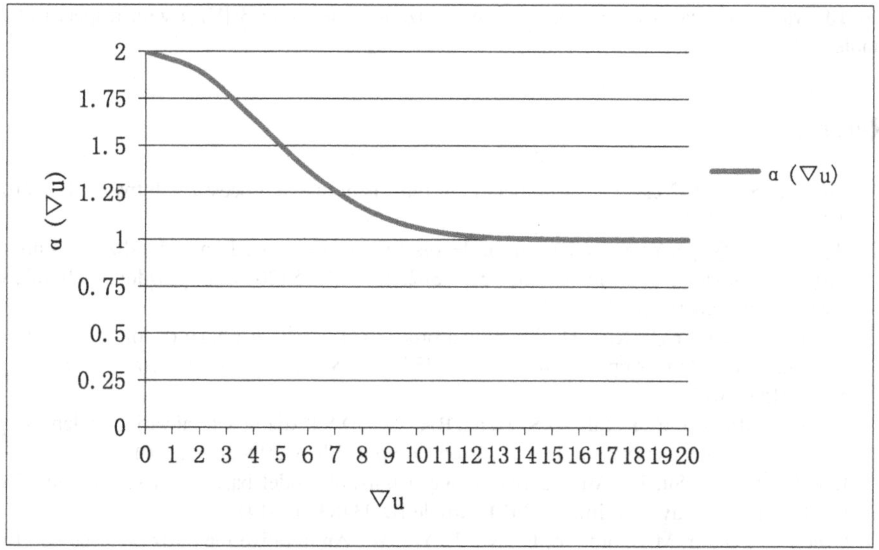

Fig. 9. Value of local feature dependent variable exponent $\alpha(|\nabla u|)$ with respect to the gradient ∇u

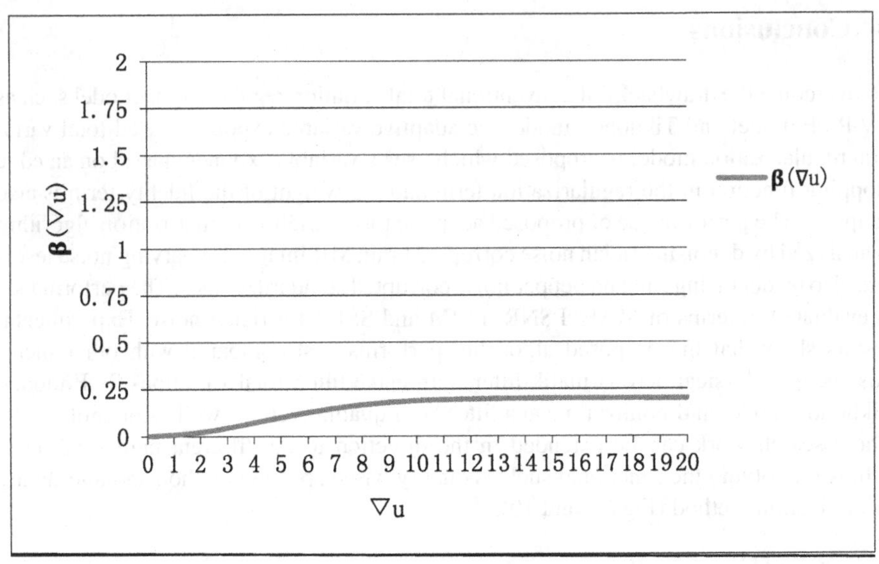

Fig. 10. Value of local feature dependent regularization parameter β(|∇u|) with respect to the gradient ∇u

References

1. Chan, T., Shen, J., Vese, L.: Variational PDE models in image processing. https://doi.org/10.21236/ada437477
2. Wang, Y.Y., Wu, S.Y.: Adaptive image denoising approach based on generalized Lp norm variational model. Appl. Mech. Mater. **556–562**, 4851–4855 (2014). https://doi.org/10.4028/www.scientific.net/amm.556-562.4851
3. Chen, D., Chen, Y.Q., Xue, D.: Fractional-order total variation image denoising based on proximity algorithm. Appl. Math. Comput. **257**, 537–545 (2015). https://doi.org/10.1016/j.amc.2015.01.012
4. Chen, Q., Montesinos, P., Sun, Q.S., Heng, P.A., Xia, D.S.: Adaptive total variation denoising based on difference curvature. Image Vision Comput. **28**(3), 298–306 (2010)
5. Liu, K., Tan, J., Su, B.: An adaptive image denoising model based on tikhonov and TV regularizations. Adv. Multimedia **2014**, Article ID 934834 (2014)
6. Osher, S., Burger, M., Goldfarb, D., Xu, J., Yin, W.: An iterative regularization method for total variation based on image restoration. Multiscale Model. Simul. **4**(2), 460–489 (2005)
7. Nikolova, M.: Minimizers of cost-functions involving non smooth data-fidelity terms. SIAM J. Numer. Anal. **40**(3), 965–994 (2002)
8. Chan, T., Esedoglu, S.: Aspects of total variation regularized L1 function approximation. SIAM J. Appl. Math. **65**(5), 1817–1837 (2005)
9. Esedoglu, S., Osher, S.: Decomposition of images by the anisotropic Rudin–Osher–Fatemi model. Commun. Pure Appl. Math. **57**(12), 1609–1626 (2004)
10. Blomgren, P., Mulet, P., Chan, T., Wong, C.: Total variation image restoration numerical methods and extensions. In: ICIP, Santa Barbara, pp. 384–387 (1997)
11. Gilboa, G., Zeevi, Y.Y., Sochen, N.: Texture preserving variational denoising using an adaptive fidelity term. In: Proceedings of the VLSM, Nice, France, pp. 137–144 (2003)

12. Blomgren, P., Chan, T.F., Mulet, P.: Extensions to total variation denoising. In: Proceedings of SPIE, San Diego, vol. 3162 (1997)
13. Yadav, R.B., Srivastava, S., Srivastava, R.: A partial differential equation based general framework adapted to Rayleigh's, Rician's, and Gaussian's distributed noise for restoration and enhancement of magnetic resonance image. J. Med. Phys. **41**(4), 254–265 (2016)
14. Kamalaveni, V., Veni, S., Narayanankutty, K.A.: Improved self-snake based anisotropic diffusion model for edge preserving image denoising using structure tensor. Multimedia Tools Appl. **76**(18), 18815–18846 (2017)
15. Yuan, Q., Zhang, L., Shen, H.: Hyperspectral image denoising employing a spectral–spatial adaptive total variation model. IEEE Trans. Geosci. Remote Sens. **50**(10), 3660–3677 (2012)
16. Kamalaveni, V., Narayanankutty, K.A., Veni, S.: Performance comparison of total variation based image regularization algorithms. Int. J. Adv. Sci. Eng. Inf. Technol. **6**(4), 419–425 (2016)
17. Yang, J., et al.: An efficient TV-L1 algorithm for deblurring multichannel images corrupted by impulsive noise. SIAM J. Sci. Comput. **31**(4), 2842–2865 (2009)
18. Beck, A., Teboulle, M.: Fast gradient-based algorithms for constrained total variation image denoising and deblurring problems. IEEE Trans. Image Process. **18**(11), 2419–2434 (2009)
19. Wang, Y., Zhou, H.: Total variation wavelet based medical image denoising. Int. J. Biomed. Imaging (2006)
20. Rudin, I., Osher, S., Fatemi, E.: Nonlinear total variation based noise removal algorithms. Phys. D Nonlinear Phenom. **60**(1), 259–268 (1992)
21. Yang, F., Chen, K., Yu, B.: Adaptive second order variational model for image denoising. Int. J. Numer. Anal. Model. **5**(1), 85–98 (2014)
22. Chopra, A., Lian, H.: Total Variation, adaptive total variation, and nonconvex smoothly clipped absolute deviation penalty for denoising blocky images. Pattern Recognit. **43**(8), 2609–2619 (2010)
23. Guo, L., Chen, W., Liao, Y., Liao, H., Li, J.: An edge-preserved an image denoising algorithm based on local adaptive regularization. J. Sens. **2016**, Article ID 2019569 6 p. (2016). https://doi.org/10.1155/2016/2019569
24. Chan, T.F., Chen, K., Tai, X.C.: Nonlinear multilevel schemes for solving the total variation image minimization problem. In: Tai, X.C., Lie, K.A., Chan, T.F., Osher, S. (eds.) Image Processing Based on Partial Differential Equations. Mathematics and Visualization, pp. 265–288. Springer, Heidelberg (2007). https://doi.org/10.1007/978-3-540-33267-1_15
25. You, Y.L., Kavesh, M.: Fourth-order partial differential equations for noise removal. IEEE Trans. Image Process. **9**(10), 1723–1730 (2000)
26. Charbonnier, P., Blanc-Feraud, L., Aubert, G., Barlaud, M.: Deterministic edge preserving regularization in computed imaging. IEEE Trans. Image Process. **6**(2), 298–311 (1997)
27. Guo, Z., Sun, J., Zhang, D., Wu, B.: Adaptive Perona–Malik model based on the variable exponent for image denoising. IEEE Trans. Image Process. **21**(3), 958–967 (2012)
28. Wang, Y.Q., Guo, J., Chen, W., Zhang, W.: Image denoising using modified Perona-Malik model based on directional laplacian. Signal Process. **93**, 2548–2558 (2013)
29. Tang, L., Fang, Z.: Edge and contrast preserving in total variation image denoising. EURASIP J. Adv. Signal Process. **2016**(1), 1–21 (2016). https://doi.org/10.1186/s13634-016-0315-5
30. Buades, A., et al.: A non-local algorithm for image denoising. In: Proceeding CVPR 2005 Proceedings of the 2005 IEEE Computer Society Conference on Computer Vision and Pattern Recognition, vol. 2, pp. 60–65 (2005)
31. Kumar, S.S., Mohan, N., Prabaharan, P., Soman, K.P.: Total variation denoising based approach for R-peak detection in ECG signals. Procedia Comput. Sci. **93**, 697–705 (2016). https://doi.org/10.1016/j.procs.2016.07.26

32. Karthik, S., Hemanth, V.K., Soman, K.P., Balaji, V., Kumar, S., Manikandan, M.S.: Directional total variation filtering based image denoising method. Int. J. Comput. Sci. **9**(2), 1694–1814 (2012)
33. Rosso, F.: Performance evaluation of noise reduction filters for color images through normalized color difference (NCD) decomposition. ISRN Mach. Vis. **2014**, Article ID 579658 (2014)

Automated Annotation and Classification of Catheters in Chest X-Rays

Akash Karthikeyan(✉) and Saravana Perumaal Subramanian

Department of Mechanical Engineering, Thiagarajar College of Engineering, Madurai, India

akashk1@student.tce.edu, sspmech@tce.edu

Abstract. Catheters are usually used to deliver drugs and medications close to the heart and to monitor the vital organs around the chest region for patients who undertook critical surgery. Radiologists often check for the presence of catheters, puncture-needles, guiding sheaths, and various other tube-like structures in interventional radiology. The clinical analysis of X-ray requires a manual pixel-wise annotation which is an excruciating process. In order to address this issue, we attempt to auto-annotate the CXRs using a Self-Supervised Learning approach. Further, the classification task on the catheter is performed based on semantic and perceptual clues (object shapes, colors, and their interactions) of color and class distributions. A generative adversarial network is utilized to learn a mapping to annotate (colorize and identify end-tip points) and classify the given grayscale CXR. The additional number of classes, custom loss function, and attention heads introduced in the model is a unique attempt to ensure robust results in the radiological inferences. It is evident that the qualitative and quantitative results of annotation and classification are viable which resembles how humans perceive such problems. The results are consistent and outperform's the state-of-the-art supervised learning models in terms of metrics and inference durations. The model being end-to-end in nature, can be integrated along with the existing in-hospital pipeline and will be ready to use instantly.

Keywords: GAN · Chest X-rays · Self-supervised learning

1 Introduction

Chest X-rays are commonly performed radiologic examination of the human body for patients kept under critical care. Portable anterior-posterior (AP) CXRs are often used to detect malpositions if any and verify the placement of catheters. These catheters are inserted through the subclavian or jugular veins and are typically blindly operated upon [12]. After placement Chest X-Rays (CXRs) are obtained to analyze their presence, and identity to avoid any mispositioning or other complications. Traditionally it requires years of training, experience, and skill-set to accomplish such a task. With the recent developments in computer

Published by Springer Nature Switzerland AG 2022
E. J. Neuhold et al. (Eds.): ICCCSP 2022, IFIP AICT 651, pp. 151–162, 2022.
https://doi.org/10.1007/978-3-031-11633-9_12

vision and the advent of Artificial Intelligence, autonomous report generation in radiology will considerably expedite clinical workload, Such a system would be able to remotely generate reports for CXRs in a matter of seconds.

Table 1. Distribution of the samples over various classes of catheters based on their position

Description		No. samples
Endo-tracheal tube	Abnormal	16
	Borderline abnormal	192
	Normal	1423
Naso-gastric tube	Abnormal	61
	Borderline abnormal	95
	Incompletely imaged	507
	Normal	887
Central venous catheter	Abnormal	640
	Borderline abnormal	1596
	Normal	4220
Swan-Ganz	Presence of Swan-Ganz catheter	139
Total classes: 11		Total: 30083

Previous attempts at producing such reports, under in-hospital conditions - lack the diagnostic interpretation and accuracy. The need for consistent and structured reports are imminent and plays a pivotal role in clinical care. Failure to report (multilabel classifications as shown in Table 1, and corresponding problems based on their positioning and insertions if any) in a clear and concise manner reflects in sub-optimal care.

The popular approach involves, the use of Deep Convolutional models. To be able to learn unique discriminative spatio-temporal features for CXRs is a difficult task. Hence recognition and classification of catheters from direct whole images yield poor results, as these needle-like structures account for less than 1% of the footprint in the whole image [12]. It is evident from the Class Activation Map as shown in Fig. 1 of traditional convolutional models struggles with classification tasks due to overlap in receptive fields. Different classes of catheters arise, owing to the difference in tip locations, functions, and the target organ as shown in Table 1.

While conventional CNNs could be used for this task, they usually require a large amount of paired data which is to be manually annotated, yet will still suffer from class imbalances. Moreover, almost all the CNNs are used to 3-channel input rather than single-channel input in the case of CXRs limiting the use of ImageNet weights of state-of-the-art models.

This paper presents an approach to address the automatic classification of unlabeled samples and the classification of peripheral and central catheter positions through a GAN model that is based on semantic and perceptual (end-tip points, pins, object shapes, colors, and their interactions) nature. We also

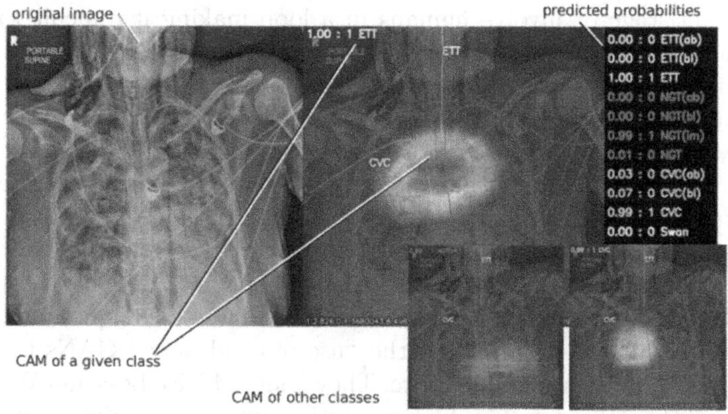

Fig. 1. Class activation maps of a multi-labelled sample, with logits

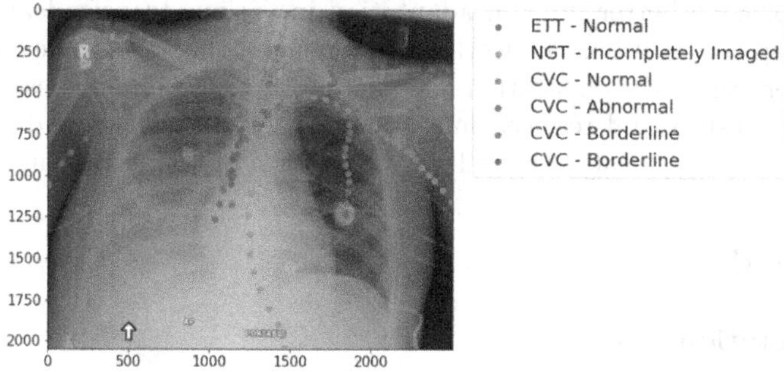

Fig. 2. Example of annotated sample, multi-labeled and annotated sample

explore how colorization affects the class distribution in CXRs. The model is designed in an end-to-end fashion and trained in a weakly supervised manner. Initial tests involving perpetual cues provided good initializations. In particular, adding color to the classification task leads to better initializations and forces the model to learn proper feature representations as seen in warm-starting of ImageNet models for various transfer learning applications.

1.1 Related Work

The absence of colors being a major reason for the failure of ImageNet models in CXRs. Colors also seemed to add class-specific semantic clues which are known to boost performance. Zhang *et al.* proposed an automatic colorization algorithm where colorization is treated as a multinomial classification problem [16] proposed a colorization model that learns to map a monochromatic image along with user-provided hints and cues that later is used to fuse along with high-level semantic information to provide realistic outputs. These processes again make the task multistage or involve humans in a loop making it difficult to build a standalone system.

"Generative Adversarial Networks (GANs) have been a popular choice to learn a mapping between gray-scale photographs. In recent times, Wasserstein GANs have been used with the gradient penalty to generate paired image-mask samples from CXRs" [10]. Authors of [2] proposed to use such generated masks to be paired along with real-time images to train in a supervised manner. A few methods were employed for non-paired data generation of medical and clinical images, entailing these data from an auxiliary imaging modality in a domain adaptation setting [8]. Performance evaluation of these techniques has not been evaluated. The author [6] proposed the "use of conditioned GANs to map the images using U-Net-based architecture. They adopted Dice Loss and Wasserstein loss to generalize the same to high-resolution images, stabilize and converge faster" [9].

Notice that GANs were essentially utilized to generate synthetic data which is used to provide better domain adaptation in various transfer learning tasks utilizing deep convolutional networks. Upon using a shared module trained in a joint manner (Semantic annotation and Classification) in an adversarial method yields better results and reduced inference period, as these learned representations aid in the classification as well acts as a form of additional supervision.

2 Method

2.1 Annotation-GAN

When the gray-scale image L which resembles the CXR, the model aims to learn a mapping $G\colon L \rightarrow c$ such that $I = (L, c)$ which represent a probable color distribution, and $\pi(z)$ denotes real image distribution. A bijective mapping such that $c = G^{-1}(z; L)$ is near the ground truth values is learned. Thus, the generated annotated sample is expected to encompass semantic, perceptual, and geometric characters to that of the ground truth image.

As in [14] a generator module learns a function G which is also invertible in nature and in an end-to-end fashion. While parallelly a discriminator module validates the similarity between the colorized output to actual ground truth. $I = (L, c)$ of L. The GAN model tries to tune the Ψ and w, parameters of the model. This ensures a conditioned GAN trained in a weakly-supervised nature using the annotated samples, with model initialized with weights from ImageNet [4], Especially when using an annotated sample $I_z = (L, c)$, the model learns the color information in a split fashion: The mono-chromatic channel L and the chrominance channels (c) similar to the method in [14].

The generator G_Ψ also tries to learn a $[nx1]$ classification matrix. The advantage of using such an approach enables us to learn the perpetual and semantic image distribution contained in L that makes the model similar to how humans perceive color. Let us subnets of generator be defined as follows, $G_{\Psi_1^1} : L \rightarrow (c)$, and $G_{\Psi_2^2} : L \rightarrow y$.

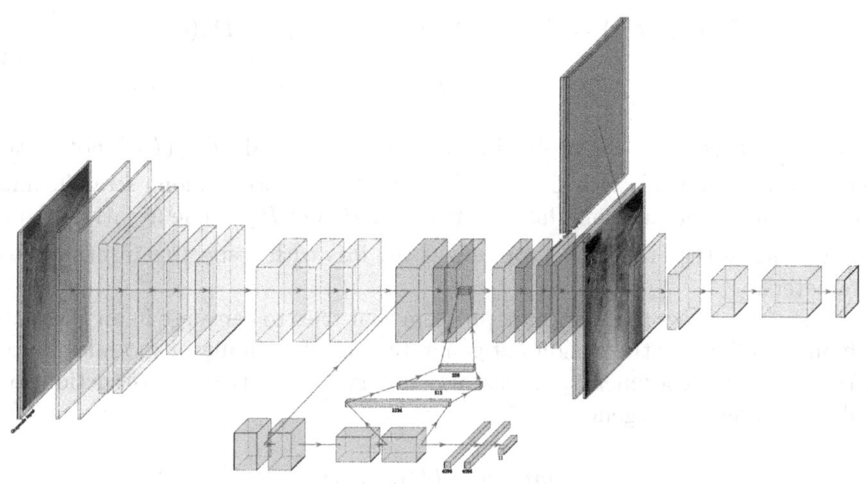

Fig. 3. Auto-Annotation GAN can colorize the tubular structures of catheters in CXR's based on different classes, It is a combination of Discriminator Network, D_Λ in pink, and the Generator Network, G_Ψ which consist of two-subnets: $G^1_{\Psi_1}$ (yellow, aqua-green, purple and gray layers) and $G^2_{\Psi_2}$ (yellow, purple and gray layers). (Color figure online)

2.2 Objective Formulation

The error function is given by:

$$L(G_\Psi, D_\Lambda) = L_\epsilon(G^1_{\Psi_1}) + \lambda_g L_g(G^1_{\Psi_1}, D_\Lambda) + \lambda_s L_s(G^2_{\Psi_2}) \quad (1)$$

The initial term represents ***reconstruction loss*** which is defined as follows:

$$L_\epsilon(G^1_{\Psi_1}) = E_{(L,c)\sim P_c}[-\log(q)(L, c')||G^1_{\Psi_1}(L) - c||^2_2] \quad (2)$$

where, P_c represents the distribution of ground truth images, the initial part represents negative log-likelihood loss added along with $||\cdot||_2$ for the euclidean norm to retain the structural similarity in the image and prevent from losing data. To improve the sensitivity to perpetual color, we use ***class distribution loss***

$$L_s(G^2_{\Psi_2}) = E_{L\sim P_z}[KL(y_v||G^2_{\Psi_2}(L)))\quad (3)$$

Herein, P_z represents the distribution of CXR input, and $y_v \in$ *labels* as in Table 1 the softmax output is obtained from VGG-16 classification branch [11]. $KL(\cdot||\cdot)$ represents the Kullback-Leibler divergence. The L_g denotes the ***WGAN loss*** which represents Wasserstein GAN [1]. WGAN provides a few niceties like avoiding vanishing gradient issues, preventing mode collapse, and faster convergence.

$$L_g(G^1_{\Psi_1}, D_\Lambda) = E_{L' \sim P_c}[D_\Lambda(L')] - E_{(c) \sim P_{G^1_{\Psi_1}}}[D_\Lambda(c, L)] \\ - E_{L' \sim P_{\hat{I}}}[(||\nabla_{\hat{I}} D_\Lambda(\hat{I})||_2 - 1)^2] \tag{4}$$

with $P_{G^1_{\Psi_1}}$ representing the probability density of the model $G^1_{\Psi_1}(L)$ denoting the generator distribution, with $L \sim P_z$. $P_{L'}$ sampled uniformly along straight lines between pairs of points from data distribution P_c and $P_{G^1_{\Psi_1}}$ The negative sign in (Eq. 4) ensures that the model minimizes the loss with respect to discriminator parameters.

This now reduces to a min-max problem that tries to converge in an alternate fashion by adjusting the weights of generator and discriminator modules. Later in the ablation experiments, it was also observed that the reconstruction loss enables quicker convergence.

$$\underset{G_\Psi}{min} \underset{D_\Lambda \in D}{max} L(G_\Psi, D_\Lambda) \tag{5}$$

Conditional GAN Loss and Adversarial Strategy L_g. The general adversarial min-max game between a generator and discriminator deals with learning suitable parameters so that the generator mimics the probability distribution of real data.

The WGAN is a better alternative to the non-overlapping supports approach. In contrast, KL divergence causes a vanishing gradient problem. The JS divergence may be non-continuous with parameters.

The results for objective formulation were in agreement with [7]. This approach outperforms the colorization produced by only L_2 or L_1 color loss terms and prevents model collapse.

Learning per-pixel probability distribution allows the use of a variety of classification losses. **Classification Loss.** The $L_s(G^1_{\Psi_1})$ Eq. 3 tries to minimize the difference between generated data with respect to actual distribution, to accomplish that we adapt convolutional layers from VGG-16 model pre-trained on ImageNet dataset. So to make the input competent with the model we create copies of the grayscale channel and reshape the input as (L, L, L) such that it could be used to generate the density distribution as stated earlier.

2.3 Model Architecture

The model architecture is as shown in Fig. 3. It is comprised of 3 sub-parts. Two of those focusing on chrominance information and classification are the same. The last one belongs to the discriminator network which to distinguishes ground truth from synthetic data.

Generator Architecture G_Ψ. The generator subnetworks $G^1_{\Psi_1}$ and $G^2_{\Psi_2}$ outputs chrominance related data, $(c) = G^1_{\Psi_1}(L)$ and classification vectors, $y = G^2_{\Psi_2}(L)$. Both the subnetworks are trained jointly through a single step backprop as in proposed in [14].

The basic blocks responsible for global feature extraction are shared by both subnets. Which is initialized with pre-trained ImageNet weights.

The first subnetwork (displayed aqua-green in Fig. 3) proceeds with a form of Convolutional(3 × 3)-BatchNorm-AReLu to learn $G^1_{\Psi_1}$ and similarly the second subnetwork (displayed purple in Fig. 3) learns the $G^2_{\Psi_2}$ using four modules of form Convolutional(1 × 1)-BatchNorm-AReLu, sufficed by fully connected layers (in purple) providing us the classification vector.

The first stage results (displayed yellow in Fig. 3) are shared to both the subnetworks and has the same architecture of VGG-16 [17] and are initialized with ImageNet weights [17]. Once $G^1_{\Psi_1}$ is learned it is used to generate useful information to help the colorization process. Later these two subnetworks are fused and are used to predict (c) by up-sampling with the help of Convolution-AReLu layers. The class distribution loss Eq. 3 only subnet $G^2_{\Psi_2}$ is affected. Whereas the color error loss Eq. 1 affects the whole network. We use AReLU [3] as activation for all layers and use a Softmax in the final layer to obtain the logits distribution. The AReLU enables a learnable activation function and formulates an element wise attention mechanism. The attention map forwards scaled positive elements which enable us to capture discriminative features amongst different classes. This amplifies positive elements and suppresses the negative ones.

Discriminator Architecture D_Λ. The discriminator is adapted from PatchGAN [7] a markovian discriminator. It operates in a sliding window fashion instead of considering the CXR as a whole to focus on local patches. Instead of classifying a whole image the discriminator convolutionally runs across the image and provides the average of those responses.

3 Experimentation and Results

Quantitatively studying the effect of colorization is a difficult task so in order to analyze how each term in the loss function affects the model, we can perform an ablation study and evaluate the different variants. *GAN* model using adversarial learning and classification approach and *GAN w/o class* $[\lambda_s = 0]$. We also compare the results with EfficientNet backbones and Knowledge Distilled models for endpoint detection and classification with custom loss function as shown in Fig. 4.

3.1 Dataset

We took the RANZCR CLiP dataset which is in-turn built upon Chest X Ray14 dataset [15], one of the largest publicly available datasets, where 30000 labeled (but non- annotated) CXRs spread across 11 different classes as in Table 1 were taken into consideration. A subset of these samples, around 950 were manually

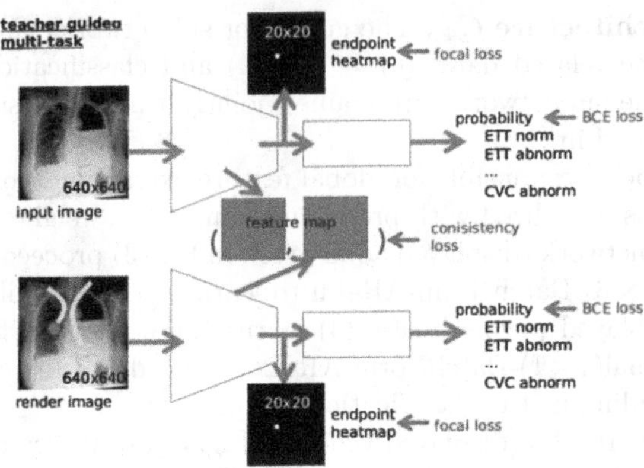

Fig. 4. Teacher - Student model with catheter enpoint heatmap, Source: kaggle

annotated with catheters and tube positions as shown in Fig. 2 to indicate pixels that belong to catheters or tubes. The class wise distribution of the labeled samples are as shown in Table 1. The CXRs are of varied resolutions (>2048 × 2048). We resize these samples to 1024 × 1024 by means of learned image resizing technique [13]. Replacing the typical linear resizers with learned resizers can substantially improve the results as they produce machine friendly visual manipulations. This resizer model is trained jointly with the classifier subnet model.

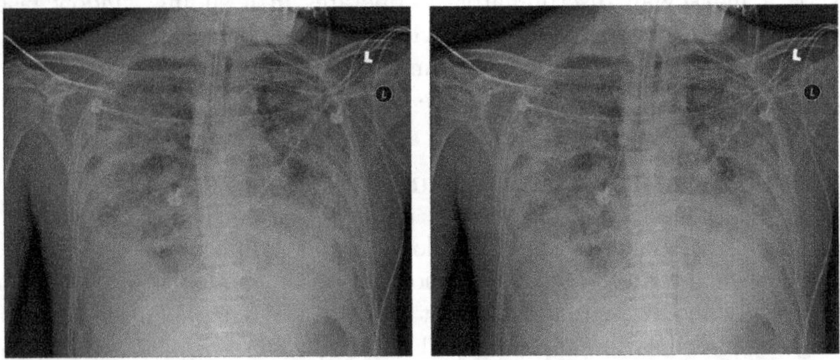

Fig. 5. Segemeted results show the presence of a multi-labeled sample (i.e. ETT - Abnormal, ETT - Borderline positive sample), Image to the left represents un-annotated sample and the one on right represents auto-annotation

3.2 Implementation Details

Table 2. Optimal Training Parameters and Hyper-parameters, Note that first and last layers consist of 7×7 kernels. With a larger kernel size allows more receptive fields, it is also verified from [13] and provides about 1–2% increase in accuracy. We also use batch normalization layers followed by AReLU activations [3].

Optimizer	
GAN: AdamW	$1e-5$
Hyperparameter	
$\lambda_g = 0.1$	$\lambda_s = 0.003$
Activation	
GAN: ReLU	$G_{\Psi_2^2}$: AReLU
Kernel	
$n = 16$	3×3
Device: NVIDIA P100	
Batch-Size: 10	

We trained the Annotation - GAN Model with about 950 annotated CXRs resized to 2048×2048 with parameters as in Table 2. A single epoch took about 5 h to train. We had to retain the original image size to make the annotations less ambiguous. The inference phase takes around 2 s Fig. 5. We minimize the objective loss using AdamW optimizer with the parameters as given in Table 2. The intensity regularization makes the model develop a mean color response over the regions of the catheter and tubes. For reliable evaluation of the data, we took a 5-fold cross-validation using F1 scores, pixel-wise precision, and recall metrics Table 3, owing to the thin structures of the catheters and tubes we enlarged the manually annotated samples to a 5-pixel dilation radius which resulted in 70% cases with over 50% of overlap.

Metrics such as Structural Similarity Index (SSIM) check for variation in contrast, luminance in high frequency region. Similarly, the Hausdorff distance measures the closeness to the ground truth thus representing the resemblance amongst the images.

Table 3. Evaluation of Auto-Annotated Samples with respect to ground truth annotation. Note these are the results of auto-annotated data averaged over a batchsize of 10.

Data	SSIM	PSNR	Hausdorf
Auto - Annotated CXR	0.98184	28.5766	4 ± 0.3
$GANw/oclass$	0.99411	33.9304	4 ± 0.5

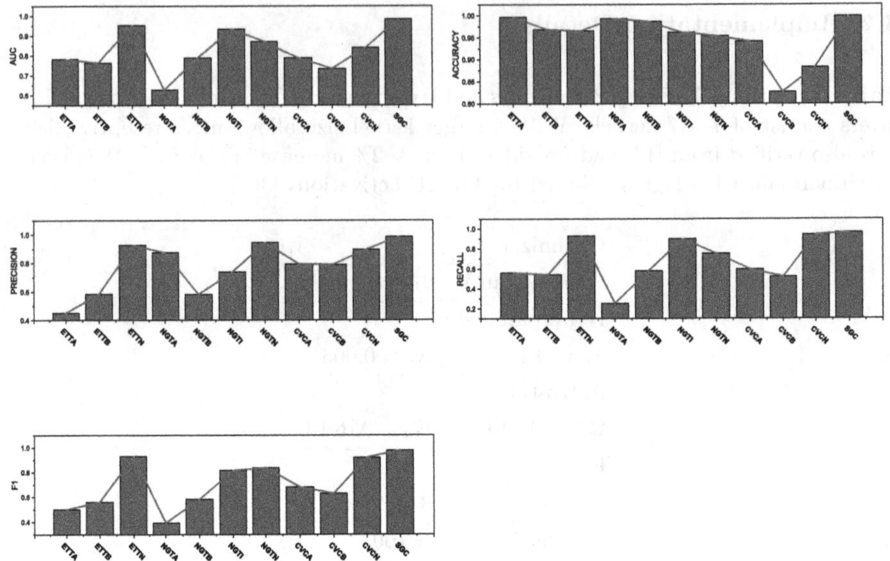

Fig. 6. Results of the Annotation GAN for each class, Mean values of the same are as shown in Table 4

3.3 Limitations

While the model offers quick inference and has a higher potential to improve workflow efficiency, there are a few drawbacks. The system confuses the catheters with tips with bone edges, often around the ribs. This can be avoided by adding additional background annotation classes (i.e., ribs, collar bones) and retraining the network so that the model will learn a differential feature to separate out the various classes.

The class imbalance can be mitigated via class frequency weights as an additional loss term. Further data augmentation techniques can be studied to provide better initializations to the model and prevent the mixing of background with labeled data.

3.4 Future Scope and Direction

Chest radiography analysis is an important stage in post-surgical care it involves detection and identification of tip locations, endpoints of catheters. The proposed model is capable of detecting tip locations of various different catheters and the inference takes about 2 s this could accelerate the mundane but essential tasks required in the health care system.

Our initial target was to detect catheter endpoints and reduce the false negatives, such as to make the solution viable in real-time applications. However, as a part of distinguishing the catheters from one another, it will work to our

Table 4. Results of the catheter classification (Mean ± standard deviation) AUC: Area under ROC, Acc: Accuracy, P: Precision, R: Recall). MTSS: Multi-Teacher Single Student trained and distilled network model with EfficientNet backbone.

Model	AUC	Accuracy	P	R	F1
Resnet200D*	0.884 ± 0.055	0.822	0.33	0.27	0.61
EfficientNet* - B0*	0.883 ± 0.055	0.732	0.4	0.39	0.62
EfficientNet - MTSS	0.917 ± 0.005	0.903	0.50	0.55	0.65
MoCo [5]	0.815 ± 0.5	0.711	0.56	0.58	0.51
AnnotationGAN	0.969 ± 0.005	0.952	0.77	0.68	0.73

benefit if we could capture all the tubular structures present in the given sample. This also aids the clinical setting without having to redesign the system to incorporate the model. The current approach involves analyzing the CXR from a single viewpoint. It could benefit us to analyze both frontal and lateral views for detecting any abnormalities.

4 Conclusion

We propose an autonomous report generation system that can autonomously classify and identify unlabeled samples and provide reports for central and peripheral catheter positions (Table 4, Fig. 6). Experiments show that our end-to-end model performs equivalent to the state-of-the-art models even though it was trained 0.033% (950 annotated samples) of labeled data. Auto-annotation GAN can further be explored with the help of shape constraints and incorporating spatial priors to improvise the results. Future prospects include autonomous report generation and validation by various trials, which results in robust reporting with minimal costs which is well under regulatory requirements. However, the proposed approach could be expanded scope for similar tasks in ophthalmology, 3D volume colorization, motion forecasting or satellite image analysis, and beyond.

References

1. Arjovsky, M., Chintala, S., Bottou, L.: Wasserstein GAN. arXiv abs/1701.07875 (2017)
2. Bailo, O., Ham, D., Shin, Y.M.: Red blood cell image generation for data augmentation using conditional generative adversarial networks. In: 2019 IEEE/CVF Conference on Computer Vision and Pattern Recognition Workshops (CVPRW), pp. 1039–1048 (2019). https://doi.org/10.1109/CVPRW.2019.00136
3. Chen, D., Xu, K.: Arelu: attention-based rectified linear unit. arXiv abs/2006.13858 (2020)

4. Deng, J., Dong, W., Socher, R., Li, L.J., Li, K., Fei-Fei, L.: Imagenet: a large-scale hierarchical image database. In: 2009 IEEE Conference on Computer Vision and Pattern Recognition, pp. 248–255 (2009). https://doi.org/10.1109/CVPR.2009.5206848
5. He, K., Fan, H., Wu, Y., Xie, S., Girshick, R.: Momentum contrast for unsupervised visual representation learning (2020)
6. Isola, P., Zhu, J.Y., Zhou, T., Efros, A.A.: Image-to-image translation with conditional adversarial networks. In: 2017 IEEE Conference on Computer Vision and Pattern Recognition (CVPR), pp. 5967–5976 (2017). https://doi.org/10.1109/CVPR.2017.632
7. Isola, P., Zhu, J.Y., Zhou, T., Efros, A.A.: Image-to-image translation with conditional adversarial networks. In: CVPR (2017)
8. Lei, Y., et al.: Male pelvic CT multi-organ segmentation using synthetic MRI-aided dual pyramid networks. Phys. Med. Biol. **66**(8), 085007 (2021). https://doi.org/10.1088/1361-6560/abf2f9
9. Nazeri, K., Ng, E., Ebrahimi, M.: Image colorization using generative adversarial networks. In: Perales, F.J., Kittler, J. (eds.) AMDO 2018. LNCS, vol. 10945, pp. 85–94. Springer, Cham (2018). https://doi.org/10.1007/978-3-319-94544-6_9
10. Neff, T.: Data augmentation in deep learning using generative adversarial networks. Ph.D. thesis, Master's thesis, Graz University of Technology (2018). https://www.tugraz.at
11. Simonyan, K., Zisserman, A.: Very deep convolutional networks for large-scale image recognition. CoRR abs/1409.1556 (2015)
12. Subramanian, V., Wang, H., Wu, J.T., Wong, K.C.L., Sharma, A., Syeda-Mahmood, T.: Automated detection and type classification of central venous catheters in chest X-rays. In: Shen, D., et al. (eds.) MICCAI 2019. LNCS, vol. 11769, pp. 522–530. Springer, Cham (2019). https://doi.org/10.1007/978-3-030-32226-7_58
13. Talebi, H., Milanfar, P.: Learning to resize images for computer vision tasks (2021)
14. Vitoria, P., Raad, L., Ballester, C.: Chromagan: adversarial picture colorization with semantic class distribution. In: The IEEE Winter Conference on Applications of Computer Vision, pp. 2445–2454 (2020)
15. Wang, X., Peng, Y., Lu, L., Lu, Z., Bagheri, M., Summers, R.: Chestx-ray8: hospital-scale chest x-ray database and benchmarks on weakly-supervised classification and localization of common thorax diseases. In: 2017 IEEE Conference on Computer Vision and Pattern Recognition (CVPR), pp. 3462–3471 (2017)
16. Zhang, R., Zhu, J.Y., Isola, P., Geng, X., Lin, A.S., Yu, T., Efros, A.A.: Real-time user-guided image colorization with learned deep priors. ACM Trans. Graph. (TOG) **9**(4) (2017)
17. Zheng, H., Fu, J., Mei, T., Luo, J.: Learning multi-attention convolutional neural network for fine-grained image recognition. In: 2017 IEEE International Conference on Computer Vision (ICCV), pp. 5219–5227 (2017). https://doi.org/10.1109/ICCV.2017.557

A Comprehensive Survey on Community Deception Approaches in Social Networks

N. Kalaichelvi(✉) and K. S. Easwarakumar

Department of Computer Science and Engineering, Anna University, Chennai, Tamilnadu, India
pnkalai@gmail.com

Abstract. Community detection techniques seek to find densely connected clusters within large networks. However, it raises privacy concerns, like the personal reveal or community member's group information, and contradicts the desire of individual or group to remain anonymous. As a result, concealing a specific community in a network to avoid the finding by methods of community detection becomes critical. Some previous work focuses on hiding some sensitive communities in order to conceal the community association of the focused vertices. Community deception is achieved by changing the links between the vertices in a network minimally so that a specific community can hide as much as possible from a community detection algorithm. This article discusses a study on previously proposed community deception techniques, as well as a discussion of the performance measures used to evaluate community deception methods.

Keywords: Social network · Community detection · Community deception · Community hiding · Modularity · Permanence

1 Introduction

As we move more and more of our activities online, the demand for social data continues to rise. Because social media is such a popular mode of communication, the massive amount of data it generates necessitates a massive level of data computation on the part of researchers and scientists. A community is a group of users who share similar characteristics and serves as the fundamental functional unit in any social network. Community detection [10] refers to the process of locating clusters of members with the same kind of interests in a network [16]. Several community detection algorithms have previously been developed [5], and research on this topic is still ongoing. Community determination is a critical task in a wide range of social network analysis applications, like customer segmentation, recommendation systems, link inference, vertex labelling, and analyzing influential members.

E. J. Neuhold et al. (Eds.): ICCCSP 2022, IFIP AICT 651, pp. 163–173, 2022.
https://doi.org/10.1007/978-3-031-11633-9_13

With the increased awareness of the importance of protecting personal privacy in online, we are now prioritizing the protection of privacy of communities in social networks instead of analyzing the information of possible communities in the networks. Community deception refers to the development of concealing techniques of the presence of a given community using community detection methods. Community deception assists users of social networks in concealing their identities from online monitoring. It also assists law enforcement organizations in criminal acts identification involving identity of online [9]. This could also be used by anti-terrorism division to insert secret agents into any terrorist network. This problem is solved by assisting the secret agents in determining with whom they can begin a fresh companionship with (adding edges) and who they must end the relationship (deleting edges) for concealing their identity of community. Paper [8] discussed deception algorithms and provided an overview of previous works on the topic.

Thus, concealing a single or more specific community in a network to avoid detection by analysis tools of social networks is extremely important. This article is a survey of previous works on community deception as well as the metrics used to evaluate community deception algorithms. Reference [6] outlines three ideal goals for measuring community privacy. As an example, consider a given network G and a specific community C, better concealing community C in G, which have three characteristics:

1. *Reachability Preservation:* To maintain information exchange, users of C must be in same connected component and reachable between them; so that, edge perturbation changes can not cut the connectivity of specific community C.
2. *Community Spread:* Users of C should be scattered across other communities in G to the maximum.
3. *Community Hiding:* Users of C must be distributed in the clusters which are most populous.

The rest of this paper is organized as follows. Section 2 explains the fundamentals of community deception. Section 3 discusses various existing deception algorithms for concealing a community. Then, evaluation parameters for measuring the deception are described in Sect. 4. Finally, Sect. 5 concludes the article.

2 Community Deception

This section briefly tells about community deception. $G = (V, E)$ denotes an undirected social network, where V is the set of nodes and E is the set of edges in the graph. The community deception algorithm for a network $G = (V, E)$ is to hide a given community C using network edge modifications by a parameter β, called budget update. As a optimization problem, it can be stated as follows:

$$\text{argmax } \eta(C, E(C), \beta, E'(C)) \tag{1}$$

where, $E'(C) = (E(C) \cup E^{add}) \setminus E^{del})$. Here E^{add} denotes the set of edges to be added and E^{del} denotes the set of edges to be deleted to hide C such that $|E^{add}| + |E^{del}| \leq \beta$.

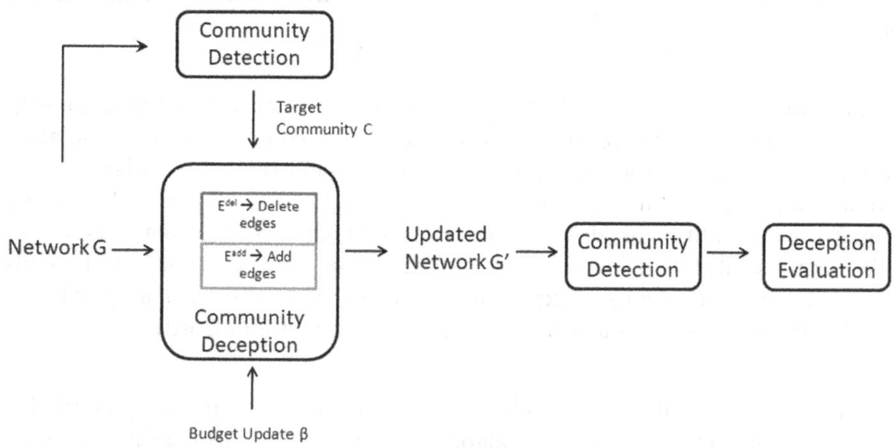

Fig. 1. Deception framework

Figure 1 shows the flow of community deception method. First, community structure is identified for the given network using a community detection technique. Then the target community from the community structure, budget update β and the network G are given to the community deception module in which β edges of the target community are modified and gives the updated network G'. Finally, the deception score is evaluated for the updated network. Various community deception algorithms are discussed in the following section.

3 Community Deception Approaches

3.1 Modularity Based Community Deception Methods

Modularity [15] is a popular metric for assessing the quality of any given community structure. It encourages structures with solid connections within communities but light connections between them. As a result, community detection algorithms are typically designed to obtain a structure with the highest modularity. Modularity is calculated by subtracting the expected number of edges placed at random from the number of links falling within groups. Modularity is denoted by:

$$Q = \frac{1}{2m} \sum_{i,j} \left[A_{ij} - \frac{k_i k_j}{2m} \right] \delta(C_i, C_j) \tag{2}$$

where, m denotes the number of links in the network, A_{ij} represents the element of the adjacency matrix of the network, i.e., $A_{ij} = 1$, if there is an relationship among i and j, $A_{ij} = 0$ or else. k_i and k_j are the degrees of vertex i and vertex j respectively. C_i and C_j are the community labels of vertex i and vertex j. Delta, the Kronecker delta function is 1 if both i and j are in one community, and 0 otherwise [11].

Nagaraja. The primary goal of a community deception algorithm is to keep hiding the community C from being revealed by any community detection algorithms. Nagaraja was the first to present this problem [14]. The author investigated how far any community can conceal by changing a few links; this approach only drives on addition of edges toward vertices which have high centrality values (like degree centrality). Vertex centrality measures are used to select the endpoints of newly added edges. Experiments were carried out on a small particular email network versus one modularity maximized detection algorithm.

DICE. Waniek et al. [17] too addressed this issue by implying a modularity based strategy. DICE, how their algorithm works is by arbitrarily removing internal links between C members and adding external links between C members and non members. It is a heuristic algorithm that hides communities by disconnecting internally and connecting externally. However, this strategy does not always result in a loss of modularity. Certainly, the edge update suggested by the author's strategy increases modularity in some cases.

D_{mod} **Algorithm.** Fionda and Pirr [9] used modularity to solve the community deception problem as well. For a network G with m edges, modularity of the community set of this network $\overline{C} = \{C_1, C_2, ...C_k\}$, is calculated by [6]:

$$M_G(\overline{C}) = \frac{\eta}{m} - \frac{\delta}{4m^2} \tag{3}$$

where $\eta = \sum_{C_i \in \overline{C}} |E(C_i)|$, $\delta = \sum_{C_i \in \overline{C}} deg(C_i)^2$.

A natural approach for attaining deception is by using the modularity loss $ML = M_G(\overline{C}) - M_{G'}(\overline{C}); G'$ is the updated network after deception. The goal here is to discover the group of β relationship changes with ML is highest. Maximizing the loss makes the splitting C provided by the community detection algorithm less ideal and thus increases the level of concealment of community C.

The maximum loss is obtained by selecting the clusters with the maximum degrees as the source and target communities for adding the links. An inter-community edge addition results in the most significant modularity loss. With respect to modularity loss, the best edge for deleting is an intra-community link in the community C_i with the least degree. This algorithm compares the two most convenient edge updates at every move and selects the update with maximum modularity loss. Understanding the degrees is required to select the change of link that will result in greatest modularity loss.

3.2 Safeness Based Community Deception Methods

D_{Saf} Algorithm. Fionda and Pirr [9] proposed a new metric called safeness and greedily optimized it in order to conceal users of a specific community from detection by community detection algorithms. They created a greedy optimization algorithm to conceal any given community depends upon the metric safeness gain, a new measure defined to find how secure a vertex is on attack. In addition to this new metric, the authors also defined a deception score to calculate the impact of the community deception method on the given network. They also confirmed that this technique outclasses other approaches depending on modularity.

Let $G = (V, E)$ be a network, $C \subseteq V$ a community, and $v \in C$. The safeness $\sigma(v, C)$ of v in G is calculated by [9]:

$$\sigma(v,C) = \frac{1}{2}\frac{|V_C^v| - |E(v,C)|}{|C|-1} + \frac{1}{2}\frac{\left|\widetilde{E}(v,C)\right|}{deg(v)} \tag{4}$$

where $V_C^v \subseteq C$ is the group of vertices accessible from v passing only through vertices in C. $E(v, C)$ represents the set of intra-community edges for a node $v \in C$ and $\widetilde{E}(v, C)$ represents the set of inter-community edges of the node v.

From this, the safeness of community C is gievn below:

$$\sigma(C) = \sum_{v \in C} \frac{\sigma(v,C)}{|C|} \tag{5}$$

Safeness of C can be defined by starting with the safeness of the elements, allowing us to find the least safe elements and modify their edges to raise the overall C safeness-score. By using the general deception formulation, the algorithm uses the safeness-gain $\xi_C = \sigma(C') - \sigma(C)$, here C' is the community after a few link updates. This algorithm employs a greedy strategy, selecting an edge modification which yields the maximum ξ_C at every stage. For additions, the algorithm only considers inter-C edges and ignores intra-C edges in order to achieve the best safeness gain.

Hs Algorithm - Community Hiding via Safeness. Chen et al. [3] used the modified safeness for community deception problem which is given below:

$$\sigma(C) = \frac{1}{2}\psi(C) + \frac{1}{2}\varphi(C) \tag{6}$$

$\psi(C)$ is Intra Community Safeness and denoted by:

$$\psi(C) = \frac{\rho(C) - 2(n-1)^2}{\sum_{k=1}^{n}(\sum_{i=1}^{n-k} i + \sum_{j=0}^{k-1} j) - 2(n-1)^2} \tag{7}$$

If $E(v, C)$ as the set of intracommunity edges for node $v \in C$ and $\widetilde{E}(v, C)$ is the set of intercommunity links, then the $\varphi(C)$ is defined as:

$$\varphi(C) = \sum_{v \in C} \frac{\left|\widetilde{E}(v,C)\right|}{deg(v)} \tag{8}$$

For the community deception problem, Chen designed a safeness-gain $\Delta(C) = \sigma(C') - \sigma(C)$, here C' is the community after few edge perturbation changes. So, this method chooses the suitable edge modification which results in the maximum $\Delta(C)$ at every step. This technique uses inter-C edge additions while adding and uses intra-C edge removals for the better safeness gain. Hs algorithm outperforms D_{saf} in most cases.

3.3 Permanence Based Community Deception Methods

Permanence is used as a measure to find how to efficiently modify any given network in order for concealing the given community [1]. Permanence is a measure that quantifies a node w's containment in a network community C [2]. The definition of permanence of w is:

$$Perm(w,G) = \frac{I(w)}{E_{max}(w)} \times \frac{1}{deg(w)} - (1 - C_{in}(w)) \tag{9}$$

This value specifies that a vertex will be in the same cluster if its internal pull $I(w)$ exceeds its external pull $E_{max}(w)$. Here, $deg(w)$ denotes the degree of node w and $C_{in}(w)$ denotes the internal clustering coefficient of w. Then the permanence of a network G is defined as follows:

$$Perm(G) = \sum_{w \in V} \frac{Perm(w)}{|V|} \tag{10}$$

NEURAL. The primary goal was to develop an algorithm capable of concealing an specific community C from a community detection method with least edge rewiring. In other words, the community detection method should not reveal the real community membership information of vertices within C. This was accomplished by rearranging the network's structure by means of a predetermined number of link updates (β - budget). Considered only intercommunity edges when adding edges, and only intracommunity edges when deleting edges.

Shravika et al., used the permanence loss as the new objective function in the NEURAL algorithm [13]. This community deception method reduced the network's durability for a specific community C to remain unseen from community detection methods. The authors proposed this because reducing a vertex's permanence would disorder its containment in the actual cluster, altering the network's community framework and building it hard for detection techniques to find the actual communities. Link updates (adding/deleting) were sought out by maximizing the permanence loss at each step, which is given below:

$$P_l = Perm(G) - Perm(\widetilde{G}) \tag{11}$$

here G denotes the actual network and $\widetilde{G}$ denotes the updated network subsequent to modifying the links, related to the given community C.

3.4 Entropy Based Community Deception Methods

REM. This raises the issue of community structure deception (CSD), which seeks methods to minimally modify the network so that a given community structure conceals from community detection methods as much as possible. Liu et al. [12] projected an approach for hiding the complete community structure (rather than just one community) with least network rewiring. They expanded the task of concealing a specific community to concealing the complete formation of the community. The authors proposed a community structure deception algorithm depending upon information theory and network entropy minimization. They approached the problem with community-based structural entropy and proposed a residual minimization (REM) algorithm.

3.5 Community Deception in Weighted Networks

SECRETORUM. The authors of [7] proposed a novel approach for deception in weighted networks using the secrecy gain like D_{saf} algorithm. They have defined the secrecy of a node v in a weighted network $G = (V, E, w)$ is:

$$\sigma_w(v, C) = \frac{1}{2}\frac{|V_C^v| - W_C^v}{|C| - 1} + \frac{1}{2}\frac{\widetilde{W_C^v}}{W^v} \tag{12}$$

where $V_C^v \subseteq C$ is the group of vertices accessible from v passing only through vertices in C. W_C^v is the sum of the weights of all intra-community edges for the node $v \in C$. $\widetilde{W_C^v}$ denotes the total weight of all inter-community edges and W^v represents the total weights of all edges adjacent to v. Then the secrecy of the community C is:

$$\sigma_w(C, G) = \sum_{v \in C} \frac{\sigma(v, C)}{|C|} \tag{13}$$

This deception technique finds the best edge modification which gives the best secrecy gain $\sigma_w(C, G') - \sigma_w(C, G)$ at each step. As usual this algorithm also considers inter-community edge additions and intra-community edges deletions for rewiring the graph.

4 Evaluation Measures for Community Deception

Evaluation metrics are used to quantify the performance of community deception algorithms. The performance indicators used in existing community deception approaches are listed below.

4.1 Deception Score

For a target community CT and a community structure $\overline{CS} = \{C_1, C_2, ...C_k\}$ detected using a community detection technique, deception score of the community is determined as below [9]:

$$H(CT,\overline{CS}) = \left(1 - \frac{|S(CT) - 1|}{|CT - 1|}\right) \times \left(\frac{1}{2}\left(1 - \max_{C_i \in \overline{CS}} \{R(C_i, CT)\}\right) + \frac{1}{2}\left(1 - \frac{\sum_{C_i \cap CT \neq \emptyset} P(C_i, CT)}{|C_i \cap CT \neq \emptyset|}\right)\right) \tag{14}$$

where $|S(CT)|$ denotes total connected components in the subgraph induced by CT's elements. H takes the value from 0 to 1. If all of the vertices in CT are present in a single component and are consealed optimally, then $H = 1$. $H = 0$ denotes that every vertex in CT is from different components. $P(C_i, CT)$ is the precision and $R(C_i, CT)$ is the recall and both are given by:

$$P(C_i, CT) = \frac{\text{\# CT's members in } C_i \text{ detected by } CD}{|C_i|} \quad \forall C_i \cap CT \neq \emptyset \tag{15}$$

$$R(C_i, CT) = \frac{\text{\# CT's members in } C_i \text{ detected by } CD}{|C|} \quad \forall C_i \in \overline{CS} \tag{16}$$

4.2 Normalized Mutual Information (NMI) and Modified NMI (MNMI)

NMI score among the actual community structure of given network with N vertices, $C_A = (C_1, C_2, ..., C_k)$, the updated community structure detected from a community detection method on the modified network, $C_B = (C'_1, C'_2, ..., C'_k)$,. This metric value ranges from 0 (no overlap of C_A and C_B) to 1 (whole overlap of C_A and C_B) [4].

$$NMI(A,B) = \frac{-2\sum_{i=1}^{C_A}\sum_{j=1}^{C_B} C_{ij} log(C_{ij}N/C_iC_j)}{\sum_{i=1}^{C_A} C_i log\frac{C_i}{N} + \sum_{j=1}^{C_B} C_j log\frac{C_j}{N}} \tag{17}$$

NMI between nodes in the target communities and their immediate neighbors' community memberships before and after the edge updates is called MNMI. It has the same frequency range as NMI.

4.3 Community Splits

This measure represents the total clusters in the new community structure CS' that contain vertices from the given community C in the modified network G' [13].

$$CommS = \sum_{C'_i \in CS'} h(C'_i, C); h(C'_i, C) = \begin{cases} 1 \; V_C \cap V_{C'_i} \neq \emptyset \\ 0 \; V_C \cap V_{C'_i} = \emptyset \end{cases} \tag{18}$$

here V_C denotes the group of vertices in C and V_{C_i} denotes the group of nodes in community $C_i \in CS'$. This metric values are from 1 (all vertices of C is in single cluster in CS') to $|CS'|$ (all nodes of C get allocated to various communities of CS').

4.4 Community Uniformity

This metric measures how vertices in the specific community C are allotted across communities in the new community structure CS' [13]. It is measured by finding the entropy of given community vertices distributed between the communities in CS' as follows:

$$CommU = \sum_{C_i' \in CS'} -\left(\left|V_{C,C_i'}\right| / \left|V_C\right|\right) \log\left(\left|V_{C,C_i'}\right| / \left|V_C\right|\right) \tag{19}$$

where $\left|V_{C,C_i'}\right|$ denotes the total vertices in C present in $C_i' \in CS'$ and $|V_C|$ denotes the total number of nodes present in C. It values are from 0 (entire nodes of C in one community of CS') to $\log\left|CS'\right|$ (entire nodes of C allocated into various communities of CS').

According to the survey, the NEURAL [13], a permanence-based community deception approach, outperforms the other existing community deception techniques in terms of the performance metrics NMI, MNMI, CommS and CommU. However, the authors did not compare the results to the deception score, which is a basic performance measure of community deception. Chen et al. [3] demonstrated that their approach outperforms the techniques proposed in paper [9] in terms of deception score and running time.

5 Conclusion

Most researchers have thus far concentrated on the development of community detection algorithms. Though, in few other situations, it is necessary to conceal the presence of a community. Community deception is the practice of preventing community detection methods from determining the community association of vertices in a specific community. We have listed the existing works that are proposed for community deception in this paper. In addition, we discussed the evaluation measures used to assess the effectiveness of community deception approaches. All of the approaches listed in this paper will be useful to other researchers in developing new methods for community deception that outperform existing methods.

References

1. Chakraborty, T., Srinivasan, S., Ganguly, N., Mukherjee, A., Bhowmick, S.: On the permanence of vertices in network communities. In: Proceedings of the 20th ACM SIGKDD International Conference on Knowledge Discovery and Data Mining, KDD 2014, pp. 1396–1405. Association for Computing Machinery, New York (2014). https://doi.org/10.1145/2623330.2623707
2. Chakraborty, T., Srinivasan, S., Ganguly, N., Mukherjee, A., Bhowmick, S.: Permanence and community structure in complex networks. CoRR abs/1606.01543 (2016). http://arxiv.org/abs/1606.01543

3. Chen, X., Jiang, Z., Li, H., Ma, J., Yu, P.S.: Community hiding by link perturbation in social networks. IEEE Trans. Comput. Soc. Syst. **8**(3), 704–715 (2021). https://doi.org/10.1109/TCSS.2021.3054115
4. Danon, L., Díaz-Guilera, A., Duch, J., Arenas, A.: Comparing community structure identification. J. Stat. Mech. Theory Exp. **2005**(09), P09008–P09008 (2005). https://doi.org/10.1088/1742-5468/2005/09/p09008
5. El-moussaoui, M., Agouti, T., Tikniouine, A., Adnani, M.E.: A comprehensive literature review on community detection: approaches and applications. Procedia Comput. Sci. **151**, 295–302 (2019). https://doi.org/10.1016/j.procs.2019.04.042. https://www.sciencedirect.com/science/article/pii/S1877050919305046. The 10th International Conference on Ambient Systems, Networks and Technologies (ANT 2019)/The 2nd International Conference on Emerging Data and Industry 4.0 (EDI40 2019)/Affiliated Workshops
6. Fionda, V., Pirrò, G.: From community detection to community deception. CoRR abs/1609.00149 (2016). http://arxiv.org/abs/1609.00149
7. Fionda, V., Pirró, G.: Community deception in weighted networks. In: Proceedings of the 2021 IEEE/ACM International Conference on Advances in Social Networks Analysis and Mining, ASONAM 2021, pp. 278–282. Association for Computing Machinery, New York (2021). https://doi.org/10.1145/3487351.3488337
8. Fionda, V., Pirró, G.: Community deception in networks: where we are and where we should go. In: Benito, R.M., Cherifi, C., Cherifi, H., Moro, E., Rocha, L.M., Sales-Pardo, M. (eds.) COMPLEX NETWORKS 2021. Studies in Computational Intelligence, vol. 1016, pp. 144–155. Springer, Cham (2022). https://doi.org/10.1007/978-3-030-93413-2_13
9. Fionda, V., Pirrò, G.: Community deception or: how to stop fearing community detection algorithms. IEEE Trans. Knowl. Data Eng. **30**(4), 660–673 (2018). https://doi.org/10.1109/TKDE.2017.2776133
10. Fortunato, S., Hric, D.: Community detection in networks: a user guide. Phys. Rep. **659**, 1–44 (2016). https://doi.org/10.1016/j.physrep.2016.09.002. https://www.sciencedirect.com/science/article/pii/S0370157316302964. Community detection in networks: a user guide
11. Nallusamy, K., Easwarakumar, K.S.: Cgram: enhanced algorithm for community detection in social networks. Intell. Autom. Soft Comput. **31**(2), 749–765 (2022). https://doi.org/10.32604/iasc.2022.020189. http://www.techscience.com/iasc/v31n2/44541
12. Liu, Y., Liu, J., Zhang, Z., Zhu, L., Li, A.: Rem: from structural entropy to community structure deception. In: Advances in Neural Information Processing Systems, vol. 32. Curran Associates, Inc. (2019). https://proceedings.neurips.cc/paper/2019/file/328347805873e9a9c700591812fb0ec2-Paper.pdf
13. Mittal, S., Sengupta, D., Chakraborty, T.: Hide and seek: outwitting community detection algorithms. IEEE Trans. Comput. Soc. Syst. **8**(4), 799–808 (2021). https://doi.org/10.1109/TCSS.2021.3062711
14. Nagaraja, S.: The impact of unlinkability on adversarial community detection: effects and countermeasures. In: Atallah, M.J., Hopper, N.J. (eds.) PETS 2010. LNCS, vol. 6205, pp. 253–272. Springer, Heidelberg (2010). https://doi.org/10.1007/978-3-642-14527-8_15
15. Newman, M.E.J.: Modularity and community structure in networks. Proc. Natl. Acad. Sci. **103**(23), 8577–8582 (2006). https://doi.org/10.1073/pnas.0601602103. https://www.pnas.org/content/103/23/8577

16. Newman, M.E.J., Girvan, M.: Finding and evaluating community structure in networks. Phys. Rev. E **69**(2), 026113 (2004). https://doi.org/10.1103/physreve.69.026113
17. Waniek, M., Michalak, T.P., Rahwan, T., Wooldridge, M.J.: Hiding individuals and communities in a social network. CoRR abs/1608.00375 (2016). http://arxiv.org/abs/1608.00375

COV-XDCNN: Deep Learning Model with External Filter for Detecting COVID-19 on Chest X-Rays

Arnab Dey(✉)

Department of Computer Science and Engineering, Kalyani Government Engineering College, Kalyani, India
arnabdey120@gmail.com

Abstract. COVID-19 is a highly infective viral disease and it is observed that the newest strains of the SARS-CoV-2 virus has greater infectivity rate. Due to the present pandemic, the economy of the country, the mental and physical state of the people and their regular lives are being affected. Medical studies have shown that the lungs of the patients who are infected by the corona virus are mostly being affected. Chest x-ray or radiography is observed to be one of the most effective imaging techniques for diagnosing problems which are related to the lungs. The study proposes a novel COV-XDCNN model with external filter for diagnosing diseases such as COVID-19, Viral Pneumonia, automatically which can assist the healthcare workers, mainly during the time of outbreak. The motivation of this research lies in designing an automated system which can aid the healthcare workers. The proposed model with external filter gives 97.86% test accuracy in classifying the chest radiography images. The model performance is examined with various other models such as NASNetMobile, ResNet50, MobileNet, VGG-16 etc. and analyzed. The model proposed in this study shows better performance than most of the existing traditional methods.

Keywords: COV-XDCNN · COVID19 · Deep learning · External filter · Chest X-ray · Data processing

1 Introduction

The World Health Organization (or WHO) have announced the COVID-19 as a pandemic during the month of March in the year 2020 after the virus has affected a large number of countries across the globe. COVID-19 disease is still a matter of huge concern as a large number of people are getting affected and many of them are also losing their lives daily across the globe. Numerous number of countries are still going through the pandemic phase. The bronchitis, common cough and cold, tuberculosis, chronic pulmonary disease, pneumonia, asthma etc. are the most commonly observed chest infections. Coronavirus disease is a kind of disease that is mainly related to chest infection. The novel corona virus disease is also familiar as severe acute respiratory syndrome coronavirus 2 (SARS-

Published by Springer Nature Switzerland AG 2022
E. J. Neuhold et al. (Eds.): ICCCSP 2022, IFIP AICT 651, pp. 174–189, 2022.
https://doi.org/10.1007/978-3-031-11633-9_14

CoV-2) [5]. As of 23 Jan. 2022, the corona virus has affected more than 35.1 crore people, about 56 lakh people died and also many people have been recovered as well. Generally, the COVID-19 disease comes into the human body as a throat infection and then the lungs gets infected. The Corona virus disease is mostly been detected with the utilization of the frequently utilized Reverse Transcriptase-Polymerase Chain Reaction (RT-PCR) method [7]. Although this procedure has a high specificity, but the RT-PCR test kits are limited, the diagnosis process is slow as it takes about one or two days for the report to come and also very costly. The RT-PCR tests may sometimes also produce an incorrect result. Chest X-rays are a commonly utilized diagnosis method which is cheaper and faster. Medical imaging [11] is considered as one of the most powerful techniques for predicting and analyzing the effects of the corona virus on the human body. With the aid of the chest radiography images and the CT images, various kinds of chest related infections or diseases can be classified. The healthcare industry needs to undergo some major technological transformation [25]. The technological innovation with the utilization of Artificial Intelligence (AI) in the healthcare will decrease the anxiety and hindrance from most of the recurring or repetitive tasks instead of replacing the trained healthcare worker or doctor. Chest x-ray can also be utilized for observing the effect of the virus on the chest after getting recovered from COVID-19 disease. The aim of this study is to classify and detect the chest x-ray images into 3 categories, namely Viral Pneumonia, Normal and COVID utilizing the Proposed COV-XDCNN model with the utilization of the external Gabor filter and other filters. For performing this research, the chest radiography images of the pneumonia, COVID affected, normal patients were collected from different sources. The proposed work is also being investigated with the deep learning models - NASNetMobile, VGG-16, MobileNet, VGG-19 and ResNet50 model for testing the performance with respect to the proposed model. It is found that utilizing the Gabor filter in the proposed COV-XDCNN model, learning duration gets reduced. Thus, it is also energy efficient. The proposed trained model is also investigated with some random labelled chest radiography images.

2 Literature Review

The literature [1] brings together numerous studies related to the field of the medical imaging technological advancements and its numerous applications. It also indicates that the ultra-modern medical imaging systems mostly comprise of the Chest radiography, Magnetic Resonance Imaging (MRI), CT scan, Ultrasound etc. and the data processing methods. In [4], the authors have utilized various Machine Learning (ML) based models for detecting COVID-19 on the chest x-ray scans. They have achieved 92% accuracy with the Random forest and 96% accuracy utilizing the SVM-based classification model. In [6], the authors have utilized the ResNet18 model for classifying disease based on CT scan images with 97.32%. In [8], various deep learning frameworks that are being utilized in medical imaging are discussed. In [10], authors mostly gave emphasis on demonstrating the coronavirus disease on the lungs of human beings and its impact. They have taken into account the chest CT images of twenty-one COVID patients in Wuhan (a popular city in China). Cohen et al. [13] have proposed a COVID-RENet model dependent on CNN and extracted the edge and region-based features for classification.

Here, the authors extract the features by applying CNN, then they have utilized SVM for improving the classification performance. The authors have utilized 5 fold cross-validation on the dataset that is gathered for predicting Covid-19 disease. Table 1 shows a comparative study of various machine and deep learning-based methods that already exist to detect COVID-19 disease.

Table 1. Comparative Study of various methods that are existing to detect COVID-19

S. No	Title/Existing Work	Feature(s)	Classifier used	Dataset	Accuracy (%)
1.	Identification of COVID-19 using Chest X-ray images with voting classifier [2]	Augmented image, Majority voting classifier, x-ray based	SVM (RBF Kernel)	Chest X-ray	82.90%
2.	Recognizing COVID-19 Pneumonia on Chest X-Ray and CT utilizing DL [3]	Glorot weight initialization, Single CNN Layer, ReLU	CNN	Chest X-ray and CT scan	94%
3.	COVID-19 classification with the Chest X-Ray images using ML [4]	Chest X-Ray, Binary classification (Covid and Normal)	Random Forest (ML based)	Chest X-ray	92%
4.	Transfer learning-based automatic detection of COVID-19 with CT scan [6]	Stationary wavelet decomposition, Normalization, Lung CT	ResNet18 (Deep Transfer Learning)	CT scan	97.32%
5.	Deep neural network model to recognize COVID-19 with chest radiography scans [7]	DCNN based, Pre-trained on Imagenet, 4-fold cross validation	Xception - CoroNet	Chest X-ray	89.6%
6.	AI on COVID-19 pneumonia detection with chest x-ray [9]	Data aggregation, Hyper parameter tuning	CNN based	Chest X-ray	90%
7.	Finding covid19 on chest x-rays utilizing Deep Learning [15]	Small dataset, Binary classification (Covid and Pneumonia)	ResNet50 and VGG-16	Chest X-ray	89.2%
8.	Detect Covid-19 with chest x-ray [17]	Pre-trained CNN model, Classification (Covid, Pne. and Normal)	CheXNet and DenseNet	Chest X-ray	90.5%

(*continued*)

Table 1. *(continued)*

S. No	Title/Existing Work	Feature(s)	Classifier used	Dataset	Accuracy (%)
9.	Efficient model for corona virus patterns detection [18]	Pre-trained CNN model, Imbalanced dataset	EfficientNet	Chest X-ray	93.9%
10.	Recognizing covid-19 utilizing Deep Learning based model [23]	DL Framework, Two step transfer learning mode, limited data size	COVID19XrayNet	Chest X-ray (189 images)	91.92%

In [14], the authors have recommended a hybrid system dependent on deep learning with Convolutional Neural Network (CNN) and the softmax classifier and implemented it for predicting COVID cases with chest radiography scan images. Another study [18], the authors utilized Efficient-Net, a pre-trained convolution neural network model and classified chest radiography images into three disease classes namely the Normal, the viral Pneumonia and Covid-19 with 93.9% accuracy. They have considered an imbalanced chest x-ray dataset for performing the study. In study [19] the authors have proposed a new deep learning based architecture to automatically diagnose Covid-19 disease with the chest radiography images to help the doctors. The authors have explored how the COVID-19 disease was exhibited as novel pneumonia infection in the Wuhan. In [20], the authors have discussed various techniques that can be used for detecting the Covid-19 disease and its challenges. There is a huge demand for developing an automated method for recognizing the Covid infection which will help to check the further spread of the disease with contact. Hemdan et al. [21], have discussed the chest x-ray based method for identifying abnormalities in the lungs. They have also shown that the healthcare industry will depend on chest radiography because of its availability and minimized infection control. Zhang et al. [23], have utilized Covid19-XrayNet framework dependent on a transfer learning approach that comprises 2-additional layers, namely Feature Smoothening layer (FSL) and another is the Feature extraction Layer (FEL) to predict the chest radiography images in 3 categories, namely viral pneumonia, normal and Covid-19 with accuracy of 91.92%. The dataset size is too small. They also have analyzed the performance of the model with the pre-trained ResNet34 model. It is observed from various existing works that the Deep Learning (DL) methods [27] performs better in most of the recognition related activities as compared to the humans beings, that showcases its numerous applications in the healthcare industry, mostly in the domain of medical imaging.

3 Materials and Methods

3.1 Dataset

The dataset selected for performing the present research has been collected from RICORD [22], Mendeley data repository [16] and [24] that comprises of the Chest radiography images of Viral Pneumonia, COVID infected and Normal patients.

The dataset taken for performing the research utilizing deep learning methodology consists of 8965 chest radiography image samples. Figure 1 shows a sample image of the chest radiography dataset of (a) person having Viral Pneumonia infection (b) COVID-19 positive person and (c) normal person. This database has been split into train set which comprises of 7968 image samples and the validation set having 997 samples of normal, COVID and viral pneumonia classes, has been utilized for analyzing the performance of the proposed model.

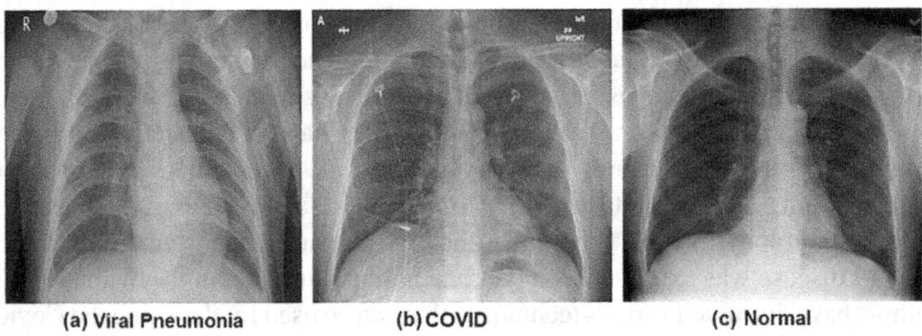

Fig. 1. Image sample taken from each class of the chest radiography dataset is shown.

The image size considered for this study is 224 × 224 that is scaled down from the original size of 299 × 299 for boosting the training process to some extent.

3.2 Proposed COV-XDCNN Model

The proposed COV-XDCNN model is being implemented with external Gabor filter in the first convolution layer for better and efficient feature extraction and the Gaussian and Sobel filters are utilized in successive convolution layers. The proposed model recommended in this study consists of 18 layers having 7 conv. layers, 2 BN layers, 4 pooling layers, 2 dense layers, 1 fully connected layer, 1 dropout layer and 1 Softmax layer. BN layer normalizes and regularizes the input layer making the training process faster. BN is the Batch Normalization. The pooling layers are utilized in the proposed model for decreasing the dimension of the feature maps. ReLU activation is utilized for introducing non-linearity in the model. In proposed model, conv. layer is considered to be the base layer. This layer with the utilization of some filter which slide across the image for extracting the low level and high level image features. The size of the input image is 224 × 224. The filter of size 3 × 3 is being utilized. The model also has a dropout layer for eliminating the overfitting effect. The parameters utilized for training

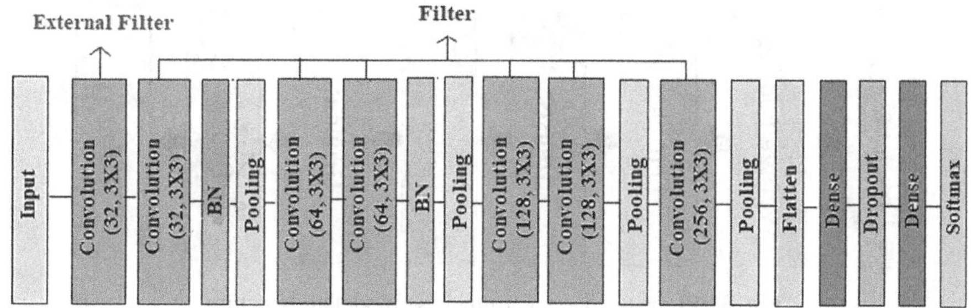

Fig. 2. Proposed COV-XDCNN model architecture

the model are selected after performing various experiments. The architecture of the model proposed in this study with external filter is indicated in Fig. 2.

The output of the conv. layer is represented in the Eq. 1. In the equation, the (*) represents the vector convolution process, c_j^l denotes the jth feature map in the layer l, f represents the function, m_r^{l-1} denotes the rth feature map in (l-1) layer, k_j^{l-1} denotes the jth kernel in the (l-1) layer, b_j^l denotes the bias factor in layer l of the jth feature map and the variable N denotes the total no. of features in the (l-1) layer.

$$c_j^l = f\left(\sum_{r=1}^{N} k_j^{l-1} * m_r^{l-1} + b_j^l\right) \tag{1}$$

The categorical cross-entropy loss function is being utilized to train the proposed model. The equation of loss function is highlighted in Eq. 2. In the equation, the term y represents the True Label and the term $\hat{y}$ denotes the Predicted labels. It is being utilized for optimizing the value of the parameters that are being utilized in the proposed model. The aim is to decrease the loss function in successive cycles of training.

$$L(y, \hat{y}) = -\left(\sum y * \log(\hat{y}) + (1 - y) * loglog(1 - \hat{y})\right) \tag{2}$$

For compiling the model, Adam optimizer is being utilized. It is a stochastic gradient descent method [29] that integrates the good features of both the AdaGrad and RMSProp algorithms for providing optimization which has the capability of handling sparse gradients on the noisy problems. To automate the training process and to control the learning process, the callback functions are being utilized.

3.3 Deep Learning Models

Some of the deep learning models which are taken for performing the efficacy testing on the chest radiography dataset are described below. The efficiency of various deep learning models is investigated by varying the base model that is shown in Fig. 3 and keeping the other layers same. The base models taken for the experiment include – NASNetMobile, VGG-16, VGG-19, ResNet50 and the MobileNet model. The models are being trained on ImageNet [28] weights.

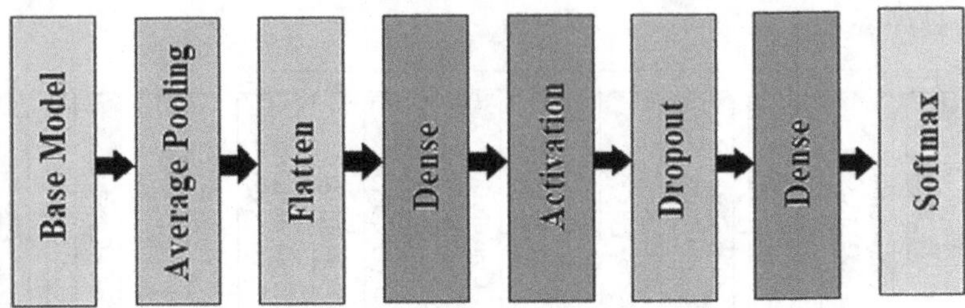

Fig. 3. Proposed deep learning base model architecture

A. NASNetMobile: It is a mobile architecture dependent on CNN known as Neural Architecture Search Network (NASNet) Mobile. The Google brain team initially developed the design of this model. The model is based on an algorithm which searches the best method for achieving the best performance on a definite task. The control architecture in NASNet is dependent on Recurrent Neural Network (RNN) that is being utilized in this model for predicting the entire structure of the network based on the two initial hidden states. Here, the base model as shown in Fig. 3 is taken as NASNetMobile model for investigating the performance with the chest x-ray images.

B. VGG-16: VGG-16 net stands for Visual Geometry Group-16 network and is based on CNN. It is named as VGG-16 due to the presence of 16 numbers of layers. The main idea behind the entire network is that the convolution layers have 3 × 3 fixed sized kernels having a stride value of one and the padding is normally selected as the same so that the size of the input image remains the same. Here, max pool layer is generally utilized after each convolution block having pool size of two and a stride value of two. The number of filter we utilize in this network generally keeps on doubling which is the working principle that is being utilized to design this model. It comprises of 12 convolution layers, 5 pooling layers and 4 dense layers including the output layer. It comprises a total of 16 layers with 5 blocks and each block is accompanied with 1 pooling layer i.e. max. Pool. The model is trained on ImageNet weights.

C. VGG-19: VGG-19 net stands for Visual Geometry Group-19 network. It is based on Convolution Neural Network. It is named as VGG-19 due to the presence of 19 numbers of layers in the net. This model is deeper than that of VGG-16 and requests more amount of memory. The main idea behind the entire network is that the convolution layers have 3 × 3 fixed sized kernels having a stride value of one and the padding is normally selected as the same so that the size of the input image remains the same. It comprises of 14 convolution layers, 5 pooling layers and 4 dense layers. The model is being trained on ImageNet weights. Here, max pool layer is generally utilized after each convolution block having pool size of two and a stride value of two.

D. ResNet-50: It stands for Residual Neural Network-50. It is a 50-layer deep Residual Neural Network (RNN). This model is an enhanced form of CNN and also an extension of the deep ResNet model. The model is dependent on the split - transform - merge approach. For solving some certain problem, the model adds shortcuts between the layers which have the capability to check the distortion that may happen when the model becomes deeper or more complex. Additionally, in this model the bottleneck blocks are being utilized for making the process of training faster.

E. MobileNet: It is 28-layer deep neural net including the depth-wise separable convolution which comprises of two layers namely the counting widthwise and pointwise convolution layers. In the model, the depth-wise conv. layer is being utilized to filter the input channels and the pointwise conv. layer is utilized for combining them for creating a new feature. It is a simple, lightweight but efficient Neural Network-based model for mobile vision applications [12]. This model is widely being utilized in various works such as fine-grained classifications, object detection etc.

3.4 Proposed Algorithm

The technique utilized to implement the COV-XDCNN model that is being proposed in this study for classifying the chest x-ray images is mentioned below:

Step 1: The data is imported from the directory.
Step 2: Data is split into the Training and Test set.
Step 3: Data Augmentation approach is being applied. The parameters used in this study are shown in Table 2. Pre-process image X (utilizing Keras data generator).

Table 2. Selected parameters utilized for data augmentation

Parameters	Value
Brightness range	0.1–0.2
Shear range	0.1
Rotation range	15
Width and height shift range	0.1
Zoom range	0.2
Horizontal Flip	True

Step 4: Give the image (224, 224) as the input to the first convolution layer with an external Gabor filter in the proposed model. And then activation (A) is applied.
Step 5: Followed by the BN, max pooling layer and various successive convolution layers. And activation function (A) is also applied after each conv. layer.
Step 6: Features are extracted in other layers using filters such as Sobel, Gaussian etc.
Step 7: Result of the ultimate conv. layer of the model is being fetched.
Step 8: Then flatten the dimensions utilizing the Flatten layer for decreasing the dimension from n to n − 1.
Step 9: A dense layer is added to the model. In Eq. 3, w represents the weights and b denotes the bias.

$$Z = w * A + b \tag{3}$$

Step 10: Then Activation function (A) is applied. The activation function and its range is highlighted in Eqs. 4 and 5.

$$\text{A} = \text{ReLU(Z)} \tag{4}$$

$$\text{where, ReLU(Z)} = \max(0, \text{x}) \tag{5}$$

Step 11: A dropout (20%) is being performed.
Step 12: An additional Dense Layer is added for introducing non-linearity.
Step 13: Softmax function is applied for classifying the chest radiography images. The equation of this function is shown in 6.

$$\text{Softmax}(\sigma_\text{z})_\text{j} = \frac{\text{e}^{\text{z}_\text{j}}}{\sum_1^N e^{z_N}} \tag{6}$$

Step 14: Model is compiled with 0.001 LR and the loss function Categorical cross-entropy and Adam optimizer is used. (LR denotes Learning Rate).
Step 15: The proposed model has been trained in 15 batches for 30 epochs with Callback functions - Early Stopping, ReduceLROnPlateau and Model Checkpoint.
Step 16: Chest x-rays are classified into 3 categories, namely COVID, Normal and Viral Pneumonia.
Step 17: The proposed model is validated on Test data.
Step 18: Plot Train and Test Accuracy curve.
Step 19: Generate the Classification report, Plot Confusion Matrix and analyze the model performance.

3.5 Data Augmentation

For the artificial creation of newer train data from the existing data, this technique is being incorporated into this research. The data augmentation methods, namely the height shift, width shift, rotation, zoom, horizontal flip and brightness are utilized before training the model. It is known that the deep neural networks require large sized database for proper training, so this method helps to overcome this issue as well.

3.6 Feature Extraction and Classification

The features of the Chest radiography images are extracted utilizing the Sobel filter, Gaussian filter, custom Gabor filter and some common edge detection filters with the proposed COV-XDCNN model. The pixel data is being converted into a higher form of representation of the texture, spatial configuration, motion and shape of the chest or its components utilizing various feature extraction approaches. Due to the use of additional filters, the features of chest X-rays are extracted more efficiently. The filters that are utilized for extracting chest radiography image features are discussed below:

A. Gaussian Filter (GF): It is a filter that is having the shape of the function Gaussian distribution (curve) for defining the weights in the kernel, that are being utilized to compute the weighted average of the neighboring points (pixels) in an image. GF also helps in extracting useful features from the chest radiography images. The canny edge detection utilizes a GF for the eliminating the noise from the image, as this noise can be presumed as edges due to sudden change in intensity with the aid of the edge detector. In this study, kernel of size 3 × 3 and std. deviation taken as 1.4 that blur the image and eliminate the noise from it. The Eq. 7 shows the equation of Gaussian filter kernel. In the equation, σ represents the std. deviation of Gaussian filter and x and y are the two components as it is a 2-D filter.

$$G_\sigma = \frac{1}{2\pi\sigma^2} e^{\frac{-(x^2+y^2)}{2\sigma^2}} \tag{7}$$

B. Sobel Filter: At present, the sobel filter is being considered as the most popular edge detection filter. It gives much better performance than most of the other edge detection approaches due to its efficient extraction of edge features from the image [26]. Utilizing edge features will definitely aid in training the proposed COV-XDCNN model and improve the disease classification performance as it is found that the edges in an image have discriminatory information.

$$K_x = \begin{pmatrix} -1\,0\,1 \\ -2\,0\,2 \\ -3\,0\,1 \end{pmatrix},\ K_y = \begin{pmatrix} -1\,0\,1 \\ -2\,0\,2 \\ -3\,0\,1 \end{pmatrix} \tag{8}$$

The derivatives Ix and Iy are being computed w.r.t x and y axis when the image is being smoothed. It is being achieved with the utilization of the Sobel-Feldman kernels convolution with image as given. Thereafter, apply the kernels K_x and K_y as represented in Eq. 8, the gradient magnitudes and the angle can be utilized for further processing. Utilizing the Eqs. 9 and 10, the magnitude and angle can be computed respectively. The Sobel filter detects the edges at the regions of the chest radiography image where there is a high gradient magnitude.

$$|G| = \sqrt{{I_x}^2 + {I_y}^2} \tag{9}$$

$$\theta(x, y) = \left(\frac{I_y}{I_x}\right) \tag{10}$$

C. Gabor Filter: These filters are mostly utilized for feature extraction, edge detection and in texture analysis. Gabor filter banks are considered to be one of the most powerful approaches for processing the chest radiography images of human beings. It is a dynamic filter.

$$g(x, y; \lambda, \theta, \psi, \sigma, \gamma) = \exp\left(-\frac{x'^2 + \gamma^2 y'^2}{2\sigma^2}\right)\exp\left(i\left(2\pi\frac{x'}{\lambda} + \right)\Psi\right)) \tag{11}$$

The filter finds a specific frequency that exists in the image along a certain orientation at a zone (local) around the region of analysis. The proposed COV-XDCNN model extracts the image sub-features utilizing this filter. It improves in extracting the features of various components of the chest and thus improves the disease detection rate. The complex form of a 2-D Gabor filter is shown in Eq. 11, it comprises of both the real and imaginary component. The orientation and frequency representations of the Gabor filters are identical to those of the human visual system. In the Eq. 11, σ represents the std. deviation of the Gaussian function utilized, λ represents the wavelet of sinusoidal factor in the eqn., γ denotes the special aspect ratio, ψ here denotes the phase-offset, θ here denotes the orientation of normal to parallel strips, $x' = xcos\theta + ysin\theta$, $y' = -xsin\theta + ycos\theta$ and k is the size of Gabor Kernel. The proposed model have been trained using varied orientations and scales.

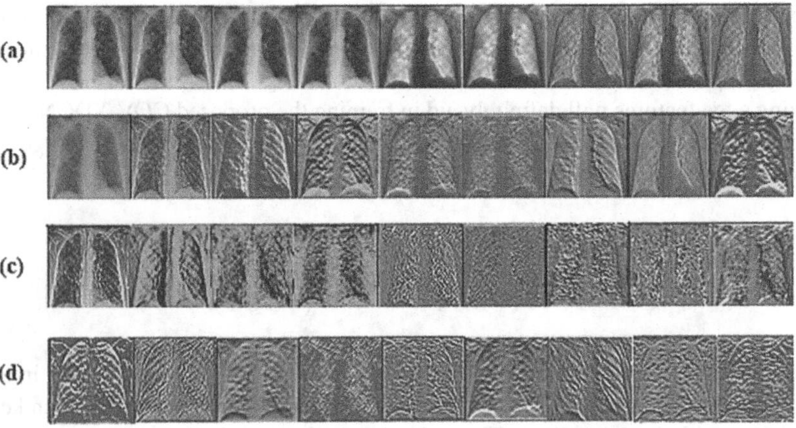

Fig. 4. Output of the Intermediate feature maps of (a) First layer (b) Fourth layer (c) Sixth layer (d) Ninth layer

The selected images from the color feature map output of some intermediate layers are shown in Fig. 4. Initially, the low level features of chest radiography are extracted and at the successive levels more complex and useful features are being extracted. It shows the responses of the filters, the activation function and pooling operations in some of the layers of the COV-XDCNN model (ext. filter) that is being proposed.

Prior to the extraction of the vital chest radiography image features, the next process is to classify the disease utilizing the trained model. The classification is carried out utilizing the Softmax function at the ultimate layer of the proposed COV-XDCNN model. The classification is considered to be a vital process. For implementation of the work, the trained COV-XDCNN model is utilized to detect random chest radiography data into 3 categories, namely COVID, Viral Pneumonia and the Normal.

4 Results and Discussion

4.1 Experimental Setup

The proposed work is implemented using the Python programming language on Spyder, Anaconda platform. The experiments and analysis were carried on a 64-bit Win. 10 Operating system having the Core i3 Processor with a clock speed of 2.0 GHz and an Intel Inbuilt GPU.

4.2 Performance Measurements

Accuracy of the Chest x-ray classification model can be described as the capacity of the model to rightly predict or classify the disease classes. The mathematical expressions of the Accuracy, Recall (Sensitivity) score, Precision score and the F1-Score or measure that are being utilized for measuring the performance of the models are shown in Eqs. 12, 13, 14 and 15 respectively:

$$Accuracy = \frac{Total\ Number\ of\ Correct\ Predictions}{Total\ Number\ of\ Predictions} \tag{12}$$

$$Recall = \frac{True\ Positive\ (TP)}{True\ Positive\ (TP) + False\ Negative\ (FN)} \tag{13}$$

$$Precision = \frac{True\ Positive\ (TP)}{True\ Positive\ (TP) + False\ Positive\ (FP)} \tag{14}$$

$$F1\ Score = 2 * \frac{Precision * Recall}{Precision + Recall} \tag{15}$$

The F1-measure is the harmonic mean of two measures, namely the Recall Score and the Precision score. Apart from the Precision and Recall score, this score is found to be very useful classification metric for understanding the performance of the model.

4.3 Accuracy Plot

The output of the Training and Test Accuracy plot of the proposed COV-XDCNN model and NASNetMobile model is shown in Fig. 5. As per the experimental observation, the proposed model in this study outperforms the NASNetMobile model.

4.4 Classification Performance

The classification report highlighted in Table 3 indicates that the proposed model has high Net Recall and Precision score of 0.97 and 0.96 respectively. Moreover, it also has a high Net F1-measure of 0.96.

All the target classes namely Normal, COVID and Viral Pneumonia are classified effectively as noticed from the classification performance report of the proposed COV-XDCNN model with the external filter.

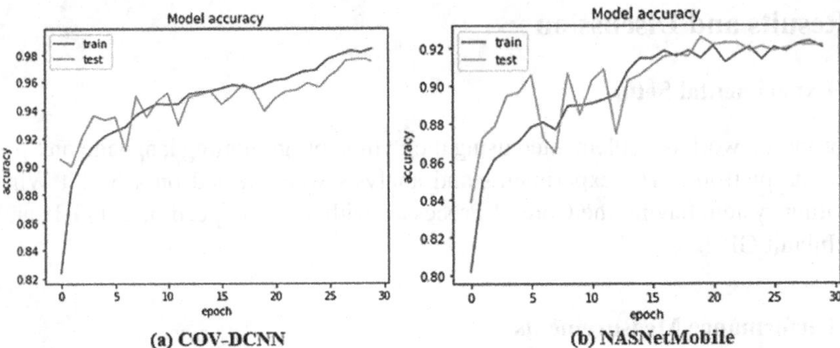

Fig. 5. Train and Test Accuracy of the (a) Proposed COV-XDCNN Model and (b) NASNetMobile Model

Table 3. Classification Report of the proposed COV-XDCNN model

Class	Precision	Recall	F1-Measure
COVID	0.96	0.97	0.96
Normal	0.98	0.99	0.98
Viral PNEUMONIA	0.94	0.95	0.94
Avg/Total	0.96	0.97	0.96

4.5 Experimental Results

The proposed COV-XDCNN model and MobileNet model perform much better in terms of classifying the chest radiography images than the other deep learning-based models being experimented as found from Table 4. The NASNetMobile and VGG-16 models also show good results. But, the proposed COV-XDCNN model with an external Gabor filter shows better performance in terms of classification, with test accuracy of 97.86% and training accuracy of 98.24% and has the highest Net F1 score.

The activation function is used to help the model for learning complex patterns. Utilizing the ReLU activation function in the proposed model better results are obtained as observed from the Table 5. Here, the LeakyReLU and SeLU activation function also performs well but it does not perform better than the ReLU activation function.

4.6 Detection Result

The output of the detection performed with the proposed COV-XDCNN Model on two sample chest radiography scans is shown in Fig. 6. It is observed that the predicted result matches exactly with the actual result in both the cases.

Table 4. Experimental Results of classification of the Chest Radiography images

S. No	Model considered	Training accuracy (%)	Test accuracy (%)	Net F1-score
1.	NASNetMobile	91.98	92.13	0.90
2.	VGG-16	92.63	94.38	0.92
3.	MobileNet	94.86	95.16	0.94
4.	VGG-19	87.38	89.40	0.86
5.	Proposed COV-XDCNN model (with ext. filter)	98.24	97.86	0.96
6.	ResNet50	89.40	90.80	0.88

Table 5. Experiment with different Act. Functions in the proposed COV-XDCNN model

Epochs (No.)	Kernel used	Initial learning rate (LR)	Activation selected (A)	Training accuracy (%)	Test accuracy (%)
30	3 × 3	0.001	ReLU	98.24	97.86
30	3 × 3	0.001	LeakyReLU	96.53	94.60
30	3 × 3	0.001	SeLU	89.46	90.30

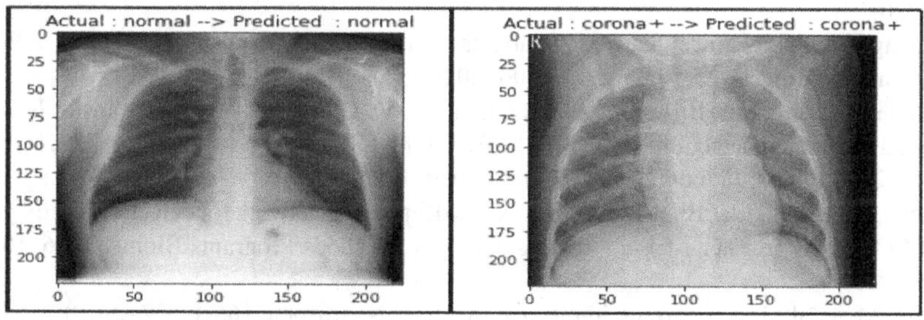

Fig. 6. Screenshot of the detection output of two sample image with the proposed model.

5 Conclusion and Future Scope

In this study, the COV-XDCNN model with external Gabor filter is being proposed for classifying the chest radiography images. The proposed model classifies and detects the chest x-ray images of human beings in three categories, namely COVID, Normal and Viral Pneumonia with 97.86% test accuracy. The Gabor filter extracts the features of chest radiography images more efficiently. Moreover, the classification performance of the model proposed is analyzed with other popular deep learning models and it is seen from experimental analysis that the proposed model shows much better performance. So, it can be employed to classify the COVID-19 affected patients using their radiography images of chest. It is also observed that the proposed COV-XDCNN model, NASNetMobile and MobileNet model takes very less training and testing time in comparison to other models being experimented. Therefore, these models are energy efficient and fast. Deep learning is a powerful method that needs to be widely utilized for automating various diagnosis tasks in the healthcare industry. In future, the classification may be carried out utilizing a more efficient model and a much bigger sized chest x-ray image dataset may be considered for training and validating the proposed model. The proposed approach may be investigated further for proving the actual case-based implementation. This research will influence new research findings on medical imaging and can be utilized as a strong reference.

References

1. Farncombe, T., Iniewski, K. (eds.): Medical imaging: technology and applications. CRC Press, Boca Raton (2017)
2. Chandra, T.B., Verma, K., Singh, B.K., Jain, D., Netam, S.S.: Coronavirus disease (COVID-19) detection in chest X-ray images using majority voting based classifier ensemble. Expert Syst. Appl. **165**, 113909 (2021)
3. Maghdid, H.S., Asaad, A.T., Ghafoor, K.Z., Sadiq, A.S., Mirjalili, S., Khan, M.K.: Diagnosing COVID-19 pneumonia from X-ray and CT images using deep learning and transfer learning algorithms. In: Multimodal Image Exploitation and Learning 2021, vol. 11734, p. 117340E. International Society for Optics and Photonics (2021)
4. Khan, N., Ullah, F., Hassan, M.A., Hussain, A.: COVID-19 classification based on Chest X-Ray images using machine learning techniques. J. Comput. Sci. Technol. Stud. **2**(2), 01–11 (2020)
5. Huang, C., et al.: Clinical features of patients infected with 2019 novel coronavirus in Wuhan China. The Lancet **395**(10223), 497–506 (2020)
6. Ahuja, S., Panigrahi, B.K., Dey, N., Rajinikanth, V., Gandhi, T.K.: Deep transfer learning-based automated detection of COVID-19 from lung CT scan slices. Appl. Intell. **51**(1), 571–585 (2020). https://doi.org/10.1007/s10489-020-01826-w
7. Khan, A.I., Shah, J.L., Bhat, M.M.: CoroNet: a deep neural network for detection and diagnosis of COVID-19 from chest x-ray images. Comput. Methods Programs Biomed. **196**, 105581 (2020)
8. Kim, M., et al.: Deep learning in medical imaging. Neurospine **16**(4), 657 (2019)
9. Baltazar, L.R., et al.: Artificial intelligence on COVID-19 pneumonia detection using chest xray images. PLoS ONE **16**(10), e0257884 (2021)
10. Chung, M., et al.: CT imaging features of 2019 novel coronavirus (2019-nCoV). Radiology **295**(1), 202–207, 26 (2020)
11. Wang, S., et al.: A deep learning algorithm using CT images to screen for corona virus disease (COVID-19). Eur. Radiol. **31**(8), 6096–6104 (2021)
12. Wang, W., Li, Y., Zou, T., Wang, X., You, J., Luo, Y.: A novel image classification approach via dense-MobileNet models. Mobile Information Systems (2020)
13. Cohen, J. P., Morrison, P., Dao, L.: COVID-19 image data collection (2020). arXiv preprint arXiv:2003.11597
14. Alqudah, A.M., Qazan, S., Alqudah, A.: Automated systems for detection of COVID-19 using chest X-ray images and lightweight convolutional neural networks (2020)
15. Hall, L.O., Paul, R., Goldgof, D.B., Goldgof, G.M.: Finding covid-19 from chest x-rays using deep learning on a small dataset (2020). arXiv preprint arXiv:2004.02060

16. Asraf, A., Islam, Z.: COVID19, Pneumonia and Normal Chest X-ray PA Dataset. Mendeley Data, V1 (2021). https://doi.org/10.17632/jctsfj2sfn.1
17. Mangal, A., et al.: CovidAID: COVID-19 detection using chest X-ray (2020). arXiv preprint arXiv:2004.09803
18. Luz, E., Silva, P.L., Silva, R., Silva, L., Moreira, G., Menotti, D.: Towards an effective and efficient deep learning model for covid19 patterns detection in x-ray images (2020). arXiv: 2004.05717
19. Hemdan, E.E.D., Shouman, M.A., Karar, M.E.: Covidx-net: a framework of deep learning classifiers to diagnose covid-19 in x ray images (2020). arXiv preprint arXiv:2003.11055
20. Ilyas, M., Rehman, H., Nait-ali, A.: Detection of Covid-19 from chest X-ray images using artificial intelligence: an early review (2020). arXiv preprint arXiv:2004.05436
21. Jacobi, A., Chung, M., Bernheim, A., Eber, C.: Portable chest X-ray in coronavirus disease-19 (COVID-19): a pictorial review. Clin. Imaging **64**, 35–42 (2020)
22. Tsai, E.B., et al.: The RSNA international COVID-19 open radiology database (RICORD). Radiology **299**(1), E204–E213 (2021)
23. Zhang, R., et al.: COVID19XrayNet: a two-step transfer learning model for the COVID-19 detecting problem based on a limited number of chest X-Ray images. Interdiscip. Sci. Comput. Life Sci. **12**(4), 555–565 (2020). https://doi.org/10.1007/s12539-020-00393-5
24. Cohen, J.P., Morrison, P., Dao, L., Roth, K., Duong, T.Q., Ghassemi, M.: Covid-19 image data collection: prospective predictions are the future (2020). arXiv preprint arXiv:2006.11988
25. Chowdhury, M.E.H., et al.: Can AI help in screening viral and COVID-19 pneumonia? IEEE Access **8**, 132665–132676 (2020)
26. Wang, R.: Edge detection using convolutional neural network. In: Cheng, L., Liu, Q., Ronzhin, A. (eds.) Advances in Neural Networks – ISNN 2016. LNCS, vol. 9719, pp. 12–20. Springer, Cham (2016). https://doi.org/10.1007/978-3-319-40663-3_2
27. Kermany, D.S., et al.: Identifying medical diagnoses and treatable diseases by image-based deep learning. Cell **172**, 1122-1131.e9 (2018)
28. Deng, R.O., et al.: ImageNet large scale visual recognition challenge (2015). arXiv preprint arXiv:14090575
29. Kingma, D.P., Ba, J.: Adam: A method for stochastic optimization (2014). arXiv preprint arXiv:1412.6980

Cyber Security

Trust Aware Secure Routing Model in MANET: Self-improved Particle Swarm Optimization for Optimal Route Selection

S. Haridas(✉) and A. Rama Prasath(✉)

Hindustan Institute of Technology and Science, Chennai, India
harigoleson@gmail.com, mraprasath@gmail.com

Abstract. In the heterogeneous network, MANETs are the collective gathering of diverse mobile devices with the ability to join and leave the network at any moment as the most prominent feature. As a consequence, mobile nodes in the decentralized network may link, interact, and transfer information to one another without the need of an intermediary router. Several academics have recently explored a variety of routing approaches to tackle issues such as packet data transmission delays and poor PDR. This paper aims to introduce a new trust-aware routing in MANET that ensures the trust level among the nodes. For this, a new trust rate estimation process is introduced based on energy and mobility of nodes exist. Thereby, a Self-Improved Particle Swarm optimization algorithm (SI-PSO) is proposed for choosing the optimal trust aware route for data transmission. The optimal route selection is performed by considering certain parameters like trust rate (security), Packet Drop Ratio (PDR) distance, congestion, energy, and as well. The performance of the adopted work is examined to the existing schemes regarding Energy, Delay, and Network Lifetime.

Nomenclature

Abbreviation	Description
BFS	Breadth-First Search Trees
AODV	Ad Hoc On-Demand Distance Vector
QoS	Quality Of Services
MANET	Mobile Adhoc Network
GA	Genetic Algorithm
SI-PSO	Self-Improved Particle Swarm Optimization Algorithm
CHS	Cluster Head Selection
GR	Global State Routing
RBT	Reputation-Based Trust-Aware Routing Protocol
TEAR	Trust Based Energy Aware Routing
RSRA	Real-Time Secure Route Analysis
WSN	Wireless Sensor Networks
TECM	Trust Enhanced Cluster Based Multipath
CH	Cluster Head
NETAR	Novel Energy Efficient Trust Aware Routing
PDR	Packet Delivery Ratio
BPSO	Binary PSO
PSO	Particle Swarm Optimization
E2E	End-To-End
OLSR	Optimized Link State Routing
FPNT	Fuzzy Petri Based Trust

Published by Springer Nature Switzerland AG 2022
E. J. Neuhold et al. (Eds.): ICCCSP 2022, IFIP AICT 651, pp. 193–212, 2022.
https://doi.org/10.1007/978-3-031-11633-9_15

1 Introduction

MANET provides a self-configuring structure comprising diverse devices that are connected via wireless network [9]. The devices linked in the MANET are generally referred to as nodes. MANET nodes include the features of mobility, infrastructure less nature, and multi-hop packet transmissions [11]. Through the direct communication link, each node communicates with the others. If the nodes are separated by a long distance, communication happens through the intermediary nodes. MANET is used in various applications, including military applications, space applications, and mobile phones, among others [10]. MANET network ensured a constant communication flow among the transmitter and receiver nodes with improved security and service quality. However, finding of the secure routing path among the MANET nodes has been emerged as the primary problem in MANET routing [12]. MANET nodes rely on one another to form a link in wireless communication. As the MANET nodes are movable, communication links fail. The MANET architecture with multipath routing prevents communication connection failure among nodes [13].

Multipath routing [14] creates several communication path among the transmitter and receiver nodes. Load balancing and route dependability are two advantages of multipath routing. The downside of multipath routing methods is topology vulnerability. The routing table of the nodes is regularly changed by multipath routing. This exposes the network to hackers, allowing them to readily obtain information from the network. During multipath routing, MANET nodes [17, 18] are exposed to a variety of assaults. Wormhole attacks, Sybil attacks, black hole attacks, and rushing assaults are examples of MANET attacks [15]. The usage of topology concealing routing protocols can cover the open topology in multipath routing. Previous research developed topology-hidden multipath routing techniques in MANETs [16]. The topology concealing paradigm conceals routing information while securely transmitting the messages over the network.

Several deterministic and stochastic models have lately been developed. The strategies which rely on the gradient technique are the predictable methods. Stochastic approaches are the multimodal problem solving methods that rely on biological entities. Many metaheuristic strategies are more helpful to solve the issues in MANET [19–22]. The clustering approach based on BFS is created to choose the lower load CHs and link the nodes with each other. Moreover, GA is implemented based on the Darwinian concept of survival of the fittest, in which it minimizes the highest load on gateway nodes. The dynamic clustering structure was determined in MANET using the PSO model [40–42]. They used a variety of CHS criteria to create stable clusters. However, the mobility of the nodes could not be handled efficiently. an energy-efficient routing approach has been done with PSO [36–39] algorithm [23, 24, 43] was presented for MANET. Still the model suffers from local optima issue, which needs an improvement to make efficiency in problem solving [25].

The main contribution of the adopted work is given in the succeeding section:

Implemented a novel optimization algorithm known as SI-PSO model which is an enhanced version of standard PSO for more trust aware secure path selection.

The optimal route selection is performed based on the constrains like the trust rate (security), distance, power, minimum congestion, and Packet Drop Ratio (PDR), respectively.

The rest of the paper is ordered as: Section 2 addresses the review on trust aware secure routing in MANET. Section 3 describes about the proposed methodology: trust aware secure routing in MANET. Section 4 portrays trust aware secure routing model in manet: defined objectives. Section 5 describes the self-improved particle swarm optimization algorithm for optimal path selection. Section 6 discusses the results acquired with the presented work.

2 Literature Review

2.1 Related Works

In 2021, Usha et al. [1] have implemented a NETAR protocol for the conventional AODV protocol for improving the 3 trust degrees between the MANET nodes by malicious behavior predictions, energy, bandwidth calculation, and neighbor-node trust rate estimation to select the reliable and efficient path. The channel capacity evaluation technique was used to estimate the intermediate nodes' residual energy, high trust rate, and bandwidth. Routing through these nodes enhances network efficiency. This was implemented using the NS2 simulator tool. When compared to GR, RBT Protocol, the proposed approach has a average delay time efficiency, throughput, less false positive, and higher PDR.

In 2018, Devi et al. [2] have introduced the TECM routing system in this work. To produce cluster formation and CHs, they employ the energy-efficient PSO method. Super CHs were chosen from trust values computed using the suggested TECM technique. Packet/frame loss ratio, received signal strength, packet/frame receiving energy, routing overhead, protocol deviation flag, average forward delay, Packet/frame forward rate, and Packet/frame forward energy was the many trust factors utilized in trust computation. The new TECM algorithm was combined with a typical multipath TECM-OLSR to evaluate its performance. The proposed TECM-OLSR protocol was extremely efficient with respect to routing overhead, loss and delivery rate, latency, and network lifespan.

In 2021, Sathyaraj et al. [3] have explored a RSRA technique in MANET for safe routing. This technique considered the strategy of intermediary nodes of discovered routes, as well as the presence of IoT devices and their trust. The approach begins via generating a list of possible paths among any transmitter and receiver. The trustworthiness of each mobile node was considered in determining the location, mobility speed, energy, and quantity of transmissions concerned, as well as their neighbor list. DS was tested for IoT devices, whereas MSRS was evaluated for mobile nodes. A single route was already chosen on the basis of DFS metric that enhances the MANET's QoS.

In 2019, Merlin et al. [4] has determined a novel TEAR technique for MANETs. The significant features of TEAR mechanism' was that it mitigates BHs via dynamic generation of different detection routes to identify BHs as feasible and attains best data route security via establishing nodal trust. Fundamentally, in the TEAR method, these multidetector routes were formed by fully using the energy in non-hotspots to increase the data route security and energy efficiency. The TEAR mechanism improves the network's lifespan by preventing black hole assaults and dramatically improves the probability of data routing.

In 2021, Anitha et al. [5] has suggested the TSVRCLPBC ensemble approach in MANET. The suggested method's major goal was to improve the secure communication with higher PDR and a lower E2E delay. The TSVRCLPBC was used to investigate node attributes including residual energy, cooperative communication, and node history. Moreover, the weak learners' results were merged to generate a powerful enhanced classifier output with weight function. To increase the Qos metric performance, the ensemble classification method in MANET computes the trustworthy nodes. Different metrics like E2E, PDR, latency, PLR, jitter, and energy consumption were used in the simulation. The simulation results have shown that the TSVR-CLPBC approaches improve PDR while reducing EC, PLR, E2E latency, and jitter than the existing methods.

In 2019, Ambekar et al. [6] has introduced the MANET's T-TOHIP method. The security element is described by four categories in the suggested routing scheme: the delay, energy, mobility, and trusted model. Based on the specified neighbor nodes, the adopted model finds the secure route among the transmitter and recipient. Ultimately, data exchange takes place via the chosen multipath. When there was an assault on the node, experimental outcomes has demonstrated that the adopted model has shown maximum throughput, latency, energy, and PDR after 50 s of simulation than the traditional system.

In 2019, Rajeswari et al. [7] has adopted a novel intelligent framework for secure routing that consists of 2 models like the TNFNS and the FBSSR algorithm. The trust based node selection method was used to provide efficient routing outcomes. The key feature of this suggested node selection mechanism was that it use trust values to separate hostile nodes from the routing process, thereby improving security. When compared to related secure routing protocol, it was shown that the suggested secured routing algorithm was more efficient in terms of enhanced PDR, reduction in delay, and FPR.

In 2019, Kukreja et al. [8] have proposed a T-SEA routing protocol for isolating the black/gray hole nodes in MANETs. The ability to conserve energy was a critical prerequisite for MANET lifetime. Black/gray hole nodes were monitored and caught using intrusion IDSs. IDS competent nodes have enough energy, a low trust value, and a large number of connections. T-SEA identified suspicious nodes throughout the data transmission phase without the need of any node into sniff mode. IDS identify a node as malicious while monitoring the present activity, current trust, and recorded behavior throughout previous transmissions. As the IDS operates on a few nodes at a time to the attack discovery, the detection approach was energy aware. The suggested approach was validated using NS-2 in this study.

3 Proposed Methodology: Trust Aware Secure Routing in MANET

3.1 Architectural Description

The roles and responsibilities of routing mechanism's involve exchanging routing path, computing the shortest route employing factors like link lifetime, least power, and hop count, collecting information concerning broken links, repairing broken links, processing power and bandwidth. MANET's routing technology is entirely dispersed and adaptable to the topological structure's frequent changes. Nevertheless, in order to reduce the packet collisions, each node in the network has a shorter route discover latency and route information with the smallest possible packets. In order to avoid the message loss and stale routes, it is critical to have reliable data transfer. As a consequence, the fundamental objective in MANET is to construct and maintain an energy-efficient optimal path to extend the network's lifetime. The nodes in geographic routing are required to discover an appropriate path for implementing the successful routing performance during the data transmission. Thereby, novel optimization techniques are used in this research to implement an adaptive routing strategy. SI-PSO [44] model a conceptual enhancement of normal PSO is introduced for more trust aware secure route selection as a novelty. Data packets are routed optimally based on the parameters like trust rate (security), minimum distance, minimum Energy, minimum congestion, and minimum PDR. Figure 1 illustrates the framework of the adopted work.

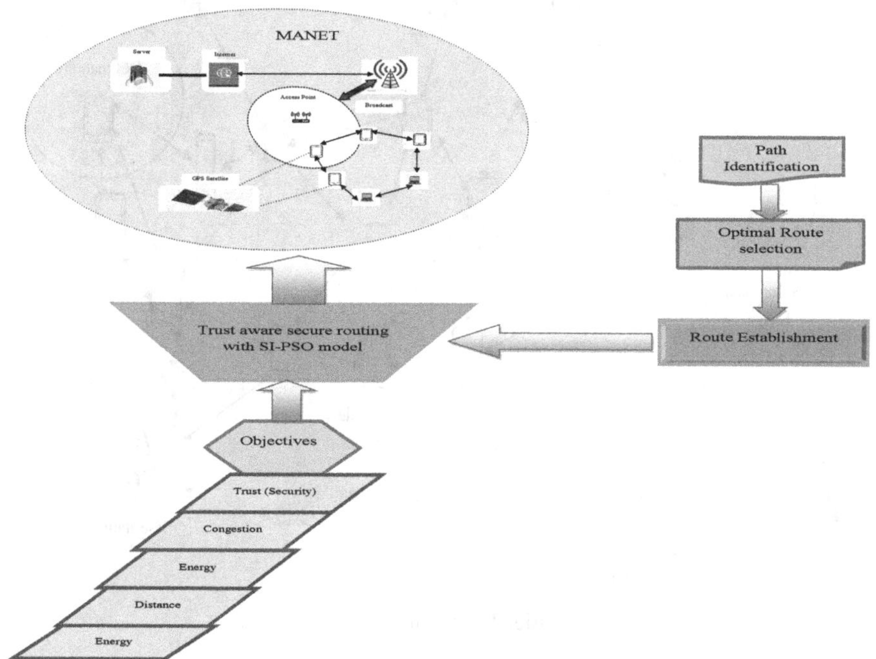

Fig. 1. Framework of the adopted work

3.2 System Model

The MANET's system model is represented in Fig. 2. Here, the count of sensor nodes is taken as $M = 100$. Moreover, the adopted network is constructed with the dimension of 500×500. Consider the graph $F(U, V)$, where $V = \{V_1, V_2, \ldots, V_l\}$ denotes the link set, and $U = \left\{U_S, U_1, U_2, \ldots, U_{R,..}U_M\right\}$ represents the nodes set. Moreover, the node sends the data packet is known as the sender U_S and the receiver U_R is one who receive the data packet. Further, the link state correlated the receiver U_R and sender U_S. It's difficult to send the message straight to the receiver because the sensor nodes are movable and have fluctuating neighbourhood conditions (nodes up to 400 m could only act as a neighbour). As a result, the sender U_S sends the message to any of its nearby neighbours that are within the radio range. That usually results in the creation of a path between among the sender U_S and the receiver U_R. The network life span with less latency, less congestion, lower packet drop ratio, and lower energy usage is a major concern with path creation. As a consequence, the shortest and most optimum path to be determined among the sender U_S and receiver U_R is critical. Further, the gateways perform as the interface among the neighboring nodes which permit to maximize the connectivity and coverage.

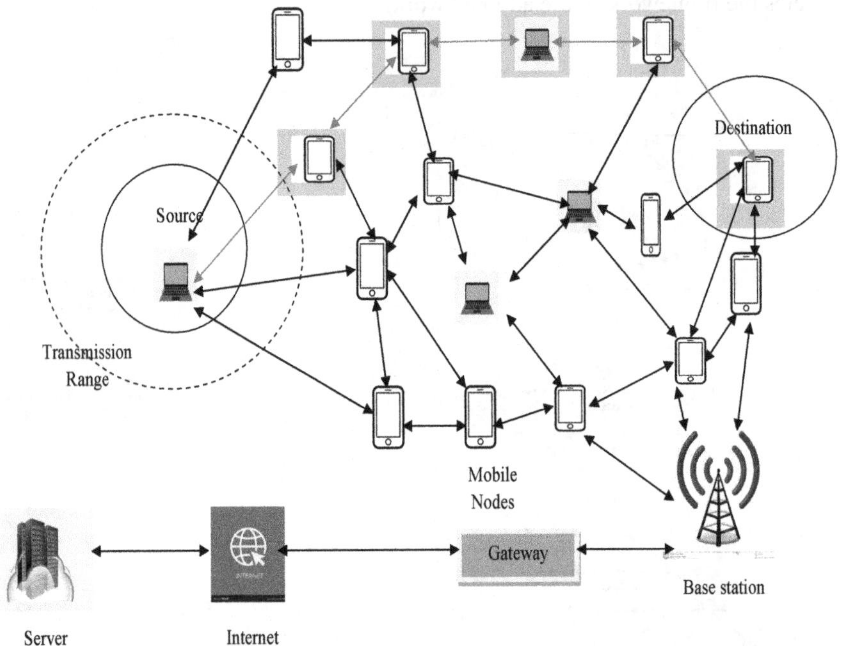

Fig. 2. System model

Route discovery, route establishment, and link break prediction are some of the steps of routing stagey. The sender U_S determines the possible routes for transmitting the message to the destination during the route discovery phase. Using the suggested optimization technique, the optimal path is selected among the possible options in the route establishment phase based on the objectives (trust rate (security), minimum distance, minimum power, minimum congestion, and minimum PDR). As the mobile nodes are dynamic, the path fixed is also dynamic and there is a risk of link breakage due to neighbour mobility. Further, the third step determines whether the route has any connection breaks. Separating all of these phases is a time-consuming but necessary task. Because all three phases function together, the network's lifetime could be extended or compressed. As a result, a novel routing algorithm is presented here to jointly select the best path that includes three phases. The routing algorithm is known as SI-PSO that is an improved version of PSO.

4 Trust Aware Secure Routing Model in MANET: Defined Objectives

4.1 Objective Function and Solution Encoding

The objective function to select the final optimal path in trust aware secure routing of MANET is given in Eq. (1).

$$Obj = w_1 \times (1 - T) + w_2(D) + w_3(E) + w_4(C) + w_5(PDR) \tag{1}$$

In Eq. (1), $w_1, w_2, w_3, w_4, and\ w_5$ are the weights of parameters ranges from 0 to 1. Here, the trust (security) is to be high. The distance, energy, congestion, and PDR are to be low.

Distance: The distance between the sender U_S and the receiver U_R is calculated through the feasible paths. Moreover, the distance matrix is expressed in Eq. (2), and it is denoted as $D(m * n)$

$$(m * n) = \begin{bmatrix} d_{M_{c1},u_1} d_{M_{c1},u_2} \cdots\cdots d_{M_{c1},u_n} \\ d_{M_{c2},u_1} d_{M_{c2},u_2} \cdots\cdots d_{M_{c2},u_n}. \\ \vdots \\ \vdots \\ d_{M_{cm},u_1} d_{M_{cm},u_2} \cdots\cdots d_{M_{cm},u_n} \end{bmatrix} \tag{2}$$

where, d_{M_c} indicates the Euclidean distance among a sender node U_S and the receiver U_R. In addition, the position of the sender and the receiver node is indicated as y and z, and the Euclidean distance $\left(d_{g,h}\right)$ is determined in Eq. (3).

$$d_{g,h} = \sqrt{(g_y - h_y)^2 + (g_z - h_z)^2} \tag{3}$$

All elements in the matrix of distance specify the distance exists within the gth sender and the hth receiver node. The packet transmission takes place and the shortest path between the sender and the receiver is selected. The distance function is indicated as D and it should be low.

Energy model (E): The nodes in MANET are utilized to transmit and receive the data with high power. Every node is assumed with maximum powers in the setup phase. The nodes with higher energy are chosen during the path selection and the nodes with lower energy are not actively takes part in the routing process. Overall power consumption should be less during the data packet transfer. Still, the energy consumed $E_{cons.}$ depends on the security level and it is determined in Eq. (4).

$$E_{cons.} = SecurityLevel * DataPackets \tag{4}$$

Also the node's energy level after transferring the data packet is specified in Eq. (5).

$$E_{remain.} = E_{node.} - E_{cons.} \tag{5}$$

In Eq. (5), $E_{node.}$ denotes the energy of the node and $E_{remain.}$ indicates the node's remaining energy.

Packet Drop ratio (*PDR*)**:** PDR is the ratio of the count of hops to the overall network nodes. Further, the congestion, link state stability, and QoS are considered during the packet transmission mechanism.

Congestion *C***:** It is a significant problem in ad-hoc networks. When the count of packets maximizes beyond the limit, it is handled via network resources that provides degradation in network performance, which is stated as congestion. A network that is congested for one user is not necessarily congested for another user. It is an unwanted situation where the network faces the difficulty of more traffic than its rated capacity results in packet loss, bandwidth degradation, waste time and energy, etc.

Link State: It is taken into account than considering the path stability. The link stability is determined for selecting the optimal path at a particular time instance. The link state for any node y to node z is given in Eq. (6).

$$link(y, z) = tfinal - tInitial \tag{6}$$

In Eq. (6), *link* indicates the time duration among the initialization and breakage in link.

QoS: For MANETs, the QoS is a complex task due to the dynamic behaviour of the network topology. QoS is the service used to allow the users and network applications to access the novel capabilities. The QoS of the packet needs to be higher for ceaseless packet transmission. Moreover, QoS network is determined based on the guaranteed count of data that a network transfers from one place to another within a certain time.

Security: The security constraint [32] is designed based on the security rank (s_{Rank}) and security demand (s_{Dem}) of the nodes. If the node is said to be more secure, only it satisfies the condition $s_{Dem} \leq s_{Rank}$. The security constraint model is defined based on the risk probability, and it is given in Eq. (7).

$$Risk_{prob} = \begin{cases} 0 & if \quad s_{Dem} - s_{Rank} \leq 0 \\ 1 - e^{\frac{(s_{Dem} - s_{Rank})}{2}} & if\ 0 < s_{Dem} - s_{Rank} \leq 1 \\ 1 - e^{\frac{3(s_{Dem} - s_{Rank})}{2}} & if\ 1 < s_{Dem} - s_{Rank} \leq 2 \\ 1 & if\ 2 < s_{Dem} - s_{Rank} \leq 5 \end{cases} \tag{7}$$

Based on the difference among the s_{Dem} and s_{Rank}, the risk probability is assigned for a node that evaluates its security level.

Trust level: The trust relation among the sensor nodes is determined. The trust level includes three types they are.

- Direct Trust
- Indirect Trust
- Social Trust

(i) *Direct Trust:* The direct trust is determined as in Eq. (8).

$$B_r(i,j) = \frac{W(i,j)}{W(i)} \tag{8}$$

In Eq. (8), $B_r(i,j) \in [0, 1]$, $W(i,j)$ indicates the degree of strength among neighboring sensors i and j, $W(i)$ indicates the overall connection strength between i and j at neighborhood distance. The similarity among neighboring nodes is computed through establishing the entire count of neighboring sensor nodes among 2 sensor nodes.

$$B(i,j) = B_r(i,j) + B_x(i,j) \tag{9}$$

$$B_x(i,j) = \sum\nolimits_{\hat{t} \in N(j) \in N(j)} \left(I\left(\hat{t}\right)\right)^{-1} \tag{10}$$

where, $I\left(\hat{t}\right)$ indicates the penetration degree of $\hat{t}$ among i and j.

(ii) *Indirect Trust:* The indirect trust is determined as in Eq. (11).

$$I_x(i,j) = \begin{cases} k\hat{t}\dfrac{B_{\max} - B_{i,j} + 1}{B_{\max}} & \text{if } B_{i,j} \le B_{\max} \\ 0 & \text{if } B_{i,j} > B_{\max} \end{cases} \tag{11}$$

The intermediate route length is calculated using $k\hat{t} = kk\left(B(i, i_1), B(i_1, i_2), \ldots\ldots, B\left(i_{\hat{n}}, j\right)\right)$ and B_{max} indicates the trust among sensor nodes with less distance.

(iii) *Social Trust:* The social trust is specified in Eq. (12).

$$ST(i,j) = f(I(i,j), G(i,j), L(i,j)) \tag{12}$$

where, $I(i,j)$ indicates the communication interval among the time duration or nodes, $G(i,j)$ denotes the communication duration or the time duration of sensor node i and j, and $L(i,j)$ refers to the context of communication that represents the communication scenario. Moreover, the overall trust is determined in Eq. (13).

$$Trust = B(i,j) + I_x(i,j) + ST(i,j) \tag{13}$$

5 Self-improved Particle Swarm Optimization Algorithm for Optimal Path Selection

5.1 Proposed SI-PSO Model

Although, the existing PSO model offers better computational efficiency with robustness and satisfactory outcomes to control parameters; still, it easily falls into local optimum from the space that affects the optimization process. For overcoming the drawbacks of traditional PSO model, the proposed SI-PSO model intends to make some enhancement on PSO that offers optimum results and better convergence. Moreover, self-enhancement is established to be capable in traditional optimization algorithms [26–31]. The objective function is fed as input to the proposed SI-PSO approach for optimal path selection and efficient data transmission. The PSO [27] algorithm was determined based on the social behavior of fish schooling and bird flocking. Every bird has a velocity and position at any time instant a. The position update is determined in Eq. (14).

$$P_o(a+1) = P_o(a) + v_o(a+1) \tag{14}$$

The proposed velocity update is given in Eq. (15).

$$v_o(a+1) = q_o v_o(a) + Z_1 e_1 (P_o^{best}(a) - P_o(a)) + Z_2 e_2 (K - Y_o(a)) \tag{15}$$

The position vector, memory vector and the velocity vector are determined as P_o, P_o^{best} and v_o, correspondingly. The random values are denoted as e_1 and e_2 in uniform manner in the interval of [0,1]. The random variables e_1 and e_2 are initialized as a single value in the PSO, they are initialized as follows.

$$e_1 = rand(A, Q) \tag{16}$$

$$e_2 = rand(A, Q) \tag{17}$$

In Eq. (16), A denotes size of the solution, and Q denotes the count of Nodes.

Moreover, K is used instead of P_o^{best} to maximize the accuracy of positional update. In the PSO, the P_o^{best} is repeated 10 times for each solution and this might increase the execution time while the count of solutions is higher. Since, the first best solution with K is kept and the rest of the solution is shuffled based on the fitness. The possibility of positional update is higher.

```
for ĩ = 2: A
        ã(1,:) = P_o^best;
    idx = randperm(node)
        X(1,:) = (1,:);
X(1, idx) = ã(1,:);
End
```

The accelerating constant is indicated as Z_1 and Z_2. The best solution is explored by all particles is determined as P_o^{best} and q_o specifies the inertia weight of the particle. At last, if the fitness of the next solution $(a+1)$ is greater than the fitness of the current solution, then the acceleration constants Z_1 and Z_2 are determined in Eq. (18) and Eq. (19).

$$Z_1 = Z_1 + 1 \tag{18}$$

$$Z_2 = Z_2 + 1 \tag{19}$$

If not, then the value of Z_1 and Z_2 are determined in Eq. (20) and Eq. (21).

$$Z_1 = Z_1 - 0.2 \tag{20}$$

$$Z_2 = Z_2 - 0.2 \tag{21}$$

The pseudo-code of the adopted SI-PSO technique is determined in Algorithm 1.

Algorithm 1: Proposed SI-PSO algorithm		
Initialize P_o, P_o^{best} and v_o		
The random values e_1 and e_2 are initialized as $e_1 = rand(A, Q)$; $e_2 = rand(A, Q)$;		
The position updated in Eq. (14)		
The velocity update is determined in Eq. (15).		
Find the K value		
	for $\tilde{i} = 2 : A$	
	$\tilde{a}(1, :) = P_o^{best}$;	
	$idx = randperm(node)$	
	$X(1, :) = (1, :)$; $X(1, idx) = \tilde{a}(1, :)$;	
	End	
	If $(Fit(a + 1)) > (Fit(a))$	
		Z_1 and Z_2 is calculated in Eq. (18) and Eq. (19)
	Else	
		Z_1 and Z_2 is calculated in Eq. (20) and Eq. (21)
	End	
	end	
Termination		

6 Results and Discussion

6.1 Simulation Procedure

The proposed trust aware secure routing with SI-PSO model in MANET was executed in MATLAB and the resultants were determined. Accordingly, the proposed SI-PSO method was computed to the extant approaches including PSO [27], GA [33], GWO [35], and WOA [34], respectively. Further, the analysis was made with respect to convergence analysis, network congestion level, E2E delay, energy consumption, link state Network lifetime, packet drop ratio, trust and risk analysis respectively for the number of nodes 100, 150, 175 and 200.

6.2 Analysis on Energy Consumption

The analysis on energy consumption based on different count of nodes is represented in Fig. 3. Moreover, the energy consumption is a major concern in the routing network. Further, the proposed SI-PSO model attains lowest energy (~0.1 $\times 10^5$) with better performance than other existing models for node count 200. Thus, for all number of nodes variation, the adopted scheme exhibits the minimal energy consumption and becomes efficient for routing.

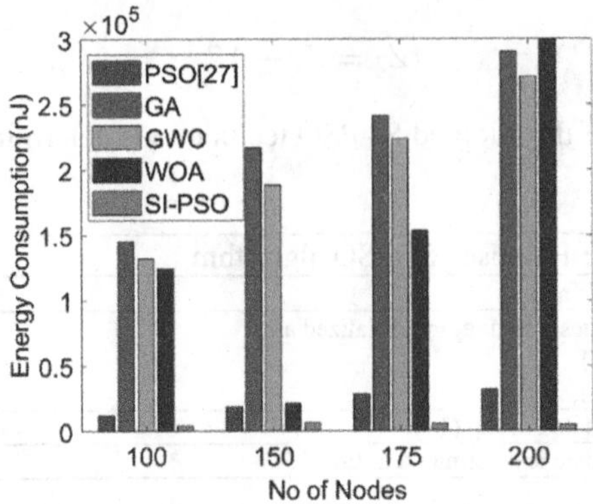

Fig. 3. Analysis on Energy consumption for adopted and traditional Models

6.3 Analysis on Network Congestion Level

Figure 4 illustrates the network congestion level of the presented scheme to the existing approaches. e GA approach has the highest level of congestion for node 100, 150, and 175; while the presented SI-PSO work has the lowest congestion level. In addition, the presented work has the lowest congestion level (~2) for node count 200 than traditional PSO, GA, GWO, and WOA approach, correspondingly.

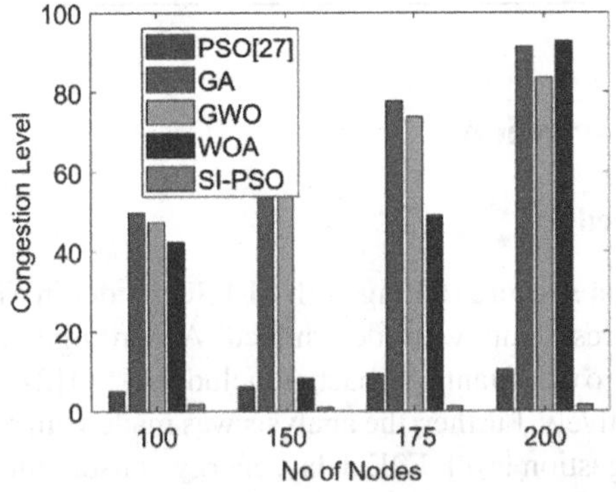

Fig. 4. Analysis on Network congestion for adopted and traditional Models

6.4 Analysis on Network Lifetime

The Lifetime ratio is utilized as the significant parameter in establishing the outcomes of adopted work. The network life span provides a decision regarding the network's transmission capability. The analysis on network lifetime by varying count of nodes is given in Fig. 5. Furthermore, the adopted SI-PSO model provides highest network lifetime than the existing works. In Fig. 5, the adopted SI-PSO model has attained (~200) alive nodes with better performance for node count 200 than other existing approaches like PSO, GS, GWO, and WOA, respectively.

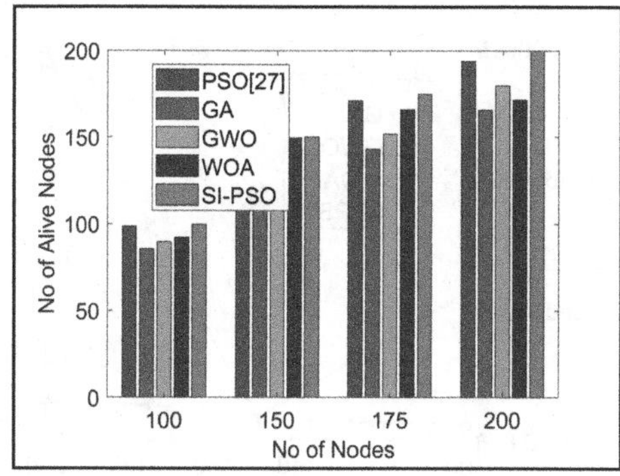

Fig. 5. Analysis on Network lifetime for adopted and traditional Models

6.5 Analysis on Link State

The graphical analysis on links state is illustrated in Fig. 6. In a routing table, the routes contain entries for the next hop neighbor and the destination node. The link-state should be lower to obtain an efficient routing. The presented SI-PSO model has shown the lowest link-state than the existing one for node 200. Further, the presented work has the lowest value (~0.1) than traditional PSO, GA, GWO, and WOA approach, correspondingly.

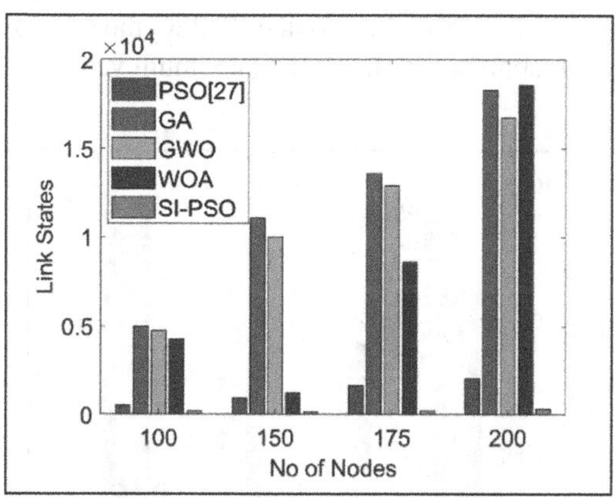

Fig. 6. Analysis on network link state for adopted and traditional models

6.6 Evaluation on E2E Delay

The E2E delay of the adopted scheme to the traditional work is exhibited in Fig. 7. The presented work has the lowest E2E delay than the existing works for all node count. In addition, the proposed SI-PSO model has attained minimum delay (~0.668) than the existing models like PSO, GA, GWO, and WOA, correspondingly for node count 140.

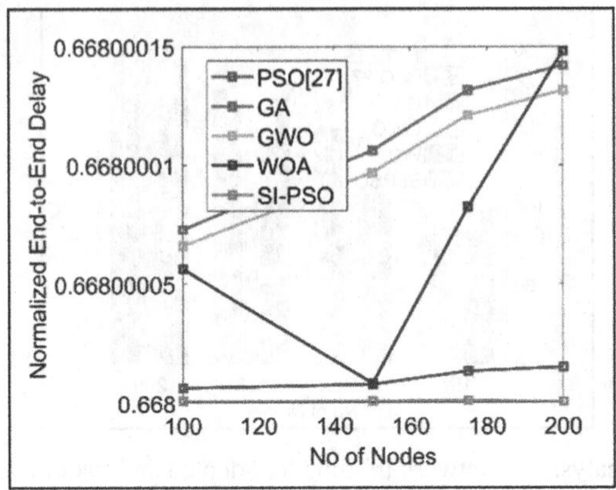

Fig. 7. Analysis on E2E delay for adopted and traditional models

6.7 Analysis on Packet Drop Ratio

The analysis of packet drop ratio is exhibited in Fig. 8. It is the ratio of the count of neighbours to the count of the overall nodes. The packet drop ratio should be minimal for a successful data transmission of packets from the source to the target. Likewise, the presented SI-PSO model attains the lowest value (~2) than other traditional models like PSO (~8), GA (~90), GWO (~80), and WOA (~52), respectively for the count of node175. As the node count = 200, the adopted SI-PSO model attained the least value and hence the traditional approaches shows the maximum value.

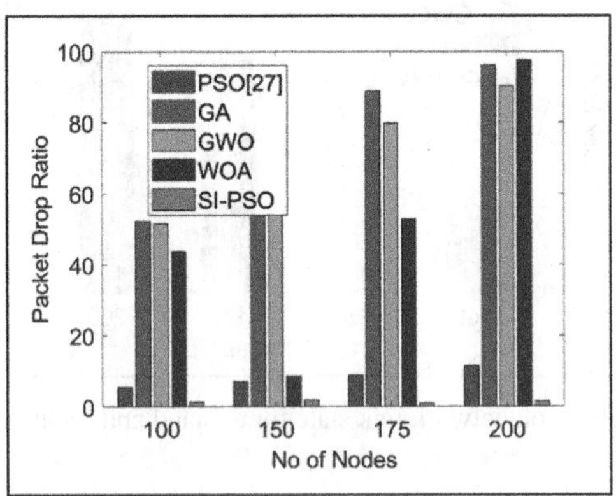

Fig. 8. Analysis on packet drop ratio for adopted and traditional models

6.8 Risk Analysis

The risk analysis for varying count of nodes is illustrated in Fig. 9. This say about the probability of the risk linked in identifying the optimal path and transmission of the data packets. Moreover, the proposed SI-PSO model holds superior outcomes than other traditional models for node 100. In all the cases, the adopted model exhibits the least value as the best model in MANET for trust aware secure routing.

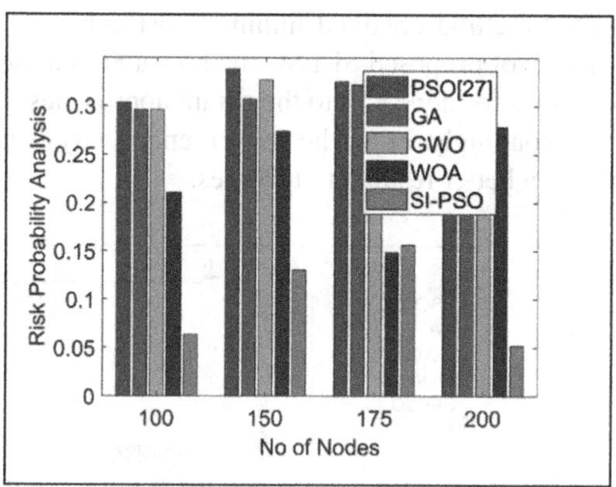

Fig. 9. Risk analysis for adopted and traditional models

6.9 Trust Analysis

Figure 10 illustrates the trust analysis of the presented scheme to the existing approaches. Here, the trust values of the proposed work are higher for all node count. In addition, the proposed SI-PSO approach achieved highest trust value for node 175; while the traditional models like PSO, GA, GWO, and WOA has lowest trust value. Further, the presented work has maximum trust value (~5.8) for node count 150 than traditional PSO, GA, GWO, and WOA approach, respectively.

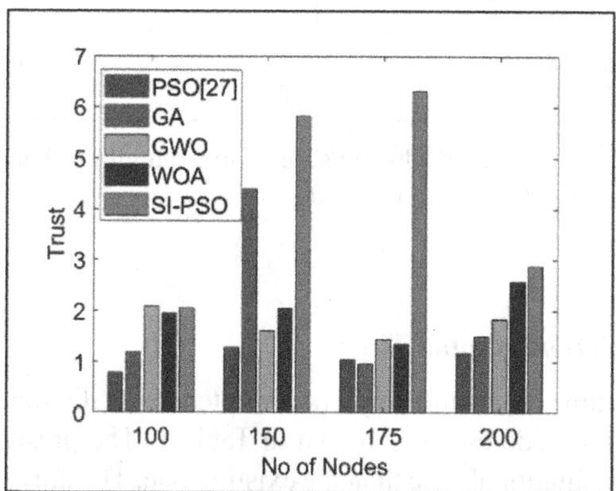

Fig. 10. Trust Analysis for adopted and traditional models

6.10 Convergence Analysis

The convergence analysis of adopted SI-PSO scheme to the extant approaches for different iterations ranges from 0, 20, 40, 60, 80, and 100 is demonstrated in Fig. 11. Fig shows a decrement of cost function with increased iterations. In the graph, it is clearly shown that the adopted SI-PSO method obtained minimal cost values than other compared methods. The performance of proposed SI-PSO method at 80th iteration is (~1.2) lower values with better outcomes for node 150 to the extant approaches including PSO, GA, GWO and WOA, correspondingly. From the convergence analysis graph, the proposed SI-PSO method has shown better resultant outcomes.

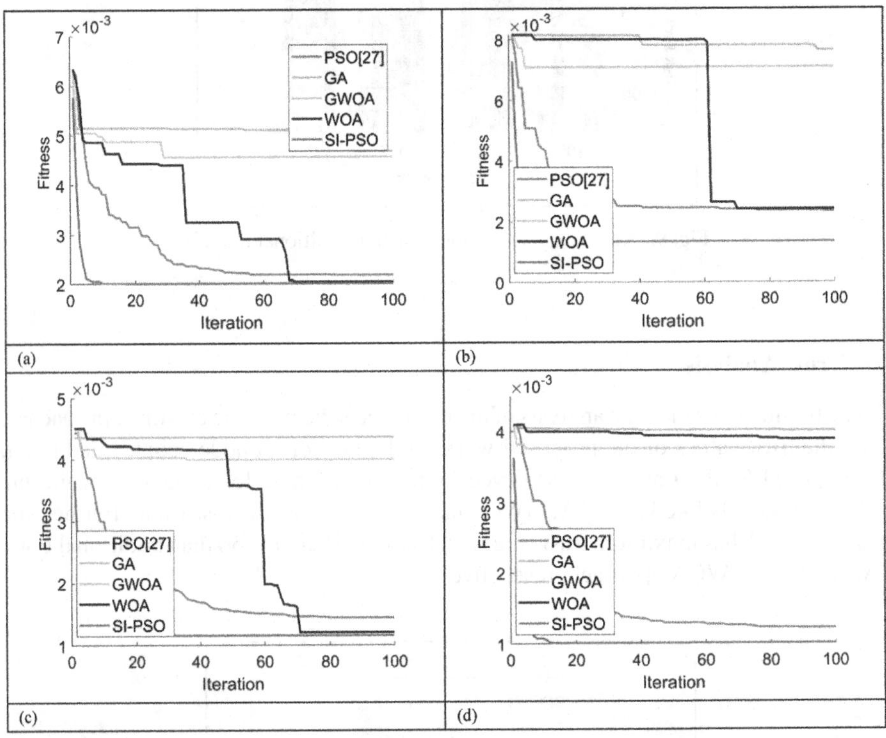

Fig. 11. Convergence analysis of the adopted scheme to the traditional approaches for (a) node 100, (b) node 150, (c) node 175, and (d) node 200

6.11 Analysis on Computational Time

The computational time consumed by the adopted SI-PSO model and the extant approaches for varying node count is shown in Table 1. The presented SI-PSO model shows the lowest computational time than the existing one. The unit of the computational time is in Seconds. In addition, the proposed SI-PSO method is (~36.85) lower values with better outcomes for node 150 than the traditional models PSO, GWO and WOA, correspondingly.

Table 1. Evaluation on computational time

Approach	Node-100	Node-150	Node-175	Node-200
PSO [27]	17.36362	37.4027	46.68733	52.28492
GA [33]	14.61194	32.91267	41.94701	52.00466
GWO [35]	140.2613	299.1416	377.7777	509.5856
WOA [34]	169.9888	292.6161	400.7701	527.9015
SI-PSO	16.94271	36.83512	47.20496	54.39663

7 Conclusion

This paper has introduced a new trust-aware routing in MANET that ensures the trust level among the nodes. For this, a new trust rate estimation process was introduced based on energy and mobility of nodes exist. Thereby, a SI-PSO algorithm was proposed for choosing the optimal trust aware route for data transmission. The optimal route selection was performed by considering certain parameters like trust rate (security), PDR, distance, congestion, energy, and as well. The performance of the adopted work was examined to the existing schemes regarding Energy, Delay, and Network Lifetime. Further, the proposed SI-PSO model attained lowest energy (~0.1) with better performance than other existing models for node count 200. Moreover, the GA approach has the highest level of congestion for node 100, 150, and 175; while the presented SI-PSO work has the lowest congestion level. Likewise, the presented SI-PSO model attained the lowest value (~2) than other traditional models like PSO (~8), GA (~90), GWO (~80), and WOA (~52), respectively for the count of node 175. Further, the mean energy of the presented SI-PSO model was the lowest value with better outcomes for node 200 than extant models like PSO, GA, GWO, and WOA, correspondingly.

References

1. Usha, M.S., Ravishankar, K.C.: Implementation of trust-based novel approach for security enhancements in MANETs. SN Comput. Sci. **2**(4), 1–7 (2021). https://doi.org/10.1007/s42979-021-00628-2
2. Devi, V.S., Hegde, N.P.: Multipath security aware routing protocol for MANET based on trust enhanced cluster mechanism for lossless multimedia data transfer. Wireless Pers. Commun. **100**(3), 923–940 (2018). https://doi.org/10.1007/s11277-018-5358-5
3. Sathyaraj, P., Rukmani Devi, D.: Designing the routing protocol with secured IoT devices and QoS over Manet using trust-based performance evaluation method. J. Ambient. Intell. Humaniz. Comput. **12**(7), 6987–6995 (2020). https://doi.org/10.1007/s12652-020-02358-4
4. Merlin, R.T., Ravi, R.: Novel trust based energy aware routing mechanism for mitigation of black hole attacks in MANET. Wireless Pers. Commun. **104**(4), 1599–1636 (2019). https://doi.org/10.1007/s11277-019-06120-8
5. Anitha Josephine, J., Senthilkumar, S.: Tanimoto support vector regressive linear program boost based node trust evaluation for secure communication in MANET. Wireless Pers. Commun. **117**(4), 2973–2993 (2020). https://doi.org/10.1007/s11277-020-07209-1

6. Ambekar, R.K., Kolekar, U.D.: T-TOHIP: trust-based topology-hiding multipath routing in mobile ad hoc network. Evol. Intel. 1–15 (2019). https://doi.org/10.1007/s12065-019-00280-z
7. Rajeswari, A.R., Kulothungan, K., Ganapathy, S., Kannan, A.: A trusted fuzzy based stable and secure routing algorithm for effective communication in mobile adhoc networks. Peer-to-Peer Netw. Appl. **12**(5), 1076–1096 (2019). https://doi.org/10.1007/s12083-019-00766-8
8. Kukreja, D., Sharma, D.K.: T-SEA: trust based secure and energy aware routing protocol for mobile ad hoc networks. Int. J. Inf. Technol. 1–15 (2019). https://doi.org/10.1007/s41870-019-00392-w
9. Veeraiah, N., Krishna, B.T.: An approach for optimal-secure multi-path routing and intrusion detection in MANET. Evol. Intel. 1–15 (2020). https://doi.org/10.1007/s12065-020-00388-7
10. Tripathy, B.K., Jena, S.K., Bera, P., Das, S.: An adaptive secure and efficient routing protocol for mobile ad hoc networks. Wireless Pers. Commun. **114**(2), 1339–1370 (2020). https://doi.org/10.1007/s11277-020-07423-x
11. Nivedita, V., Nandhagopal, N.: Improving QoS and efficient multi-hop and relay based communication frame work against attacker in MANET. J. Ambient. Intell. Humaniz. Comput. **12**(3), 4081–4091 (2020). https://doi.org/10.1007/s12652-020-01787-5
12. Jamaesha, S.S., Bhavani, S.: A secure and efficient cluster based location aware routing protocol in MANET. Clust. Comput. **22**(2), 4179–4186 (2018). https://doi.org/10.1007/s10586-018-1703-4
13. Hemalatha, R., Umamaheswari, R., Jothi, S.: LF distribution and equilibrium optimizer based fuzzy logic for multipath routing in MANET. Wireless Pers. Commun. **120**(2), 1837–1861 (2021). https://doi.org/10.1007/s11277-021-08537-6
14. Tamil Selvi, P., Suresh GhanaDhas, C.: A novel algorithm for enhancement of energy efficient zone based routing protocol for MANET. Mobile Netw. Appl. **24**(2), 307–317 (2018). https://doi.org/10.1007/s11036-018-1043-x
15. Desai, A.M., Jhaveri, R.H.: Secure routing in mobile Ad hoc networks: a predictive approach. Int. J. Inf. Technol. **11**(2), 345–356 (2018). https://doi.org/10.1007/s41870-018-0188-y
16. Janani, V.S., Manikandan, M.S.K.: Efficient trust management with Bayesian-Evidence theorem to secure public key infrastructure-based mobile ad hoc networks. EURASIP J. Wirel. Commun. Netw. **2018**(1), 1–27 (2018). https://doi.org/10.1186/s13638-017-1001-5
17. Rajashanthi, M., Valarmathi, K.: A secure trusted multipath routing and optimal fuzzy logic for enhancing QoS in MANETs. Wireless Pers. Commun. **112**(1), 75–90 (2019). https://doi.org/10.1007/s11277-019-07016-3
18. Pushpalatha, K., Karthikeyan, M.: A generalized framework for disruption tolerant secure opportunistic routing during emergency situations using MANETs. Clust. Comput. **22**(4), 9905–9913 (2018). https://doi.org/10.1007/s10586-018-1849-0
19. Kukreja, D., Dhurandher, S.K., Reddy, B.V.R.: Power aware malicious nodes detection for securing MANETs against packet forwarding misbehavior attack. J. Ambient. Intell. Humaniz. Comput. **9**(4), 941–956 (2017). https://doi.org/10.1007/s12652-017-0496-2
20. Nagendranath, M.V.S.S., Babu, A.R.: An efficient mobility aware stable and secure clustering protocol for mobile ADHOC networks. Peer-to-Peer Netw. Appl. **13**(4), 1185–1192 (2020). https://doi.org/10.1007/s12083-019-00868-3
21. Kushwah, R., Tapaswi, S., Kumar, A.: A detailed study on internet connectivity schemes for mobile ad Hoc network. Wireless Pers. Commun. **104**(4), 1433–1471 (2018). https://doi.org/10.1007/s11277-018-6093-7
22. Srivastava, A., Gupta, S.K., Najim, M., Sahu, N., Aggarwal, G., Mazumdar, B.D.: DSSAM: digitally signed secure acknowledgement method for mobile ad hoc network. EURASIP J. Wirel. Commun. Netw. **2021**(1), 1–29 (2021). https://doi.org/10.1186/s13638-021-01894-7

23. Kumar, S.: Prediction of node and link failures in mobile ad hoc network using hello based path recovery routing protocol. Wireless Pers. Commun. **115**(1), 725–744 (2020). https://doi.org/10.1007/s11277-020-07596-5
24. Vatambeti, R.: A novel wolf based trust accumulation approach for preventing the malicious activities in mobile ad hoc network. Wireless Pers. Commun. **113**(4), 2141–2166 (2020). https://doi.org/10.1007/s11277-020-07316-z
25. Selvakumar, K., Seethalakshmi, N.: Secure group key management protocol for mobile ad hoc networks. Clust. Comput. **22**(5), 11989–11995 (2018). https://doi.org/10.1007/s10586-017-1535-7
26. Rajakumar, B.R.: Impact of static and adaptive mutation techniques on genetic algorithm. Int. J. Hybrid Intell. Syst. **10**(1), 11–22 (2013). https://doi.org/10.3233/HIS-120161
27. Manickavelu, D., Vaidyanathan, R.U.: Particle swarm optimization (PSO)-based node and link lifetime prediction algorithm for route recovery in MANET. EURASIP J. Wireless Commun. Netw. **2014** (2014)
28. Rajakumar, B.R.: Static and adaptive mutation techniques for genetic algorithm: a systematic comparative analysis. Int. J. Comput. Sci. Eng. **8**(2), 180–193 (2013). https://doi.org/10.1504/IJCSE.2013.053087
29. Swamy, S.M., Rajakumar, B.R., Valarmathi, I.R.: Design of hybrid wind and photovoltaic power system using opposition-based genetic algorithm with cauchy mutation. In: IET Chennai Fourth International Conference on Sustainable Energy and Intelligent Systems (SEISCON 2013). Chennai, India (2013). https://doi.org/10.1049/ic.2013.0361
30. George, A., Rajakumar, B.R.: APOGA: an adaptive population pool size based genetic algorithm. In: AASRI Procedia - 2013 AASRI Conference on Intelligent Systems and Control (ISC 2013), vol. 4, pp. 288–296 (2013). https://doi.org/10.1016/j.aasri.2013.10.043
31. Rajakumar, B.R., George, A.: A new adaptive mutation technique for genetic algorithm. In: Proceedings of IEEE International Conference on Computational Intelligence and Computing Research (ICCIC), pp. 1–7, December 18–20. Coimbatore, India (2012). https://doi.org/10.1109/ICCIC.2012.6510293
32. Liu, H., Abraham, A., Snášel, V., McLoone, A.: Swarm scheduling approaches for work-flow applications with security constraints in distributed data-intensive computing environments. Inf. Sci. **192**, 228–243 (2012)
33. Vrionis, T.D., Koutiva, X.I., Vovos, N.A.: A genetic algorithm-based low voltage ride-through control strategy for grid connected doubly fed induction wind generators. IEEE Trans. Power Syst. **29**(3) (2014)
34. Mirjalili, S., Lewis, A.: The whale optimization algorithm. Adv. Eng. Softw. **95**, 51–67 (2016)
35. Mirjalili, S., Mirjalili, S.M.: Andrew Lewis. Grey Wolf Optimizer" Advances in Engineering Software, vol. 69, pp. 46–61 (2014)
36. Murugan, T.K.S.: Hybrid weed-particle swarm optimization algorithm and C- mixture for data publishing. Multimedia Res. **2**(3), 33–42 (2019)
37. Srinivas, V., Santhirani, C.: Hybrid particle swarm optimization-deep neural network model for speaker recognition. Multimedia Res. **3**(1), 1–10 (2020)
38. Cristin, R., Gladiss Merlin, N.R., Ramanathan, L., Vimala, S.: Image forgery detection using back propagation neural network model and particle swarm optimization algorithm. Multimedia Res. **3**(1), 21–32 (2020)
39. Rajeshkumar, G.: Hybrid particle swarm optimization and firefly algorithm for distributed generators placements in radial distribution system. J. Comput. Mech. Power Syst. Control **2**(1), 41–48 (2019)
40. Gayathri Devi, K.S.: Hybrid genetic algorithm and particle swarm optimization algorithm for optimal power flow in power system. J. Comput. Mech. Power Syst. Control **2**(2), 31–37 (2019)

41. Roy, R.G.: Economic dispatch problem in power system using hybrid Particle Swarm optimization and enhanced Bat optimization algorithm. J. Comput. Mech. Power Syst. Control **3**(3) (2020)
42. AlBalushi, F.M.: Chaotic based hybrid artificial sheep algorithm - particle swarm optimization for energy and secure aware in WSN. J. Network. Commun. Syst. **2**(2), 37–48 (2019)
43. Deotale, N., Kolekar, U., Kondelwar, A.: Self-adaptive particle swarm optimization for optimal transmit antenna selection. J. Netw. Commun. Syst. **3**(1), 1–10 (2020)
44. Haridas, S., Prasath, A.R.: Enhancement of network lifetime in MANET: improved particle swarm optimization for delayless and secured geographic routing. J. Adv. Res. Dyn. Control Syst. **12** (07) (2020)

Emulation and Analysis of Software-Defined Networks for the Detection of DDoS Attacks

Sanjana Prasad[1], Ashwani Prasad[1](✉), Karmel Arockiasamy[1], and Xiaohui Yuan[2]

[1] Vellore Institute of Technology, Chennai 600127, Tamil Nadu, India
{sanjana.prasad2019,ashwani.prasad2019}@vitstudent.ac.in,
karmel.a@vit.ac.in

[2] University of North Texas, Denton, TX 76203, USA
xiaohui.yuan@unt.edu

Abstract. Development in digital infrastructure have resulted in distributed denial of service attacks to become increasingly widespread and target large number of host machines in organizations, that crashes down access when requested by the user. Such attacks when deployed on a larger scale, can result in a wastage of time and resources. With increasing complexity, these attacks have become more sophisticated and complex, leading to the emergence that has led to the rise of several algorithms and tools, that uses SDN (Software-Defined Networking) networks, in the domain of network security. Through this paper, we have surveyed what is a DDoS attack, its different forms and the use of software-defined networking tools such as Mininet and HPE VAN SDN controller, to analyze some basic topologies. Four different topologies were created namely Single, Linear, Tree and Torus, and experiments were performed to analyze the flow of traffic in these topology networks. From these experiments performed, the ping statistics in terms of minimum, maximum, average and minimum deviation Round-Trip Time (RTT) in milliseconds were computed for each of the given topologies. The values obtained as ping statistics were tabulated and represented graphically. A visual analysis between number of nodes and average round-trip time for the three topologies were done graphically. We have compared and analyzed several open-source tools, on their basis of efficiency of detecting the attack. Apart from this, a study of several instances of DDoS attacks in organizations regarding the mitigations and step initiated to withstand the intensity of these attacks, has also been done.

Keywords: Distributed denial of service · Software-defined networks · Mininet · OpenFlow · Cyber-attacks · Topology

1 Introduction

With booming technologies such as big data, cloud computing and SaaS (Software as A Service) becoming emergent, we have reached a data rich era, where organizations utilize and mine tons of data from various sources to analyze and offer a variety of services as

Published by Springer Nature Switzerland AG 2022
E. J. Neuhold et al. (Eds.): ICCCSP 2022, IFIP AICT 651, pp. 213–231, 2022.
https://doi.org/10.1007/978-3-031-11633-9_16

per the requirements specified by the customers. With the usage of data mining, customer segmentation and predictive analytics having a rising trend, there is a burgeoning need for a well-defined-network infrastructure that will be able to handle and facilitate the needs and requirements of such complex technologies in order to be deployed in a turbulent manner, to ensure its smooth functioning. Software-defined networks are an interface that leverages the use of software modelling in the form of interfaces and applications to interact with the base hardware and regulate the traffic mechanism in a traditional network. By using such an organized paradigm, we are able to virtualize the network, in order to fulfil the demands of any complex and robust technologies that require a smooth, hassle-free functioning network. Though, the demands of a well efficient network infrastructure have been emphasized, there is also a pressing need, for a well-developed, robust and a fool-proof system that can successfully detect any kind of threat and malicious activity that can cause hindrance to a network.

The most common attacks that are launched on most of the services today are the Denial of Service (DoS) and the Distributed Denial of Service (DDoS). When such attacks are successfully launched, they target a particular system network that could potentially cause a system to temporarily shut down or crash, restricting access to the users, intending to avail the service [1]. This task of suspending the service is achieved by increasing the traffic at the target host, thereby jamming the network by transmitting data packets that trigger breakdown. In this manner, a successful DoS attack launched denies access to services requested by the user. Though the severity of such an attack may not be critical, it can result in hefty loss of time and money. A DDoS attack is a version of a DoS attack, that deploys multiple hosts, for flooding the network with humongous traffic. In order to achieve a voluminous scale of attack, The attacks are launched using crawlers and botnets, these botnets can be used to leverage substantial amounts of infected machines, to flood the host machines with voluminous traffic. A botnet, comprises of several devices that are connected as a network, these devices could be an IoT device or a PC etc., wherein the security is controlled by a third party. Though DDoS attack is a type of DoS attack, it is used on a large scale due to its innate features, that sets it apart. When launched, a DDoS attack, shall be executed on a massive scale, due to a vast network of infected computers or a zombie army, controlled by the attacker. This makes it difficult to detect the location of the attacking party and the target host machine, shall find it tough to detect the incoming traffic, due to the random distribution of attacking systems [2]. The disastrous impacts and outcomes, its diversity, and several types of these attacks, have resulted in the design and evolutions of systems, that can make analysis, detection, and mitigation of these attacks on the top most priority [3].

Apart from various methodologies that include the implementation of algorithms for detecting the DDoS attacks, there have been many advancements that have leveraged the use of software-defined networks (SDNs). Many methodologies have proposed the usage of solutions with SDNs, leading to widespread deployment in the field of cyber security, as it enables the central control of the network by being programmed manually and also controls and distributes incoming traffic [4]. Such a technology enables dynamic network configuration to facilitate the network performance and promote efficient management similar to a cloud computing environment.

The main outcomes of this paper can be summarized as follows:

- Study and analyze the different varieties of DDoS attacks and hence survey the various kinds of SDN controllers, that have been experimented to mitigate the attack.
- Study and understand the topologies of virtual SDNs.
- Use of HPE VAN SDN controllers to study and experiment the topologies of virtual SDNs.
- Conduct experiments to study the topology created and analyze the runtime.

The rest of the paper is organized as follows: In Sect. 2, we shall survey and study the diverse types of DDoS attacks and a variety of mitigation techniques that have been deployed by organizations to handle large scale attacks and survey various topologies, tools used and the accuracy achieved in detecting the attack. Section 3 gives the details about the SDN architecture. Section 4 talks about tools used for conducting the experiments and its theoretical methods. Section 5 deals with the creation of the several network topologies. Section 6 illustrates two experiments which forms the base of this research work. Section 7 comprises of the tabulated results from the conducted experiments. Finally, Sect. 8 concludes this research work and gives ideas for future implementation.

2 Related Work

With the emergence of technologies, that support a well-developed infrastructure, the variety, complexity, and the diversity of the type of attacks also increases, leading to a plethora of tools and models that can handle the intensity of the attacks. The many types of DDOS attacks are: UDP flood, ICMP flood, SYN flood, Ping of Death (POD), NTP amplification and HTTP flood. With a diverse variety in DDoS attacks, there are several mitigation tools that are on the rise, that varies with the intensity of the attack. While most of the tools are similar in terms of architecture, the mitigation tools of DDoS can be classified into IRC based DDoS tools and agent-based DDoS tools [5]. In [6], Trinoo, is an open-source tool that has been widely used. It is a bandwidth depletion attack tool, that can launch a UDP flood attack against many IP addresses [7]. Trinoo is known to support IP address spoofing. The research work in [8] talks about TFN, Tribal Flood Network, offers the attacker an option to launch bandwidth and resource depletion attacks. It involves the usage of a command line interface, that serves as a medium of interaction between the attacker and the master program, but offers no encryption between the target host and the attacker.

Common attacks than can be launched by TFN are smurf, UDP flood, TCP Syn flood etc. Further, [9] elaborates on the TFN2K based on the TFN architecture and adds an encrypting message medium between various attack components [10]. The communication between the attacker and the master program takes place using an encryption algorithm CAST-256, that is key based [11]. In [12], Mstream is a tool that uses spoofing of TCP packets and ACK flags to attack the target network. It is a simple tool with point-to-point communication, wherein communication takes place through TCP and UDP packets and the primary node is connected via a telnet and zombie. A DOS attack can be designed as an attack launched to hinder the normal functionality of offering service to the clients [13]. A DoS attack is a resultant of a one-way blockage between the host user on one end and the target system on the other end, when there is an intentional blockage of service from one end. In such an attack, there is no damage that is caused to the data, but instead there is a denial to access the requested service at a particular instant of time.

Most DOS attacks are target the bandwidth of the network, which results in high traffic amongst the network, leading to more resources being consumed, due to which the request of the user is denied upon permission. SDN is an abstract networking paradigm, where in the entire system is seen as a distributed model, where there is a distinction between the data and the control planes. The data plane comprises of physical devices such as routers and switches, that are involved in transferring the data packets, while the control plane comprises of the controller. An SDN controller is usually the brain of the network, that will be able to adapt to changes and modifications, if any in the network, and performs several computations [14]. Depending upon the approach, protocols, and many other programmable features, Several SDN controllers can be contrasted on the basis of their performance using Chench, an OpenFlow tool [15]. An initial survey was conducted in [16] featuring a limited number of controllers such as Beacon, Maestro and NOX-MT where the only criteria for evaluation has been the performance, however these have become obsolete and have been replaced with new ones like OpenDayLight and FloodLight.

In [17], the criteria considered for the performance of SDN controllers: TLS support, GUI, RESTful API, Open-Flow Support etc. This study was done using the Analytic Hierarchy process, through an extrapolation mechanism that matches the parameter of these values to a pre-defined scale. Using this technique, five controllers have been compared and "RYU" was classified to be the most suitable as per requirements. Besides, the work presented in [18] surveyed SDN OpenFlow controllers, where in an analysis of widely used controllers such as NOX, POX and Beacon was done on the basis of their efficiency. It was therefore concluded that these controllers posed some threats when it came to security and presented mismatches with workload and beacon was one of the most productive controllers in terms of output. Lastly, [19] takes into account, the operating modes namely-Reactive and Proactive, wherein proactive presents a much greater performance than reactive, since instructions are loaded onto the switch in the initial phase of Proactive mode and the switch receives a data packet, with no rule in flow table.

As increased organizations adopt evolving technologies like big data, SaaS and cloud computing, organizations are constantly scaling up their network infrastructure, DDOS attacks are a common way of disruption by hackers. Since the attacks are easy to organize and execute, the intensity of recent attacks has become more complex with time. There have been multiple instances, where renowned organizations have witnessed such attacks, that has lasted for a longer time, many organizations are ramping up, leveraging the use of several algorithmic models to mitigate these attacks. Some of the infamous DDoS attacks are summarized in Table 1. In [20] An intrusion deduction system methodology was used to predict the malicious DDOS attacks in the SDN adaptation by using Machine Learning Algorithms namely, the Random Forest, Support Vector Machines, Decision tress and The Multiple Layer Perceptron. Scapy tool was used to launch the attack and Mininet tool with a POX controller tool performed the simulation. In [21] a classification algorithm and an entropy-based method was implemented, wherein, a two-class classification task distinguished normal flows from attacks.

Table 1. Some notable DDoS attacks in the past

Organization	Description of the attack
Amazon [22, 23], 2020, February	The attack was the largest attack, that had an intensity of 2.3 Tbps. Relied on attacking CLDAP servers, to amplify the traffic. AWS shield, was successfully used for mitigation
GitHub [24], 2018, February	This attack did not involve botnets, but a technique called meme caching was used, wherein a vulnerable server is a target and receives a spoofed request, that can intensify the traffic. The attack lasted for about 20 min, but was shortened owing to better mitigation plans and preparedness
DYN [25], 2016, October	An organization, that provided network database services to tech giants, massive botnets were created to launch an attack through interconnected IOT devices
BBC [26], 2015, December	A group called "New World Hacking" launched a 600 Gbps attack, and the tool used to launch it involved using cloud computing resources from two AWS servers

Apart from DDoS attacks, ransomware attacks are a widespread threat that poses risks to the confidential data secured in a network infrastructure. In such an attack, the attacker deploys various methodologies to capture the confidential data of the user to confiscate hefty amounts from the user. Such an attack, is more severe in intensity due to the financial losses incurred to the industries [27]. There are two different forms of Ransomware attack which are Locker and crypto ransomware [28]. Such attacks, impact the network infrastructure negatively and in turn confiscates confidential data. [29] talks about the usage of intelligent algorithms in detecting ransomware attacks. Such a methodology classifies the algorithms as random forests, decision trees and deep learning algorithms. In [30], Random Forest classifier potentially identifies threats in windows, Virtual Box and other android based operating systems. In [31] decision tree algorithms were proposed to detect ransomware in windows. Such an algorithm works by mining the features of the infected network through its traffic conversations. In [32] decision tree was used to detect multiple variants of ransomware attacks. In [33] a hybrid model comprising of Classical Auto Encoder (CAE), a Variational Auto Encoder (VAE) and a deep neural network with batch normalization detected ransomware threats in the Internet of Things (IoT).

3 SDN Architecture

This section explains about a typical software-defined networking architecture with its various components and layers. In addition, an account on the HPE VAN SDN Controller with its essential features is also provided.

A typical SDN Architecture comprises of the following components. Figure 1 shows a simple schematic representation of the components and the layers of the SDN architecture.

a) **Applications:** These are programs that are used to directly convey the network requirements and its characteristics to the central repository (SDN controller) via an interface.
b) **Controller:** It holds the responsibility of providing a view of the entire network layers to the applications.
c) **Datapath:** Expresses complete control of incoming and forwarding data in the form of packets across the entire network.
d) **Data Plane:** An intermediary interface between the controller and the datapath, that apart from facilitating communication, is responsible for processing data transfers and notifying the network about incoming packets and transfers.
e) **North-bound interfaces:** Provides an entire overview of the network and analyses the communication and requirements of the network.
f) **South-bound interfaces:** Enables communication between controllers and switches and other network nodes, which is with the lower-level components of the SDN.

The centralized controller assumes the responsibility of the control plane and distributes the flow of data onto the entire network. The OpenFlow protocol, between the control and the data plane facilitates the communication between the data plane and the control plane [34]. SDN experiments are usually stimulated out on an open-source platform, The Mininet, an application that runs in a virtualized environment. This tool assists with creating new topologies and networks in a virtualized environment, and allows users to visualize the live functioning and experimentations on a network at no costs, as the tools are open-source [35]. Since it runs on a virtualized network, it may be slower than the actual ones. SDN networks, enables users to interact with the network by creating topologies, and customizes it in a manner to detect any interactions in the network [36]. The Software-Defined Networking (SDN) architecture is built in a way that makes it unable to independently manage the network by itself.

The architecture relies on a software called as a SDN controller, which manages the network with the aid of network administrators. In other words, a SDN controller is an application in the SDN environment that manages the flow control for better management of the network and improved application performance. The SDN controller is usually deployed on a server where it runs and manages several protocols to mediate the network traffic between switches and hosts. In addition, the controller software is responsible for communicating with applications with northbound APIs and the network infrastructure with southbound APIs. In essence, SDN controller acts like the "brain" of a software-defined network. To perform all the necessary tasks of the controller, a SDN Controller Platform is required, which is essentially a set of assembled software modules. This is illustrated with an example in Fig. 2, wherein we have considered the control plane of the SDN architecture.

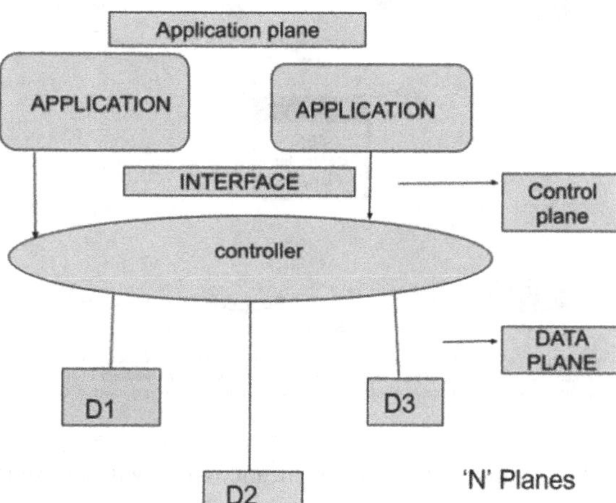

Fig. 1. Layers of SDN architecture

There are numerous SDN controllers used for dictating the behaviour of the network. Some of the prominent ones include ONOS [37], OpenDayight [38], RYU [39] and OpenMUL [40]. However, we discuss the features of am OpenFlow-enabled network controller, namely the HPE VAN SDN Controller, which shall be used for the experiment in this paper. The HPE VAN SDN Controller acts as a single point of control in an OpenFlow-enabled network, simplifying maintenance, provisioning, and orchestration while allowing the delivery of a new generation of application-based network services. The control and data planes of the network are separated in the Hewlett Packard Enterprise Software Defined Networking (SDN) architecture, centralizing network intelligence, and abstracting the underlying network infrastructure from applications. The industry-standard OpenFlow protocol is used by controller software to provide physical and virtual switches under its management. The visibility of network ports, connections, and topologies allows for centralized policy administration and more effective path selection based on a dynamic, global picture of the network. For both mobile clients and servers, this greatly simplifies the orchestration of multi-tenant systems and the enforcement of network policies.

The HPE VAN SDN Controller is a premium software which is versatile in its usage. It is designed to operate in several computing environments including the service provider, public cloud, campus, private cloud, and data centers. Some of the highlight features of the controller are as follows:

a) Provides a platform for delivering a wide range of network improvements that is enterprise-class.
b) Provides a controller architecture that is extendable, scalable, and robust.
c) Compliance with OpenFlow 1.0 and 1.3 protocols.

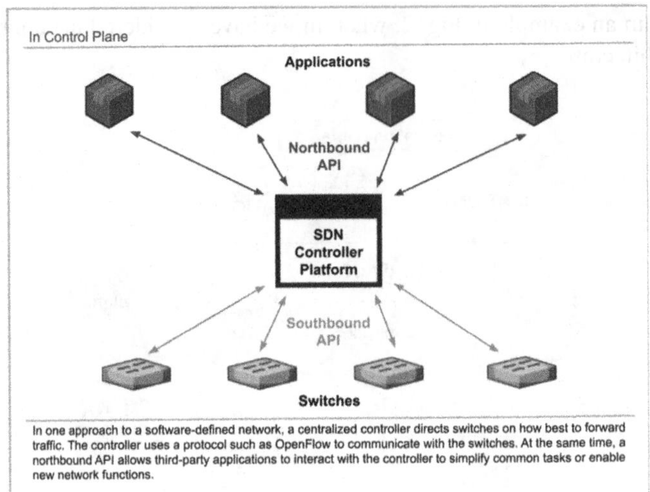

Fig. 2. SDN controller communicating with applications and switches using appropriate APIs

d) Hewlett Packard Enterprise and H3C OpenFlow-enabled switches are supported.
e) Uses a local or distant Keystone server for secure authentication.
f) Teams up controllers for a distributed platform scalability and high availability.
g) Common network services are provided by embedded applications.
h) Uses either specialized Java programs or general-purpose RESTful control interfaces, including functions to expand the controller REST API and UI, open APIs enable SDN application developers to create creative solutions that dynamically integrate business requirements to network infrastructure.
i) Integrates the HPE Intelligent Management Center (IMC) which manages and monitors the whole controller application life cycle, as well as providing better reporting and SDN network visibility [41].

The HPE VAN SDN Controller also provides a controller User Interface (UI) which acts the SDN Controller Platform for the users. The console UI can be used as follows:

a) View notifications and logs, as well as OpenFlow data including data flow details, topology of identified switches and end nodes, including shortest path, and OpenFlow classes that application programs have registered.
b) Acknowledge alerts, add, or enable applications, export log data, and enter licensing information, among other things.
c) Set key values for alert policies and other components of the SDN controller.
d) The SDN controller also has REST APIs that can be used to program or configure the controller, as well as construct applications that could be run on the controller.
e) There are some premium features (in the form of apps) offered by the controller that can be installed on the console from the HP SDN App Store.

4 Materials and Methods

To virtually demonstrate the effect of a DDoS attack in software-defined network, we shall need to create a virtual software-defined network first. In this section, we propose the materials and methods used to create a typical software-defined network. Section 4.1 describes the software technologies and tools that are used for creating such networks in contemporary times. The tools implemented concerning this research paper is also explained. Next, Sect. 4.2 and 4.3 highlights the advantages and limitations of the Mininet tool respectively.

4.1 Tools for Creating a Software-Defined Network

As far as this research paper is concerned, we discuss the features and functions of two software tools viz. The Mininet (a network emulator) and the HPE VAN SDN Controller (a SDN controller as discussed in Sect. 3), both of which shall be used in the topology creation process in Sect. 5. The reasons behind using these tools are:

- Mininet is an open-source tool which is easily accessible and can run on most of the Linux-based operating systems. For this research work the experiment was conducted in Linux environment.
- The commands in Mininet are easy to understand and implement.
- HPE VAN SDN controller is a user-friendly controller as compared to the rest.

Network emulators are software programs which runs on a standalone machine, and takes an abstract description of an actual network traffic. They are used by software developers for analyzing the response times, sensitivity to packet loss of clients and server applications and to emulate specific network access with different bit error rate, network dropouts, round-trip time, application dropouts and throughput. Emulators come in many different forms including integrated development environment appliances and browser-based network emulators. Some of the widely used network emulators include Mininet, UNetLab, Coolnix, Common Open Research Emulator (CORE), Marionnet and VNX. Since we shall be focusing on implementing a SDN network using the OpenFlow protocol, we choose Mininet as the network emulator to perform the experiments in this paper.

Mininet is a network emulator which has been extensively used for creating realistic virtual networks. It is a useful tool for the creating virtual networks based on Software-Defined Networking using OpenFlow and P4. This enables us to experiment with and understand the working mechanism of the same. Besides, it can also be used for running switch, kernel, controller, links, and application code on a single laptop, computer, or any other machine (virtual machines, cloud). The Mininet hosts run on a standard Linux network software. Because, it is easier to learn the functioning of Mininet, with its interactive command line interface, ease of customization, sharing and deployment, Mininet has been used by many researchers, teachers, and development groups for building networks, prototyping, debugging, testing, and experimenting with custom experimental networks [42].

4.2 Significant Characteristics of Mininet

a) Customizable, because it supports random custom network topologies, and consists of a basic set of parameterized topologies.
b) Extensible, because it a simple and extensible Python application programming interface (API) for creating and experimenting virtual networks. It also supports various other APIs.
c) Applicability, as the correct implementation source codes of prototype should be used in any arbitrary real network based on hardware requirements with negligible changes in the source code.
d) Interactivity, as the simulation of virtual networks should be comparable to real-time networks
e) Scalability, as the prototype networks must be capable to handle a vast network with numerous switches on a single machine.
f) Realistic, as the virtual prototype networks must resemble real-time networks with realistic behaviour, so that all applications and protocols can be used without any changes in the source code.
g) Shareable, as the created virtual networks should be easily shareable with other users or collaborators who can run the same and modify the experimental prototype as per their requirements.
h) Supporting concurrency, as it allows multiple developers to work independently on the same topology simultaneously.
i) Easily testable, as system-level regression tests, can be implemented with ease and get packaged. There is support of complex testing of the topology virtually, without any requirement of physical hardware [42, 43].

In addition to above characteristics, Mininet can be viewed as a package of useful features of various simulators, emulators, and hardware testbeds. In contrast to complete system virtualization procedure (emulator approach), Mininet boots faster, scales larger, provides more bandwidth, and can be installed easily. On the other hand, comparing to simulators, Mininet connects to realistic networks, runs practical and original code, and provides collaborative interface. Lastly, Mininet is better fit for use as compared to the hardware testbeds as it is inexpensive, always available, and can be easily reconfigured. It can also be easily restarted if any failure occurs.

Mininet works on the principle of process abstraction to virtualize the computer system resources. It runs several hosts and switches on a single operating system kernel using process-based virtualization. Network namespaces, a lightweight virtualization feature that enables individual processes with distinct network interfaces, routing tables, and ARP tables, have been supported by Linux since version 2.2.26. To enable complete OS-level virtualization, the full Linux container design adds "chroot()" jails, process and user namespaces, and CPU and memory limitations, however Mininet does not require these features. To connect switches and hosts, Mininet uses "virtual ethernet (veth) pairs." Furthermore, Mininet has a scope of supporting other operating systems with process-based virtualization as well, besides its current support for Linux kernel. Most of the code of Mininet is written in Python with a short implementation of C utilities [42].

4.3 Limitations of Mininet

a) It cannot run switches or other applications which are not Linux-based.
b) Though it runs on a single machine, it does impose resource limits of the system. For instance, it cannot surpass the CPU or bandwidth available on the given machine or server.
c) All the Mininet hosts share the PID space with the host file system, by default. This can cause some processes to be arbitrarily killed if care is not taken.
d) Since all the measurements re in real time, Mininet-based networks cannot be used to emulate faster-than-real-time results (e.g., networks with 100 Gbps or more bandwidth).
e) In order to create, custom switching or routing behaviour, Mininet lacks the ability to create a controlled for the user. One must arrange a controller if such networking behaviour is deemed necessary.

5 Topology Creation

This section shows the usage of the Mininet tool in creating topologies using specific commands.

A network in Mininet can be created with a single CLI command. The network topologies are created using the "sudo mn" command. Diverse options can be appended with the "sudo mn" command such as "--topo=linear, 8". To integrate with the HPE VAN SDN Controller, the "--controller" option is used. In this case, the controller is running on a server with IP address 192.168.1.114;

```
~$ sudo mn --controller=remote,ip=192.168.1.114 --topo=linear,8
```

The above command creates a network of eight OpenFlow switches and eight hosts (PCs). The hosts need to send traffic so that they can be discovered by the SDN controller. This can be achieved using the "pingall" command in Mininet. The following command creates a network consisting of a single switch and eight hosts. All the eight hosts are connected to the same switch.

```
~$ sudo mn --controller=remote,ip=192.168.1.114 --topo=single,8
```

A single switch is used in a tree topology, with others connected to it based on a fanout number. A fanout value of 3 indicates that the core switch is connected to three switches, each of which may have three switches connected to it. This process is repeated based on the given depth. The number of hosts connected to each leaf or edge switch is also determined by the fanout value. The following command creates a network with tree topology with depth of 3 and fanout of 2. Each leaf switch has two hosts connected to it.

```
~$ sudo mn --controller=remote,ip=192.168.1.114 topo=tree,depth=3,fanout=2
```

The following command creates a network with torus topology with dimensions 3 × 3.

```
~$ sudo mn --controller=remote,ip=192.168.1.114 --topo=torus,3,3
```

Figures 3(a–d) depict the linear, single, tree and torus topologies respectively, created by the using the aforementioned commands. The blue boxes represent the switches with their MAC addresses and the brown boxes represent the hosts with their IP addresses. The port numbers are also mentioned in the topology for each kind of network. The following figures are taken from the HPE VAN SDN Controller UI console.

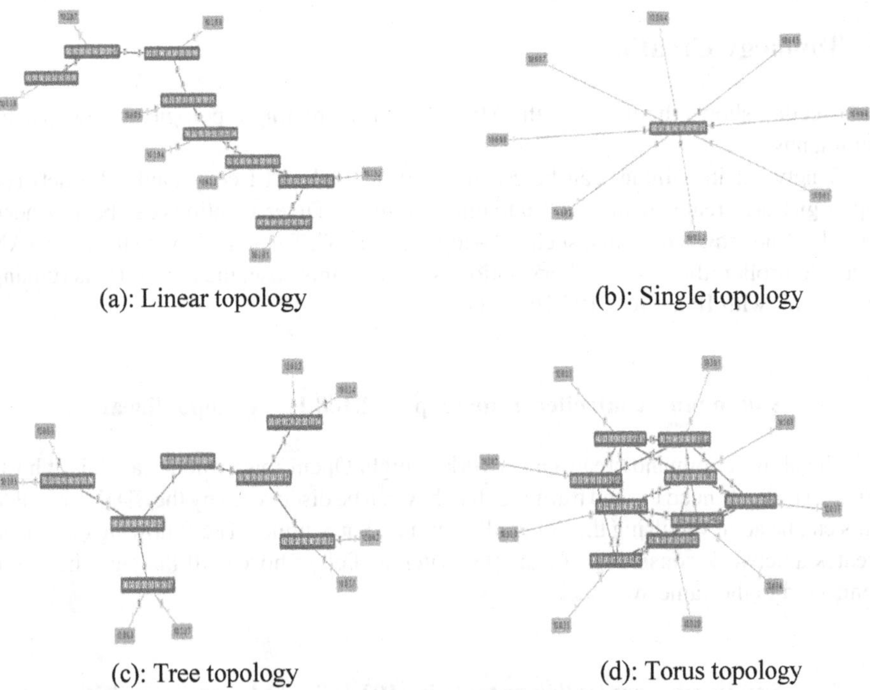

Fig. 3. Typical linear, single, tree and torus topologies created on HPE VAN SDN Controller UI console

6 Methodology for Experimental Analysis

In this section, the methods for performing the experimental analysis for three different types of network topology are explained.

Two experiments were performed to analyze and compare the traffic flow in three different types of topologies viz. linear, single, and tree topology. The two experiments described in the sub-Sects. 6.1 and 6.2 was performed on a HP Laptop 14s-cr1005TU PC with the following specifications used; Intel(R) Core (TM) i5-8265U CPU @ 1.60 GHz 1.80 GHz, 8.00 GB of RAM running the Windows 10 (Version 21H1) 64-bit operating system and Oracle VM VirtualBox version 6.1.28.

The guest operating systems used on the VM: Linux operating system Ubuntu 14.04.4 LTS (64-bit) for the "mininet-vm tty1" with 1 GB of base memory. The HPE VAN SDN Controller was installed on Linux operating system Ubuntu 12.04.5 LTS (64-bit) with 1 GB base memory. Both the guest operating systems were managed by the VirtualBox Manager. Further, the HPE VAN SDN Controller UI console was accessed via https://192.168.1.114:8443/sdn/ui on Google Chrome Version 96.0.4664.45 (Official Build) (64-bit) web browser.

6.1 Experiment - Testbed - 1

In the first experiment, the total number of hosts in each type of network topology is set to 8. The network topologies are created using the following CLI commands:

```
~$ sudo mn –controller=remote,ip=192.168.1.114 --topo=linear,8

~$ sudo mn –controller=remote,ip=192.168.1.114 --topo=single,8

~$ sudo mn –controller=remote,ip=192.168.1.114 -topo=tree,depth=3,fanout=2
```

For each topology, 10 packets are sent between the source host (h1) and the destination host (h2) using the "h1 ping –c10 h8" command. As a result, ten ICMP packets with sequence number starting from 1 with 64 bytes of data is pinged from h1 to h8. The ping statistics are obtained at the destination host, which has been tabulated in Sect. 7.

6.2 Experiment - Testbed - 2

In the second experiment, for each type of topology the relationship between the number of nodes and average round-trip time (RTT) in milliseconds (ms) is observed. The number of hosts are increased exponentially; 2n where n = 1 to 8. For each case of simulation with a given number of nodes (hosts and switches), 5 packets were pinged from the first host to the last host in the network. The results are tabulated in Sect. 7.

7 Results and Discussion

For the first experiment, the ping statistics in terms of minimum, average, maximum, and minimum deviation round-trip time (RTT) in milliseconds (ms), for each of the three topologies is provided in the Table 2. The ping statistics of the first experiment is also graphically presented in Fig. 4.

Table 2. Ping statistics for the first experiment

Topology	Minimum RTT (ms)	Average RTT (ms)	Maximum RTT (ms)	Min. Deviation of RTT (ms)
Linear	0.085	0.432	1.679	0.596
Single	0.054	0.230	1.568	0.446
Tree	0.046	0.299	1.368	0.429

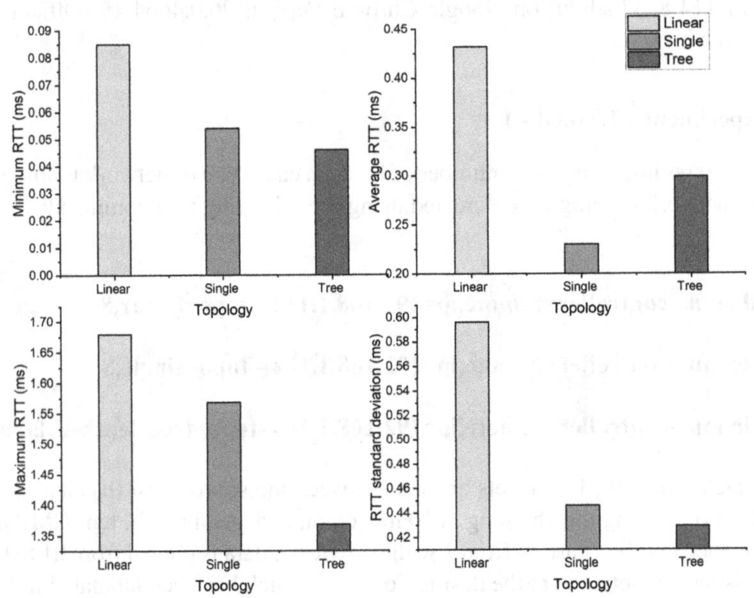

Fig. 4. Comparison of ping statistics between the linear, single, and tree topologies.

In the first quadrant of Fig. 4, we observe that minimum RTT is the least for tree topology. In the second quadrant, the single topology has the least average RTT. Further in the third and fourth quadrants, the tree topology has the least maximum RTT and minimum deviation in RTT. The results obtained from the second experiment are shown in Table 3 for the tree topology, in Table 4 for the single topology and in Table 5 for the linear topology. The results for these three tables are visualized in Figs. 5(a–c).

Table 3. Second experiment scalability results for the tree topology

Topology	Number of nodes	Number of hosts	Number of switches	Average RTT (ms)
Tree	3	2	1	0.137
Tree	7	4	3	0.196
Tree	15	8	7	0.201
Tree	31	16	15	0.256
Tree	63	32	31	0.317
Tree	127	64	63	0.381
Tree	255	128	127	1.423
Tree	511	256	255	2.479

Table 4. Second experiment scalability results for the single topology

Topology	Number of nodes	Number of hosts	Number of switches	Average RTT (ms)
Single	3	2	1	0.157
Single	5	4	1	0.158
Single	9	8	1	0.135
Single	17	16	1	0.122
Single	33	32	1	0.133
Single	65	64	1	0.111
Single	129	128	1	0.123
Single	257	256	1	0.120

Table 5. Second experiment scalability results for the linear topology

Topology	Number of nodes	Number of hosts	Number of switches	Average RTT (ms)
Linear	4	2	2	0.130
Linear	8	4	4	0.182
Linear	16	8	8	0.257
Linear	32	16	16	0.814
Linear	64	32	32	1.067
Linear	128	64	64	2.096
Linear	256	128	128	3.147
Linear	512	256	256	5.141

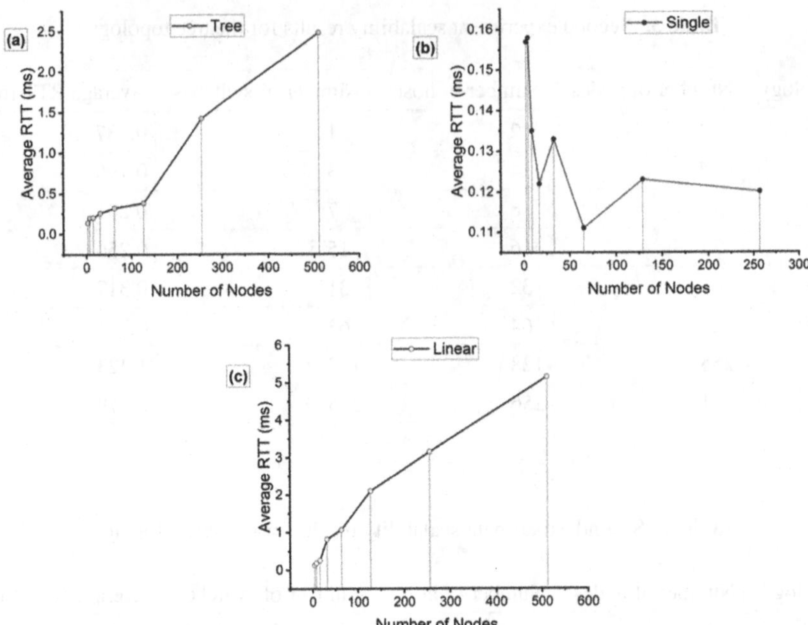

Fig. 5. Graphical analysis between number of nodes and average round-trip time for the three topologies.

From the Figs. 5(a) and 5(c), we observe that as the number of nodes increase the average RTT also increases sharply. But in Fig. 5(b), there is overall decline in average RTT as the number of nodes increase.

8 Conclusion and Future Work

Through this paper, we have analyzed the features of the tools namely, Mininet and HPE VAN SDN controller. The architecture of an SDN controller was analyzed in detail, and different topologies such as linear, tree topology, were simulated using the commands in the console. Several parameters were derived from the simulation, such as average, minimum and maximum round trip Time in milliseconds. The ping statistics were visualized by plotting a graph, that compares the topology and the round-trip time and the second experimental analysis visualized a graphical relationship between the number of nodes and the average round trip time.

The future work for this research work can be aimed towards the actual simulation of distributed denial of service attacks in the virtual networks created by Mininet. Besides, we can also analyze the behaviour of DDoS attacks in varying topologies of the virtual software-defined network in its control plane. Several other tools could also be incorporated besides the one used in this research work to choose the attack node and simulate the attack successfully. Ransomware attacks could also be studied using similar topologies. Lastly, the sophisticated torus topology still needs to be researched thoroughly to study its behaviour in terms of round-trip time and the behaviour of DDoS attack in similar kinds of complex topology.

References

1. Ottis, R.: Analysis of the 2007 cyber attacks against Estonia from the information warfare perspective. In: Proceedings of the 7th European Conference on Information Warfare, p. 163 (2008)
2. Hoque, N., Bhattacharyya, D., Kalita, J.: Botnet in DDoS attacks: trends and challenges. IEEE Commun. Surv. Tutor. **99**, 1 (2015)
3. Bawany, N.Z., Shamsi, J.A., Salah, K.: DDoS attack detection and mitigation using SDN: methods, practices, and solutions. Arab. J. Sci. Eng. **42**(2), 425–441 (2017). https://doi.org/10.1007/s13369-017-2414-5
4. Jain, S., et al.: B4: experience with a globally-deployed software defined WA. ACM SIGCOMM Comput. Commun. Rev. **43**(4), 3–14 (2013)
5. Douligeris, C., Mitrokotsa, A.: DDoS attacks and defense mechanisms: classification and state-of-the-art. Comput. Netw. **44**(5), 643–666 (2004)
6. Criscuolo, P.J.: Distributed Denial of Service Trin00, Tribe Flood Network, Tribe Flood Network 2000, and Stacheldraht CIAC-2319, Department of Energy Computer Incident Advisory (CIAC), UCRL-ID-136939, Rev. 1, Lawrence Livermore National Laboratory, 14 February 2000. http://ftp.se.kde.org/pub/security/csir/ciac/ciacdocs/ciac2319.txt
7. Dittrich, D.: The DoS Projects "trinoo" Distributed Denial of Service attack tool, University of Washington, 21 October 1999. http://staff.washington.edu/dittrich/misc/trinoo.analysis.txt
8. Dittrich, D.: The Tribe Flood Network Distributed Denial of Service Attack Tool. University of Washington, 21 October 1999
9. Barlow, J., Thrower, W.: TFN2K—an analysis (2000). http://security.royans.net/info/posts/bugtraq_DDoS2.shtml
10. CERT Coordination Center, Center Advisory CA-1999-17 Denial of Service tools. http://www.cert.org/advisories/CA-1999-17.html
11. Adams, C., Gilchrist, J.: The CAST-256 encryption algorithm, RFC 2612, June 1999. http://www.cis.ohio-state.edu/htbin/rfc/rfc2612.html
12. Dittrich, D., Weaver, G., Dietrich, S., Long, N.: The mstream Distributed Denial of Service attack tool, May 2000. http://staff.washington.edu/dittrich/misc.mstream.analysis.txt
13. Moore, D., Voelker, G., Savage, S.: Inferring internet denial of service activity, In: Proceedings of the USENIX Security Symposium, Washington, DC, USA, pp. 9–22 (2001)
14. Yan, Q., Yu, F.R., Gong, Q., Li, J.: Software-Defined Networking (SDN) and Distributed Denial of Service (DDoS) attacks in cloud computing environments: a survey, some research issues, and challenges. In: IEEE Communications Surveys and Tutorials, vol. 18, issue number 1, pp. 602–622, First quarter 2016. https://doi.org/10.1109/COMST.2015.2487361
15. Salman, O., Elhajj, I. H., Kayssi, A., Chehab, A.: SDN controllers: a comparative study. In: 2016 18th Mediterranean Electrotechnical Conference (MELECON) (2016).https://doi.org/10.1109/melcon.2016.7495430
16. Tootoonchian, A., Gorbunov, S., Ganjali, Y., Casado, M., Sherwood, R.: On controller performance in software-defined networks. In: USENIX Workshop on Hot Topics in Management of Internet, Cloud, and Enterprise Networks and Services (Hot-ICE), vol. 54 92012)
17. Khondoker, R., Zaalouk, A., Marx, R., Bayarou, K.: Featurebased comparison and selection of Software Defined Networking (SDN) controllers. In: 2014 World Congress on Computer Applications and Information Systems (WCCAIS), pp. 1–7 (2014)

18. Shalimov, A., Zuikov, D., Zimarina, D., Pashkov, V., Smeliansky, R.: Advanced study of SDN/OpenFlow controllers. In: Proceedings of the 9th Central and Eastern European Software Engineering Conference in Russia, p. 1. ACM (2013)
19. Kalkan, K., Gur, G., Alagoz, F.: Defense mechanisms against DDoS attacks in SDN environment. IEEE Commun. Mag. **55**(9), 175–179 (2017)
20. Santos, R., Souza, D., Santo, W., Ribeiro, A., Moreno, E.: Machine learning algorithms to detect DDoS attacks in SDN. Concurr. Comput. Pract. Experience **32**(2019). https://doi.org/10.1002/cpe.5402
21. Banitalebi Dehkordi, A., Soltanaghaei, M., Boroujeni, F.Z.: The DDoS attacks detection through machine learning and statistical methods in SDN. J. Supercomput. 1–33 (2020). https://doi.org/10.1007/s11227-020-03323-w
22. Amazon says it mitigated the largest DDoS attack ever recorded - The Verge. https://www.theverge.com/2020/6/18/21295337/amazon-aws-biggest-DDoS-attack-ever-2-3-tbps-shield-github-netscout-arbor. Accessed 8 Feb 2022
23. Amazon 'thwarts largest ever DDoS cyber-attack' - BBC News. https://www.bbc.com/news/technology-53093611. Accessed 8 Feb 2022
24. DDOS attacks and the GitHub case» IRIS-BH. https://irisbh.com.br/en/DDoS-attacks-and-the-github-case/. Accessed 8 Feb 2022
25. Cyber Case Study: The Mirai DDoS Attack on Dyn - CoverLink Insurance|Ohio Independent Insurance Agency. https://coverlink.com/case-study/mirai-DDoS-attack-on-dyn/. Accessed 8 Feb 2022
26. DDoS attack on BBC may have been biggest in history|CSO Online. https://www.csoonline.com/article/3020292/DDoS-attack-on-bbc-may-have-been-biggest-in-history.html. Accessed 8 Feb 2022
27. Bello, I., et al.: Detecting ransomware attacks using intelligent algorithms: recent development and next direction from deep learning and big data perspectives. J. Ambient. Intell. Humaniz. Comput. **12**(9), 8699–8717 (2020). https://doi.org/10.1007/s12652-020-02630-7
28. Reshmi, T.R.: Information security breaches due to ransomware attacks - a systematic literature review. Int. J. Inf. Manage. Data Insights **1**(2), 100013 (2021). https://doi.org/10.1016/j.jjimei.2021.100013
29. Digital Guardian: A history of ransomware attacks: the biggest and worst ransomware attacks of all time (2019). https://digitalguardian.com/blog/history-ransomware-attacks-biggest-and-worst-ransomware-attacks-all-time. Accessed 17 Dec 2019
30. Agrawal, R., Stokes, J.W., Selvaraj, K., Marinescu, M.: Attention in recurrent neural networks for ransomware detection. In: Paper Presented at the ICASSP 2019—2019 IEEE International Conference on Acoustics, Speech and signal Processing (ICASSP) (2019)
31. Alhawi, O.M.K., Baldwin, J., Dehghantanha, A.: Leveraging machine learning techniques for windows ransomware network traffic detection. In: Dehghantanha, A., Conti, M., Dargahi, T. (eds.) Cyber Threat Intelligence. AIS, vol. 70, pp. 93–106. Springer, Cham (2018). https://doi.org/10.1007/978-3-319-73951-9_5
32. Alrawashdeh, K., Purdy, C.: Ransomware detection using limited precision deep learning structure in FPGA. In: Paper Presented at the NAECON 2018-IEEE National Aerospace and Electronics Conference (2018)
33. Cusack, G., Michel, O., Keller, E.: Machine learning-based detection of ransomware using SDN, pp 1–6 (2018). https://doi.org/10.1145/3180465.3180467
34. Open Networking Foundation. https://www.opennetworking.org/sdndefinition. Accessed 12 Nov 2021
35. Wang, S.-Y.: Comparison of SDN OpenFlow Network Simulator and Emulators. EstiNet vs. Mininet
36. Lantz, B., Heller, B., Mckeown, N: A Network in a Laptop: Rapid Prototyping for Software-Defined Networks

37. Open Network Operating System (ONOS) SDN Controller for SDN/NFV Solutions. https://opennetworking.org/onos/. Accessed 12 Nov 2021
38. Platform Overview - OpenDaylight. https://www.opendaylight.org/about/platform-overview. Accessed 12 Nov 2021
39. Ryu SDN Framework. https://ryu-sdn.org/. Accessed 12 Nov 2021
40. Saikia, D., Malik Jaffe, N., White Paper, T.: Whitepaper Openmul An Introduction to OpenMUL SDN Suite (2014). www.openmul.org. Accessed 12 Nov 2021
41. Introduction to the HPE VAN SDN Controller. https://techhub.hpe.com/eginfolib/networking/docs/sdn/sdnc2_7/5200-0910prog/content/c_sdnc-pg-intro.html. Accessed 12 Nov 2021
42. Mininet: An Instant Virtual Network on Your Laptop (or Other PC) - Mininet. http://mininet.org/. Accessed 11 Nov 2021
43. Keti, F., Askar, S.: Emulation of software defined networks using mininet in different simulation environments. In: Proceedings of the 6th International Conference on Intelligent Systems, Modelling and Simulation (2015)

Collision Elimination for Random Behavior Nodes in Ad Hoc Wireless Network Using Early Backoff Announcement (EBA)

D. Prabhu, T. Anitha, G. Logeswari(✉), S. Bose, and P. Venkatasubramani

Department of Computer Science and Engineering, College of Engineering, Anna University, Guindy, Chennai, India
logeswarig4@gmail.com

Abstract. Due to the detrimental repercussions of hidden terminals, collision avoidance is essential in contention-based media access control systems for multi-hop adhoc networks. Currently, the most common collision-avoidance strategies are four-way sender-initiated schemes. Although many research has been done to assess the performance of these schemes, the most of it has focused on single-hop ad hoc networks or networks with a limited proportion of hidden terminals. This research presents an enhancement to the existing IEEE 802.11 Distributed Coordination Function (DCF) MAC that reduces collisions, medium idle time, and overall network speed. The modification utilizes the existing Early backoff announcement (EBA) mechanism. The frame header in EBA is used by a station to indicate its upcoming backoff time; the backoff value is determined at random. This reduces collisions but no care has been taken to improve the throughput directly. In this paper, an algorithm for selecting the post backoff value based on certain criteria is proposed. The post backoff selection is selected through a round robin scheduling between the number of stations currently being transmitting. This reduces unnecessary wait time for stations that want to transmit back-to-back.

Keywords: Ad hoc networks · Distributed coordination function · Point coordination function · Collision avoidance · Early backoff announcement

1 Introduction

The IEEE 802.11 standard is a commonly used wireless local area network technology. The IEEE 802.11 MAC standard distinguishes between two strategies: the contention-based Distributed Coordination Function (DCF) and the optional polling-based Point Coordination Function (PCF) [1]. DCF is the most extensively utilized MAC approach in IEEE 802.11-compliant products at the time. IEEE 802.11 uses the Carrier Sense Multiple Access (CSMA) approach and other contention-based MAC algorithms. If the medium is considered idle, a station may transmit in CSMA. The goal is to keep any station from broadcasting and interfering with an already broadcast transmission [15].

Published by Springer Nature Switzerland AG 2022
E. J. Neuhold et al. (Eds.): ICCCSP 2022, IFIP AICT 651, pp. 232–245, 2022.
https://doi.org/10.1007/978-3-031-11633-9_17

The collision prevention mechanism executes random backoff before every frame transmission attempt. Because two or more stations can complete their backoff procedures around the same time, random backoff can reduce the likelihood of collisions, but it cannot completely eliminate them. The primary access strategy of EBA is that the next backoff period bnext is computed and notified to all stations sooner, without negatively impacting any other MAC procedure [16]. The backoff value is determined at random. The MAC frame header is piggybacked with future backoff information. All nearby stations receive the frame containing the EBA data, including the endpoint, depending on the nature of radio transmissions. The DCF requires a station to accept it is in the sleeping state, it should decode all incoming frames and at least the MAC header section. When a station gets an EBA frame, it is notified with the current transmitting station's next frame transmission time, which is saved in the station's Reservation Windows.

In this paper, a priority scheme that enhances the existing EBA mechanism that improves throughput is proposed. The back off value can be selected immediately after the current transmitting slot if other stations do not reserve the slot. If the slot is reserved then the next available slot can be selected. In addition to the above, a set of slots in the reservation window can be reserved. This is to avoid other stations utilizing the same set of slots. This scheme reduces unnecessary wait time for stations that want to transmit back-to-back.

2 Related Work

For IEEE 802.11, the current DCF protocol has been renamed Location Enhanced DCF (LED) by the authors of paper [2]. Other stations sharing the communication channel can better identify interference and analyse blockage using the proposed approach, which incorporates position information in IEEE 802.11 DCF frame exchange sequences. To improve performance, Location Enhanced DCF provides additional communication characteristics, particularly the locations of transmitters and receivers, than the basic 802.11 DCF frames compatible with DCF. Wu et al. introduced a DCF+ scheme in article [3], which is a reliable WLAN transfer protocol. The authors also suggested a Markov chain-based analytical model for calculating the throughput performance of IEEE 802.11 DCF and DCF+.

Using the assumption that there are a finite number of terminals and ideal channel conditions, Giuseppe Bianchi [4] constructed a simple but very reliable mathematical model for predicting 802.11 DCF throughputs. This study focuses on DCF's packet transmission systems' basic and RTS/CTS access techniques. The authors of the paper [5] suggested the design of OSU-MAC, a MAC protocol based on the physical layer features and restrictions of a narrow-band wireless modem test bed currently under development at Ohio State University. Black-burst (BB) contention, a distributed MAC technique that provides QoS real-time access to ad hoc CSMA wireless networks, has been defined and researched by Joao L. Sobrinho et al. [6]. Real-time nodes compete for channel access via energy pulses known as BBs, whose duration are a function of the node's latency until the channel becomes idle in this technique. In carrier sense ad hoc wireless networks, BB contention is a distributed MAC technique for QoS real-time traffic support.

The Fast Collision Resolution (FCR) algorithm, introduced by Younggoo Kwon et al. [7], is an innovative and efficient contention-based MAC protocol for wireless local area networks. This algorithm is built on the following ground-breaking concepts: to reduce the time it takes to resolve collisions, actively redistribute the backoff timers for all active nodes and to reduce the average number of idle slots fixed number of consecutive idle slots are discovered, reduce the backoff timers exponentially quickly. Tamer Nadeem and Ashok Agrawala [8] suggested an upgraded BEB technique that improves IEEE 802.11 by allowing it to distinguish between different sorts of failed transmissions. Chong gang Wang and Weiwen Tang [9] have proposed a 802.11 DCF, a probability-based technique is used to update the contention window. It's based on the fact that following every successful transfer, 802.11 DCF reduces the contention window to its original value, implying that each successful transmission indicates that the system is under low traffic load.

The Exponential Increase Exponential Decrease (EIED) backoff method proposed by Nai-Oak Song et al. [10] is an easy to build backoff algorithm that improves network performance is significantly better than BEB's. For performance comparison, another hackoff approach called Multiple Increase Linear Decrease (MILD) backoff algorithm is investigated. Shaohu Yan et al. [11] presented a new backoff technique for IEEE 802.11 DCF termed the priority backoff algorithm (PBA). The primary idea behind PBA is that while sensing the channel, each station should collect statistical data from the transmissions of other stations and keep a Sent Data Table for the entire network.

In paper [17], the researchers have conducted various studies in order the enhance the performance of IEEE 802.11 MAC layer in MANET. The authors proposed a novel technique to handle throughput issues, packet delivery rate in adhoc environment. The performance comparison was done with several algorithms such as BEB of the IEEE 802.11 DCF and opposite Exponential Backoff (OBEB). The paper offers a novel technique for detecting Denial of Service (DoS) attacks on wireless networks with hidden nodes, which frequently employ the widely used IEEE 802.11 Distributed Coordination Function (DCF) protocols [18]. [19] described how the transmission scheduling approach is used by the node scheduling algorithm. The authors provide a few OBSP strategies for determining the node's status and various levels. To offer resilient streaming in the event of link failures, many pathways are discovered using an efficient genetic algorithm. The server employs dynamic encoding techniques to react to changing network conditions depending on network feedback Handoffs are also predicted ahead of time, and mobile agents containing buffered data are delivered to the anticipated base station [20].

3 Proposed Methodology

In this paper, a priority scheme that enhances the existing EBA mechanism that improves throughput is proposed. The backoff value can be selected immediately after the current transmitting slot if other stations do not reserve the slot. If the slot is reserved, then the next available slot can be selected.

In addition to the above, round robin scheduling could be implemented between the stations currently transmitting. For example, if there is a single station transmitting, then it can reserve the next slot. If there are two stations currently transmitting, then it can reserve the slot after a gap of one slot. It can be expressed, as the selection of the next slot on the reservation window could be the nth slot, where n is the number of stations currently doing the transmission. The number of station currently transmitting could be identified based on the node id. If there is a new node entering into the transmission, then the counter value shall be increased. If the node has completed the transmission then the counter shall be decreased. To fulfill this requirement, each node announces the end of transmission to other stations. This could be added along with the other EBA information. This scheme reduces unnecessary wait time for stations that want to transmit back-to-back. The system architecture of EBA architecture is shown in Fig. 1.

3.1 EBA System Architecture

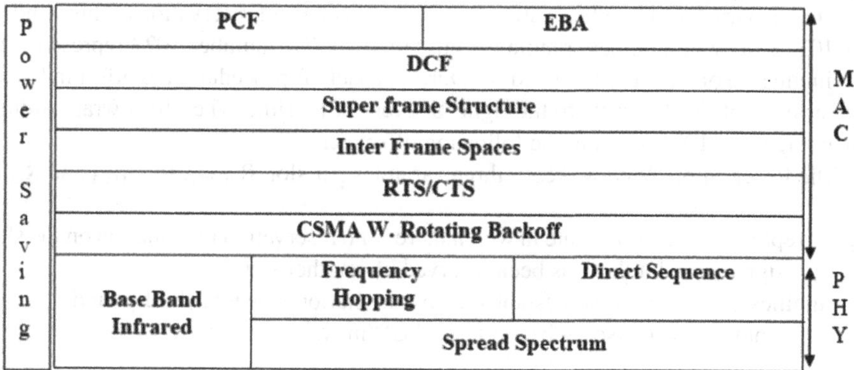

Fig. 1. System architecture of EBA

The Early Backoff Announcement (EBA) is an improvement to the existing 802.11 DCF protocol. The improvement is mostly done at the MAC level. EBA station chooses its next backoff period before broadcasting the frame, not after getting the ACK. This future backoff information, known as the EBA information, is then piggybacked into the MAC frame header. Because radio communications are transmitted, the frame holding the EBA data is broadcasted to all surrounding stations, including the target. Unless a station is in the resting state, DCF requires it to collect all arriving frames and decode at least the MAC header part. When a station receives an EBA frame, it is notified of when the presently broadcasting station will broadcast the next frame and this information is recorded in their Reservation Windows.

3.2 Reservation Window

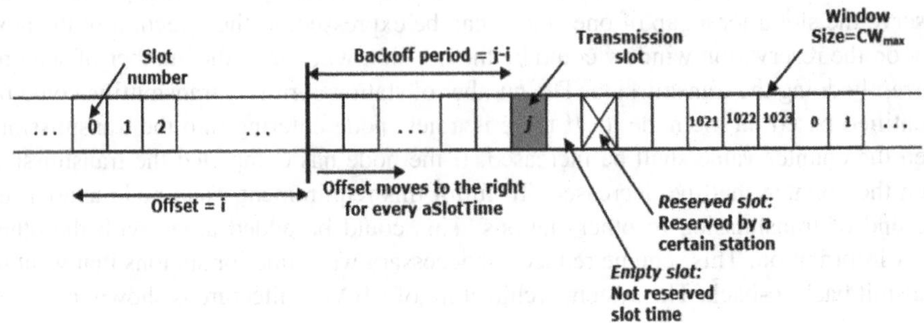

Fig. 2. Reservation window

Figure 2 explains the reservation window scheme. The Reservation window is being used to keep track of the other stations' and its own channel reservations. This window has 1024 slots with numbers ranging from 0 to 1023. The number 1023 represents the maximum size of a contention window. During a backoff procedure, the offset indicates the current slot, which shifts to the right for every aSlotTime. The offset wraps around when it reaches 1023, making the following offset zero.

The Reservation Window keeps three variables per slot: R_{empty}, $R_{reserved}$ and R_{tx}.

R_{empty} represents the initial state in which there is no reservation information on the slot.
$R_{reserved}$ signifies a slot that has been reserved by another station.
R_{tx} signifies the broadcast slot established by the station's own backoff period.
R_{tx}- slot's number = (offset + backoff) mod CWmax.

The receiving station reads the reservation information from the MAC header and marks the slot as $R_{reserved}$ when it receives a frame. If the offset matches the slot with the value R_{tx}, transmission will begin. The channel reservation information is shared by each station with the other stations. This action allows a station to reserve a transmission time as well as notify other stations of its plan to send a frame at the given time, ensuring that other stations do not begin broadcasting a frame at the same time. The system flow for transmitting packet is shown in Fig. 3.

In order to implement the EBA Algorithm, the following notations are employed, where T denotes the current time,

TxQ (Qt1 = m, Qt2 = n): the condition of a station with a TxQ (transmission queue) of m at slot time t1 and n at slot time t2.

TxQidle, busy station: a station that was idle previously and is now busy (newly transmitting station).

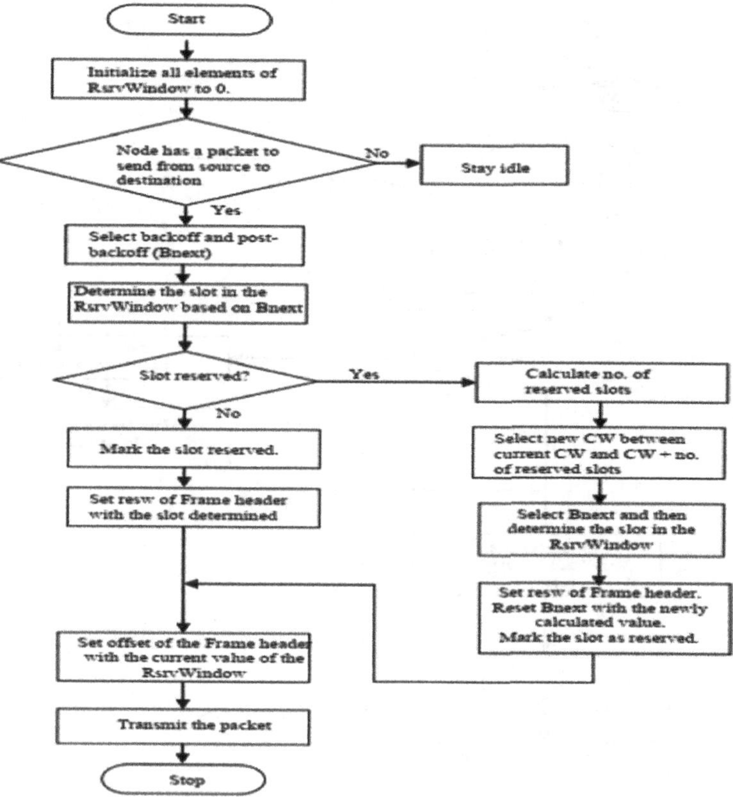

Fig. 3. System flow for transmitting packet

TxQbusy, idle station: indicates a station that was formerly busy but is now idle (a station that will perform post backoff procedure).

TxQbusy, busy station: indicates a station that was broadcasting previously and is presently transmitting (station making successive broadcasts).

TxQidle, idle station: a station that is idle.

One of the two Backoff selection strategies can be used in the Early Backoff Announcement (EBA).

EBA – I

EBA – I is a straightforward MAC with slight modifications to the IEEE 802.11 DCF. It is compatible with earlier DCF versions. In the same WLAN, EBA – I and DCF stations can coexist peacefully. Figure 4 depicts the system flow for accepting packets.

EBA – II

EBA – II is a refined version of EBA – I with increased throughput over EBA – I and DCF. It is EBA – I backward compatible.

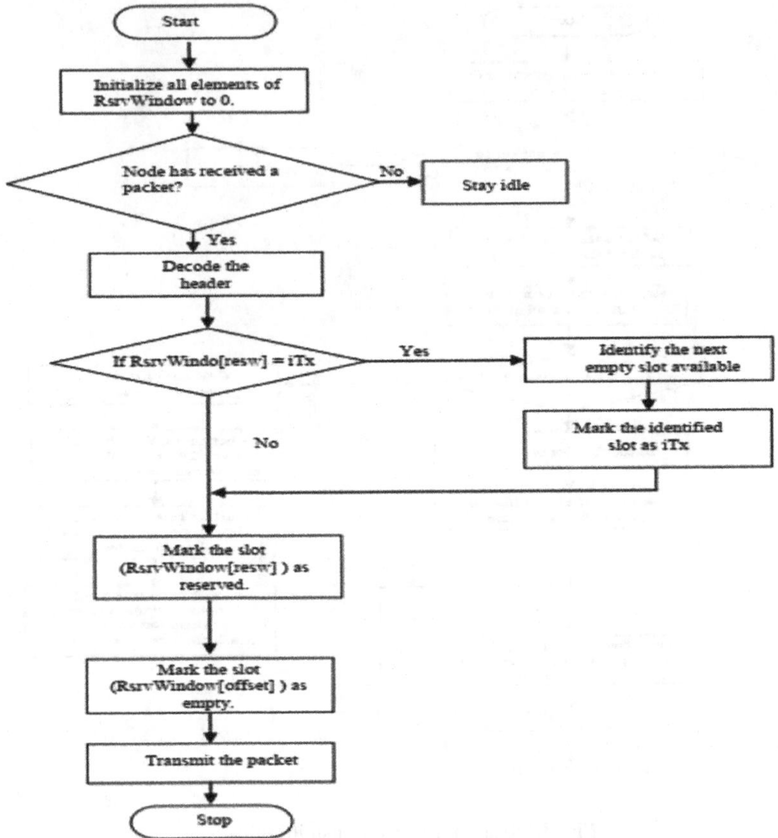

Fig. 4. Receiving a packet

3.3 EBA Backoff Mechanism

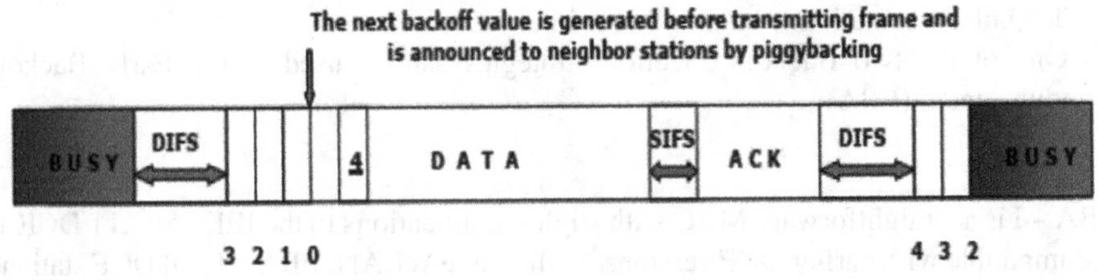

Fig. 5. Basic operation of EBA

The basic operation of EBA is pictorially presented in Fig. 5. The method of picking the next backoff value in EBA – I is nearly identical to the IEEE 802.11 DCF backoff selection mechanism. In this case, the backoff value bnext for a non-reserved slot is chosen at random from the range [0, CW]. For each unsuccessful transmission, the CW value is doubled. The distinction is that the station uses its own Reservation Window (Rempty slot), which is an empty slot, to select only non-reserved backoff periods.

After choosing the (offset + bnext)th slot in the Reservation Window, the station inserts the next backoff period bnext into the transmitted frame header (EBA FIELD) and sets the (offset + bnext)th slot in the Reservation Window to Rtx.

It's likely that the 0 through CW slots will be full if there are more stations than the CW number. In this situation, a backoff value is picked at random from the non-reserved slots in the range [CW, CW + CWreserved], where CWreserved is the number of Reservation Windows reserved slots.

3.4 Additional Collision Prevention Options

Because other stations do not broadcast during the time slot, a station that booked the channel via EBA can send its frame during the specified time without causing a collision. As a consequence, the reserving station obtains a frame to transmit during the reserved time slot, signalling that it is a TxQbusy,busy station. In contrast, the reserving station, i.e. a TxQbusy, idle station, may not include a frame for the reservation. In this case, the access mechanism is identical to that of DCF. TxQbusy, idle stations have no frames to broadcast in the allocated slot while having a reserved channel through EBA. As a result, the channel will be inactive throughout the slot.

Additionally, since TxQbusy, idle stations do not offer any reservation information to their neighbours for their next transmission, they will be unable to reserve the following channel access period. Consider what happens when this station, which corresponds to TxQidle, busy station, tries to transmit a new frame after such an idling interval. Other stations are uninformed of the station's backoff value because it did not reserve the channel for its scheduled transmission, letting them to pick a backoff value that will result in a collision with this station. The following additional algorithms can be used to reduce the likelihood of a collision in such situations.

3.5 Non-reserved Transmission of TxQidle, Busy Stations

Consider the following scenario: station X has been idle for some time and now has to broadcast a new frame, so it sets its backoff counter to a value, and station X is a TxQidle,busy station. After one slot time TxQbusy, busy station A starts transmitting and reserves its next channel access time by setting its next backoff value to the same as station X's. Station X has now seen that station A is attempting to broadcast at the same time as it. Because it is difficult to persuade station A to change its backoff value, we believe station X is accountable for averting the anticipated accident.

Station X converts its existing Rtx-slot to Rreserved-slot and selects another Rempty-slot for its new backoff period as a result. Station X does not choose at random; instead, it advances the Rtx-slot to the left until it finds a Rempty-slot and switches it to the Rtx-slot. If a Rempty-slot does not exist on the left side, it selects the Rempty-slot on the right side that is closest to the original Rtx-slot.

3.6 Newly Arriving Station

Consider the following scenario: a new station joins the WLAN. The Reservation Window for this new station provides no reservation information for its new neighbors. In this case, the station calculates a backoff value and initiates the backoff operation. Consider the case when station Y enters the network and chooses a backoff value for its transmission. Station Y begins transmission after this backoff value and reserves the following channel access period by declaring its next backoff value. However, station B has already reserved this backoff amount. This occurs because station Y was unaware that station B had previously reserved the slot time.

Station B determines that after obtaining the EBA information, station Y intends to transmit at the same time. Station B surrenders the reservation to Station Y by withdrawing its own reservation and selecting the next vacant neighbour slot on the left side as a new backoff value to avoid a collision. In this way, the risk of a collision caused by a newly arrived station can be avoided.

4 Implementation and Results

The proposed model is implemented in Parsec programming language. Glomosim simulator environment is used to implement and evaluate the performance of the proposed protocol over the existing 802.11 DCF. The following parameters is used for the simulation.

Parameters	Values
OS	Fedora 13
Simulator	GloMoSim
Application	Telnet
No. of nodes	49,64
Mobility model	Random way point

4.1 Performance Evaluation

Output for 49 Nodes

The output generated using Glomosim simulator is presented in a Table 1. Table 1 is organized as: First two columns represent EBA and its collision details at the corresponding nodes. Next two columns represent the output generated for the existing 802.11 DCF protocol.

Figure 6 represents the performance comparison of existing 802.11 DCF protocol with the EBA protocol for 49 nodes configuration. The X-axis denotes the nodes and the Y-axis denotes the corresponding collisions occurring at each node. As evident from Fig. 6, the number of collisions occurring at each node using EBA is comparatively less than the legacy DCF protocol.

Table 1. Output for 49 nodes configuration.

EBA		DCF		EBA		DCF	
Node	Collisions	Node	Collisions	Node	Collisions	Node	Collisions
Node 0	44	Node 0	183	Node 25	33	Node 25	102
Node 1	165	Node 1	276	Node 26	0	Node 26	11
Node 2	205	Node 2	292	Node 27	30	Node 27	67
Node 3	28	Node 3	107	Node 28	0	Node 28	15
Node 4	24	Node 4	77	Node 29	1	Node 29	5
Node 5	1	Node 5	45	Node 30	109	Node 30	206
Node 6	2	Node 6	25	Node 31	0	Node 31	0
Node 7	1	Node 7	45	Node 32	49	Node 32	81
Node 8	40	Node 8	107	Node 33	90	Node 33	197
Node 9	41	Node 9	118	Node 34	65	Node 34	99
Node 10	76	Node 10	156	Node 35	7	Node 35	49
Node 11	1	Node 11	14	Node 36	0	Node 36	11
Node 12	7	Node 12	40	Node 37	0	Node 37	0
Node 13	0	Node 13	11	Node 38	159	Node 38	263
Node 14	18	Node 14	157	Node 39	7	Node 39	54
Node 15	35	Node 15	161	Node 40	0	Node 40	1
Node 16	2	Node 16	21	Node 41	177	Node 41	332
Node 17	1	Node 17	23	Node 42	74	Node 42	256
Node 18	1	Node 18	13	Node 43	93	Node 43	170
Node 19	8	Node 19	27	Node 44	1	Node 44	15
Node 20	135	Node 20	321	Node 45	40	Node 45	105
Node 21	32	Node 21	62	Node 46	4	Node 46	33
Node 22	3	Node 22	32	Node 47	1	Node 47	13
Node 23	29	Node 23	68	Node 48	49	Node 48	162
Node 24	213	Node 24	345				

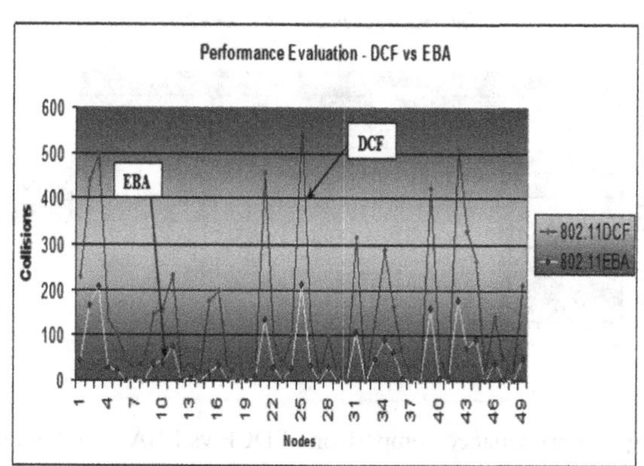

Fig. 6. Performance comparison of DCF vs EBA for 4 nodes

Output for 64 Nodes

The output generated using Glomosim simulator is presented in Table 2. Here the number of nodes is configured to be 64. Table 2. is organized as: First two columns represent EBA and its collision details at the corresponding nodes. Next two columns represent the output generated for the existing 802.11 DCF protocol.

Table 2. Output for 64 nodes configuration.

EBA		DCF		EBA		DCF	
Node	Collisions	Node	Collisions	Node	Collisions	Node	Collisions
Node 0	71	Node 0	277	Node 32	20	Node 32	33
Node 1	186	Node 1	292	Node 33	134	Node 33	300
Node 2	274	Node 2	354	Node 34	106	Node 34	218
Node 3	107	Node 3	293	Node 35	174	Node 35	273
Node 4	73	Node 4	152	Node 36	3	Node 36	9
Node 5	12	Node 5	82	Node 37	0	Node 37	0
Node 6	179	Node 6	235	Node 38	186	Node 38	309
Node 7	12	Node 7	78	Node 39	144	Node 39	287
Node 8	44	Node 8	121	Node 40	5	Node 40	34
Node 9	43	Node 9	150	Node 41	188	Node 41	329
Node 10	61	Node 10	184	Node 42	160	Node 42	316
Node 11	1	Node 11	19	Node 43	337	Node 43	576
Node 12	241	Node 12	389	Node 44	8	Node 44	33
Node 13	34	Node 13	89	Node 45	44	Node 45	110
Node 14	101	Node 14	277	Node 46	9	Node 46	45
Node 15	350	Node 15	591	Node 47	4	Node 47	34
Node 16	4	Node 16	24	Node 48	369	Node 48	544
Node 17	200	Node 17	375	Node 49	13	Node 49	37
Node 18	75	Node 18	155	Node 50	94	Node 50	208
Node 19	111	Node 19	195	Node 51	193	Node 51	291
Node 20	251	Node 20	449	Node 52	162	Node 52	349
Node 21	11	Node 21	13	Node 53	117	Node 53	273
Node 22	87	Node 22	196	Node 54	201	Node 54	347
Node 23	68	Node 23	104	Node 55	4	Node 55	32
Node 24	239	Node 24	395	Node 56	222	Node 56	400
Node 25	214	Node 25	418	Node 57	109	Node 57	282
Node 26	35	Node 26	69	Node 58	4	Node 58	26
Node 27	39	Node 27	60	Node 59	6	Node 59	41
Node 28	2	Node 28	30	Node 60	136	Node 60	316
Node 29	11	Node 29	89	Node 61	116	Node 61	262
Node 30	190	Node 30	397	Node 62	140	Node 62	306
Node 31	2	Node 31	9	Node 63	89	Node 63	230

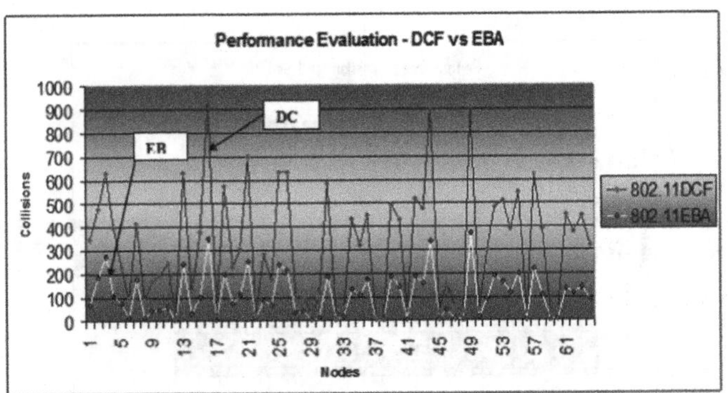

Fig.7. Performance comparison of DCF vs EBA for 64 nodes

Figure 7 represents the performance comparison of existing 802.11 DCF protocol with the EBA protocol for 64 nodes configuration. The X-axis denotes the nodes and the Y-axis denotes the corresponding collisions occurring at each node. As evident from Fig. 7, the number of collisions occurring at each node using EBA is comparatively less than the legacy DCF protocol. Also with the number of contending stations increasing the collision factor gets greatly reduced.

Figure 8 and Fig. 9 shows the overhead and delivery ratio of DCF and EBA for 64 nodes.

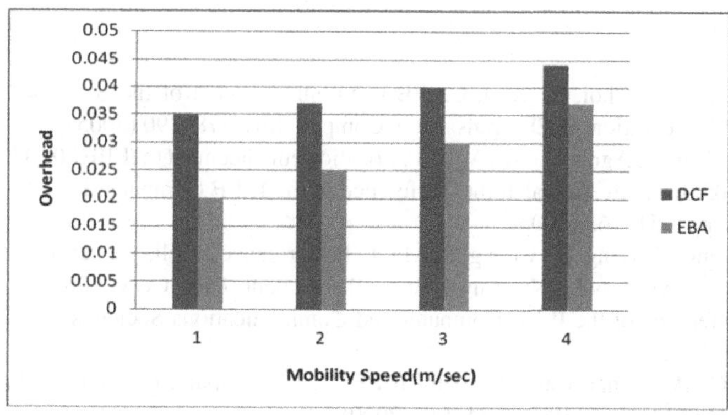

Fig. 8. Overhead of DCF vs EBA for 64 nodes

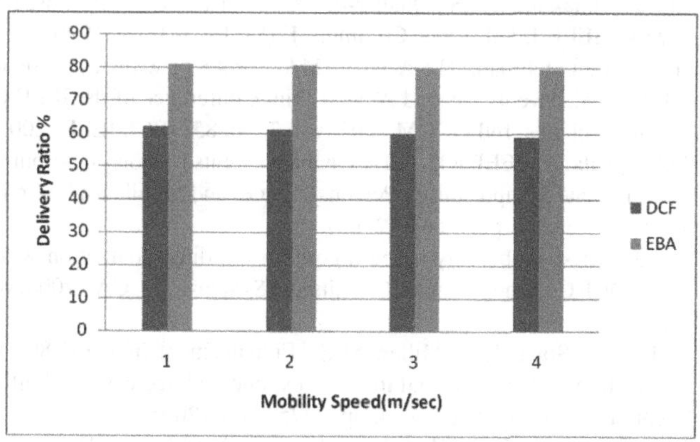

Fig. 9. Delivery Ratio of DCF vs EBA for 64 nodes

5 Conclusion and Future Work

The proposed work is an enhancement to the existing IEEE 802.11 DCF protocol. This scheme is compatible with existing DCF and EBA [1] protocols. The priority scheme enhances the existing EBA mechanism to reduce collisions and improve throughput. The backoff value selection used in this model improves channel usage by allowing stations to transmit back-to-back without any wait time due to post backoff. It provides better performance improvement over the legacy DCF. Some techniques, in addition to random selection, might be used for backoff selection as a future development to the EBA. Scheduling algorithms such as round robin can be used to provide scheduling by reserving channel access time in FIFO order. Instead of a random number, the backoff value might be decided straight after the final reserved slot, saving time at the station that transmits frames back-to-back.

References

1. Choi, J., Yoo, J., Choi, S., Kim, C.: EBA: an enhancement of the IEEE 802.11 DCF via distributed reservation. IEEE Trans. Mob. Comput. **4**(4), 378–390 (2005)
2. Nadeem ,T., Ji, L., Agrawala, A., Agre, J.: Location enhancement to IEEE 802.11. DCF INFOCOM 2005. In: 24th Annual Joint Conference of the IEEE Computer and Communications Societies, pp. 651–663 (2005)
3. Wu, H., Peng, Y., Long, K., Cheng, S., Ma, J.: Performance of reliable transport protocol over IEEE 802.11 wireless LAN: analysis and enhancement. INFOCOM 2002. In: 21st Annual Joint Conference of the IEEE Computer and Communications Societies, vol. 2, pp. 23–27, 599–607 (2002)
4. Bianchi, G.: Performance analysis of the IEEE 802.11 distributed coordination function. IEEE J. Sel. Areas Commun. **18**(3), 534–547 (2000)
5. Baldwin, R.O., Davis, N.J.I., Midkiff, S.F.: A real-time medium access control protocol for adhoc wireless local area networks. ACM Mob. Comput. Commun. Rev. **3**(2), 20–27 (1999)
6. Sobrinho, J.L., Krishnakumar, A.S.: Quality-of-service in adhoc carrier sense multiple access wireless networks. IEEE J. Sel. Areas Commun. **17**(8), 1353–1368 (1999)
7. Kwon, Y., Fang, Y., Latchman,, H.: A novel MAC protocol with fast collision resolution for wireless LANs. In: Twenty-Second Annual Joint Conference of the IEEE Computer and Communications Societies, INFOCOM 2003, vol. 2, pp. 853–862. IEEE (2003)
8. Nadeem, T., Agrawala, A.: IEEE 802.11 DCF enhancements for noisy environments. In: 2004 15th IEEE International Symposium on Personal, Indoor and Mobile Radio Communications, 5–8 September 2004, vol. 1, pp. 93–97 (2003)
9. Wang, C., Tang, W.: A probability-based algorithm to adjust contention window in IEEE 802.11. In: 2004 DCF Communications, Circuits and Systems, ICCCAS 2004, vol. 1, pp. 418–422 (2004)
10. Song, N.O., Jae, B., Song, K.J., Miller, M.E.: Enhancement of IEEE 802.11 distributed coordination function with exponential increase exponential decrease backoff algorithm. In: Vehicular Technology Conference, vol. 4, pp. 2775–2778 (2005)
11. Yan, S., Zhuo, Y., Wu, S., Guo, W.: Priority backoff algorithm for IEEE 802.11 DCF. In: International Conference on Communications, Circuits and Systems, ICCCAS 2004, vol. 1, pp. 423–427 (2004)
12. Ko, Y.B., Shankarkumar, V., Vaidya, N.H.: Medium access control protocols using directional antennas in ad hoc networks. In: IEEE INFOCOM 2000, pp. 142–152 (2000)
13. Wang, Y., Garcia-Luna-Aceves, J.J..: Collision avoidance in multi-hop ad hoc networks. In: Proceedings of the 10th IEEE International Symposium on Modeling, Analysis, and Simulation of Computer and Telecommunications Systems (MASCOTS 2002) (2002)
14. Nasipuri, A., Ye, S., You, J., Hiromoto, R.E.: A MAC protocol for mobile ad hoc networks using directional antennas. In: Proceedings of the IEEE Wireless Communication and Networking Conference (WCNC) 2000, pp. 200–213 (2000)
15. Albalt, M., Nasir, Q.: Adaptive backoff algorithm for IEEE 802.11 MAC protocol. Int. J. Commun. Netw. Syst. Sci. **2**(4), 300–317 (2009)
16. Rafsanjani, M.K., Fatemidokht, H., Balas, V.E.: Modeling and optimization of quality of service routing in mobile Ad hoc networks. Open Phys. **14**(1), 498–507 (2016)
17. Zerguine, N., Aliouat, Z., Mostefai, M., Harous, S.: M-BEB: enhanced and fair binary exponential backoff. In: 2020 14th International Conference on Innovations in Information Technology (IIT), pp. 142–147(2020)
18. Joseph, S.: DoS detection in IEEE 80211 with the presence of hidden nodes. J. Adv. Res. **5**(4), 415–422 (2014)

19. Susila Sakthy, S., Bose, S.: Dynamic model node scheduling algorithm along with OBSP technique to schedule the node in the sensitive cluster region in the WSN. Wireless Pers. Commun. **114**(1), 265–279 (2020). https://doi.org/10.1007/s11277-020-07362-7
20. Bose, S., Kannan, A.: Adaptive multipath multimedia streaming architecture for mobile networks with proactive buffering using mobile proxies. J. Comput. Inf. Technol. **15**(3), 215–226 (2007)

Novel Hybrid Technique Enhancing Data Privacy and Security

Y. Sunil Raj[1(✉)], S. Albert Rabara[1], A. Arun Gnanaraj[1], and S. Brito Ramesh Kumar[2]

[1] Department of Computer Science, St. Joseph's College (Autonomous), Affiliated to Bharathidasan University, Trichy 2, India
ysrsjccs@gmail.com

[2] Qanawat L. L. C, Dubai Media City 502299, Saudi Arabia

Abstract. Internet of Things is playing a major role by connecting everything via Internet to the Cloud. Data from things are collected at gateways and processed at the application servers. The processed data is sanitized and masked to preserve it on Cloud. The security and privacy issues such as data misuse, loss or theft make IoT Cloud more untrusted. While providing numerous benefits IoT Cloud help the business organizations grow by limiting the time and economy. Fixing the security and privacy issues would enhance the use of these technologies. This work is aimed at proposing a novel DNA based algorithm to enhance the security and privacy of data on cloud. The detailed study is conducted on the existing security schemes. Finally, clear picture on the pits and holes in existing IoT Cloud based security schemes have been presented. The proposed scheme has been tested by implementing it using opensource tools. Results generated depicts the level of security and privacy provided by the proposed scheme. This would also help researchers to analyse the efficiency of existing hybrid security schemes.

Keywords: IoT · ECC DNA · Cloud computing · TPA · Privacy · Security

1 Introduction

Internet of Things (**IoT**) connects the devices and sensors over the Internet. Objects with intelligent sensors, and a number of connectivity protocols help connecting things together [1, 2]. As the devices are of low capability, the connecting protocols include, CoAP, MQTT, AMQP, and XMPP [3–5]. Data thus transferred by this **IoT** network, will be converted to HTTP by the gateway. This data finally reaches cloud for processing, analysis or storage.

Cloud Computing (**CC**) provides services in a distributed fashion despite of the geographical locations. Therefore business/firms are saving a huge space and large amount of time. Major transactions are done using the protocols such as HTTP, POP, SMTP, FTP and so on. Most services have direct link with **IoT's**, where they send request using protocols such as CoAP/MQTT. Working on the request Cloud would respond with its own language (HTTP). In this scenario any point of time eavesdroppers or malicious users may initiate an attack [6].

Published by Springer Nature Switzerland AG 2022
E. J. Neuhold et al. (Eds.): ICCCSP 2022, IFIP AICT 651, pp. 246–264, 2022.
https://doi.org/10.1007/978-3-031-11633-9_18

Availing lot of advantages, greatest problem in cloud is security threats [23–27]. The security and privacy issues that arise as **CC** leads to lack of manual control and implements virtualization. This may lead to integrity, consistency and privacy issues. The attacks such as spoofing, replace, DOS, eavesdropping and man in the middle attack could expose the data privacy. Privacy of data in **IoT** Cloud can be achieved by handling privacy at device level, storage level, processing level and transit level [29]. Therefore, proper security mechanism is to be devised to enhance the security by strengthening the authentication and encryption techniques [7].

User authentication combined with audit mechanisms and proper encryption could enhance the security and privacy [29–32] to a larger extent. The encryption schemes in Hybrid form perform better. **DNA** coding-based encryption is performing better with **ECC** [8–12]. It is revealed that **DNA** is more efficient and would be predominantly used in **IoT** Cloud [13]. This strengthens the security using subsequent substitution and **ECC** does the rest. For enhancing the security but reducing the computing power the **DNA** encoding mechanism stands first. As the research is on the go **DNA** may be undertaking every area. This work is intended to have a detailed review on the security mechanisms employed in **IoT** Cloud and to propose a novel **DNA** based security mechanism.

The paper is organized as follows: Section 2 presents the review of literature, Section 3 presents the proposed algorithm, Section 4 showing the result and analysis, Section 5 concludes the work.

2 Review of Literature

The review exhibits the recent security techniques that exist to protect the IoT network. As **DNA** cryptography requires substitutions as Caesar ciphers, they reduce computational complexity and assure security. Here data is transformed to genomic sequence which resembles a **DNA** strand.

In [25] a lightweight encryption based on **DNA** sequence for **IoT** device's is proposed by the authors. Here authors have used **DNA** sequence to generate secret key, that is used to encrypt images. Hence mixing it with the classical cryptographic scheme such as symmetric or asymmetric would provide strong security [14, 15, 22].

Novel methods have been proposed to enhance security of data, using Huffman with **DNA** cryptography [4, 16]. The proposal exhibits multiple level of encoding. **DNA** coding scheme include an advantage of better authentication, storage, and digital signatures. In [9, 21] authors have tried securing the data using digital signatures and **DNA** cryptography. Here public-key algorithm is implemented in the form of **DNA** sequencing. In [10] a **DNA** based method is realized on **IoT's**. After implementation of proposal efficiency in energy consumption was detected.

[11] Presents **DNA** and **ECC** based hybrid scheme. After sequence selection, sorting is applied and then resultant is replaced with **DNA** codes. Now the data is converted into binary after which they are encrypted using **ECC**. To provide to **IoT** environment another approach by [12], uses **DNA ECC** for reducing the processing time in **IoT** devices and reducing the size of memory in **IoT** devices.

In [24] author have designed an algorithm based on composite chaos map for securing image. After XOR operation using composite chaotic map, **DNA** encoding which results in image being less prone to attacks. [28] have proposed a system to secure the data in transit with integrity and availability mechanisms. To enhance the data confidentiality a **DNA** cryptography is used along with AES.

The Table 1, accounts few recent proposals **ECC** and **DNA** based hybrid algorithm. In [17] authors have found that **DNA** and **ECC** make difference in **IoT**. The framework is employed with double layered security, first is **DNA** followed by **ECC**. On combining cryptography with steganography [18] have used SHA512, **ECC**, **DNA** and CM-CSA. To hide data behind video, initially the data is compressed using IHE. Multilevel encrypted data is put in pixel points behind frames. The steganographic process is done to enhance security of data.

On suggesting a double level of encryption authors in [19] authors have used two keys for encoding. The first key is generated using **ECC**, and Gaussian kernel (GKF). The other key being generated based on random injective mapping. In [20] authors have proposed **ECC** based hybrid technique. This provides solution for secure communication between nodes. Authors have implemented the scheme as two parts, where the first is encrypting the data with play fairs. And the second is hiding the encrypted data behind **DNA** in a random location using **ECC**.

In [26] authors have proposed an architecture to improve the level of security in **IoT** Cloud. They have adopted a hybrid **DNA** based mechanism with **ECC**. Also, authors have implemented an audit mechanism to monitor data integrity.

Table 1. DNA based hybrid security – existing approaches

	Proposal	Technique
[11]	Framework	DNA & ECC
[12]	Framework	DNA & ECC
[17]	Framework	ECC, RSA, DNA
[18]	Algorithm	DNA, SHA512-ECC
[19]	Algorithm	DNA, ECC, DES, GKF
[20]	Algorithm	DNA, ECC
[26]	Architecture	DNA, ECC, TPA

Hybrid encryption schemes being the security experts, Table 1, shows the way algorithms are combined for enhancing the security in **IoT** Cloud. The attacks that are raised by the anonymous or malicious users are dealt with these schemes. Though the proposals are providing better security, there is no prominent approach to resist data privacy and security attacks on **IoT** Cloud. Hence the proposed security mechanism.

3 Proposed Work

The proposed mechanism enhances the security as it is composed of four components including, **DNA** **P**rocessing **C**enter (**DPC**), **S**ecurity **M**anagement (**SM**), Trusted **TPA** on **C**loud (**TPAC**) and Secure **DNA** Bank (**SDB**). The devices such as sensors/ actuators communicate with each other while it is under clouds boundary.

3.1 Functionality of the Proposed Architecture

User Registration and Authentication. Registration is the initial level where service user is adopted to the **IoT C**loud platform through the **DNA G**ateway (**DG**). Such users are allowed to use the services. The registration will be done with credentials including Name, DoB, MSISDN, MAC, E-mail and so on. The User ID is provided for authenticating the user later. For any user to access the service, have to be authenticated which largely increase the security and privacy of user data. The authentication is done by sending and validating the OTP.

Device Registration and Authentication. Any authenticated user allowed to register their **IoT** Device. The required credentials are IMEI, location, service, name and type. Things Manager (TM) receives the credentials and passes it Things Registry (TR). An key is generated and split into two. First few bits are sent via **DNA G**ateway and the remaining sent to users' mobile. If the authentication is successful, the key is stored. As the TR forwards the device id generated to the certificate registry (CR) it generates a Device Certificate (DC) based on ECDSA. Once the device is registered it is ready for use on successful authentication by the user. The process of device authentication is done by the verification of DC.

Data on Transit. After the successful authentication of User at DG and device authentication at TM, on verifying the service certificate the Service Registry (SR) provides the user with the service. The data is encrypted using **ECC DNA** and hash of the data is generated using SHA1. The cypher text and signature merged together is sent to the cloud through the application. The application server after extracting the encrypted text calculates the signature and compares the same with the signature received. This process at the receiving end ensures the privacy and integrity of data. After the user and application specific process the data is again encrypted to be stored at SDB.

DNA Bank/Data at Rest. The data from the Data Owner (Do) is allowed to be stored as blocks. These blocks contain encrypted data, signature of data and signature of the next block of data. As the data enters the cloud the Third Party Audit Manager (TPAm) makes an entry on the device and the user involved in the process. TPAm also records the signature. While a request is received from the Data Users (D_U), TPAm verifies the access rights and transfers the control to Third party Auditor for user (TPAu). TPAu handles the process of requesting the Do through TPAo. Only after recording the credentials such as signature along with device and user credentials the access is provided.

TPAC. Third Part Auditors monitor the access to keep the non-repudiation. The TPA_u hold the user's privileges and other related credentials while monitoring the activities of Du. The TPA_0 monitor the activities of Do. Also providers are also included in the process of auditing as they are treated as an user. Thus TPAC by verifying TPAs and CSP's could enhance the privacy and integrity of data on **IoT C**loud environment Fig. 1.

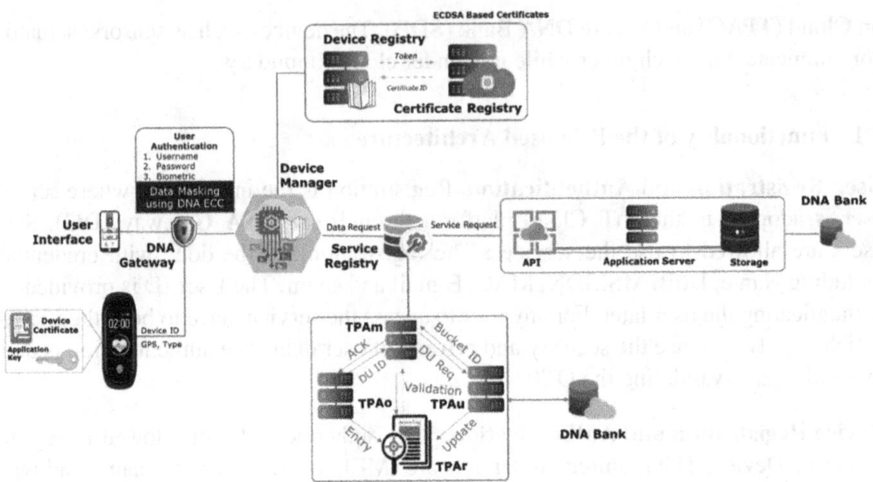

Fig. 1. IoT cloud framework with enhanced data privacy and security

3.2 Encryption Technique

The data is encoded using **DNA** which then transfers it through **DG**. The device authentication is the key to enter the process. After authentication application token is generated. As the authentication becomes successful, the device manager generates a unique session token to handle the user access. The process of encryption is depicted here below and Table 2, shows the symbols used and their meanings.

Table 2. Symbols used to represent data

Symbols	Meaning
ϑ	Set containing ascii
ω	Variable holding a set of binaries
α	Set containing set of paired binaries
gc	Set containing genomes and associated binary values
β	Resultant of first cycle of substitution
γ	Set holding the grouped pairs of genomes into 4's
∞	Resultant of second cycle of substitution
ε	Vectors containing odd elements
ε'	Vector holding matrix associated ε
δ	Holds even set of data
δ'	Used to store matrix representing δ

Step 1: Initially ASCII equivalent for the input data is retrieved, as depicted in the Eq. 1. Here d is the data that is received at the **DPC**, $\mathbf{f_{asc}}$ is the function that converts it into ASCII, and ϑ represents the array that is generated.

$$\vartheta = fasc(d) \tag{1}$$

Process of Substitution
According to the ANSI standards every character in a given set is assigned with unique numbers as in the following Table 3.

Table 3. ASCII value substitution

Characters	Associated values
0–9	48–57
A–B	65–90
a–b	97–122
Symbols and Blank Space characters	Rest of the values between 0 and 256

For Example
Let 'DNA', be the input value the resultant value after the process of calculation is 687797 as per the standard. For any integer value between 0 to 9 the ASCII will be between 48 and 57 respectively.

This phase of encoding works at an order of O(n), and at the successful conversion of data ϑ is passed for the further encoding process.

Step 2: After the retrieval of ASCII values, the binary equivalent is retrieved as Eq. 2, shows the conversion of ϑ into binary sequence. The ω hold the binary sequence retrieved by f_{bin} from the ASCII elements in ϑ.

$$\omega = fbin(\vartheta) \tag{2}$$

Process of Substitution
The binary equivalent of any integer can be calculated easily by subsequent division of the value by 2.

For instance,
Assume the number 687797 the ASCII value generated. This is changed into binary:

- Modulo divide the 68 and store the binary value (remainder) in an array
- Divide the number 68 and store the quotient value to the same variable
- Repeating the process will arrive with a final result, the resultant can be of any size and an eight-bit representation of the given character is 01000100 01001101 00011000.

Higher and random sized binary enhance the security, as it is hard to be guessed. Higher the randomization and bit size also increase the processing time.

Step 3: Binary equivalent is in ω, as in the Eq. 3, the process of encoding starts by grouping input in pairs of two elements. Here ω, presents its contents to the pairing function f_{par} that chops the entire contents into pair of twos.

$$\alpha = fpar(\omega) \tag{3}$$

The process of conversion is expanded as in Eq. 4. The sequence of elements represented as, $\omega(i)_j$ to $\omega(n)_m$. Here i represent the starting element in ω and n represent the last element in the set ω. And j count the bits in two's, and m the last bit. The f_{par} could be expanded as, $\alpha_i = \omega_i + \omega_{i+1}$, which forms a pair iterating till ω_n the upper limit reaches. The final set α, could be written as in Eq. 4.

$$\sum\nolimits_{i=0}^{n} \alpha = \sum\nolimits_{j=0}^{m} \omega_j \; \omega_{j+1} \tag{4}$$

where i, the initial value of α and increases until n is reached at ω_n. And j is initialized with 0 stepping higher till m, while passing only two binary elements such as $\omega_j and \omega_{j+1}$. The routine takes O(n * 2) for the successful partitioning of ω.

For example,
If the input value is 01100001, the binary sequence is generated as follows,

01	00	01	00	01	00	11	01	00	01	10	00

Step 4: Now binary pairs are encoded using the fixed set, of values as in the following table. The encoding is done based on the set generated. After the verification of pairs, the associated nucleotide is substituted replacing the binary pair. This the coding table is generated as in Eq. 5.

$$\sum\nolimits_{i=0}^{4} gc = \sum\nolimits_{i=0, j=0}^{1} (i + j) \tag{5}$$

The generated table is depicted in Table 4. The set actually contain A, T, C, or G, which actually means adenine, thymine, cytosine and guanine respectively.

Step 5: The process of substitution $fdse$ is represented in Eq. 6, where each and every pair of elements is replaced with the genome as in Eq. 7. The encoded message is at β,

$$\beta = fdse(\alpha) \tag{6}$$

$$\sum\nolimits_{i=0}^{n} a = \sum\nolimits_{i=0}^{m} gc \tag{7}$$

To understand the process, let us consider the example here,

Table 4. Nucleotide table for substitution

Code	Genome
00	A
01	T
10	C
11	G

If the input value is 01100001, the substitution of the genomes would result in the following set of values,

T	A	T	A	T	A	G	T	A	T	C	A

Step 6: Next process is to group the genome into pairs of four. This is achieved using the algorithm as represented in Eq. 8, and the process it does is equated in Eq. 9.

$$\gamma = fnuc(\beta) \tag{8}$$

$$\sum_{i=0}^{n} \gamma = \sum_{i=0}^{m} \beta_j \beta_{j+1} \beta_{j+2} \beta_{j+3} \tag{9}$$

For example, let us consider the genomic sequence generated recently,

For the input TATATAGTATCA, the substitution of the genomes would result in the following set of values,

TATA	TAGT	ATCA

Step 7: Generate nucleotide table, for the four-digit genomic sequence. The series is tabulated with an initial value a random number as represented in Eq. 10.

$$f_{ntbl}(\text{rand}(1, \text{len(a)}), \boldsymbol{len(\alpha) + 2}) \tag{10}$$

Here to construct nucleotide coded set a random number between 1 and length of the actual data is taken. The set generated by f_{ntbl} is as described in Table 5. The order of time taken by f_{ntbl} to complete the process is calculated as O (n * 4).

The message encoded using table is more secured, as random number is random. This is because random number depends on the size of the message that changes based on the application.

Step 8: The set β, is grouped in pairs of four by f_{nuc} as in Eq. 8. This is done by merging the set of elements, as $\gamma_i = \beta_i + \beta_{i+1} + \beta_{i+2} + \beta_{i+3}$, here γ is a set containing grouped

Table 5. Nucleotide generated for the message

Text	DNA	Text	DNA	Text	DNA	Text	DNA	Text	DNA	Text	DNA
101	ATAA	109	AGGA	115	CTAA	123	ACAA	131	GATA	139	TAGT
102	TCTA	110	CAAA	116	GCTA	124	CTCA	132	GTAA	140	TACT
103	GCGA	Start	TTGA	117	GTCA	125	TGTA	133	ATGA		
104	GTGA	Stop	TAAA	118	CGTA	126	GAGA	134	AGTA		
105	AGAA	111	ACTA	119	CTGA	127	TATA	135	GACA		
106	CGCA	112	CATA	120	TGCA	128	CACA	136	GCAA		
107	ATTA	113	TCAA	121	TCGA	129	TGAA	137	AGCA		
108	ACCA	114	TACA	122	ATCA	130	TAGA	138	ACGA		

message. Thus, the data are grouped and are stored in γ. The message γ thus encoded is ready for further encoding with the generated f_{nuc} by the module f_{enc} as in Eq. 11.

$$\infty = fenc(\gamma, fntbl()) \tag{11}$$

For each and every entry of γ is replaced with associated index of f_{nuc} This actually generates the set of digits by fully hiding the message. The time taken for this process is in the order of O(n), this actually sustaining the speed of the process. The process is formulated as:

$$\sum_{i=0}^{n} \infty = \sum_{j=0}^{m} fntbl(j), \quad if\ \gamma_j <> \{\theta\} \tag{12}$$

where, *i* representing the index of the resultant message set ∞, and *j* representing index of input set. Here both *i* and *j*, starts with 0 and the iteration steps with one till the value reaches *m* and *n*. The message is stored in ∞ as in Eq. 12.

Here let us consider the grouped sequence of genomes,

For the input TATA/TAGT/ATCA, the substitution of the cyphertext would result in a set of values as follows,

127	139	122

Step 9: As in the Eq. 13 and 14, f_{split}, takes ∞ as input and finds the odd numbers which are then stored into ε. The calculation is done with the simple mathematical calculation of modulo division. After modulo division with the digits, data that do not generate a 0 as result is stored at ε. And for each entry of ε, a separate vector ε' is generated by replace every non zero values with 1's as represented in Eq. 13.

$$\varepsilon = fsplit(\infty) \tag{13}$$

$$\delta = fsplit(\infty) \tag{14}$$

Thus, f_{split} could separate every odd value in the message. In Eq. 12 input calculated for separating the even numbers. The f_{split}, takes ∞ as input and finds the even numbers which are then stored into δ by applying modulo division. The numbers that generate 0 is stored in δ. Parallely each entry in ε, a separate vector $\delta^{'}$ is generated by replace every non zero values with 1's as in Eq. 14. Thus, f_{split} separate every odd value in message.

$$\varepsilon' = fsplit(\varepsilon) \tag{15}$$

$$\delta' = fsplit(\delta) \tag{16}$$

After splitting the converted message in to two set of integers and matrix representation is generated, as in Eq. 15 and 16, f_{mdd} takes odd set ε, even set δ. The resultant denoted by μ, hold the message ready for undergoing the final phase of encoding process by **ECC**. Data Retrieval Matrix looks as in the following example:

$$\begin{vmatrix} 127 & 139 \\ & \end{vmatrix} \quad \begin{vmatrix} & \\ 122 & \end{vmatrix} \quad \begin{vmatrix} 1 & 1 \\ 0 & 0 \end{vmatrix} \quad \begin{vmatrix} 0 & 0 \\ 1 & 0 \end{vmatrix}$$

V 2 V 1

Example - Data Retrieval Matrix

Step 10: Now the hash for the both the odd (ε) and even (δ) set is calculated using **SHA512** as represented in Eq. 17 and 18. The DRM is stored with the generated hash as the reference. This DRM set is stored in gateway for the use during decryption.

$$dh_1 = {}^{f}{}_{sha}(\varepsilon) \tag{17}$$

$$dh_2 = {}^{f}{}_{sha}(\delta) \tag{18}$$

Step 11: Before encryption, the process of key generation is done by f_h, The curve generated based on the curve Eq. 19, contains y, x, ax and b, of which (x, y) represent a point on the curve.

$$y2 = x3 + ax + b \tag{19}$$

The domain parameters of curve are a, b, h, p, N, G, and r. Here 'p' representing prime number, 'a' and 'b' representing coefficients. The 'G' represents point, 'N' represents prime factor, 'h' represent the cofactor and 'r' representing random integer that is less than 'N'. Since NIST specifies the 'p' to be greater than 2^160, the Eq. 19 is rewritten as in Eq. 20, by assuming.

$$y2 = x3 + ax + bmodp(p > 2160) \tag{20}$$

To encrypt any given input, sender choses a random number 'r'. Using this 'r', point is calculated towards encrypting the text with the receiver's Public Key (**Pu**).

$$C = [(r.G), (M + \mathrm{r}.Pu)]$$

Example for the key generation is depicted, by assuming the pain text as "W" which is represented by a value 4,433.

$$y^2 = x^3\text{-}ax\text{+}b \text{ (mod 997)}, a = (\text{-}3), b\text{=}3$$
$$y^2 = (\text{-}3)^3\text{+}1 \text{ (mod 997)}$$
$$G = 17{,}427$$
$$Pr = 11$$
$$Pu = 37, 620$$
$$r = \text{Random Number} = 7$$

Step 12: The final phase of encryption is done by passing the data $\mu 1$ *and* $\mu 1$ to the f_{ecc} along with the pu is depicted in Eq. 21 and 22 subsequently. After data is **DNA** encoded and encryption process is over signature (**dnaSig**) is recorded. After the completion of process of encryption of f_{ecc}, the data is sent to the cloud for storage.

$$d_1\text{'}=\boldsymbol{fecc}(\mu, pu) \tag{21}$$

$$d_2\text{'}=\boldsymbol{fecc}(\mu, pu) \tag{22}$$

After the successful encoding, the data is again passed through another set of encoding process where a random salt (**Es**) is used to generate the code as the user request to store the data. This salt is named here as encryption salt (**Es**), which will be used to construct a sequential array of numbers associated to the **DNA** codes generated in the previous cycle. The partitioned data will be separated as odd and even set, where the odd set of data will have its associated matrix generated and even set of data will have its own set of matrices generated. After the signature is calculated using SHA 512, the cipher text will be grouped in to two portions and two set of matrices are generated to handle both the portions of data separately.

DNA data is converted into the digital form which is partitioned into two groups $\mathbf{data_{si}}$ and $\mathbf{data_{sj}}$. The encrypted data along with the necessary credentials such as unique signature reach the cloud storage after the validation of **TPAo**. The cloud storage gateway after verifying the data with the received signature (**dnaSig**), allocates the buckets for the data after processing. Thus, communication between **IoT** and cloud application are encrypted in a much-secured manner.

3.3 Secure Data Decryption

The request from the device at the **IoT** Environment is taken to cloud along with device certificate. The **CR** validates the certificate by extracting the device information, based on the credentials stored in the certificate registry. The firewall after making the entry on its device log, directs the request to the **TPAu**, while **TPAo** after making the entry on the log including the device credentials of the client and user credentials, sends the request to the **Do**. **Do** may provide the **A**ccess **T**oken (**Acct**). Now the **Acct** is transferred to **Du** through **TPAu**, for authorizing the requestor. After making the entry on the **TPAr**, **TPAu** verify the signature in the register with the signature of the data on the storage. After verifying the signature, the data will be transferred from the storage.

To decrypt of the data is done by the receiver, as it multiplies the first point of the ciphertext pair (r.G) with the private key (**Pr**). Now this result is added to the second point of the ciphertext pair.

$$M = (M + r.Pu) - (Pr\ (r.G)) = (M + r.\ Pr\ G) - (Pr\ (r.G))$$

After authentication of application token, session token and user credentials the encrypted data is decrypted and send to the client through the firewall reaching the **DNA** Gateway. As the gateway receives the data after verifying the **dnaSig**, it first merges the **DNA** matrix $\mathbf{data_{si}}$ and $\mathbf{data_{sj}}$, together $\mathbf{data_m}$ with the help of matrix created. Once identifying the code pattern generated for the data with the help of application id and the session id stored, it multiplies the even numbered **DNA** matrix with the n that is randomly chosen, where $n > 1 < 10$. Then it merges the **DNA** matrix together so that the actual **DNA** message.

The **DNA** data that is received would never require further processing but decoding based on the standard table that was generated for an application.

$$code_{si} => data_{si} \&\& code_{sj} => data_{sj} \quad \text{----------------} \ 18$$

$$data_m = data_{si} + data_{sj} \quad \text{------------------------------} \ 19$$

The next level of decryption involves merging the data together that can be decoded using that generated table. The **DNA** data thus calculated is combined to form a string altogether, from where the further process of decryption could proceed decoding the **DNA**'s. As the **DNA**'s are calculated using the generated application specific nucleotide code, final phase of decryption is done. After actual data is decoded out, the **dSig** is compared with calculated signature of data that is retrieved.

If verification successful the data is sent to client, or an error token *eT* is generated. The *eT* intimates the replace attack to **TPAo**, who further will keep **DOw** informed.

4 Result and Analysis

The implementation is done using opensource tools such as PHP and MYSQL. The interface is designed using HTML5 and CSS3. The cloud sim is used to evaluate the performance of the proposed framework.

4.1 Analysis on ECC DNA

The implementation of the work algorithm is done and results are generated. The input and the output, of the system is recorded to analyse the performance. The sample of the results generated by the proposed algorithm is present here in Fig. 2.

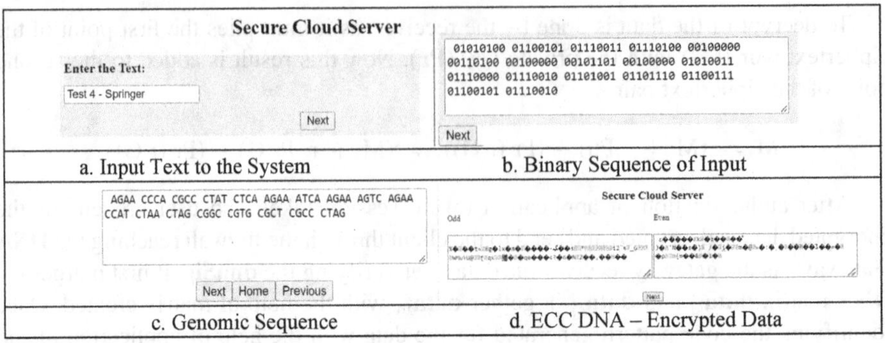

Secure Cloud Server
Enter the Text:
Test 4 - Springer
Next

01010100 01100101 01110011 01110100 00100000 00110100 00100000 00101101 00100000 01010011 01110000 01110010 01101001 01101110 01100111 01100101 01110010
Next

a. Input Text to the System

b. Binary Sequence of Input

AGAA CCCA CGCC CTAT CTCA AGAA ATCA AGAA AGTC AGAA CCAT CTAA CTAG CGGC CGTG CGCT CGCC CTAG
Next Home Previous

Secure Cloud Server
Odd
Even
Next

c. Genomic Sequence

d. ECC DNA – Encrypted Data

Fig. 2. Sample input and output – proposed ECC DNA

The Fig. 2a, shows the inputs text of size 16 characters, Fig. 2b, displays the binary sequence of every character. On subsequent conversion the binary is converted into nucleotides as in Fig. 2c. Finally, the Fig. 2d, shows the final cypher text ready for transmission. The analysis on the proposed **DNA** algorithm is presented here by sampling the data. The efficiency of the algorithm on the basis of time taken is analysed as in Table 6.

Table 6. Analysis on encryption of data-sample 1

Test	Plain text	Cipher text	Key size	Time (MS)
Test 1	10	80	1024	0.07
Test 2	20	160	1024	0.12
Test 3	50	400	1024	0.17
Test 4	120	960	1024	0.23
Test 5	240	1920	1024	0.32

The key size chosen is 1024 bits and at various input sizes the time taken is analysed. At a maximum of 240 characters of data is encrypted in 0.32 ms. The resultant cyphertext is of size 1920 bits.

The process of decryption is done after the implementation of the algorithm. The sample data set for analysis of the results generated is presented here in Table 7. The time taken for encryption is analyzed and is summarized as follows:

The Fig. 3, describes the time taken by the encryption algorithm for encrypting the plain text. Test conducted is based on two key patterns, first is with 1024 bit key and next is using 2048 bit key. As per the results generated by the system the average time taken for encrypting 10 byte of data is 7.5 ms. The maximum size reported for this work is 240 byte, for which an average time of 32.5 ms is recorded. Therefore, the **ECCDNA** proves better for encryption.

Table 7. Analysis on encryption of data - sample 2

Test	Plain text	Cipher text	Key size	Time (MS)
Test 6	10	80	2048	0.08
Test 7	20	160	2048	0.12
Test 8	50	400	2048	0.20
Test 9	120	960	2048	0.24
Test 10	240	1920	2048	0.33

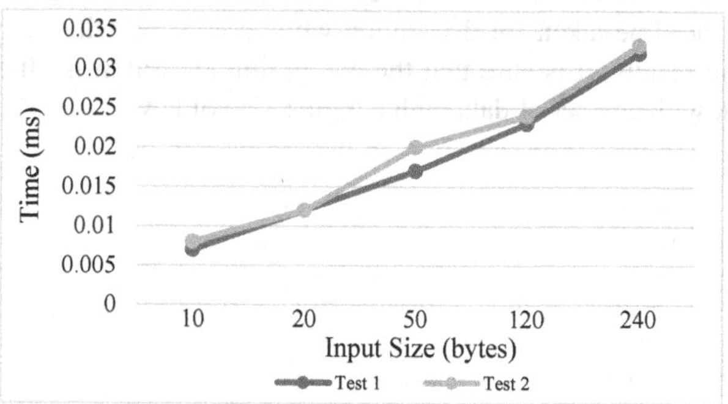

Fig. 3. Time taken by the ECC DNA for encryption

Table 8. Analysis on decryption of data - sample 1

Test	Cipher text	Plain text	Time (MS)
Test 1	80	10	0.08
Test 2	160	20	0.14
Test 3	400	50	0.16
Test 4	960	120	0.26
Test 5	1920	240	0.31

The implementation is tested to verify its efficiency during data decryption and results generated are sampled as in Table 8. Algorithm performed the decryption process in an efficient manner. The variable length data is used as input to check the efficiency. The minimum size of data is performed at an average of 9 ms and the data with about 1920 bytes is performed at an average of 35 ms.

Table 9. Analysis on decryption of data - sample 2

Test	Cipher text	Plain text	Time (MS)
Test 6	80	10	0.09
Test 7	160	20	0.13
Test 8	400	50	0.18
Test 9	960	120	0.23
Test 10	1920	240	0.35

The efficiency of data decryption process is described in Table 9, which shows a consistency in the time taken for decryption while compared with the previous set of data. As per the results, it is sure that the encryption algorithm is efficient and faster enough to work with any set of data with a higher size of key.

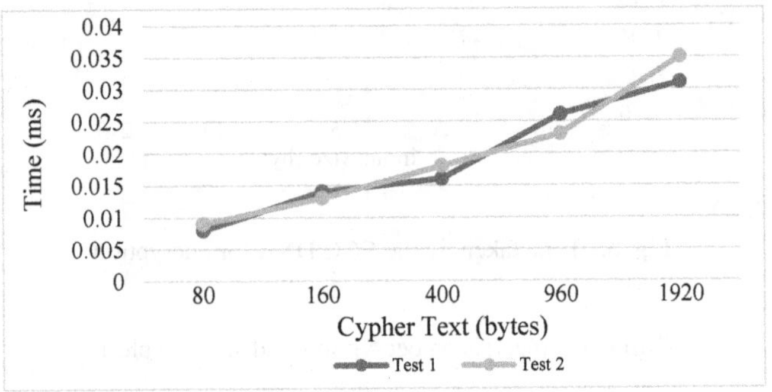

Fig. 4. Time taken by the ECC DNA for decryption

The Fig. 4, describes the time taken by the encryption algorithm for encrypting the plain text. As per the results generated by the system the average time taken for decryption for 80 byte encrypted input data is 8.5 ms. The time taken is to decrypt the data of size 1920 bytes, for which an average time taken is recorded as 33 ms.

The proposed work while compared with the existing approaches found to have better performance. The approach included RC4 along with **DNA**. The comparison is presented here below in Table 10.

The results depict the efficiency of the proposed algorithm as the key size increases the time taken for encryption also increases. Among the present scenario, such situation the proposed **ECC DNA** after testing with higher key sizes 1024 and 2048 could perform better up to 0.023 ms and 0.033 ms respectively. Therefore, the proposed **ECC DNA** proves performing better at encryption.

Table 10. Comparison with existing proposals

	RC4	RC4 – DNA	Proposed ECC – DNA
Plain Text (bytes)	128	128	120
Key Size (bytes)	256	256	1024
Encryption Time (ms)	0.414	0.584	0.23
Plain Text (bytes)	256	256	240
Key Size (bytes)	256	256	2048
Encryption Time (ms)	0.576	0.69	0.33

4.2 Analysis of Proposed Framework

Test is conducted using an opensource tool Cloud Analyst. The load test, response time and throughput were recorded. Series of requests were generated to test performance of the system as in Fig. 5. It shows that the system could accept multiple request if the system is implemented.

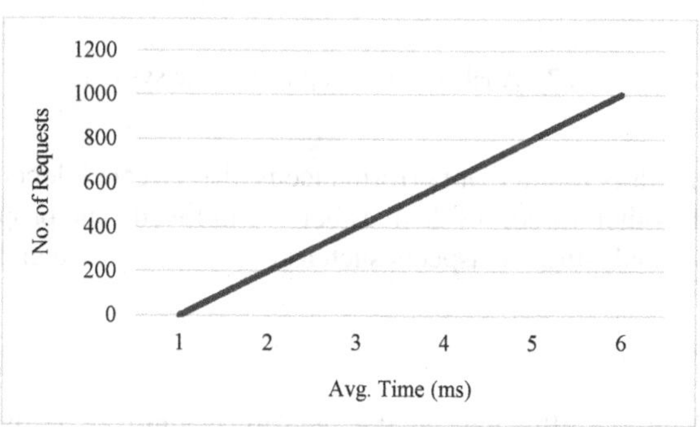

Fig. 5. Analysis of the parrel requests

As any request to have a task done response time of the system is recorded and found to be reasonable as in Fig. 6. After the series of requests are received, the calculation is done with the input and the response is sent back. The minimum time taken to respond is 6.8 ms and a maximum of 16.5 ms.

During the communication, network show up throughput as the request and response are higher. On the analysis of throughput is depicted as in Fig. 7. It also depends on the

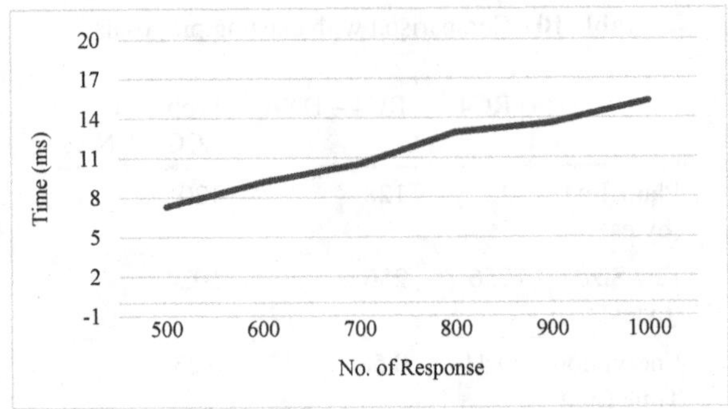

Fig. 6. Analysis on the response time of the system

type of network used, here the throughput recorded is between 2.2 ms to 4.4 ms on an average.

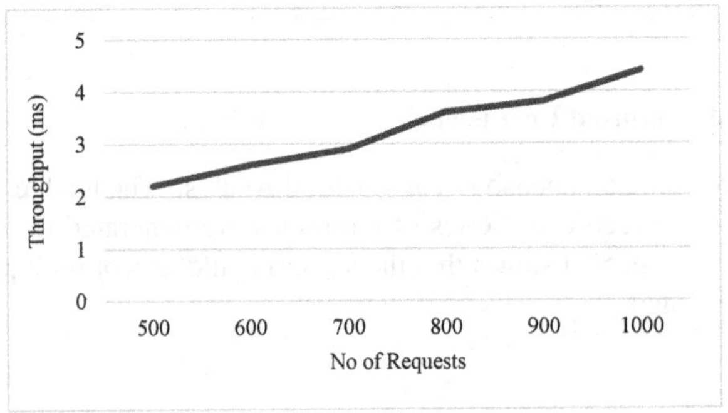

Fig. 7. Analysis of throughput of the system

As per the study it is found that performance is also affected depending on medium that is used and the other aspects of devices being employed. The proposed mechanism performs better on analysing the aspects such as request, response and throughput.

5 Conclusion

The analysis reflects the efficiency of the security techniques as the privacy attacks such as data leakage is mitigated. As described in [4, 8–12] that **DNA** based security algorithms with **ECC** provide better security at **IoT** level. Hybrid algorithms proposed could encrypt the data as fast as 0.033 ms as the size of key is 2048. The decryption time stands equally faster up to 0.035 ms. Data privacy and integrity stands high as security is strong. **DNA** is efficient in such a way that it could enhance the security and privacy as it is prominent at data hiding and the proposed architecture enhance the privacy and security by enforcing authentication and repudiation using TPAC. As per the results generated, it is clear that using Hybrid encryption could enhance the security in **IoT** Cloud.

References

1. Van Kranenburg, R.: The Internet of Things: A Critique of Ambient Technology and the All-Seeing Network of RFID. Institute of Network Cultures, Amsterdam, The Netherlands (2007)
2. Tan, L., Wang, N.: Future internet: the internet of things. In: Proceedings of the. 3rd International Conference on Advanced Computer Theory and Engineering (ICACTE) , pp. 376–380. Chengdu, China (2010)
3. Wu, Y., Sheng, Q.Z., Zeadally, S.: RFID: opportunities and challenges. In: Chilamkurti, N. (ed.) Next-Generation Wireless Technologies. CCN, pp. 105–129. Springer, New York (2013). https://doi.org/10.1007/978-1-4471-5164-7_7
4. Vijayan, V., Elias, E.P.: Hybrid method for securing data in IoT cloud. Int. J. Innov. Technol. Explor. Eng. (2019)
5. Swamy, S.N., Jadhav, D., Kulkarni, N.: Security threats in the application layer in IOT applications. In: International Conference on I-SMAC (2017)
6. Joel, J.P.C., et al.: Enabling Technologies for the Internet of Health Things. IEEE (2018) ISSN: 2169-3536
7. Kanthavar, S.: Design of an Architecture for Cloud Storage to Provide Infrastructure as a Service (IaaS). IEEE (2017)
8. Hussein, N.A., Shujaa, M.I.: DNA computing-based stream cipher for internet of things using MQTT protocol. Int. J. Electric. Comput. Eng. **10**(1), 1035–1042 (2020)
9. Cherukupalli, N.S., Maruvada, S.S.: Securing data in IoT devices using DNA cryptography. Int. J. Mod. Trends Sci. Technol. **6**(8S) (2020)
10. Agarwal, N., Mahendran, A., Lakshmanan, R.: Trusted third party auditing for cloud security using digital signature and DNA cryptography. IJSTR **8**(12) (2019)
11. Tiwari, H.D., Kim, J.H.: Novel method for DNA-based elliptic curve cryptography for IoT devices. ETRI J. **40**(3) (2018). http://wileyonlinelibrary.com/journal/etrij)
12. Barman, P., Saha, B.: DNA encoded elliptic curve cryptography system for IoT security. Int. J. Comput. Intell. IoT **2** (2019)
13. Prabhu, D., Adimoolam, M.: Bi-serial DNA Encryption Algorithm. https://pdfs.Semanticscholar.org/1754/f0eb5852500598a70af4002e186cd2f3c6ce.pdf
14. Ning, K.: A Pseudo DNA Cryptography Method. arXiv:0903.2693, [cs.CR]. Cornell University Library (2009)
15. Gupta, K., Singh, S.: DNA based cryptographic techniques: a review. Int. J. Adv. Res. Comput. Sci. Softw. Eng. **3**(3) (2013)
16. Harish Kumar, N., Patil, R.M., Deepak, G., Murthy, B.M.: A novel approach for securing data in IoTCloud using DNA cryptography and huffman coding algorithm. In: 2017 International Conference on Innovations in Information, Embedded and Communication Systems (ICIIECS) (2017)
17. Bansal, M., Gupta, S., Mathur, S.: Comparison of ECC and RSA algorithm with DNA encoding for IoT security. In: Proceedings of the Sixth International Conference on Inventive Computation Technologies (ICICT 2021). IEEE Xplore (2021)
18. Jose, A., Subramaniam, K.: DNA based SHA512-ECC cryptography and CM-CSA based steganography for data security. Materials Today: Proceedings, Elsevier (2020)
19. El-Latif, E.I.A., Moussa, M.I.: Information hiding using artificial DNA sequences based on Gaussian kernel function. J. Inf. Optimiz. Sci. (2019). ISSN: 0252-266
20. Ahmed, Z., Adil, S., Al-Alak, S.M.K.: ECC based blind steganography-DNA for hidden information. J. Eng. Appl. Sci. **14** (2019)
21. Kumar, M.: Implementation of DNA cryptosystem using Hybrid approach. Res. J. Comput. Inf. Technol. Serv. **6**(3) (2018)

22. Rathi, M., Bhaskare, S., Kale, T., Shah, N., Vaswani, N.: Data security using DNA cryptograph. Int. J. Comput. Sci. Mobile Comput. **5**, 123–129 (2016)
23. Abusaimeh, H.: Security attacks in cloud computing and corresponding defending mechanisms. Int. J. Adv. Trends Comput. Sci. Eng. **9**(3), 4141–4148 (2020)
24. Aditya, K., Mohanty, A.K., Ragav, G.A., Thanikaiselvan, V., Amirtharajan, R.: Image encryption using dynamic DNA encoding and pixel scrambling using composite chaotic maps. IOP Conf. Ser. Mater. Sci. Eng. **872**(1), 12045 (2020)
25. Al-Shargabi, B., Al-Husainy, M.A.F.: A new dna based encryption algorithm for Internet of Things. In: International Conference of Reliable Information and Communication Technology, IRICT 2020, pp. 786–795 (2021)
26. Raj, Y.S., Rabara, S.A., Ramesh, K.S.B.: A security architecture for cloud data using hybrid security scheme. In: Proceedings of the Fourth International Conference on Smart Systems and Inventive Technology (ICSSIT-2022), pp. 1803–1811, IEEE (2022). ISBN: 978-1-6654-0117-3
27. Raj, Y.S., Rabara, S.A.: An integrated architecture for IoT based data storage in secure smart monitoring environment. Int. J. Sci. Technol. Res. **8**(10) (2019). ISSN: 2277-8616
28. Kolate, V., Joshi, R.B.: An information security using DNA cryptography along with AES algorithm. Turkish J. Comput. Math. Educ. **12**(1S), 183–192 (2021)
29. Alferidah, D.K., Jhanjhi, N.Z.: A review on security and privacy issues and challenges in Internet of Things. IJCSNS Int. J. Comput. Sci. Network Secur. **20**(4) (2020)
30. Yu, Y., Li, Y., Tian, J., Liu, J.: Blockchain-based solutions to security and privacy issues in the Internet of Things. IEEE Wirel. Commun. **25**(6), 12–18 (2018)
31. Yang, Y., Wu, L., Yin, G., Li, L., Zhao, H.: A survey on security and privacy issues in Internet-of-Things. IEEE Internet Things J. **4**(5), 1250–1258 (2017)
32. Assiri, A., Almagwashi, H.: IoT security and privacy issues. In: 2018 1st International Conference on Computer Applications & Information Security (ICCAIS), pp. 1–5 (2018)

Internet of Things

SMADE - Smart Medical Assist Device for Elders

Muvva Durga Samhitha[1(✉)], E. Umamaheswari[2], Rudra Pratap Singh[1], and Souranil Das[1]

[1] Vellore Institute of Technology, Chennai 600127, India
muvvadurga.samhitha2019@vitstudent.ac.in
[2] Center for Cyber Physical Systems, Vellore Institute of Technology, Chennai 600127, India
umamaheswari.e@vit.ac.in

Abstract. This paper presents the implementation and working of a smart medical assist device for the elderly. The Internet of Things (IoT) is attracting attention for applications in various fields. The elderly people of the society are currently facing their inability to understand the proper medication schedule. Pandemic made things harder than usual. Especially during this period, even the caretakers/medical assistants don't tend to travel outside and meet their clients. We looked into no contact medical assistance and chose that as the main objective, along with the intention of providing them with proper medical scheduling for intake and adding the advantage of tracking the amount of medicine. The research paper will handle the medicines' schedule from any place when entered manually. It informs the pharmacy and doctor to see the complete status of medicines with the elderly. The device checks the quantity of medication left and alerts when required.

Keywords: Elder assistance · Arduino UNO · Blynk application · Pills · Microcontroller

1 Introduction

The Internet of Things (IoT) has been such a powerful paradigm in making the activities of a user easier on a daily basis. The quality of being able to communicate the software with the hardware or usable things is providing the solutions to all kinds of problems. This is progressively becoming the most wanted technology. The numerous research works in this field are making the IoT a more innovative technology nowadays. The extensive work carried out in bringing the sensors more and more close to the software is making it more efficient to work to bring out the best and useful products into the market. One of the major problems that elderly people of the society are facing currently is their inability to understand the proper medicines schedule, even though the doctor prescribes the medicine schedule. As the pandemic hit us hard, we are trying to avoid contact with other people. Statistics say that most of the elders tend to behave as their brain is not ready to adapt to any new changes.

Published by Springer Nature Switzerland AG 2022
E. J. Neuhold et al. (Eds.): ICCCSP 2022, IFIP AICT 651, pp. 267–280, 2022.
https://doi.org/10.1007/978-3-031-11633-9_19

The proposed idea of helping the elderly to find an easier way in knowing their medicines along with their daily schedule by reminding them with a beep alarm makes the task of the people who are taking care of the elderly easier, with the additional quality of reminding the medical assistants when the amount of the medicine is on the edge of completion. The whole prototype is incorporated with all the mentioned qualities, making it a smart assistive medical device.

The project prototype can be implemented in any circumstances. The research paper features no restrictions or rules to implement the features. Since the device performs multiple operations, the features are trained to work one by one. The process flow happens one by one. Initially, the scheduling and choosing the medicines of the respective slots is performed manually. The scheduling is fed into the system. The device, then linked to the Arduino, performs the task. The device gives a beep sound when it's time for the medicines and dispenses out the same. The ultrasonic sensor evaluates the distance of the medicine and alerts when they are on the edge of completion. Sensing and evaluating the medicine amount can further be extended in an error-free manner by using other sensors, though costly to give out the proper output. The prototype, if implemented on iOS and Android, will make usability accessible to various users.

The research paper has various topics, starting with a section describing the background work performed to finalize the problem solution and related work describing the existing problem and the solutions related to the problem. Section 3 has the methodology proposed, and the architecture used to set up the hardware components. Section 4 has the set-up work the paper required to bring out the final solution to the issue found in a detailed manner followed by implementation. The results and outputs are described in the next section, which has the visual proofs of the process performed. The last section has the conclusions and future scope of the project, explaining the outcome of the paper and the future advancements possible.

2 Background and Related Work

2.1 Background Work

A typical elderly person expects someone to be there when it comes to notifying and explaining to them about the medication schedule and the respective intake. Even though they get a properly aligned give-out prescription along with a physician/caretaker, the elderly who aren't educated have difficulty with understanding the schedule and medicines allotted. Even if the elderly is educated, studies show that they are facing a hard time in remembering their intake time and the medicine due to their deprived health conditions. Additionally, the pandemic is added to the list of the problems. Though the families are hiring caretakers, they are not willing to travel and take care of their patients during this phase. When the issues are all identified properly, a product prototype with the following features is designed and implemented.

2.2 Related Work

Medication for Elders. Elders have been known to have issues with taking regular medication due to either their health issues, or loss of memory power. This, along with being dependent on others just for medication, is a big concern. This has been looked into by a number of papers [1–4].

Technological Acceptability. This has always been a challenge faced by a lot of people, most important being feasibility [5]. The devices should also have considerations on time [6]. The time taken for setup [7], and the device control has been a significant factor [8]. There is also the factor of acceptance by elders [9]. This can lead to a lot of problems, such that there is no need for a helper for setup. Pharmacies should be able to set up the schedules in the device directly after prescribing their medicines [10, 11].

Automatic Dispensing. The automatic dispensing of the medicines is also a significant factor [12]. The correct selection and use of motors, and the containers where the medicines are to be dispensed, is also a significant factor [13]. The control of such a mechanism was explored [14, 15].

Remote Interface Control. The control of the system was inspired by baby monitors [16]. The system is similar to such an elder medication system. The connections are done through a smartphone app [14] including an alarm system with dispenser time scheduling and control was also observed, for ease of access. The systems were observed on other similar devices [17, 18].

3 Proposed Methodology and Architecture

Medical Dispensing. Our prototype is designed in such a way that the medicine once loaded into the slot will itself dispense the medicine without guiding it for every single dosage.

Medicine Alerts. One of the major difficulties the elderly face is they tend to forget the medicine timing and the respective medicine. So an alert or a reminder will be a cue to them that it's time for medicine. So the prototype also has the feature of alerting the user reminding their medicine time. That's when the device will dispense out the medicine as per the schedule it will be programmed. Additionally, one more alert will be sent to the medical assistant when the box of medicines is on the edge of completion. This is added so that the elderly doesn't have to miss the medicines because of the reason that they missed checking their device. Hence, are programmed into the device.

Medicine Scheduling. Manual work is dominant in this scenario when compared to technical work. The prototype needs a UI interface to feed in the memory of the medicine and the schedule for the user. A UI has to be created in such a way that the caretaker and a medical shop assistant can use it to fill the medicine and set up the reminder alert in the interface, which will be interlinked with the hardware components and setup.

New Innovation. It is almost impossible to have the scheduling done by a device. Various sources and research works have been evaluated, and a proper conclusion has been drawn that, in order to have a device schedule the medicines, a new product has to be designed and fed in the memory of the patient's problem and a doctor's appointment. The whole concept extends as a separate problem statement leading to a separate project. If considered, it can be extended and used to design an entirely new prototype for scheduling alone. The existing medical dispenser's working models have been evaluated and concluded that with a touch of new advancements, the prototype can be carried away to the next level. Though various solutions are existing, not even a single solution provides the proper and multiple efficient features. Each of the existing products provides the solution to one or two problems. Additionally, none of the existing products checks the expiry dates of the medicines. All the papers are verified and conclude that there is no such product that dispenses, schedules, alerts, checks the medicine quantity and manufacturing date.

Bedridden Patients. Majority of the elderly are bedridden and even find it difficult to understand technology and the idea of the SMADE is to make the medicine intake easier for them. The setup however is designed in such a way that the caretaker or sons/daughters sets up the medicine slot and time for dispensing in the application. Once the setup is made, the major part left is dispensing the medicine at the right time by alerting the elderly. The SMADE has to be placed in the reach of bedridden elders so that they just take the medicine whenever it comes out without any help required. The SMADE will pop out the medicine container and the elderly should be educated whenever the container pops out, they take the medicine in that particular container. There is no fixed distance to maintain between the device and the elderly people. They can keep the device at any distance depending on their ease.

Setup. The set-up mentioned in this paper has two parts, the hardware, and the software.

Hardware System. The hardware system consists of Items as mentioned (Table 1).

1. The hardware system performs three functions:
2. Dispensing Medicines according to set time
3. Alerting while dispensing
4. Getting information about Medicine quantities

Software System. The software system consists of Items as mentioned (Table 2). The Software System performs two functions:

1. Display Dispense Events Log
2. Setup time for each medication
3. Turn on or off each medication
4. Alert when the Quantity of medication is low and needs refilling.

Workflow. The system communicates according to the Flow Chart defined above.

1. For Setup, the timing for each of the medicines available is set.
2. The required buttons for each medicine in the app are turned on.
3. The Hardware requires being on and connected to the Blynk server.

Table 1. Hardware system

Hardware	Description
Arduino UNO	Main microcontroller
DS3231 RTC module	Clock synchronization module
Piezo electronic buzzer	Alert buzzer
LED lights	Alert lights
LCD1602	16 × 2 display
SG90 servo motor(s)	Rotary actuator for dispensing
HC-SR04 ultrasonic sensor	Distance sensor for quantity check

Table 2. Software system

Hardware	Description
Blynk	Library and application for wireless control
Android/iOS	Mobile OS

4. When it is time for dispensing medicine(s), The Arduino dispenses the required medicine, provides visual and auditory alerts, and checks for the quantity of medicine left in the dispensed container.
5. The quantity is checked against a certain value, depending on the size of the container, and if it is below a certain level, the information is sent to the application as alerts.

The setup mentioned in this research paper used many components as per the requirements. The setup used I2C LCD to display the output and RTC for real-time clocks, which will be saving time. The Buzzer and Led are used to alert the user, and a detailed description of the alert will be shown on the LCD used.

The servo motor is used to dispense the medicine, this will be connected in such a way that whenever scheduled medicine time has reached then the servo will open the container where medicine will be stored, and it will dispense the medicine. The ultrasonic sensor is just used to detect the distance between the sensor and medicine, and this will alert the user when the medicine level is down (Figs. 1 and 2).

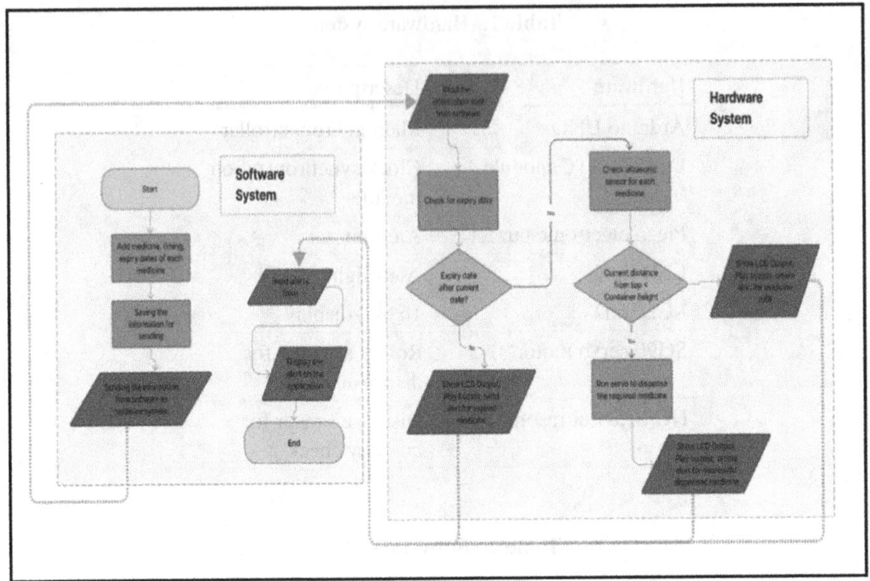

Fig. 1. Flow diagram of the system

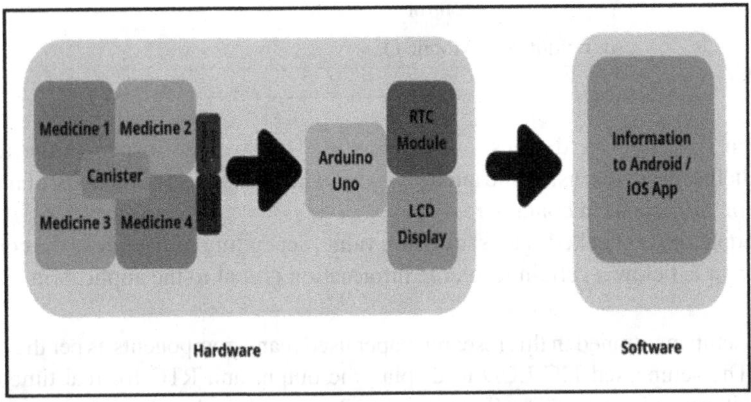

Fig. 2. The framework of the system

Setup. In this schematic as presented in Fig. 3 and circuit diagram as presented in Fig. 4, the connections of the component are as follows:

For Ultrasonic Sensor 1.
Echo Pin is Connected to Pin 8 of Arduino
Trig Pin is Connected to Pin 9 of Arduino

For Ultrasonic Sensor 2.
Echo Pin is Connected to Pin 10 of Arduino
Trig Pin is Connected to Pin 11 of Arduino

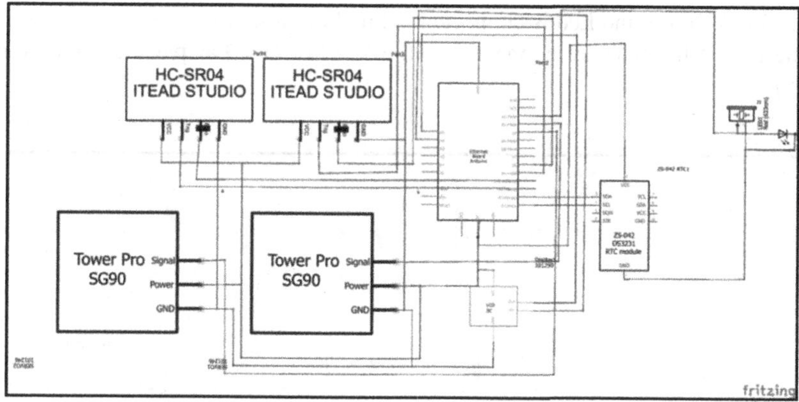

Fig. 3. Schematic diagram

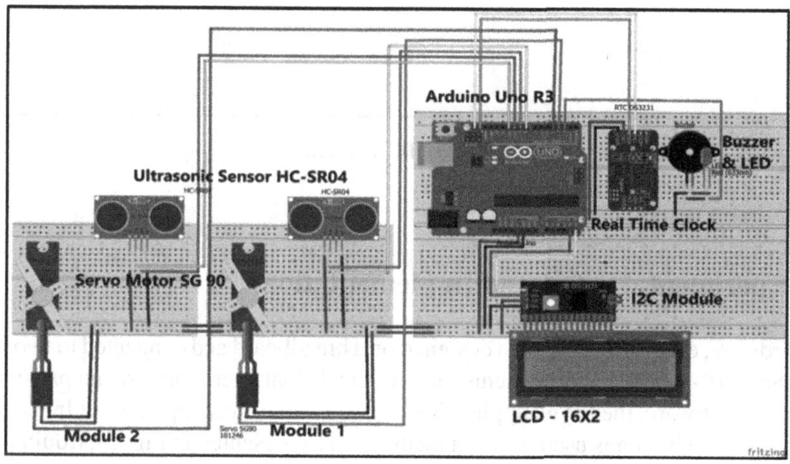

Fig. 4. Circuit diagram

For Servo Motor 1.
Signal Pin is Connected to Pin 3 of Arduino

For Servo Motor 2.
Signal Pin is Connected to Pin 4 of Arduino

For LCD Display.
SDA is Connected to Pin A4 of Arduino
SCL is Connected to Pin A5 of Arduino

For RTC Module.
SDA is Connected to the default SDA pin of Arduino
SCL is Connected to the default SCL pin is Arduino

For Buzzer and LED.

Power pin of buzzer and Led is connected is Pin 2 of Arduino

The rest of the pins are connected to the VCC or GND as per their requirements (Fig. 5).

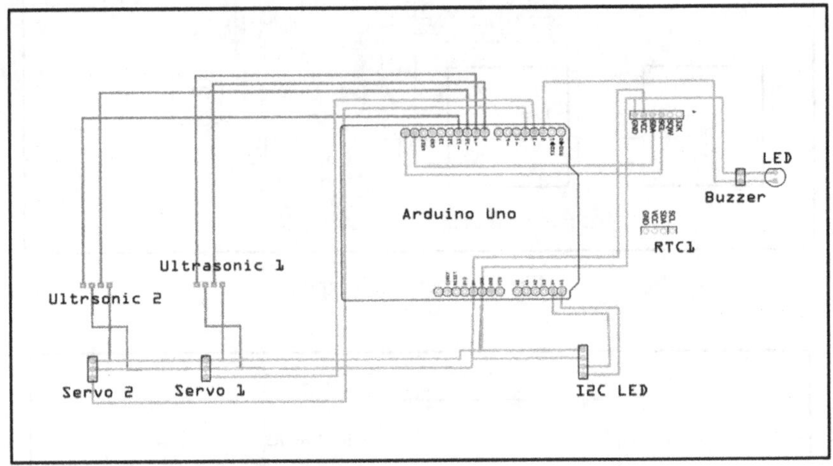

Fig. 5. PCB design

4 Experimental Setup and Implementation

For hardware, everything has been designed on a breadboard and connected to two Ultrasonic Sensors - Servo Motor Systems for 2 Medical Containers support and presented in Fig. 6. For software, the Blynk application is used, where the setup of Time Input and an Enable/Disable button is used for each medication as presented in Fig. 7. Arduino UNO has been used as the microcontroller to configure the device, and this can be replaced by any board depending upon the need of the user and industry requirements. As SMADE is a modular device, it can be configured with any number of medicine slots, and replaced with any microcontroller in place of the Arduino UNO.

4.1 Default Time Display

When alerts, or no dispense or quantity check options are triggered, the default display mode of the device is set to a time display mode. This shows the time and the date, and changes when there is a medicine to dispense as presented in Fig. 8.

4.2 Application Setup

The android app is set up to initiate once every x day's a week, and the time can also be set. The expiry option is also present, which checks for the expiry month of medicine and alerts when it has expired as presented in Fig. 9.

Fig. 6. Hardware implementation

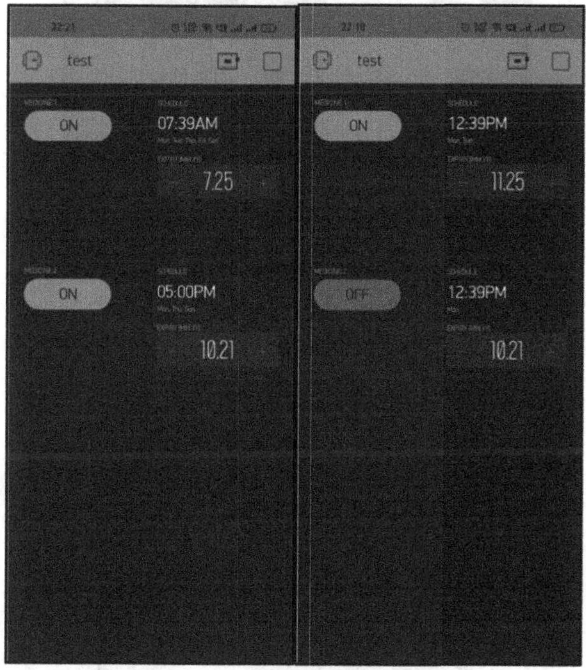

Fig. 7. Software application implementation

4.3 Medicine Time Alert

When it is time for dispensing medicines, the timer runs, and alerts. This is done by checking the configurations provided in the Android app as presented in Fig. 10.

Fig. 8. Time for medicine 1

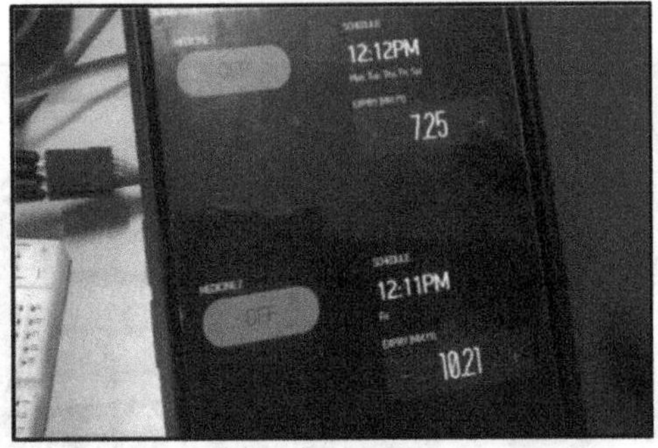

Fig. 9. Application setup

Fig. 10. Time for medicine 1

4.4 Medicine Level Alert

Medicine levels are checked after every dispense and alerts are scheduled accordingly.

When the quantity is below 20%, a "Refill" alert is initiated as presented in Fig. 11. When the quantity is below 10%, a "Mandatory refill alert" is initiated.

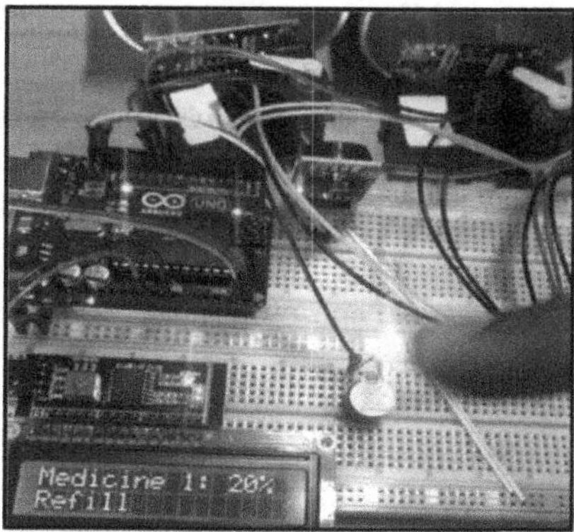

Fig. 11. Medicine 1 quantity alert

The following picture Fig. 12 shows the average medical delivery services as per the sources and most of them are internet and mobile-based, making this paper more visual proof of a better outreach.

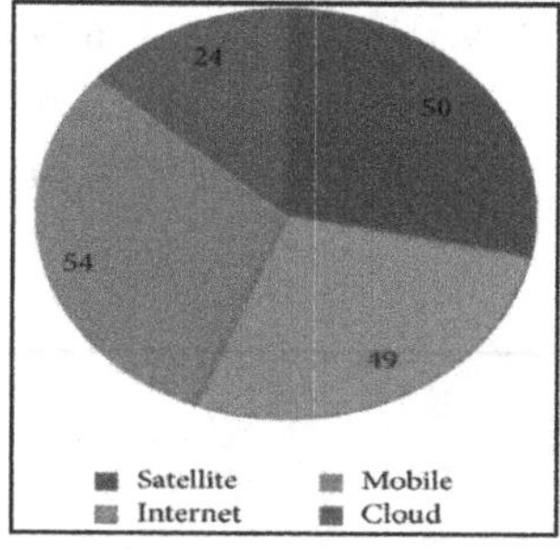

Fig. 12. Medical delivery services

By allowing the user to choose the dosage of the medicine and the time of the dosage, the device relieves the user from constantly forgetting their medicine cycle and intake. By dispensing the medicine as per the schedule the software is fed into, the device is completely taking up the task of the scheduler/medical assistant going to the elder to give the medicine.

5 Result Analysis

The proposed application tested with 5 elder volunteers, and it was found that most of them were able to handle the device without any difficulty. The medicines were dispensed, and the average data among volunteers for certain age groups.

The details for the analysis as given in Table 3 show the average delay for three main aspects of operation: Scheduled time, dispensed delay, and intake delay. The data is also shown as a plot in Fig. 12. The time is plotted on the X-axis and the blue line describes the scheduled time whereas the orange line represents the delay caused in dispensing medicine. The gray line shows the delay caused by the patient in taking the medicine. As per the data, the device was able to dispense the medicines on time, with 99% accuracy, and the confirmation notifications were being sent to the caretakers and doctors via the Blynk application. The dispensed delay is close to 2 s which is an accurate delay as it can be considered as the time taken by device to pull out the slot (Fig. 13).

Table 3. Average testing delays

	Dispensed delay (s)	Intake delay (s)
Elder 01	2.51	5.6
Elder 02	2.44	8.45
Elder 03	2.12	10.42
Elder 04	2.32	9.45
Elder 05	2.95	6.67
Elder 06	2.68	7.9
Elder 07	2.91	5.32
Elder 08	2.29	6.29
Elder 09	2.43	6.98
Elder 10	2.92	9.89

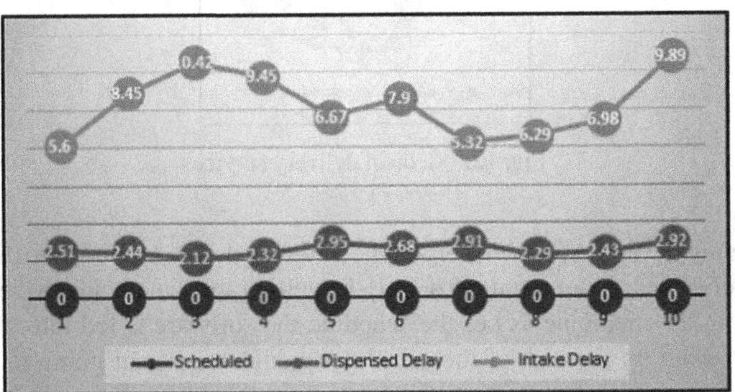

Fig. 13. Average operational delays

The quantity of medicines is dependent on the size of container used, and can be customized based on use cases and requirements, and whenever the quantity was below preset levels, the notification was sent to the caretakers and pharmacies for a refill, based on the doctor's confirmation the medicine slots can be refilled by the pharmacies.

6 Conclusion and Future Work

The proposed software implementation is minimal, and the UI design is extremely easy for the user to choose and work on. The prototype itself performs multiple tasks including scheduling, alerting, and dispensing the medications. Every feature implemented in the prototype reduces the burden of the user in one or another way. Blynk made the software interface easier to program than the authors analyzed.

The background work evaluated gave birth to the new idea of designing a proper prototype for feeding the medicine schedules too. The above designed product needs manual work to feed the medicine dosage and time. If analyzed properly by identifying the loopholes and numerous ways of implementing a smart scheduler, the project can be extended further. With the introduction of smart scheduling algorithms along with proper medical treatment strategy, the same project can be extended further to develop a Smart Medicine Input Scheduler.

Technical Upgrades:

1. PCB Model Printing and Implementation
2. 3D-Printed Case for the PCB Designed.
3. Identifying Expiry dates from medicine Strips visually.

An additional feature is where the device visually scans the medical strip and evaluates the expiry date based on the time allotted. To proceed with the further coding, proper scanning algorithms have to be incorporated into the hardware setup.

1. Full-Scale Android/iOS Application.
2. An additional feature where alerts can be incorporated as currently, we are working on the medicine dispensing part only so we have included all the possible features related to medication dispensing.

The proposed work currently uses the Blynk application to create a user interface that takes the user timings and medicine slots. Instead of using Blynk, a proper android or iOS application can be designed for better and easier access to the hardware device.

Acknowledgement. This work is supported by the management of Vellore Institute of Technology, Chennai under the guidance of Dr. E. Umamaheswari. The authors wish to thank the management for all the encouragement we received in taking our ideas further.

References

1. de Beer, R., Keijers, R., Shahid, S., Al Mahmud, A., Mubin, O.: PMD: designing a portable medicine dispenser for persons suffering from Alzheimer's disease. In: Miesenberger, K., Klaus, J., Zagler, W., Karshmer, A. (eds.) ICCHP 2010. LNCS, vol. 6179, pp. 332–335. Springer, Heidelberg (2010). https://doi.org/10.1007/978-3-642-14097-6_53
2. Haynes, R.B., McKibbon, K.A., Kanani, R.: Systematic review of randomized trials of interventions to assist patients to follow prescriptions for medications. Lancet **348**(9024), 383–386 (1996)

3. Coughlin, S.P.: Medicament dispensing cell. U. States. US, Scriptpro, LLC, Mission, KS, pp. 202–209 (2002)
4. Dhukaram, V., Baber, C.: Elderly cardiac patients' medication management: patient day-to-day needs and review of medication management system. In: 2013 IEEE International Conference on Healthcare Informatics, pp. 107–114 (2013). https://doi.org/10.1109/ICHI.2013.20
5. Ahadani, M.A., De Silva, L.C., Petra, I., Hameed, M.F.A., Wong, T.S.: Low cost robotic medicine dispenser. Procedia Eng. **41**, 202–209 (2012)
6. Lin, A.C., Huang, Y.C., Punches, G., Chen, Y.: Effect of a robotic prescription-filling system on pharmacy and prescription-filling time. Am. J. Health-Syst. Pharm. AJHP **64**(17), 1832–1839 (2007)
7. Patil, A., Darshan, B.G., Ashoka, D.V., Nethravathi, B.: IoT based medicine dispenser. Int. J. Eng. Res. Technol. (IJERT) **8**, 2289–2292 (2020)
8. Tsai, P.-H., Chen, T.-Y., Chi-Ren, Y., Shih, C.-S., Liu, J.W.S.: Smart medication dispenser: design, architecture and implementation. IEEE Syst. J. **5**(1), 99–110 (2011). https://doi.org/10.1109/JSYST.2010.2070970
9. Ziefle, M., Wilkowska, W.: Technology acceptability for medical assistance. In: 2010 4th International Conference on Pervasive Computing Technologies for Healthcare, pp. 1–9 (2010). https://doi.org/10.4108/ICST.PERVASIVEHEALTH2010.8859
10. HongLeiChe, C.Y., Zang, J.: Design and implement an automatic pharmacy system. In: International Conference on CSEE, vol. 214 (2011)
11. Liu, X., Yun, C., Zhao, X., Wang, W., Ma, Y.: Design and application for automated depositing and dispensing system of pharmacy. In: ICCSIT, 2nd IEEE International Conference of Computer Science and Information Technology, pp. 332–336 (2008). https://doi.org/10.1109/ICCSIT.2008.20
12. Kudera, K.W., Guerra, L.E., Leonard, R.A.: Medicament dispensing cell with dual platens (2000)
13. Boquete, L., Rodriguez-Ascariz, J.M., Artacho, I., Cantos-Frontela, J., Peixoto, N.: Dynamically programmable electronic pill dispenser system. J. Med. Syst. **34**(3), 357–366 (2009). https://doi.org/10.1007/s10916-008-9248-3
14. Othman, N.B., Ek, O.P.: Pill dispenser with alarm via smartphone notification. In: 2016 IEEE 5th Global Conference on Consumer Electronics, pp. 1–2 (2016). https://doi.org/10.1109/GCCE.2016.7800399
15. Chawla, S.: The autonomous pill dispenser: mechanizing the delivery of tablet medication. In: 2016 IEEE 7th Annual Ubiquitous Computing Electronics & Mobile Communication Conference (UEMCON), pp. 1–4 (2016). https://doi.org/10.1109/UEMCON.2016.7777886
16. Jen, Y.-K.E.: Design and development of wireless baby monitors. BioMed Res. Int. **2012**, 10 (2012). https://doi.org/10.1155/2012/381493.Article ID: 381493
17. Jabeena, A., Kumar, S.: Smart medicine dispenser. In: International Conference on Smart Systems and Inventive Technology (ICCSIT), pp. 410–414 (2018). https://doi.org/10.1109/ICSSIT.2018.8748601
18. Kassem, A., et al.: A comprehensive approach for a smart medication dispenser. Int. J. Comput. Digit. Syst. **8**(02), 131–141 (2019)
19. Kumar, K.D., Umamaheswari, E.: Prediction methods for effective resource provisioning in cloud computing: a survey. Multiagent Grid Syst. **14**(3), 283–305 (2018)
20. Kumar, K.D., Umamaheswari, E.: HPCWMF: a hybrid predictive cloud workload management framework using improved LSTM neural network. Cybern. Inf. Technol. **20**(4), 55–73 (2020)
21. Kumar, K.D., Umamaheswari, E.: EWPTNN: an efficient workload prediction model in cloud computing using two-stage neural networks. Procedia Comput. Sci. **165**, 151–157 (2019)

An Intelligent Intrusion Detection System Using Hybrid Deep Learning Approaches in Cloud Environment

Andrea Sharon, Prarthna Mohanraj, Tanya Elizabeth Abraham, Bose Sundan, and Anitha Thangasamy(✉)

Department of Computer Science and Engineering, College of Engineering, Anna University, Guindy, Chennai, India
ani.astt18@gmail.com

Abstract. An Intrusion Detection System (IDS) detects suspicious activities and sends alerts when they are found. Based on these alerts, the issue is investigated, and appropriate actions are taken to remediate the threat. The traffic in a network is examined by a network-based intrusion detection system using various traffic tools that collect and analyse traffic data utilizing detection algorithms. Virtualization is used to construct the cloud infrastructure, which renders the virtual network flow between the virtual machines and it is mostly unidentifiable by typical intrusion detection systems. Previous studies proposed a software-defined network technology to reroute network traffic to a Snort IDS for detection of malicious attacks. However, this is incapable of detecting unknown attacks and adapting to large-scale traffic. Deep learning algorithms are used automatically to extract essential features from raw network data, which can then be fed into a shallow classifier for effective malicious attack detection. The main objective of the proposed system is to utilize a combination of a sparse autoencoder and stacked contractive autoencoder (S-SCAE) along with a Bi-DLDA (Bi-directional LSTM followed by a dense layer, a dropout layer, and a layer with attention mechanism) for detecting intrusions in a cloud environment. Moreover, a cloud intrusion detection system that designed to collect the data traffic from the NSL-KDD dataset and applies the S-SCAE + Bi-DLDA algorithm to determine if the received packet is malicious or non-malicious. To assess the proposed system's detection performance, a variety of measures were used such as precision, recall rate, and accuracy. The proposed model achieves precision, recall rate, and accuracy of 99%, 98%, and over 98% respectively, according to simulation findings.

Keywords: Attack detection · Bi-directional LSTM with dropout and attention layer · Cloud computing · Distributed denial of service · Long short-term memory · One-hot encoding · Sparse autoencoder - stacked contractive autoencoder

1 Introduction

Society has embraced rapid advancements in technology. These advancements have been incorporated into everyday life by people for personal use and by organizations for their

Published by Springer Nature Switzerland AG 2022
E. J. Neuhold et al. (Eds.): ICCCSP 2022, IFIP AICT 651, pp. 281–298, 2022.
https://doi.org/10.1007/978-3-031-11633-9_20

internal operations and business solutions. However, this rapid technological growth has increased vulnerabilities, threats, and cyber-crime. Organizations have implemented several mechanisms to protect themselves from these computer system intrusions such as a firewall and an antivirus. A firewall is a type of security device used to monitor inbound and outbound network traffic. Antivirus software examines the data (files, software, web pages, and applications) travelling to a device on which the software is. It also schedules automatic scans and deletes harmful code/software. Although these mechanisms can protect computer systems from malicious attacks, intrusion detection systems are more effective and efficient.

Cloud Computing has arisen a standard platform in the current year for sharing data in a large pool and it also offers several user-friendly characteristics [15]. Moreover, it defined a model, which allows sharing a configurable pool of computing resources like servers, networks, services, applications, and storage that can quickly release with minimum user effort. Profits of making services exist at anywhere at any time and making resources to be added or removed are one the big advantage of the cloud. The majority of cloud computing services are available on a pay-as-you-go basis, with each user assigned an individual collection of devices for the extraction of data. The services of cloud computing classification illustrated in Fig. 1 [9]. Service Delivery Model depends on the kind of provided cloud service and it is grouped into three categories are expressed in Fig. 1.

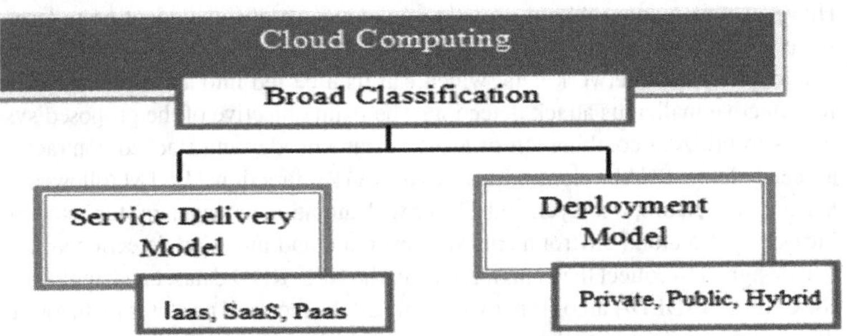

Fig. 1. Classification of cloud computing [4]

Whereas the deployment model depends on cloud deployment is sub-divided into the private, hybrid, and public cloud. Data protection from cybercriminals is among the most challenging aspects of a cloud platform because the majority of the data is public. There are several attacks and threats in a cloud environment, which illustrated in Fig. 2.

An Intrusion Detection System (IDS) monitors network traffic and generates notifications whenever suspicious activity is detected. This type of security system collects data and information from various network sources and four systems. The data collected, then analyzed to detect if an activity may constitute an intrusion or attack on the system and helps system administrators and computer systems to prepare and deal with attacks or intrusions aimed at their network(s). In addition, intrusion detection systems used to identify anomalies before hackers can make any or a considerable amount of damage

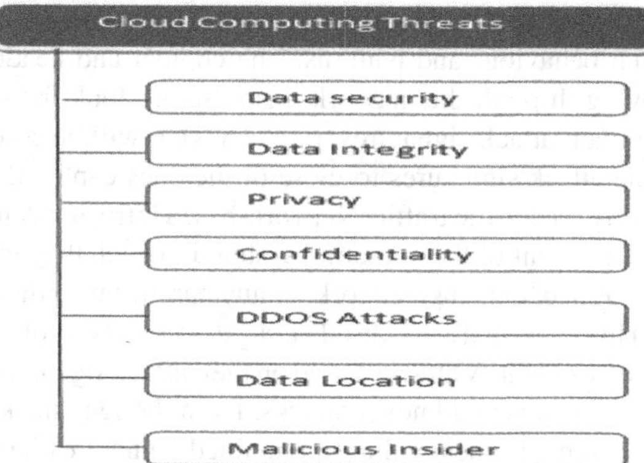

Fig. 2. Types of threats in cloud computing [4]

to a network. There are 2 different types of intrusion detection systems: host-based and network-based. This categorization done based on the source of information.

A host-based intrusion detection system [3] has been used in a single host system and it can only serve the system in which it is installed. Host-based agents, sensors, installed on a machine that found to be susceptible to possible attacks on the system. A separate sensor is required for each machine. Sensors collect data on the events occurring, which are being monitored. This type of IDS assesses the host system's security performance and analyzes the log information. Generally, Logs are typically basic text files in which a few lines are written at a time while events and processes take place. Host-based intrusion detection systems are advantageous for many reasons. Host-based systems can monitor access to information ("who accessed what"). In simple terms, these systems can trace harmful or malicious activities to a specific user. This aspect helps identity whether a person within an organization is responsible for the improper use of resources. Host-based systems are very versatile since they can operate in encrypted environments and over a switched network topology. This type of intrusion detection system can also distribute the load across the available hosts on large networks, cutting the deployment cost. When the network traffic becomes too large, this feature of host-based systems provides a benefit by spreading the load evenly over a network. Host-based systems also present several disadvantages. Host-based sensor systems are not portable. Since the sensors are host-based, they must be compatible with the platform, which they are running over. Setting up this type of system can be very costly. The management and deployment costs for this type of intrusion detection system are more costly because each host requires its sensor. An additional disadvantage of a host-based intrusion detection system is that it can't "see" network activity and relies significantly on the host operating system. The integrity of host-based sensors can be weakened by vulnerabilities.

On the other hand, a network-based intrusion detection system (NIDS) [8] verifies network traffic using traffic tools that capture and analyse traffic data using detection algorithms. Unlike a host-based intrusion detection system, information gathered from a whole network rather than from each separate host. NIDS are deployed with one or many prominent points throughout a network to monitor traffic on a network from together with all of the network's devices. An analysis performed on the network traffic to look for abnormal behaviour and patterns. The content and header information, of all the packets moving through the network, inspected to look for signs of an attack. Network sensors contain attack signatures, rules on what will be considered an attack. Sensors compare the attack signatures to those of the ones captured from the network traffic and then identify the hostile traffic. Network-based intrusion detection systems are portable and are independent of the operating system in which they installed. Similarly, it can be introduced into an existing network, or any part of one, efficiently with minute disruptions if any. However, there are disadvantages to this type of intrusion detection system. Network sensors identify attacks based on their attack signatures, which based on data, collected from previous and known attacks. Even though attacks with recognized signatures can be prevented, ones without predefined signatures have the potential to create a great amount of damage. Another major issue with a network-based intrusion detection system is scalability. Every packet that passes through the segment on which it is placed is inspected by network monitors. This type of IDS has difficulty keeping up with a 100 Mbps environment. High-speed networks are becoming more and more common; attackers will target to exploit this weakness. Encryption is also a problem with these IDS. If network traffic is encrypted, then agents will not be able to scan the contents of those plackets.

Cloud infrastructure built with virtualization renders virtual network traffic across VMs undetectable and unmanageable by standard intrusion detection systems. Previous studies have reported that network traffic be redirected to a Snort IDS for detection of malicious attacks using software-defined network (SDN) technologies [13]. Snort is a network intrusion prevention and detection system that is free and open source that detects any unlawful behaviour using a versatile rule-based language comprised of signature, protocol, and inspection approaches. Snort records the packet in a human-readable form. It has the capability of detecting worms and it exploits the port, which scans and detects suspicious activity through protocol analysis, pre-processors, and content searching. Snort, on the other hand, is incapable of identifying unknown attacks or adjusting to massive amounts of traffic.

Anomaly-based, misuse-based, and hybrid-based intrusion detection systems can also be distinguished by the detection process. An anomaly is an outlier or something, which deviates from the expected. This type of intrusion detection system discovers patterns that are far from normal and labelled as intrusion. Anomaly detections can be characterized by static and dynamic detectors. Anomaly-based IDS been well built to differentiate anomalous traffic from normal traffic and the detection of unknown attacks. However, because some intrusion might simulate normal activities, it is also associated with a high false alarm rate. A misuse-based IDS creates a database that stores several attacks. It is also known as signature-based detection because it employs a set of recognised patterns stored in a database. The patterns, used in a misuse-based intrusion detection system, are a collection of sequences of activities that have a possibility of being harmful. The time taken to match with a pattern from the database is minimal. The benefit of this type of system is that the patterns can be easily understood if the network behaviour is familiar or recognized. Misuse-based intrusion detection systems are especially suited for intrusions where the attack patterns have already been saved in the database, but they might handle attacks with human interference and perhaps self-modifying behavioural characteristics. Although misuse-based IDS is not suited for detecting novel attacks, it does enable very accurate detection of previously identified anomalous activities. Lastly, the hybrid method combines both anomaly-based and misuse-based methods.

The main contribution of the work is as follows:

- To utilize a combination of Sparse Autoencoder and Stacked Contractive Autoencoder (S-SCAE) along with a Bi-DLDA (Bi-directional LSTM followed by a dense layer, a dropout layer, and a layer with attention mechanism) for detecting intrusions in a cloud environment.
- To design a cloud IDS, which collects the data, traffic from the NSL-KDD dataset and applies the S-SCAE + Bi-DLDA algorithm to determine if the received packet is malicious or non-malicious.

The remaining section of this article, titled Sect. 2, discusses the detection of DDoS attacks using various approaches like Sparse Autoencoder - Stacked Contractive Autoencoder, Bi-Directional LSTM with Dropout and Attention Layer, etc. The proposed system architecture for detecting DDoS attacks is mainly explained in Sect. 3 with the Sp-SCAE and the Bi-DLDA method. In Sect. 4, the findings of the experimental results and the comparison analysis are briefly presented and finally in Sect. 5, the conclusion and future work has been discussed.

2 Related Work

In this related work section will be discussing on a comprehensive examination of most advanced intrusion detection technologies, which intended to lessen the risk of DDoS attacks. Self-taught learning (STL)-IDS, a powerful deep learning approach based on the STL framework, has been presented. The sparse autoencoder technique was used to generate the model, which is an efficient unsupervised method of learning for reconstructing novel feature representations. The proposed method used to learn features and reduce dimensionality. The SAE-SVM algorithm, used to [1], employs a 1-n encoding scheme to convert non-numerical attributes to numbers before the application of STL. Because most of the NSL-KDD dataset's features have very huge ranges between the minimum and maximum values, those values of features are contradictory and inappropriate for computation. Those features are then normalized to the range [0,1]. The proposed method significantly lowers the amount of time spent on training and testing while effectively improving the predictive performance of SVM about attacks. The advantage is that this model uses a sparse autoencoder, which is more robust to noise because of which the important features from the data extracted easily but the disadvantage of using this proposed model in this paper has a lower accuracy when compared to the other existing models.

[2] developed new self-organizing map algorithms that successfully updated neighbourhood laws and learning rates to govern basic SOM weight vectors are randomly assigned and have a static architecture as well as the initial data size of the weight vector. Performance metrics such as detection rate and false alarm rate were pre-owned to evaluate the novel technique.

The developing classifier for IDS using the DL method [5] has been contributed in this paper. The most appropriate optimizer is chosen among 6 optimizers for LSTM RNN is utilized to predict intrusion. Experimental result shows LSTM RNN with Nadam optimizer gives better result than previous work.

The proposed TLS-BLSTM (Transfer Learning-depended on Stacked-BLSTM) [6] network detect the quality of air for newly emerged stations which have to lack data. The proposed technique combines a transfer-learning plan and deep learning methods to use concepts from the current air quality station to the new station for boosting the forecast. Experimental results depicts that the proposed technique lowest RMSE for a sample of 3 pollutants in the new station. [7] presents a solution for predicting botnet activity inside network and consumer IOT devices. The deep learning method utilized to create a prediction model depending on Bidirectional (BLSTM-RNN). Word embedding utilized to recognize text and to convert attacked packed to the format of tokenized integer. Experiments show that the proposed method proves a better model over some time.

D-Sign is a deep learning-powered solution [10] for identifying hybrid intrusions and developing signatures for unknown web vulnerabilities. D-Sign is divided into three tiers: the Misuse Detection Engine, Signature Generation Engine and the Anomaly Detection Engine. The detection engine analyzes the traffic captured by the honey pot servers, decoy servers that are set up to attract the attacker and monitor/log activities, and detects attacks. The misuse detection engine uses a rule-based approach and deployed after the honey pot servers to filter the suspicious traffic collection for known threats. The anomaly detection engine builds a profile of normal behaviour. A normal profile consists of patterns or descriptive statistic from the network traffic's non-harmful community. The signature generation engine continues to generate content-based attack signatures from a malicious collection of packets. With a high degree of sensitivity, precision, and specificity, D-Sign can successfully detect and generate attack signatures. Here the web-based attacks must be detected and signatures to be generated. The proposed model is a strong defense methodology that detects new threats within a short amount of time from its launch and with a minimal amount of damage to information. The advantage of using the multilayer LSTM model overcomes long-term dependency, the vanishing gradient problem, and the drawback of this LSTM model works at a slow speed when compared to some other models.

The scalable outlier decoder was [11] introduced, which is a combination of LSTM and hierarchical clustering (HC). Where HC give scalability to the outlier detectors by computing correlated sensors. LSTM is combined with M-estimator, robust statistics to accurately predict outliers in time-series data. The simulation result expresses that the proposed method has higher accuracy for various attacks.

[12] proposes a BAT model to address the issues of less accuracy and model evaluation in Bi-LSTM intrusion detection and an attention mechanism are combined with the BAT model. The network flow vector, which mainly composed of packet vectors created by the Bi-LSTM model and may acquire critical components for traffic flow detection, was tested using the attention mechanism. The proposed model consists of an input layer, multiple convolution layers, a BLSTM layer, an attention layer, and an output layer. In the input layer, the input that has been transformed into numerical features

using the one-hot encoding method. Then, a standard scalar is used to normalize the data into the range [0,1]. After pre-processing occurs on the input data, the convolution layer captures the local features of the traffic data. This layer creates different feature maps. The BLSTM layer, an enhanced version of the LSTM layer, connects a forward and backward LSTM to extract coarse-grained characteristics. The time series feature of a data packet acquired via the BLSTM layer. From the BLSTM to the attention layer, forward propagation is carried out. Following that, the attention layer will know the relationships between the packet vectors. The BAT-MC model eliminates the issue of conventional design features. The advantage of this model is that the Bi-LSTM algorithm is faster at learning and better at remembering new features and forgetting older features as compared to other existing algorithms. The attention mechanism is useful in obtaining accurate and reasonable features from the output vectors of the Bi-LSTM algorithm. The main disadvantage is that the model proposed in this paper does not account for over-fitting of data.

[14] proposed novel DL techniques for the prediction of real-time threats in IOT systems with the use of BLSTM RNN. The proposed method had been employed over python programming language and Google Tensor Flow framework. The experiment conducted on UNSW-NB15 datasets and the results shows in terms of intrusion prediction, the suggested strategy outperforms previous methods.

[16] suggested LSTM network depended on numerous-feature layers. Primarily, layer stage feature is presented where historical data is saved and computed to discover variable duration's various stages numerous stage attacks. Then layer time-series feature is utilized to relate autonomous attack stages to see if current data fits under the attack interval. The experiment represents the proposed scheme had the lowest positive rate compared to the existing scheme.

[17] describe a model using SCAE and SVM for detecting intrusion attacks. The SCAE used for feature extraction and the extracted features are used for training the SVM classifier. SCAE is comprised of multiple hidden layers for encoding. For decoding, the SCAE consists of a set of symmetrical layers. Here, the output of one layer is the input for the next layer in these layers. On the NSL-KDD dataset, five distinct kinds of SCAE + SVM models were created (SCAE1 + SVM, SCAE2 + SVM, SCAE3 + SVM, SCAE4 + SVM, and SCAE5 + SVM). Out of all five models, SCAE4 + SVM had the better categorization performance. As a result, SCAE can extract the best features and meet the aim of dimensionality reduction. The SCAE approach can be used to continuously train better and more robust low-dimensional features from raw network traffic. The SCAE + SVM classifier detects whether the given online traffic or testing data considered normal or an attack (i.e., DOS, Probe, R2L, U2R). Research with the use of KDD Cup 99 and NSL-KDD, two well-known intrusion detection evaluation datasets, reveal that the proposed SCAE + SVM technique outperforms three other state-of-the-art approaches in terms of detection rate. The advantage of this model produces a high accuracy rate as compared to earlier models. The disadvantages of using this SVM classifier model the new attacks in the testing dataset are not effectively recognised.

This study proposes [18] an IDS model based on AE and LSTM cells. The autoencoder (AE) be a feature compression approaches that usually done by a neural network. The autoencoder's encoding step will reduce the number of features and translate the high-dimensional input into a low-dimensional space. This is possible due to the bottleneck structure present in the autoencoder. The data will be re-constructed during the decoding process so that it can be given to the neural network again with a loss function for network training. The gradient descent process relies heavily on the loss function. The ability of the autoencoder will enhanced by using a stacked autoencoder, multiple autoencoder is stacked together. A feature extractor, a classifier, and an evaluation block are all part of the intrusion detection model's overall design. The input data pre-processed by feature transformation and normalization before feature extraction. The nominal feature transformed into numerical values using feature transformation. More precise and deeper representation of features permitted by the LSTM and the multi-layer neural network. Lastly, the softmax layer used to classify the extracted features. By using LSTM cells is that it excels in extracting information that is more latent. The main advantage of the LSTM algorithm is better at learning new features as compared to other existing algorithms but the disadvantage of the model proposed in this paper produces a high false alarm rate.

Policy repository methodology proposed [19] to store the policies attached with each file. With the help of the Policy Enforcement Engine, Policy Enforcement Agent starts enforcing the policy on the uploaded file. The Policy Management Module is in charge of creating, modifying, deleting, and enforcing policies for each file or group. For each data piece saved, a correct data retention policy to be handle. The computation made more efficient by using a Hadoop framework operating on the private cloud to check the retention duration of samples mixed to each file.

[20] proposed solution relied on a technique called univariate ensemble feature selection, which is used to choose valuable minimized feature sets from incursion datasets. Ensemble classifiers, on the other hand, are capable of competently fusing to create a robust classifier, combine separate classifiers utilizing the voting process. The preferred solution, which based on an ensemble, accurately distinguishes between normal and malicious network traffic pattern.

3 Proposed Methodology

Data traffic obtained from the NSL-KDD cloud dataset. This dataset, which contains 43 features per record, is the global standard for current internet traffic. Of those 43 features, 41 of them refer to the traffic input themselves. The remaining two features are the classification of the attack and the score (severity of the traffic input). Intrusion Detection Systems classify traffic into 4 categories as intrinsic, content-based, time-based, and host-based based on the information obtained through traffic features. The proposed system uses pre-processing techniques and algorithms for detecting malicious attacks. i.e. identifying whether the cloud network traffic behavior is malicious or normal. Suppose the traffic is Denial of Service (DOS), or User to Root (U2R), or Probe, or Root to Local (R2L), that will be considered malicious. The proposed system Fig. 3 uses list of modules as Collection of Data, Data Pre-Processing, Sparse Auto Encoder – Stacked Contractive Auto Encoder (S-SCAE), and Bi-Directional LSTM with Dropout and Attention Layer (Bi-DLDA).

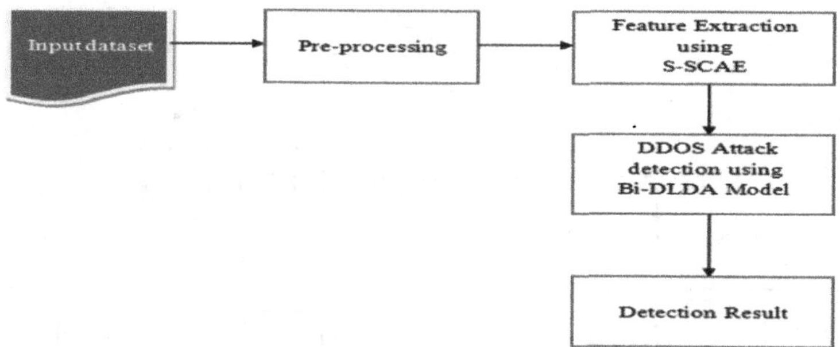

Fig. 3. The architecture of DDoS attack detection based on S-SCAE + Bi-DLDA

3.1 Pre-processing the Dataset

One-Hot Processing

The One-Hot Processing method, used for transforming the symbolic features into numerical features. This necessitates the mapping of category variables to integer values. Except for the integer's index, which is specified with 1, each integer value is shown with vector consisting completely of zero values.

Standardisation

The Standardisation method, used for scaling every feature into a well-balanced range. This method is done to remove the bias in favour of features with higher values along with lower value 0. Standardisation is done using the Z-Score method.

3.2 DDoS Feature Extraction using Sparse Auto Encoder – Stacked Contractive Auto Encoder (S-SCAE)

S-SCAE algorithm used for extracting features from the raw network traffic data. It consists of a sparse auto encoder followed by a stacked contractive autoencoder (SCAE). The sparse autoencoder Fig. 3. employs sparsity to achieve an information bottleneck. The pre-processed data passed to the input vector of the Sparse Autoencoder. This data encoded using a weight matrix and passed to the inner hidden layer. From here, the data is decoded using a tied weight matrix and is outputted to a reconstruction vector. Figure 4 describes the overall framework of the proposed DDoS attack detection model.

Next, the data from the Sparse Autoencoder passed to the Stacked Contractive Autoencoder Fig. 5. Here, the data undergoes pre-training wherein a greedy layer-by-layer strategy is employed for training a series of basic Contractive Autoencoders individually. Each CAE network's output has now become the following CAE network's input.

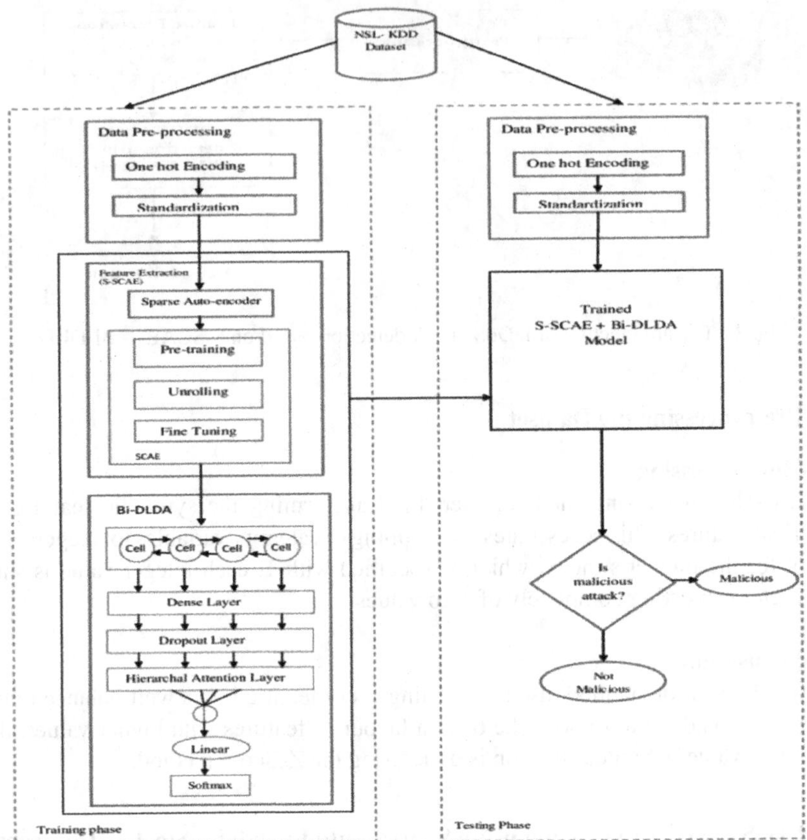

Fig. 4. The overall framework of the proposed DDoS attacks detection model

Layer (type)	Output Shape	Param #
input_1 (InputLayer)	[(None, 117)]	0
dense (Dense)	(None, 52)	6136
dense_1 (Dense)	(None, 26)	1378
dense_2 (Dense)	(None, 26)	702
dense_3 (Dense)	(None, 117)	3159

Total params: 11,375
Trainable params: 11,375
Non-trainable params: 0

Fig. 5. Structure of the sparse autoencoder

The next step is unrolling, in which the hidden layer of each Constructive Autoencoder network is unrolled and stacked to a deep or stacked Constructive Autoencoder network Fig. 6. The final step in the process is fine-tuning in which the parameters are adjusted using a multi-class cross-entropy function.

Layer (type)	Output Shape	Param #
input_2 (InputLayer)	[(None, 117)]	0
dense_4 (Dense)	(None, 52)	6136
dense_5 (Dense)	(None, 26)	1378
dense_8 (Dense)	(None, 52)	1404
dense_9 (Dense)	(None, 26)	1378
dense_10 (Dense)	(None, 26)	702
dense_11 (Dense)	(None, 117)	3159

Total params: 14,157
Trainable params: 14,157
Non-trainable params: 0

Fig. 6. Structure of the stacked contractive autoencoder

3.3 Proposed Bi–Directional LSTM with Dropout and Attention Layer (Bi-DLDA) Attack Detection

The Bi-DLDA Classifier trained with the essential features extracted by the S-SCAE algorithm. The structure of the Bi-DLDA Classifier described in Fig. 7. Bi-LSTM used for learning the features of each packet and obtaining a characteristic vector related to that packet. The packet vector is passed on to a dense followed by a dropout layer, and then to an attention layer where to extract the detailed features, an attention mechanism is required to carry out feature learning on the packet sequence. The S-SCAE + Bi-DLDA classifier outputs whether the selected packet is malicious or not.

In the context of proposed Bi-DLDA, classification model based IDS learn cloud network connection features from existing data and perform classification tasks on unseen network traffic by categorizing them as normal or malicious. This malicious traffic can be either DoS, probe, R2L, or U2R.

Step-by-Step procedure for Bi-DLDA Learning Method:

Step 1: The extracted features from the S-SCAE passed onto the Bi-DLDA for the classification of the packet.
Step 2: First, data fed into a Bi-LSTM where the input passed in both the forward and backward directions. This employs the use of two activation and candidate values (one for each direction). Both activation values considered while calculating the output value of each cell.
Step 3: The Bi-LSTM uses a Dropout layer, which randomly sets input units to 0, thereby preventing over fitting.
Step 4: The output passed to the attention mechanism layer. Feature learning is carried out on sequential data made up of data packets in this scenario.
Step 5: From here, we obtain our result stating whether the given packet is malicious or not.

```
Layer (type)                 Output Shape              Param #
=================================================================
input_3 (InputLayer)         [(None, 117, 1)]          0

bidirectional (Bidirectional (None, 117, 234)          111384

dropout (Dropout)            (None, 117, 234)          0

hierarchical__attention (Hie (None, 234)               27612

dense_12 (Dense)             (None, 2)                 470
=================================================================
Total params: 139,466
Trainable params: 139,466
Non-trainable params: 0
```

Fig. 7. Structure of the Bi-DLDA module

4 Experimental Results

The experiments on S-SCAE + Bi-DLDA were performed by Tensor flow and Keras are used to implement the intelligent intrusion detection system in the cloud environment, which is provided by IBM Watson studio. 80 and 20% of the NSL-KDD dataset used to train and test the network respectively. Thus, 18,036 packets used for training the model and 4,509 packets used for testing. The dataset with 43 features used in the experiments. Two characteristics ignored throughout the classification process because they have no bearing on the effectiveness of DDoS attack detection.

In the validation process, we compare the proposed algorithm S-SCAE + Bi-DLDA with other models such as SAE + SVM and SCAE + SVM. To evaluate each approach, we use the 'Precision,' 'Recall,' 'F Measure,' and 'Accuracy' measures, all of which have been used widely in the literature.

The model accuracy and loss score obtained by our system after training with 18,036 packets is 98.32% and 0.0561 respectively while the model accuracy and loss obtained after testing with 4,509 packets is 98.58% and 0.0540 respectively. The model accuracies at each epoch for the training and testing phases are depicted in Fig. 8. The model loss scores at each epoch for the training and testing phases are depicted in Fig. 9.

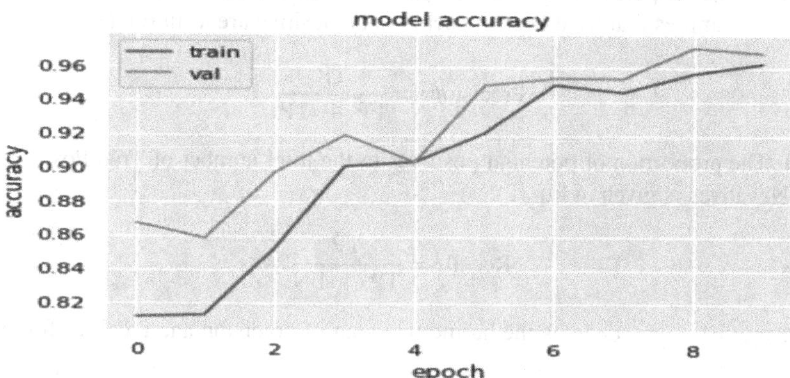

Fig. 8. Graphical representation of the model accuracy

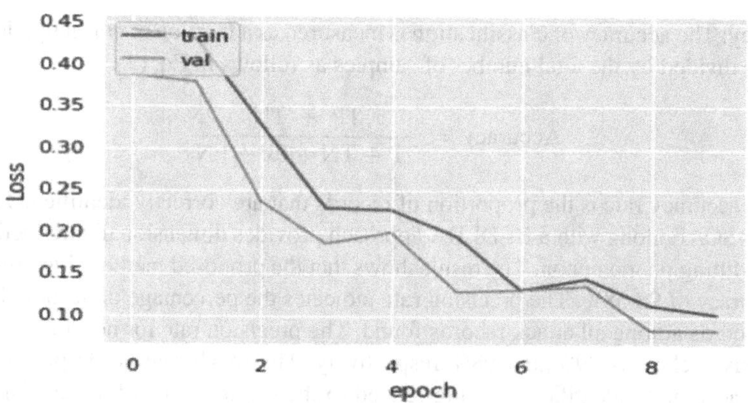

Fig. 9. Graphical representation of the loss

4.1 Evaluation Metrics

For the comparison of the above-proposed model with the previously proposed models, to evaluate each approach, we widely used measurements such as 'Precision,' 'Recall,' 'F Measure' and 'Accuracy' throughout the literature.

The four basic properties of the confusion matrix, which depict the actual and predicted classes, are used to generate all of these evaluation measures. These confusion matrix elements are:

True Negative (TN): number of correctly predicted instances as normal packets.

False Negative (FN): number of incorrectly predicted instances as normal packets.
False Positive (FP): number of wrongly predicted instances as malicious.
True Positive (TP): number of correctly predicted instances as malicious.

The comparison measures are defined as:

Precision: The proportions of samples that have been correctly categorised to the total number of samples that have been expected to be positive are as in Eq. (1).

$$\text{Precision} = \frac{\text{TP}}{\text{FP} + \text{TP}} \tag{1}$$

Recall: The proportion of potential positives to the total number of True Positives and False Negatives is given in Eq. (2).

$$\text{Recall} = \frac{\text{TP}}{\text{TP} + \text{FN}} \tag{2}$$

F-measure: F1-score, denotes the harmonic mean of precision and recall as follows in Eq. (3).

$$\text{F-Measure} = \frac{2 * (\text{Recall} * \text{Precision})}{(\text{Recall} + \text{Precision})} \tag{3}$$

Accuracy: The accuracy of classification is measured as a fraction of correctly identified samples divided by the total number of samples as follows in Eq. (4).

$$\text{Accuracy} = \frac{\text{TP} + \text{TN}}{\text{TP} + \text{TN} + \text{FP} + \text{FN}} \tag{4}$$

The accuracy rate is the proportion of records that are correctly identified. The proposed S-SCAE along with a Bi-DLDA approach provides dimensionality reduction and no over-fitting phenomenon. The result shows that the proposed methodology improves the accuracy of 98.58%. The precision rate indicates the percentage of accurately identified records among all attack records found. The precision rate for non-malicious and malicious packets is 99% and 98% respectively. The recall rate is the proportion of records accurately identified as being related to the original type of attack. The recall rate for non-malicious and malicious packets is 98% and 99% respectively. The harmonic mean of the precision and recall rate is represented by the f-measure. The f-measure for non-malicious and malicious packets is 98% and 99% respectively. Using a confusion matrix M, the above metrics can be obtained. The confusion matrix's leading diagonal members represent the number of records properly predicted. Finally, the ROC - curve displays the true positive rate (TP) and false positive rate (FP) to show classification performance. The higher the TP and the smaller the FP, the greater the area under the ROC curve. In Fig. 10 the confusion matrix for our proposed system is depicted below:

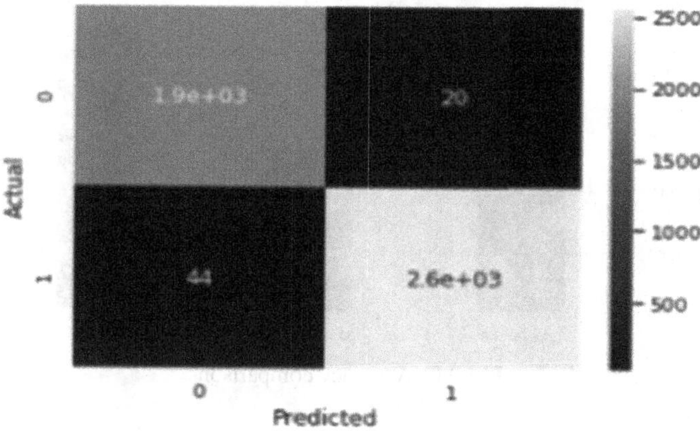

Fig. 10. Confusion matrix of proposed system

The true positive rate for this system was found to be 97.7%. The false-positive rate for this system is determined to be 0.7%. The false-negative rate is 2.3%. Lastly, the true negative rate is found to be 99.2%.

Table 1. Comparison of Accuracy, Precision, Recall and F-score in %

	Accuracy	Precision	Recall	F-Score
SAE + SVM [18]	85.09	85.78	85.09	84.83
SCAE+SVM [18]	88.73	89.87	88.73	88.04
S-SCAE+BI-DLDA	**98.58**	**99**	**98**	**99**

The 'Accuracy,' 'Precision,' 'Recall,' and 'F Measure' for each previously suggested approach in the context of intrusion detection such as the SAE + SVM model and the SCAE + SVM model [18] is compared with the S-SCAE + Bi-DLDA model and the various results in % are reported in Table 1.

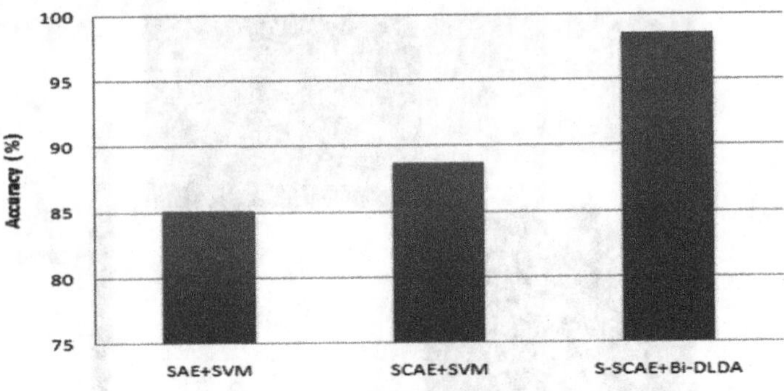

Fig. 11. Accuracy comparison

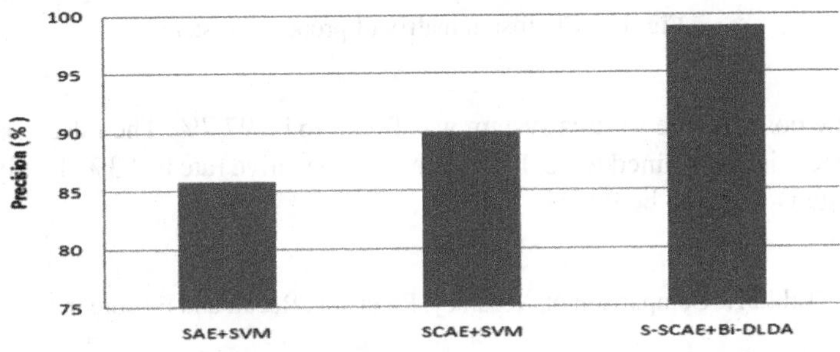

Fig. 12. Precision comparison

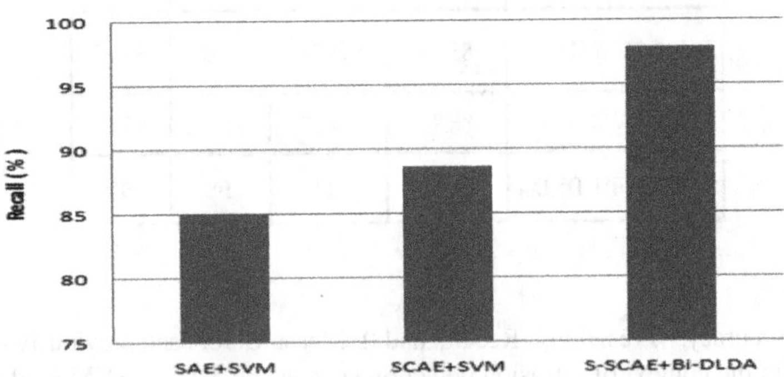

Fig. 13. Recall comparison

Figure 11, 12, 13, and 14 show the graphical representation of the comparisons of the 'Accuracy' 'Precision', 'Recall' and 'F-score' for each previously proposed method such as the SAE + SVM model and the SCAE + SVM model with the S-SCAE + Bi-DLDA model respectively.

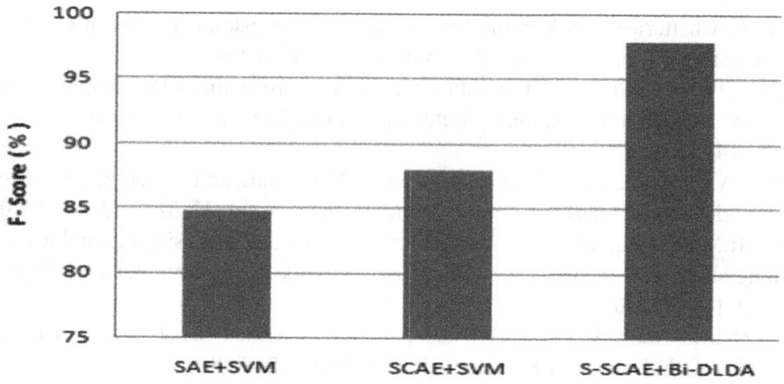

Fig. 14. F-score comparison

5 Conclusion and Future Work

Major losses in the cloud computing environment have occurred due to security concerns. In addition, these concerns have led to the loss of confidence in users on cloud computing. An intrusion detection system is a cost-effective way to safeguard cloud computing environment against unwanted intrusions. We have proposed an intelligent intrusion detection system that uses a sparse auto encoder – stacked contractive autoencoder (S-SCAE) for feature extraction and a Bi-Directional LSTM with Dropout and Attention Layer (Bi-DLDA) for classification of the packets. By the NSL-KDD dataset, we have proposed highly efficient IDS with accuracy higher than 98%. In the future, a cloud computing context, powerful deep learning techniques can be used to detect assaults.

References

1. Al Qatf, M., Lasheng, Y., Al Habib, M., Al Sabahi. K.: Deep learning approach combining sparse autoencoder with SVM for network intrusion detection. IEEE Access **6**, 52843–52856 (2018)
2. Aneetha, A.S., Bose, S.: The combined approach for anomaly detection using neural networks and clustering techniques. Comput. Sci. Eng. Int. J. **2**(4), 37–46 (2012)
3. Khraisat, A., Gondal, I., Vamplew, P., Kamruzzaman, J.: Survey of intrusion detection systems: techniques, datasets and challenges. Cybersecurity **2**(1), 1–22 (2019). https://doi.org/10.1186/s42400-019-0038-7
4. Dhanapal, A., Nithyanandam, P.: The slow HTTP distributed denial of service attack detection in cloud. Scalable Comput. Pract. Exper. **20**(2), 285–297 (2019)
5. Le, T., Kim, J., Kim, H.: An effective intrusion detection classifier using long short-term memory with gradient descent optimization. In: 2017 International Conference on Platform Technology and Service (PlatCon), pp. 1–6 (2017)
6. Wang, W., Du, X., Wang, N.: Building a cloud IDS using an efficient feature selection method and SVM. IEEE Access **7**, 1345–1354 (2019)
7. McDermott, C.D., Majdani, F., Petrovski, A.V.: Botnet detection in the internet of things using deep learning approaches. In: International Joint Conference on Neural Networks (IJCNN), pp. 1–8 (2018)

8. Prwez, T., Chatterjee, K.: A framework for network intrusion detection in cloud. In: IEEE 6th International Conference on Advanced Computing (2016)
9. Osanaiye, O.A.: Short paper: IP spoofing detection for preventing DDoS attack in Cloud computing. In: 2015 18th International Conference on Intelligence in Next Generation Networks, pp. 139–141 (2015)
10. Qureshi, A.S., Khan, A.K., Shamim, N., Durad, M.H.: Intrusion detection using deep sparse auto-encoder and self-taught learning. Neural Comput. Appl. **32**, 3135– 3147 (2020)
11. Shukla, R.M., Sengupta, S.: Scalable and robust outlier detector using hierarchical clustering and long short-term memory (LSTM) neural network for the Internet of Things. Internet Things **9**, 1–18 (2020)
12. Su, T., Zhu, J., Wang, S., Li, Y.: BAT: deep learning methods on network intrusion detection using NSL-KDD Dataset. IEEE Access **8**, 29575–29585 (2020)
13. Badotra, S., Panda, S.N.: SNORT based early DDoS detection system using Opendaylight and open networking operating system in software defined networking. Clust. Comput. **24**(1), 501–513 (2020). https://doi.org/10.1007/s10586-020-03133-y
14. Roy, B., Cheung, H.: A deep learning approach for intrusion detection in internet of things using bi-directional long short-term memory recurrent neural network. In: 2018 28th International Telecommunication Networks and Applications Conference (ITNAC), pp. 1–6 (2018)
15. Velliangiri, S., Karthikeyan, P., Vinoth Kumar, V.: Detection of distributed denial of service attack in cloud computing using the optimization-based deep networks. J. Exp. Theor. Artif. Intell. **33**, 405–424 (2020)
16. Xu, M., Li, X., Ma, J.F., Zhong, C., Yang, W.: Detection of multi-stage attacks based on multi-layer long and short-term memory network. In: ICC 2019–2019 IEEE International Conference on Communications (ICC), pp. 1–4 (2019)
17. Yan, Y., Qi, L., Wang, J., Lin, Y., Chen. L.: A network intrusion detection method based on stacked autoencoder and LSTM. In: ICC 2020 - 2020 IEEE International Conference on Communications (ICC), pp. 1–6 (2020)
18. Wang, W., Du, X., Shan, D., Qin, R.: Cloud intrusion detection method based on stacked contractive auto-encoder and support vector machine. IEEE Trans. Cloud Comput. 1–14 (2020)
19. Varghese, L.A., Bose, S.: Efficient data storage model to overcome the storage problems in industries. Dyn. Syst. Appl. **30**(6), 994–1002 (2021)
20. Krishnaveni, S., Sivamohan, S., Sridhar, S.S, Prabakaran, S.: Efficient feature selection and classification through ensemble method for network intrusion detection on cloud computting. Cluster Comput. **24**(3), 1–19 (2021)

Smart License Approval Using AIOT

Anika Jagati and Maheswari Raja(✉)

School of Computer Science and Engineering, Vellore Institute of Technology, Chennai, India
maheswari.r@vit.ac.in

Abstract. In India, a driving test consists of only a short duration test on an empty track which does not really assess a person's driving skills when it comes to driving on an actual road. Figures tell that on an average, 415 deaths are recorded per day in road accidents in India. This is relatively a very high number and there is an urgent need to address this issue. On studying the situation carefully, it is observed that the most common reasons for the increasing road accidents in India are distracted driving, over-speeding, not wearing seat belts, breaking traffic rules and tailgating. As pointed out earlier, the driving test conducted to grant a license is not enough to know a person's driving capability and thus, there has to be an additional test in order to monitor the person in a much more realistic and natural environment. With the advancements in technology, this task is highly feasible. Sensors to monitor tailgating, drowsiness detection system to check alertness, deep learning models to detect distraction caused by the use of mobile phones, belt and speed sensors together can be fitted on cars and the candidate put under observation for a period of 1–2 days. Certain parameters that the candidate has to pass in order to obtain the license are laid. The process being fully automated is faster and more wholesome as it monitors the candidate's actual driving on a road.

Keywords: Road accidents · License approval · Internet of Things · Sensor technology · Data collection · Automation

1 Introduction

The rapidly increasing road accidents in India are a matter of concern [4]. 83.38% of publications on road traffic accidents have been written by the Indian authors which shows the severity of the issue [13, 14]. In 2019, 4,49,002 road accidents were recorded all over India out of which 1,51,113 people succumbed to injuries [6]. Out of the fatal road accidents, cases in which the drivers were at fault account for about 56.2% [10]. It is suggested that without any new reforms made, the total number of deaths caused by road accidents is expected to cross the margin of 250,000 by 2025 [11]. There are many other countries with much higher vehicle ownership rates than India but RTI fatality lower rates [12] i.e., increase in vehicle ownership does not account for increased accidents. There is an urgent need to make certain reforms to curb the situation. The case studies suggest some of the major reasons for such accidents to be unethical and distracted driving [1, 2]. Obtaining a driving license brings with it a lot of responsibilities which

Published by Springer Nature Switzerland AG 2022
E. J. Neuhold et al. (Eds.): ICCCSP 2022, IFIP AICT 651, pp. 299–313, 2022.
https://doi.org/10.1007/978-3-031-11633-9_21

not only include driving safely but staying alert and keeping the cars moving around you also safe. Therefore, the parameters assessed to issue a license should be much more than driving on an empty track. The candidate should be evaluated based on his alertness, adherence to rules, distraction extent while driving. The current driving license obtainment procedure does not cover the evaluation of all the above mentioned parameters. Thus, many candidates who lack practical sense to drive on roads are granted the license [3]. The license approval procedure needs to be reformed in order to ensure that licenses are issued to responsible drivers.

The solution aims to promote safe driving on roads and check if the drivers are aware of the road ethics before being granted the license. The proposed solution suggests an additional test that should be conducted along with the existing procedure. The additional test should be conducted without any manual intervention to evaluate the candidate in his most natural state. This will help us know the actual driving instincts of the candidate. The test should be conducted in the candidate's personal vehicle fitted with sensors and cameras to record every movement for the duration of the test. The candidate would be expected to drive the vehicle for a stipulated amount of time in the monitoring period of two days. Each time the vehicle is started, the person driving the car is validated using the camera and checked if he is the same applicant as registered. The camera will record the alertness and distraction of the candidate while driving. The sensors include a belt sensor in the form of a LED light, to know if the belt is worn before driving or not. This will be recorded only once as the engine is started. The other sensors are the speed sensor to record the speed of the car throughout the session and a proximity sensor to measure the distance the car keeps from the car in front of it. The camera monitors the alertness with the help of a drowsiness detection model [8] which stores the timestamp when the candidate's eyes were found to be closed. The candidate is considered to be distracted if he is found to be talking over his phone while driving which is a bad practice. The camera uses a Tensorflow model trained to detect mobile phones in the video frame and each time the phone is detected, the time instance stored. The data collected is further analyzed using the grading system laid beforehand. The rules are laid such that higher priority parameters are evaluated first and then the lesser ones. The observation period for each candidate can be for one to two days and data recorded for each session when the car is drove. The entire process is made automated to ease the monitoring and the result generation task and to help in faster processing of license approval. In the current scenario, one slight error, a single instance of over speeding would result in the candidate failing the test whereas the increased monitoring period suggested in the proposed solution would be beneficial to them as the average speed at which he drove the vehicle would be considered and a considerable number of penalties would be allowed. The proposed grading system carefully assesses the parameters necessary for safe driving and if a person fails to meet the parameters, he is not fit for a license issue. If the number of license approvals are reduced by this method, it is because the applicants are unaware of safe driving practices and thus, incapable of driving on roads. The test cannot guarantee that the person won't repeat the action in future and installing the cameras in personal vehicles permanently to have a constant check on the drivers is not possible. But, having a test for a longer duration wherein the parameters which are very crucial to satisfy while driving safely on roads are assessed does give us a better understanding about the candidate's driving. Thus, by incorporating the proposed solution, the license granting procedure is expected to be more robust and dynamic.

2 Literature Survey

2.1 Aggressive Driving Case Studies and Mitigation in India

This paper deals with the increasing road rages in India. In this, road rages have recently been cited as equalling alcohol-impaired driving in the number of resultant motor vehicle accident related injuries and fatalities. Presently Indian roads and driving conditions are a point of discussion as it is regarded highly unsafe. The paper mainly focuses on the reasons which make Indian roads a death trap. The prime reason for the same tends to be the poor implementation of the set laws [1].

2.2 They do not just Drive When They are Driving: Distracted Driving Practices Among Professional Vehicle Drivers in South India

Driving is a complex task, requiring coordination between multiple mental and physical faculties. Distractions lead to delayed recognition of information needed to drive safely. This paper deals with how certain avoidable distractions taken up by drivers during the course of them being occupied mentally and physically in driving leads to accidents in which they as well as the innocents suffer [2].

2.3 Obtaining a Driver's Licence in India: An Experimental Approach to Studying Corruption

This paper focuses on the ill practices which are prevalent in the licence issuing system of the Indian traffic industry. It highlights the ill practices prevalent present in the system which are making the roads a not so safe place to be in. Corruptions and other such malpractices are being practiced at a very high rate in this industry which has led to its major downfall [3].

2.4 Road Safety in India: Challenges and Opportunities

The paper deals with identifying countermeasures for areas in which the total harm caused by crashes can be substantially and readily reduced. The report focuses on two aspects of traffic safety in India: challenges and opportunities. The major challenges mentioned here are limiting the traffic on the roads and improving the law enforcement infrastructure. Another major highlight of this paper is the improvement in the quality of drivers on the roads as what we see around is quantity but not quality [4].

2.5 A Review on Road Traffic Accident and Related Factors

This paper regards India as one nation which experiences the highest rate of road accidents. The core reason again comes out to be the negligence shown by the under qualified drivers abundant on Indian roads and improper law enforcement. This paper reviews various factors and statistics related to road accidents occurring in various countries and also studies different safety measures suggested by researchers [5].

Based on the literature review conducted coupled with the general on road observations, the below listed factors are needed to be dealt in order to improve the driving standards and road safety in India.

The factors are:

1. Improving the law enforcement infrastructure
2. Improving the quality of drivers on the road.

3 Existing Driving License Issuing System in India

The current driving license issuing system in India is a very simple and straightforward process. A driving test consists of only a short duration test on an empty track which does not really evaluate a person's driving skills when it comes to driving on an actual road.

Description of the existing system [7]:

1. The person applies for DL through a government website.
2. On the website, they first register themselves for the issue of an LL (learner's license).
3. The person gets a date to give the LL test.
4. The test consists of 10 MCQ based traffic laws questions. You need to score a minimum of 60% that is 6 marks to clear the test.
5. Post clearance you are issued an LL for one month.
6. On the completion of the one month, you are eligible for the driving test.
7. The candidate is given a date for the test.
8. On the day of the test, the candidate is required to be present with his/her car and park in a fixed space or go around a circular track or move the car around in a H shape track.

The above mentioned license obtainment procedure only evaluates a person capability to drive slowly on tracks with some turns. Whereas, on driving in a realistic situation on a road full of traffic, the driver has to take care of many things apart from driving slowly. The driver has to take care of tailgating i.e., not drawing too close to the car in front of him and always maintain a safe distance. He also has to be fully alert while driving; not fall asleep, be on his/her phone or involved in any other distraction. The driver should abide by the traffic rules, always wear a seat belt and avoid any kind of rash driving. The driver should always be within the speed limits and avoid over-speeding at all times. All these parameters to assess are overlooked in the existing license obtainment procedure.

4 Proposed Methodology

The proposed solution is to test the drivers in real life driving conditions over a period of time. The focus is to keep the driver in his/ her natural state and then collecting the drive data. The candidate is expected to drive within city limits therefore, expected to drive the vehicle carefully while avoiding any bad practices like over speeding, tailgating and distraction. Monitoring can be done for one or two days within different sessions during different times of the day. The candidate can be asked to drive the car for a certain number of hours on different hours of the day so as to collect enough data for analysis. Based on the collected drive data, a study or an analysis should be conducted and with regard to its output, the license should be granted to the candidate.

In order to collect the drive data, we would require sensors and cameras fitted in a car to record:

1. Speed
2. Distance maintained from other vehicles on the road
3. Belt worn or not
4. Distraction using phones
5. Drowsiness while driving

4.1 Scoring Pattern

The model developed gives scores to the person taking the test based on these parameters. Higher priority is given to more important parameters and only if they are satisfied or within a certain threshold, we move down to check other parameters.

The scoring pattern has been discussed below.

Parameter 1- Belt status

If belt not worn at the start of the session
->FAIL
Only if the belt is worn, the next parameter is assessed.

Parameter 2 - Distraction

The phone usage is monitored and the time stamps recorded,
If more than once,
->FAIL
If not, assess the next parameter.

Parameter 3 - Speed
The person is expected to drive within the city limits, therefore average speed is expected to be between 30 to 50 -> Points =10
If above 60 -> FAIL
If above 50 -> Points = (60 – average speed)
If below 30 -> Points = 3

Parameter 4 - Alertness
The drowsiness timestamps recorded are divided into drowsiness sessions; if difference between two recordings are between 1.5 seconds ~ same session, else ~ drowsiness session(count) incremented
If count > 5 -> FAIL
Else 2 points deducted for each count

Parameter 5 - Distance kept from cars

Ideal distance to be kept from vehicle ahead is told to be at least half of your car speed, otherwise it is considered tailgating.
If violated more than 5 times -> FAIL
Else 2 points deducted for each violation
From sides, 1.5 m to be maintained else 1 point deducted for each after >10 violations

Total points

After all parameters are monitored, the total points awarded are out of 30.
If >20 obtained - PASS
Else - FAIL

4.2 Process Workflow

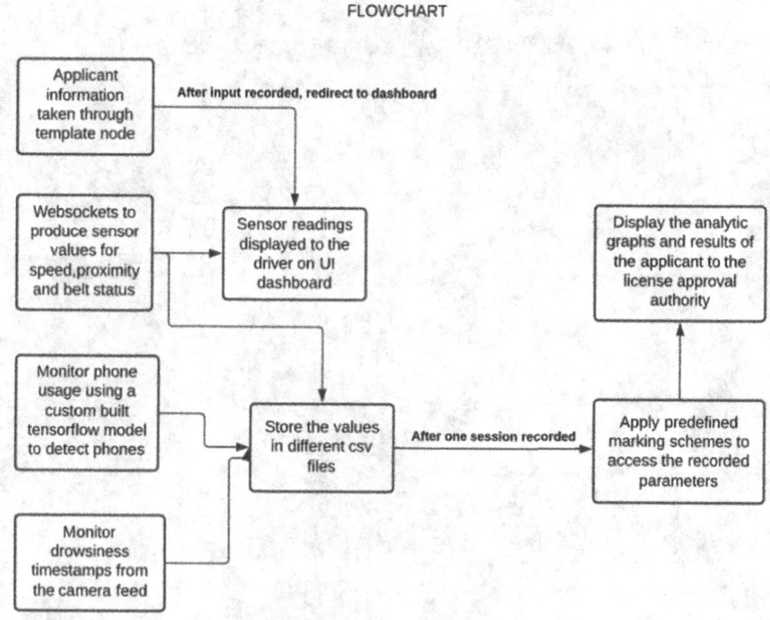

Fig. 1. Flow of the process

Figure 1 represents the complete flow of the Smart License Approval system.

Sensor Data Generation Using Web Socket. As this project involved no hardware, the sensor readings were generated using web sockets. Three server python files were created to generate data for belt status (IN/OUT), speed, and proximity sensor for all four sides of the car. After a client connection is established, through the node-red http request node, the data generation is done and the values generated through a random function between a certain range, is sent to the node-red flow for displaying the same on the UI dashboard and also written to CSV files to facilitate analytics for result generation. The code facilitating the data generation is shown in Fig. 2.

Applicant Interface. Node-red was used to simulate the applicant side of information. It consists of taking the applicant information through a template node and storing it in the backend to help in the result generation. The UI dashboard helps the user view the visual representation of the sensor readings: belt sensor, speed sensor and proximity sensor.

The flow handling the data collection and the applicant's details such that it can be utilized for result generation is shown in Fig. 3.

Drowsiness Detection. A drowsiness detection model uses the eye_aspect_ratio function to determine the ratio of distances between the vertical eye landmarks and the

```
host = '127.0.0.1'
port = 6990
s = socket.socket()
s.bind((host, port))
s.listen(5)
c, addr = s.accept()
data2 = "HTTP/1.1 200 OK\n"+"Content-Type: text/html\n"+"\n"+"connection established"
c.send(data2.encode())
data = c.recv(1024)

c.close()

while True :
    try:
        c, addr = s.accept()
        #generate a random speed instance between the range 20-60
        x = random.randint(20, 60)

        sensor="HTTP/1.1 200 OK\n"+"Content-Type: text/html\n"+"\n"+str(x)
        c.send(sensor.encode())
        data = c.recv(1024)

        with open(filename, 'a',newline='') as csvfile:
            row=[datetime.datetime.now()]
            row.append(x)

            csvwriter = csv.writer(csvfile)
            # writing the data to the csv file
            csvwriter.writerow(row)
    except KeyboardInterrupt:
        break

c.close()
print("\n connection closed!")
```

Fig. 2. Generating sensor data using socket programming

horizontal eye landmarks. The eye aspect ratio stays constant when the eye is open and rapidly decreases towards zero on blinking [9]. If the eye is found to be closed, it will become very small. When the eye is found to be closed using the above mentioned function, the timestamp for the same is recorded and stored in a CSV file to be used for result generation.

Distraction Caused by Phone Usage. To capture the distraction of the applicant, a Tensorflow MobileSSD model was trained to exclusively detect a mobile phone in the video frame. MobileSSD model was chosen as it is a comparatively light weight model and doesn't use up a lot of resources while running.

Result Generation. The sensor data collected through the web sockets and the data collected from the camera feed is analyzed using the scoring pattern mentioned earlier, the points scored calculated for the candidate and the graphs rendered to give some insights into the analysis carried out on the data.

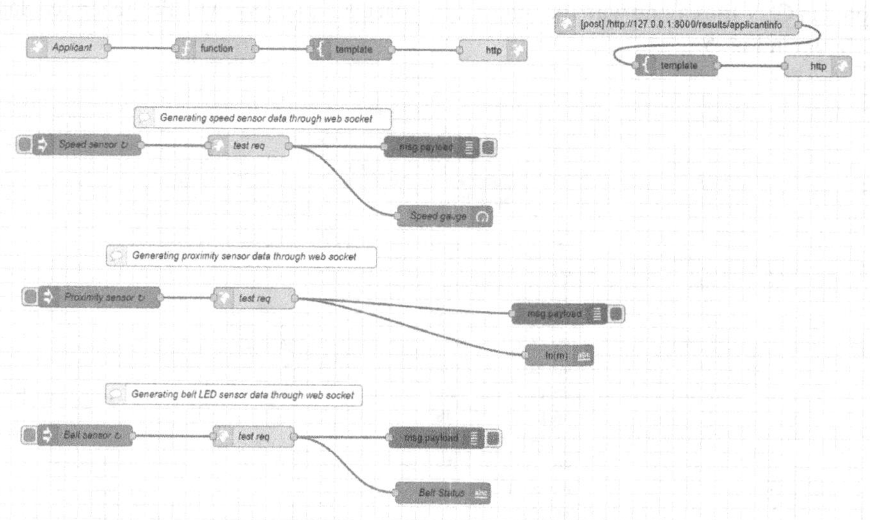

Fig. 3. Flow of information and sensor data collection

5 Experiment

The experiment was carried out by building a Django application along with node-red to show the working of the proposed system.

The applicant's details were collected using a registration form, shown in Fig. 4, such that it could be used throughout the application process and help keep a track of whose application is being processed.

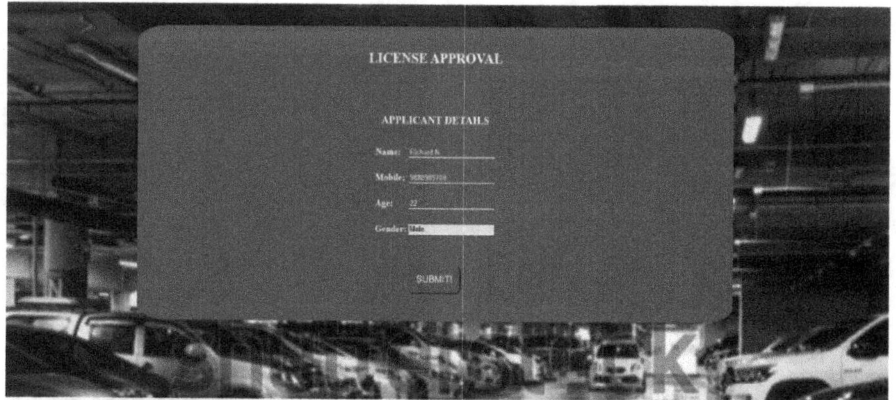

Fig. 4. Applicant details collection form

The sensor data was generated by making appropriate connections to the server script from the http request node to generate data. The generated values were continuously stored in CSV files along with the timestamps. An example CSV with the generated data is shown in Fig. 5.

A2 — 27-11-2021 12:46:07

	A	B	C	D	E
1	Time	Speed			
2	46:07.2	20			
3	46:08.3	47			
4	46:09.3	24			
5	46:10.3	34			
6	46:11.3	33			
7	46:12.3	41			
8	46:13.3	44			
9	46:14.3	48			
10	46:15.3	48			
11	46:16.3	23			
12	46:17.3	33			
13	46:18.3	32			
14	46:19.4	54			
15	46:20.4	55			

Fig. 5. CSV file generated for the speed of the candidate's vehicle at different instances.

The Django application consisted of three modules – detecting phone usage, detecting drowsiness and to view results. The phones usage and drowsiness detection modules used the webcam to detect any mobile phone present in the video frame and monitor if the person's eyes are closed respectively. The timestamps of the instance when the candidate's eyes were found to be closed were also stored in a CSV file.

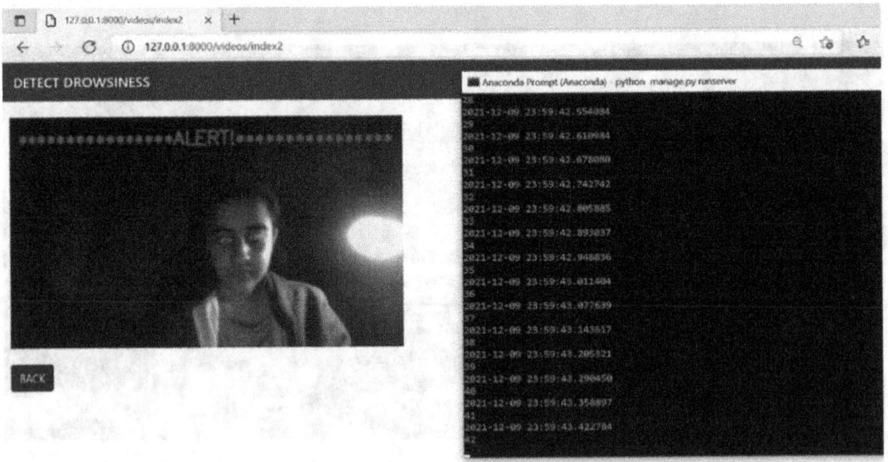

Fig. 6. Timestamp recorded when candidate found to be drowsy.

Figure 6 shows the recorded timestamps displayed in the command prompt.

The live camera feed is taken and the Tensorflow model detects any mobile phones present in the captured frame. Both the modules were tested in a low-lighted environment to test the performance and accuracy of the detection systems. The outputs for the same are shown in Fig. 7 and Fig. 8.

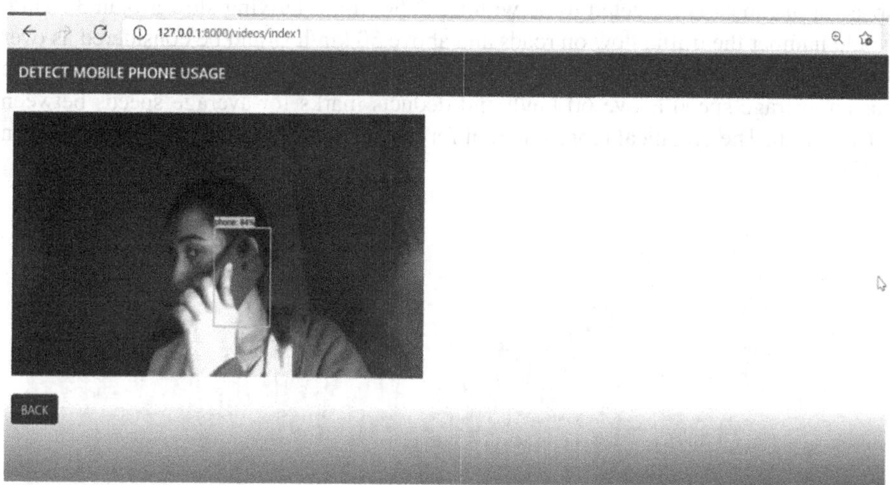

Fig. 7. A visual representation showing the working of distraction monitoring of the applicant. Here, the phone is fully visible in the video frame and detected by the model.

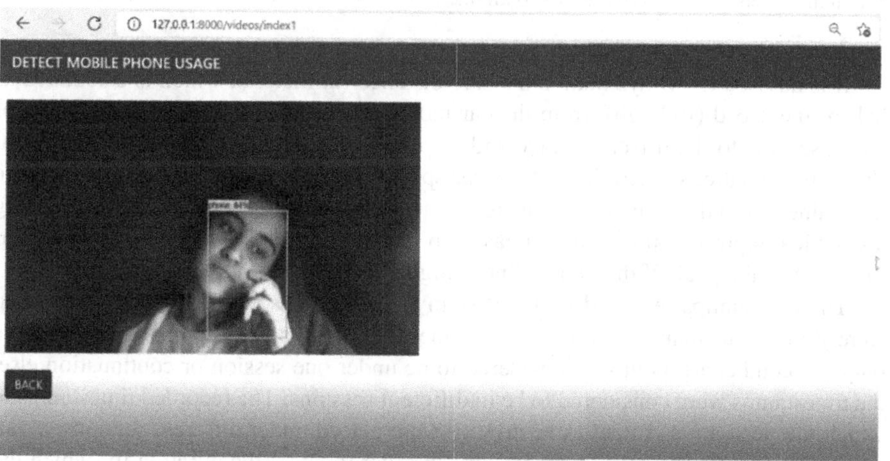

Fig. 8. A visual representation wherein the phone although visible very slightly is still detected by the model with an accuracy of 84%.

6 Results

The collected data is processed and graphical representations provided to facilitate better understanding of the result generation.

The candidate is expected to be driving within city limits therefore, his average speed at all times is expected to be within 30–50 km/h. Driving slower than 30 km/h would hamper the traffic flow on roads and above 50 km/h would be considered as over speeding. Therefore, the scoring pattern directly evaluates the candidate as failed if he has an average speed above 60 km/h and deducts marks for average speeds between 50–60 km/h. The graphical representation for the candidate's speed variations is shown in Fig. 9.

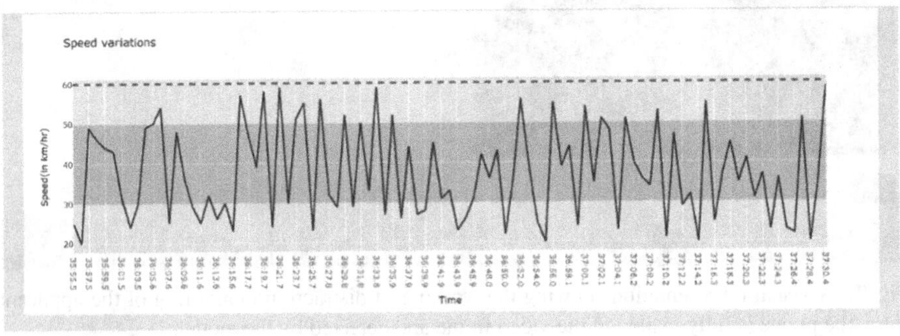

Fig. 9. The speed variations datapoints are plotted and ideal speed expected to be maintained is within the green box i.e. between 30–50 km/h.

It is advised to always maintain a safe distance (in meters), which is calculated as half of the speed (in km/h), from the car moving in front of you to provide ample of response time to the driver to brake and stop his car if required. The graph in Fig. 10 shows the situations where half of the car speed (in km/h) is greater than the distance maintained from the vehicle in front are considered to be instances of tailgating. Having a graphical representation makes it easier to find such instances as on those particular timestamps, the peak of the orange line is higher than that of the blue line.

The timestamps recorded by the system when the person was found to be asleep were grouped to make sessions of drowsiness i.e., if two timestamps recorded were only a second apart, both are considered to be under one session or continuation else, the timestamps were considered to be in different sessions. The recorded timestamps in which the person was found to be drowsy were placed under different sessions which helped in merging the various timestamps in order to count the duration for which the person fell asleep as shown in Fig. 11. Frequently falling asleep would result in failing the driving test as lack of attention is risky for the driver as well as other vehicles on the roads.

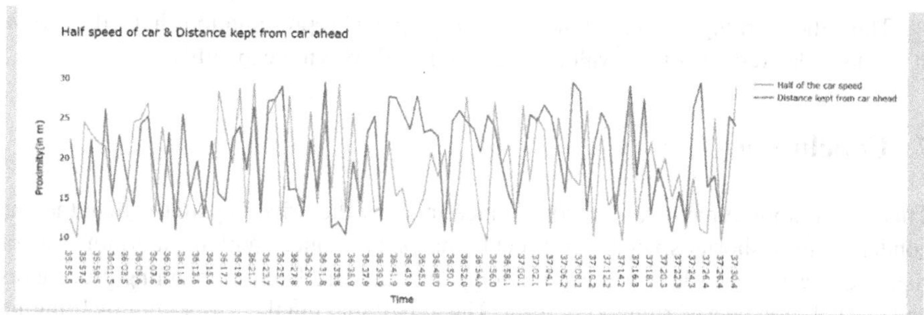

Fig. 10. Plot showing half of the car speed (in km/h) and distance maintained from car in front (in m). (Color figure online)

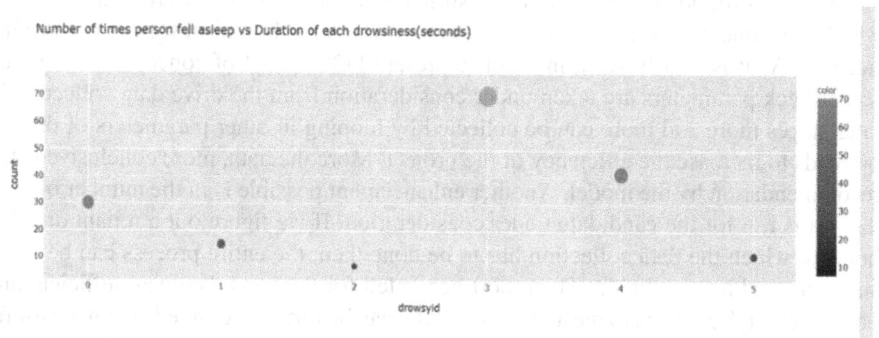

Fig. 11. The recorded drowsiness sessions of the candidate during the assessment.

The candidate's data obtained from the CSV files was evaluated using the scoring pattern as mentioned in Sect. 4, and the final scores obtained after each parameter check added to mark a total score out of 30. The score obtained is displayed on the license authorities' interface along with the candidate's details and the status of his license obtainment test; showing whether he cleared the test or not. On not being able to clear the test, the person is asked to re-appear/apply for the test after 14 days as shown in Fig. 12.

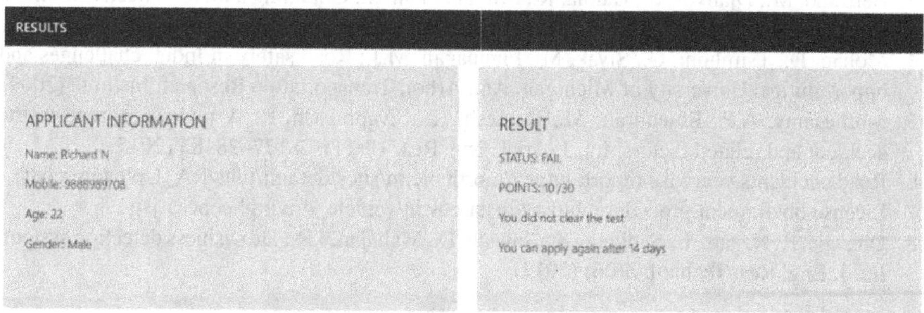

Fig. 12. Auto-generated consolidated report of the candidate

Thus, the marking schema along with the graphical representations helped to arrive at a consolidated decision to evaluate the candidate's driving capability.

7 Conclusion

This test is more dynamic and records much more of the driver's patterns than the one conducted for a shorter span under direct human surveillance. With the alarming rate of rising road accidents, there is a need to refine the standard license obtaining procedures and this solution be a starting point for it. The aim of making the roads safer by bringing in the reliable class of drivers out on the road by the observational test would be achieved if the proposed solution is adapted in its true state without any malpractice encouraged by the citizens and the regulatory authorities.

Although the idea proposed is self-sufficient enough yet there are many ways in which the same can be improved and made a more reliable tool in rolling out driving licenses. As it is clearly seen, in order to present POC (proof of concept) only certain basic check parameters are taken under consideration from the drive data collected. In later stages more and more can be collected by looping in other parameters of driving on roads to increase the efficiency of the project. More the data, more conclusive is the recommendation by the model. Another enhancement possible is in the number of days the test is run for the candidate under consideration. If we figure out a reliant drivable hour for which the data collection has to be done then, the entire process can be made smoother and more reliable. The report generated for the candidate was sufficient and provide enough analysis to the authorities and it can be further extended and made useful to the candidate as well by forwarding the analysis charts to the concerned candidate's email along with his score and some additional comments to help him understand the reason for the not being able to clear the test.

References

1. Chakrabarty, N., Riku, R.: Aggressive driving case studies and mitigations in India. Int. J. Sci. Res. Publ. **3**(2), 1–10 (2013)
2. Abdulkader, R.S., Madhan, C., Jeyashree, K.: They do not just drive when they are driving: distracted driving practices among professional vehicle drivers in South India. Indian J. Commun. Family Med. **5**(1), 34 (2019)
3. Bertrand, M., Djankov, S., Hanna, R., Mullainathan, S.: Obtaining a driver's license in India: an experimental approach to studying corruption. Q. J. Econ. **122**(4), 1639–1676 (2007)
4. Mohan, D., Tsimhoni, O., Sivak, M., Flannagan, M.J.: Road safety in India: challenges and opportunities. University of Michigan, Ann Arbor, Transportation Research Institute (2009)
5. Muthusamy, A.P., Rajendran, M., Ramesh, K., Sivaprakash, P.: A review on road traffic accident and related factors. Int. J. Appl. Eng. Res. **10**(11), 28177–28183 (2015)
6. Road accidents yearwise report. https://morth.nic.in/sites/default/files/RA_Uploading.pdf
7. License obtainment procedure. https://tnsta.gov.in/vehicle_drivinglicence1.jsp
8. Dhawde, P., Nagare, P., Sadigale, K., Sawant, D., Mahajan, J.R.: Drowsiness detection system. Int. J. Eng. Res. Technol. **3**(06) (2015)

9. Mehta, S., Dadhich, S., Gumber, S., Jadhav Bhatt, A.: Real-time driver drowsiness detection system using eye aspect ratio and eye closure ratio. In: Proceedings of International Conference on Sustainable Computing in Science, Technology and Management (SUSCOM). Amity University Rajasthan, Jaipur-India (2019)
10. Singh, H., Kushwaha, V., Agarwal, A.D., Sandhu, S.S.: Fatal road traffic accidents: causes and factors responsible. J. Indian Acad. Forensic Med. **38**(1), 52–54 (2016)
11. Singh, S.K.: Road traffic accidents in India: issues and challenges. Transport. Res. Procedia **25**, 4708–4719 (2017)
12. Mohan, D., Tiwari, G., Bhalla, K.: Road Safety in India: Status Report 2019. New Delhi: Transportation Research & Injury Prevention Programme. Indian Institute of Technology Delhi (2020). www.iitd.ac.in/-tripp
13. Hugar, D., Jayaprakash, G., Naseer, M.M., Waris, A., Khan, M.A.: Road Traffic Accident Research in India: A Scientometric Study from 1977 to 2020 (2018)
14. Goli, S., Shruti, Siddiqui, M.Z., Gouda, J.: High spending on hospitalised treatment: Road traffic accidents and injuries in India. Econ. Political Weekly **53**(14), 52–60 (2018)

Automatic Identification of Heart Abnormalities Using PCG Signals

V. Pravin, Narendran Srinivasan(✉), Palukuri Rohith, U. Vishnu Arvind, and Devi Vijayan

Department of Electronics and Communication Engineering, Amrita School of Engineering, Amrita Vishwa Vidyapeetham, Coimbatore, India
cb.en.u4ece18233@cb.students.amrita.edu, v_devi@cb.amrita.edu

Abstract. A phonocardiogram (PCG) signal holds aural information generated by the heart during a cycle. A close examination of the PCG signal can reveal valuable cardiac information thereby allowing detection of abnormalities and diagnosis of heart diseases. An automation-aided analysis of PCG signals can play a vital role in the medical field, especially in remote patient monitoring, apart from being a very efficient approach. In this study, PCG signals are classified under 5 different classes based on the features extracted. The five classes are normal, mitral stenosis, mitral regurgitation, mitral valve prolapse, aortic stenosis (N, MS, MR, MVP, AS). Mel-Frequency Cepstral Coefficients (MFCCs) are extracted from the PCG audio signals and fed into a deep learning based convolutional neural network (CNN). The proposed approach achieves a maximum accuracy of 99.64% which outperforms the existing state-of-the-art approaches.

Keywords: Mel-Frequency Cepstral Coefficients · 2-D Convolutional Neural Network · Cross Validation

1 Introduction

Among all the necessities for the normal functioning of the human body, a healthy heart is the most important. It is the heart that carries out mechanical and electrical activities to ensure blood is pumped to all parts of the body. A problem in the functioning of the heart can therefore be devastating. Cardiovascular diseases (CVDs) are a very common cause of demise for individuals. According to WHO surveys, approximately 33% of all deaths are related to CVDs. An early and accurate detection of abnormalities or diseases can essentially save the lives of countless individuals. Amidst the most popular modalities that exist to monitor the health of a functioning heart are electrocardiogram (ECG), photoplethysmography (PPG) and phonocardiogram [12] (PCG). An ECG signal is a recording of the electrical activity of the heart; a PPG estimates the blood flow rate by employing light based sensors; PCG signals are audio recordings of heart sounds and murmurs present in one cardiac cycle.

Published by Springer Nature Switzerland AG 2022
E. J. Neuhold et al. (Eds.): ICCCSP 2022, IFIP AICT 651, pp. 314–324, 2022.
https://doi.org/10.1007/978-3-031-11633-9_22

A PCG signal is obtained using a machine called phonocardiograph. It uses a high-fidelity microphone to record the sounds and murmurs made by the heart. There are two fundamental heart sounds in every PCG signal - S1 and S2. These are caused by the atrioventricular and semilunar valves during their closure, and are also what we generally associate with the 'lub-dub' sound our hearts make. The interval between S1 and S2 is called systole ('lub') and the vice versa is called diastole ('dub'). A normal PCG signal contains only S1 and S2, however abnormalities cause other sounds or murmurs to arise and can be labeled as S3, S4 and so on.

Traditionally, a doctor analyses the sounds produced by the heart using a stethoscope and tries to identify any abnormality in the rhythm or the sound. This is a very difficult skill that requires years of exposure to gain proficiency at. Also, there are a myriad of limitations to the human ear as it ages that make detection of pathological symptoms quite inaccurate.

In this paper, MFCCs [4, 14] have been employed because of the similarities in properties that PCG signals have with speech signals. 26 such coefficients are extracted from a single frame. After extraction of features, a 2-D convolutional network ensues that classifies each audio signal into one of the five classes mentioned earlier.

The following graphical representation depicted in Figs. 1, 2, 3, 4 and 5 are PCG signals from individuals having N, MR, MS, MVP and AS conditions.

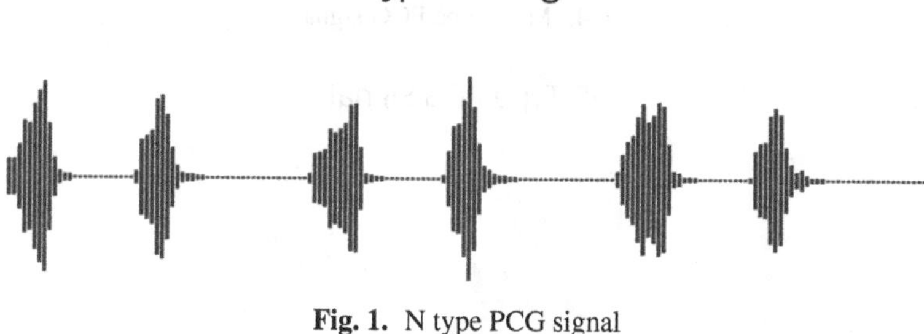

Fig. 1. N type PCG signal

Fig. 2. MR type PCG signal

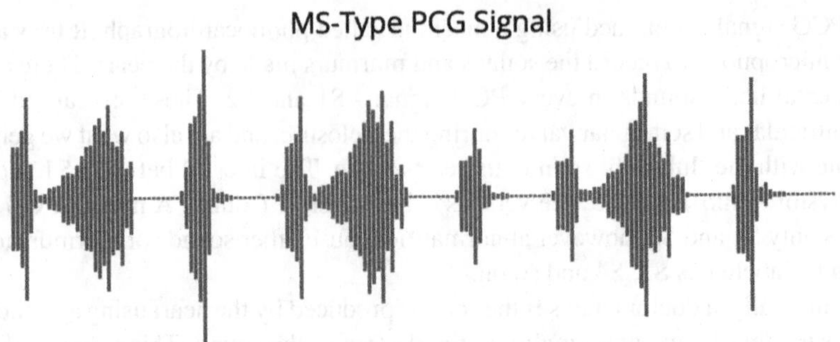

Fig. 3. MS type PCG signal

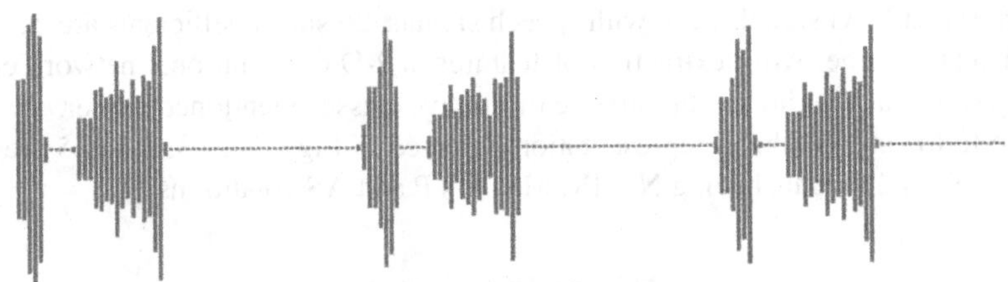

Fig. 4. MVP type PCG signal

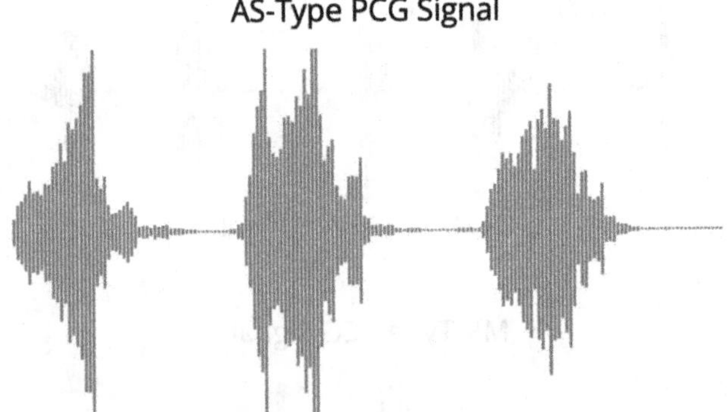

Fig. 5. AS type PCG signal

2 Related Work

Chowdhury et al. [1] employs DWT to decompose the PCG signals into multiple sub-bands having different frequencies. The sub-bands which contain unnecessary noise are dropped. For feature extraction, MFCC and Mel-scaled power spectrograms (Mel- Scale) are used. The latter is then fed through a 5-layered feed-forward DNN model trained by keras. The model has an accuracy, specificity and sensitivity of 97.10%, 94.86% and 99.26% respectively.

K. Poudel et al. [2] encountered a problem of an unbalanced dataset and employed a pre-processing method called SMOTE (Synthetic Minority Over-Sampling Technique) to counter it. Mel-Scale and MFCCs have been used for feature extraction from the PCG signals. They then pass this to a 1-D CNN model that has 4 hidden layers. The layers have been implemented with the ReLu activation function having filters of sizes 128 to 1024, with each increment doubling in size. The PCG signal is then classified in the database. The authors have used Shannon energy envelopes to develop a segmentation technique. The model has an accuracy of 93.20%, specificity of 94.20% and sensitivity of 89.20%.

Alkhodhari et al. [3] have used the combination of CNN and Bi-LSTM for the automatic extraction of features from the PCG signals. The VHD classes namely AS, MR, MVP, MS were preprocessed by MODWT and z-scoring normalization. The model was tested and trained using a 10-fold cross validation with CNN-Bi-LSTM network as well as CNN and Bi-LSTM individually. The model has an Accuracy of 99.32%, specificity of 99.58% and Sensitivity of 98.30%

The work of N. Baghela et al. [4] proposes a machine learning model to automatically diagnose CVDs using PCG signal. The model has a combination of 1-D CNN layers and Dense layers. Extensive preprocessing such as pitch correction, amplitude normalization, etc were done along with augmentation to increase the dataset size. The model was trained and evaluated using 10-fold cross validation, with an accuracy of 98.6%.

Shuvo et al. [5] have employed automatic detection of CVDs under the classes - N, AS, MR, MS and MVP using raw PCG signals. They use a CRNN architecture for this. Their model has representational and sequence residual learning phases. The time invariant features of the PCG signal are extracted using Adaptive Feature Extractor (AFE), Frequency Feature Extractor (FFE) and Pattern Extractor (PE), which are all included under representational learning. The latter includes bidirectional connections, which is used for the extraction of temporal features. Their model achieved 99.6% accuracy in the GitHub dataset and 86.57% in the Physionet dataset.

Li Oh et al. [6] proposed the WaveNet model which consisted of 6 residual blocks. 1000 PCG signals were collected from an open database which consisted of signals from 5 different classes. The signals were resampled at 8 Khz and were then normalized between -1 to 1. The model was cross-validated using 10 folds. It was trained for 3 epochs and the optimization algorithm used was Adam. The learning rate was set to 0.0005. The model has an average accuracy of 97%.

3 Proposed Methodology

2-D CNNs [13] are widely used in image recognition and object detection. For audio signals, 1-D convolutions are preferred as the kernel is only expected to slide across the time axis. In this paper, we extracted Mel Frequency Cepstral Coefficients from the audio signals. MFCCs are represented as 2-D data, with one axis representing the coefficient and the other axis representing time. We extracted 26 such coefficients. The magnitude of the frequency is represented by color. As a result, the MFCCs can be considered as a 2-D image. We have used 2048 samples in a window with a hop length of 512. The proposed methodology is depicted in Fig. 6.

3.1 Block Diagram

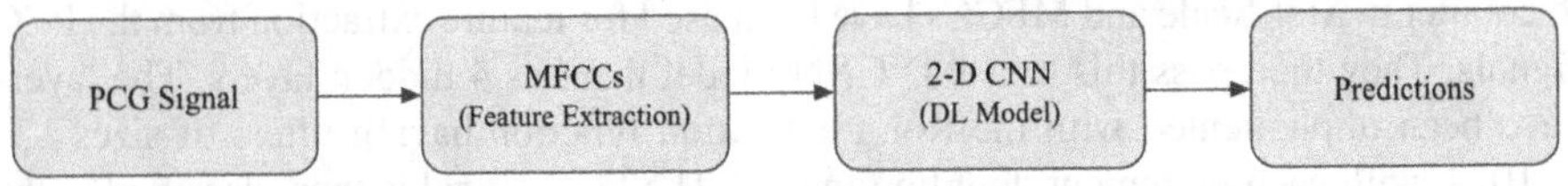

Fig. 6. Block diagram

3.2 Architecture and Training

Table 1. Model architecture

Layer	#Filters, Size	#Neurons	Strides, Padding	Activation
2-D Convolution	32, (3,3)		1, 'Same'	ReLu
2-D Convolution	32, (3,3)		1, 'Same'	ReLu
2-D Max Pooling	-, (2,2)		(2,2), None	-
2-D Convolution	64, (3,3)		1, 'Same'	ReLu
2-D Max Pooling	-, (2,2)		(2,2), None	-
2-D Convolution	128, (3,3)		1, 'Same'	ReLu
2-D Max Pooling	-, (2,2)		(2,2), None	-
2-D Convolution	64, (3,3)		1, 'Same'	ReLu
Dense		512	-	ReLu
Dense		256	-	ReLu
Dense		5	-	Softmax

- Input layer: 32 filters of dimensions 3 × 3 with stride size set to 1 and padding set to 'same' and activation function set to relu, resulting in an output dimension of (26, 44, 32) (Table 1).
- Hidden Layer 1: 32 filters of dimensions 3 × 3, stride size set to 1, padding set to 'same' and activation function set to relu.
- Hidden Layer 2: 64 filters of dimensions 3 × 3 with stride size set to 1, padding set to 'same' and activation function set to relu.

- Hidden Layer 3: 128 filters of dimensions 3 × 3 stride size set to 1, padding set to 'same' and activation function set to relu.
- Hidden Layer 4: 64 filters of dimensions 3 × 3 with stride size set to 1, padding set to 'same' and activation function set to relu. The output is flattened.
- Hidden Layer 5: Dense layer comprising 512 units and activation function as relu.
- Hidden Layer 6: Dense layer comprising 256 units and activation function as relu.
- Output Layer: Dense layer comprising 5 units and activation function as softmax.

The model was trained for 15 epochs on a Tesla K80 GPU. The loss function used was categorical cross entropy, with Adam being the choice of the optimizer with a learning rate of 0.001.

4 Results and Discussion

The dataset (link included) used in this study includes a total of 1000 PCG signals from patients (inclusive of both sexes and all age groups) with normal and 4 different valvular heart diseases (MS, MR, MVP, AR). The 1000 signals are divided into the 5 classes of 200 signals each. The duration of each signal is fixed at 2 s. To evaluate the performance metrics of the model, cross validation with fold size 10 has been used.

Table 2 shows the results of the cross validation with accuracy as the parameter.

Table 2. Training and validation accurary of each fold

Fold	Training Accuracy	Validation Accuracy
1	100%	100 %
2	100 %	99.49 %
3	100 %	98.97 %
4	100 %	100 %
5	100 %	100 %
6	100 %	98.46 %
7	100 %	100 %
8	100 %	99.49 %
9	100 %	100 %
10	100 %	100 %
	Average	**99.64 %**

Table 3. Parameter values of each fold

Fold	Parameters	AS	MR	MS	MVP	N
1	Precision	1.00	1.00	1.00	1.00	1.00
	Recall	1.00	1.00	1.00	1.00	1.00
	F1-Score	1.00	1.00	1.00	1.00	1.00
2	Precision	1.00	0.97	1.00	1.00	1.00
	Recall	1.00	1.00	1.00	0.97	1.00
	F1-Score	1.00	0.99	1.00	0.99	1.00
3	Precision	0.98	1.00	1.00	0.97	1.00
	Recall	1.00	0.97	1.00	0.97	1.00
	F1-Score	0.99	0.99	1.00	0.97	1.00
4	Precision	1.00	1.00	1.00	1.00	1.00
	Recall	1.00	1.00	1.00	1.00	1.00
	F1-Score	1.00	1.00	1.00	1.00	1.00
5	Precision	1.00	1.00	1.00	1.00	1.00
	Recall	1.00	1.00	1.00	1.00	1.00
	F1-Score	1.00	1.00	1.00	1.00	1.00
6	Precision	0.98	1.00	1.00	0.97	0.98
	Recall	1.00	0.95	1.00	0.97	1.00
	F1-Score	0.99	0.97	1.00	0.97	0.99
7	Precision	1.00	1.00	1.00	1.00	1.00
	Recall	1.00	1.00	1.00	1.00	1.00
	F1-Score	1.00	1.00	1.00	1.00	1.00
8	Precision	1.00	1.00	1.00	0.97	1.00
	Recall	1.00	1.00	0.97	1.00	1.00
	F1-Score	1.00	1.00	0.99	0.99	1.00
9	Precision	1.00	1.00	1.00	1.00	1.00
	Recall	1.00	1.00	1.00	1.00	1.00
	F1-Score	1.00	1.00	1.00	1.00	1.00
10	Precision	1.00	1.00	1.00	1.00	1.00
	Recall	1.00	1.00	1.00	1.00	1.00
	F1-Score	1.00	1.00	1.00	1.00	1.00
Average	Precision	0.99	0.99	1.00	0.99	1.00
	Recall	1.00	0.99	0.99	0.99	0.99
	F1-Score	0.99	0.99	0.99	0.99	1.00

The lowest validation accuracy was 98.46% and the highest validation accuracy was 100%. The mean validation accuracy across all the folds was 99.64%.

Table 3 shows the performance of the model for each class on metrics such as precision, recall and F1-scores for all 10 folds. The following parameters are calculated as follows:

$$Precision = \frac{TP}{FP + TP} \tag{1}$$

$$Recall = \frac{TP}{TP + FN} \tag{2}$$

$$F1\text{-}Score = 2 * \frac{Precision * Recall}{Precision + Recall} \tag{3}$$

Table 3 shows the parameter values for all the folds while Table 4 compares the model presented in this paper with other models.

The following figures present the confusion matrices for folds that do not have a validation accuracy of 100%.

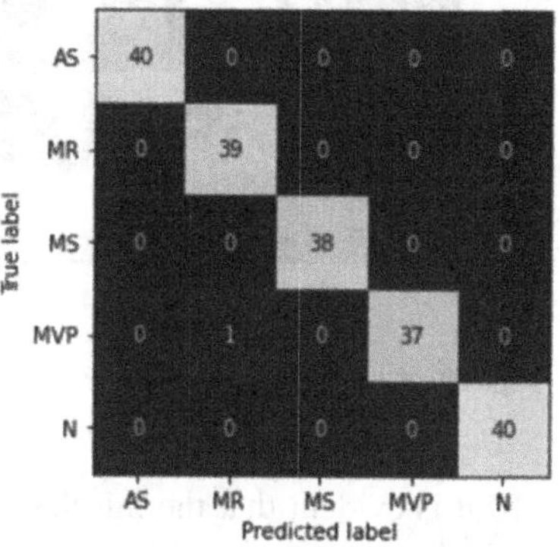

Fig. 7. Confusion matrix for Fold 2

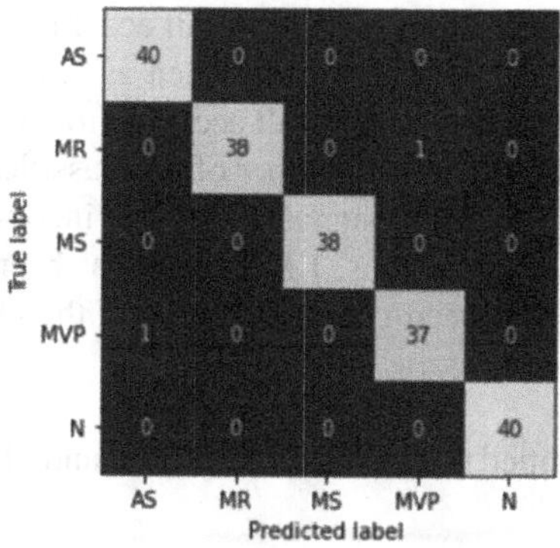

Fig. 8. Confusion matrix for Fold 3

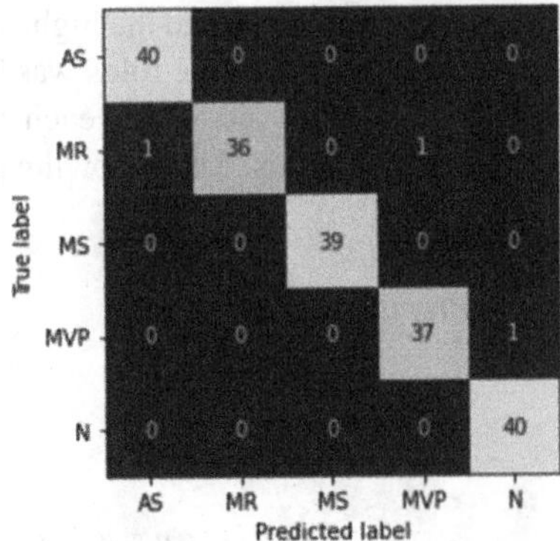

Fig. 9. Confusion matrix for Fold 6

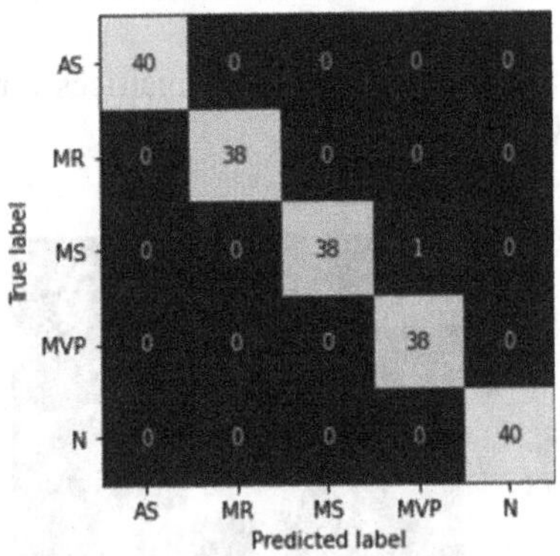

Fig. 10. Confusion matrix for Fold 8

From Figs. 7, 8, 9 and 10 it is evident that the misclassifications have occurred at certain instances.

- In the confusion matrix for fold 2, as shown in Fig. 7, 1 signal attributed to MVP has been misclassified as MR, resulting in an overall accuracy of 99.49%.
- For fold 3, 1 MVP signal has been misclassified as AS and 1 MR signal has been misclassified as MVP, lowering the overall accuracy to 98.97%.
- Fold 6 shown in Fig. 9 has the most number of misclassifications and hence the least overall accuracy of 98.46%. 2 MR signals have been incorrectly classified as AS and MVP respectively. In addition to this, 1 MS signal has been misclassified as N.
- In fold 8, 1 MS signal has been classified as MVP thereby resulting in an overall accuracy of 99.49%.

MR is incorrectly classified three times, while MVP and MS signals are misclassified twice.

Even though MFCCs are not traditional two-dimensional images, the 2-D CNN model was able to perform surprisingly well. It matches and even surpasses the performance of 1-D CNN and LSTM [15] in some cases.

Table 4. Study comparison

Model	Features	Accuracy
MD Chowdhury et al. [1]	MFCC, Mel-Scale	97.10%
M. Chowdhury et al. [2]	MFCC	93.20%
Li Oh et al. [6]	Deep Learned	97.00%
Yaseen et al. [9]	MFCC, Wavelet	87.2%
P.Lubaib et al. [10]	MFCC, envelope detection	99.01%
Ghosh et al. [11]	Chirplet transform	98.33%
Proposed Study	**MFCC, 2-D CNN**	**99.64%**

5 Conclusion

Manual detection of heart abnormalities is a challenging and time-consuming task that requires specific expertise. This study proposes a computer aided diagnosis (CAD) system using 2-D CNN for classification of cardiovascular diseases. 2-D CNNs are uncommon in the audio domain, but continue to gain traction. The proposed method achieves an average 10-Fold cross validation accuracy of 99.64%, which surpasses many other state of the art models in this dataset. This model does not require extensive pre-processing and is relatively light-weight. The overall accuracy of the model may be further improved by performing data augmentation.

The main limitation of the proposed work is the lack of multi-class PCG datasets. While there are multiple datasets for binary PCG signal datasets, it is not the case for non-binary datasets.

References

1. Chowdhury, T.H., Poudel, K.N., Hu, Y.: Time-frequency analysis, denoising, compression, segmentation, and classification of PCG signals. IEEE Access **8**, 160882–160890 (2020). https://doi.org/10.1109/ACCESS.2020.3020806
2. Chowdhury, M., Poudel, K., Hu, Y.: Detecting abnormal PCG signals and extracting cardiac information employing deep learning and the shannon energy envelope. IEEE Signal Process. Med. Biol. Symp. **2020**, 1–4 (2020). https://doi.org/10.1109/SPMB50085.2020.9353624
3. Alkhodari, M., Fraiwan, L.: Convolutional and recurrent neural networks for the detection of valvular heart diseases in phonocardiogram recordings. Comput. Methods Programs Biomed. **200**, 105940 (2021). https://doi.org/10.1016/j.cmpb.2021.105940
4. Baghel, N., Dutta, M.K., Burget, R.: Automatic diagnosis of multiple cardiac diseases from PCG signals using convolutional neural network. Comput. Methods Programs Biomed. **197**, 105750 (2020). https://doi.org/10.1016/j.cmpb.2020.105750. Epub 2020 Sep 10 PMID: 32932128

5. Shuvo, S.B., Ali, S.N., Swapnil, S.I., Al-Rakhami, M.S., Gumaei, A.: CardioXNet: a novel lightweight deep learning framework for cardiovascular disease classification using heart sound recordings. IEEE Access **9**, 36955–36967 (2021). https://doi.org/10.1109/ACCESS.2021.3063129
6. Oh, S.L., et al.: Classification of heart sound signals using a novel deep WaveNet model. Comput. Methods Programs Biomed. **196**, 105604 (2020). https://doi.org/10.1016/j.cmpb.2020.105604. Epub 2020 Jun 12 PMID: 32593061
7. Ismail, S., Siddiqi, I., Akram, U.: Localization and classification of heart beats in phonocardiography signals—a comprehensive review. EURASIP J. Adv. Sig. Process. **2018**(1), 1–27 (2018). https://doi.org/10.1186/s13634-018-0545-9
8. Yang, T.-C., Hsieh, H.: Classification of acoustic physiological signals based on deep learning neural networks with augmented features. In: 2016 Computing in Cardiology Conference (CinC), pp. 569–572 (2016)
9. Yaseen, Son, G.-Y., Kwon, S.: Classification of Heart Sound Signal Using Multiple Features. Appl. Sci. **8**, 2344 (2018). https://doi.org/10.3390/app8122344
10. Lubaib, P., Ahammed Muneer, K.V.: the heart defect analysis based on PCG signals using pattern recognition techniques. Procedia Technol. **24**, 1024–1031, ISSN 2212–0173. https://doi.org/10.1016/j.protcy.2016.05.225
11. Ghosh, S.K., Ponnalagu, R.N., Tripathy, R.K., Acharya, U.R.: Automated detection of heart valve diseases using chirplet transform and multiclass composite classifier with PCG signals. Comput. Biol. Med. **118**, 103632 (2020). https://doi.org/10.1016/j.compbiomed.2020.103632. Epub 2020 Jan 30 PMID: 32174311
12. Kesav, R.S., Bhanu Prakash, M., Kumar, K., Sowmya, V., Soman, K.P.: Performance improvement in deep learning architecture for phonocardiogram signal classification using spectrogram. In: Singh, M., Tyagi, V., Gupta, P.K., Flusser, J., Ören, T., Sonawane, V.R. (eds.) ICACDS 2021. CCIS, vol. 1440, pp. 538–549. Springer, Cham (2021). https://doi.org/10.1007/978-3-030-81462-5_48
13. Kishore, S.L.S., Sidhartha, A.V., Reddy, P.S., Rahul, C.M., Vijaya, D.: Detection and diagnosis of Covid-19 from chest X-ray images. In: 2021 7th International Conference on Advanced Computing and Communication Systems (ICACCS), pp. 459–465 (2021). https://doi.org/10.1109/ICACCS51430.2021.9441862
14. Supriya, P., Jayabarathi, R., Jeyanth, C., Ba, Y., Sarvesh, A., Shurfudeen, M.: Preliminary Investigation for Tamil cine music deployment for mood music recommender system. In: 2020 6th International Conference on Advanced Computing and Communication Systems (ICACCS), pp. 1111–1115 (2020). https://doi.org/10.1109/ICACCS48705.2020.9074249
15. Sujadevi, V.G., Soman, K.P., Vinayakumar, R., Sankar, A.U.P.: Deep models for phonocardiography (PCG) classification. In: 2017 International Conference on Intelligent Communication and Computational Techniques (ICCT), pp. 211–216 (2017). 10.1109/ INTELCCT.2017.8324047

Self Driving Car in a Constrained Environment

B. Harish and Durairaj Thenmozhi(✉)

SSN College of Engineering, Chennai, India
harish17049@cse.ssn.edu.in, theni_d@ssn.edu.in

Abstract. The purpose of the research is to build a machine learning model which can drive a car on the tracks of Udacity's Car simulator without any human intervention. This is achieved by mimicking the human driving behaviour in the training mode on a track. A dataset is generated by the simulator based on the human driving behaviour in the training mode and a deep learning model is built using this dataset which is then used to drive the car autonomously on any unseen track. Initially the model performed well only on the already seen track and failed to perform well on new unseen tracks. The simulator track in which the car was trained with didn't consist of any sharp turns or elevations or any other road barriers, but the real world tracks do contain them, so in order to overcome this problem image processing techniques like zooming, changing brightness, flipping images, panning were used and in order to avoid over-fitting problem more dataset was generated using data augmentation techniques. Finally a model was built which was able to generalise the tracks and drive the car autonomously on the unseen track of the simulator.

Keywords: Self-driving car · Deep learning · Automation · Machine learning · Udacity · Unity · Track · Roads · ELU activation function · Constrained environment

1 Introduction

This section describes the need of autonomous cars and the objectives of our research work.

1.1 Motivation

Today, driving has become a stress full job, people going on long trips get tired because of driving and lose their focus many times due to which accidents happen, this can be solved through model-based and learning-based [3] approaches in order to achieve full vehicle autonomy without or with minimum human intervention. Perceiving the scenes, controlling the vehicles and choosing a best and

Published by Springer Nature Switzerland AG 2022
E. J. Neuhold et al. (Eds.): ICCCSP 2022, IFIP AICT 651, pp. 325–339, 2022.
https://doi.org/10.1007/978-3-031-11633-9_23

safe path to drive remains a challenge. A machine learning model is needed which can aid the car to drive autonomously in the real world tracks which has lot of constraints like pot holes, elevations, speed breakers etc. With advancement in technologies and many things getting automated it's time to automate the driving task by building a model which can handle a lot of edge cases and the error produced by it should be extremely small.

1.2 Objectives

The governing objectives of the study are:

- To create a driving dataset using Udacity Simulator which can provide high definition pictures and video for the development of a deep learning model, similar to the famous NVIDIA model [1].
- To identify the right tools and techniques which can help in providing a safe vehicle autonomy.
- The car must be capable of driving within the lanes of the track.

2 Related Work

Muddassir Ahmed Khan [2] has undertaken this research work 4 years ago. For data generation, images were picked from the metadata provided driving_log.csv file and passed through the augmentor to get the training data. The top and bottom 25 pixels of the images are ignored, in order to get rid of the front of the car from the images, he has used various augmentation techniques like image flipping, brightness variation, adding shadows to the images. When he trained the network using such data alone the network went off the track and wasn't able to drive properly. He then included the left and right images with various offsets such as 0.3, 0.2, but these values led to large shifts in the steering and the car would wear off the track. 0.3 worked fine when training the network for few epochs but when the number of epochs was increased the vehicles started to move in a zig-zag fashion across the road with more and more hard turns. At the last moment he changed the offset to 0.09 and started getting better results.

In 2017, Albin Falk and David Granqvist from Chalmers University of Technology, University of Gothenburg [8], Sweden proposed that by integrating deep learning and conventional computer vision based techniques, redundancy can be introduced and it can minimize the unsafe behaviour in autonomous vehicles. A control algorithm was constructed to combine the advantages of a lane detection algorithm with a deep neural network which ensures the vehicle stays within the appropriate lane. The proposition makes it evident that the system shows better performance when a combination of the two technologies were run in a simulator than using them independently.

In 2018, Aditya Babhulkar from California State University, Sacramento has undertaken this research work [9]. The dataset was collected by driving the car on Track_1 of the simulator in the training mode, and the simulator provided the dataset in a csv file which consisted of steering angle and the path to then directory in which the images of the track were stored. During the autonomous mode the simulator acts as a server and the images captured from the single center camera of the car are sent to the client python program which uses the built neural network model and send back a steering angle to the car to drive autonomously on the Track_2 of the simulator in autonomous mode. The model was built using sequential models provided by Keras.

3 Proposed Methodology

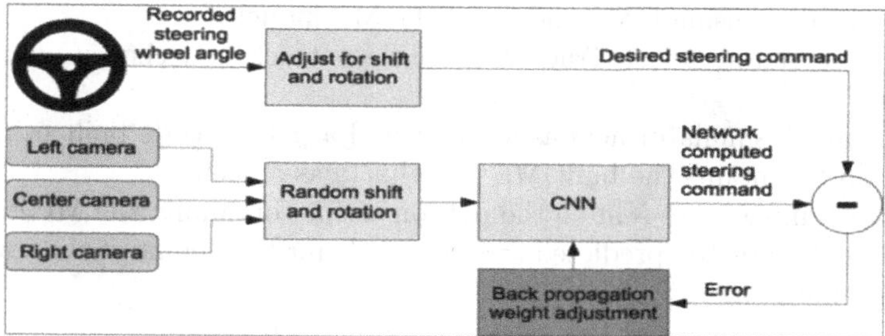

Fig. 1. Bird's eye view of the system's working

Figure 1 shows an overview of our system. The images from the three cameras attached to the car in the training mode of the simulator, are fed to the CNN model which predicts a steering angle for that part of the track, this predicted steering angle is compared to the desired steering angle proposed by human for that part of the track. And the weights of the CNN are adjusted to bring the CNN output closer to the desired output. Weight adjustment is accomplished using back propagation. Once trained, the network is able to generate steering commands for driving left, straight or right from the video images of a single center camera provided by the simulator in autonomous mode. Figure 2 shows this configuration.

4 Algorithm

- Open Unity Self Driving car simulator powered by Udacity.
- Select Track-1, the primitive track and choose training mode.
- Turn on recording mode and start collecting the data - track images and steering angle.
- Perform Data Manipulation i.e. changing or altering the collected data.
- Perform Data Augmentation.
- Pre-process the data.

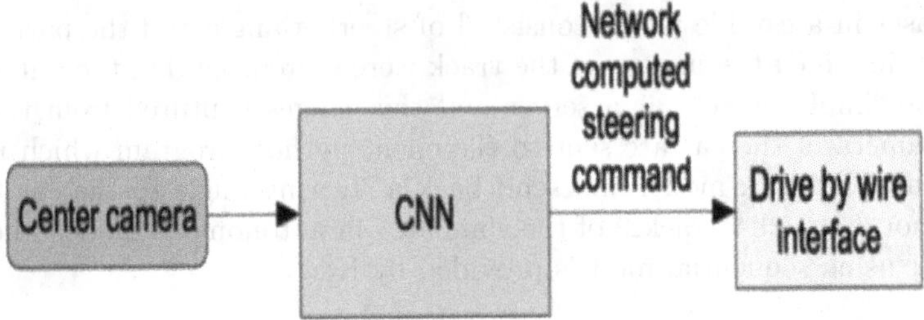

Fig. 2. The CNN predicts a steering angle for the images from the single center camera of the car in the autonomous mode of the simulator.

- Train the data using CNN and build the ML model.
- In the simulator, select Track-2 the unseen track and choose autonomous mode.
- In this mode simulator acts as a server and a python code built using Flask framework contains the built ML model acts as a client.
- The track images are sent to the python script containing the ML model.
- ML model sends the predicted steering angle for that point of the track back to the simulator.
- Test the performance of the model in the simulator.

4.1 Udacity Simulator

Unity simulator by Udacity [7] is used for training the self-driving car. The simulator provides two types of tracks, Track-1 is a circular track with a few sharp turns and no elevations, this is the track which was used for data collection purposes. Track-2 is a very complex track with a lot of sharp turns, ups and downs through out the end of the track, this is the track where we tested the car using the built machine learning model. The simulator has two modes - Training mode, where an user can move the car using his keyboard and Autonomous mode where the car is moved by instructions given by ML model. The car in the training mode has 3 cameras attached to it and in autonomous mode has a single camera attached to it.

4.2 Assumptions and Limitations

- No other cars are present along the track.
- No speed breakers are present.
- No human interventions along the track.
- Performance is affected by hardware specification, performance will be good only if run on machines with atleast 8 GB of Ram and quad cores.
- No split lanes in the track. Assuming just a one way track.
- Udacity has released a newer version where we can train the car to handle the lane changes, it will be considered in the future works.

- Road traffic with few vehicles, hurdles and risks will be considered in the future works.
- A speed limit variable is set to control the speed of the car while driving autonomously. It's value can range from 5 MPH to 30 MPH (max speed of the car).

4.3 Data Collection

Steps involved in the data collection are

- Training mode is turned on for Track-1 and data collection process is started.
- Various images of the track are captured.
- The simulator also records the Steering angle and speed of the car.
- The simulator provides the recorded data in CSV format.
- Size of the collected dataset = 25641 images of Track-1
- Amount of data used for Training = 15384
- Amount of data used for Testing on Track-2 = 10257

4.4 Data Manipulation

The car provided by the simulator in the training mode contains 3 cameras attached in it's front part. The cameras are located on the left, center and right side in the front part of the car. The idea is to make the images captured by the left and the right cameras as though they were captured by the center camera, this is done by adding a bias to their steering angles, this is necessary because in the autonomous mode the simulator provides only a single center camera to the car. Also by utilizing all the 3 cameras we get a bigger dataset of the track images to train our model, which helped in improving the accuracy of our machine learning model. The distance-arc length between center and left camera (or right camera) is called as bias After trial and error we came up with 0.09 bias, which gave good predictions when trained with our machine learning model. For the images captured by the left camera, 0.09 bias was added to it's steering angle. For the images captured by the right camera, −0.09 bias was added to it's steering angle. These images from left and right cameras after adding the bias were appended to the images captured by the center camera.

In Fig. 3, x-axis shows the range of steering angle and y-axis shows the count of images for that particular steering angle.

Since amount of images available for 0.0, 0.09 and −0.09 steering angle is more, our model will always tend to predict these steering angles making our model predict poorly, so, we deliberately delete some images containing these steering angles from various parts of the track, Fig. 4 depicts the new distribution of steering angle after that deletion.

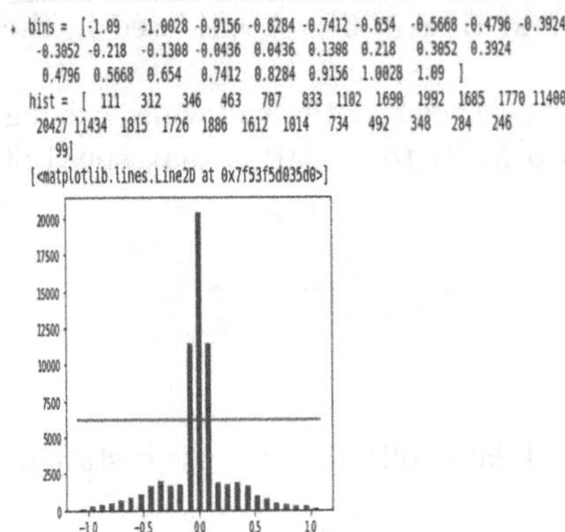

Fig. 3. Histogram of steering angle-1

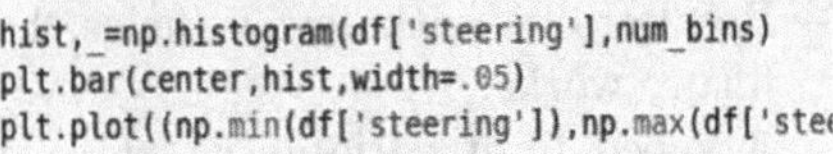

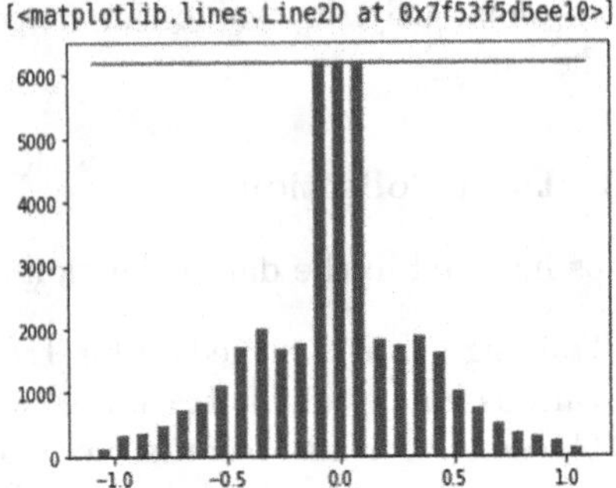

Fig. 4. Histogram of steering angle-2

4.5 Data Augmentation

The biggest challenge was to generalize the car behaviour on Track_2 (unseen track) of the simulator. In real world, we can never train a machine learning model for every available track as it will require a humongous amount of data to train and process it. Real world contains a variety of weather conditions, and it is impossible to build a dataset for all such weather conditions and roads, however by using data augmentation techniques we can create a dataset closer to the real world.

Zooming. Images were zoomed, to get a better view of the track. OpenCV techniques were used to achieve this. Figure 5 shows the original and zoomed track.

Changing Brightness. By changing the brightness of the track images we can generalize the weather conditions. By increasing brightness we can get a track which looks as if it was captured during a sunny day and by decreasing the brightness we can make the track image look like as though it was captured during night time or a cloudy day or a shadow of a building/tree falls on the track. The change in brightness for various images of the track can be seen in the Fig. 6.

Panning/Translation. The image is moved along the x-axis or y-axis, which make the neural network to look everywhere in the image to capture the vital data. The original and translated images are shown in Fig. 7.

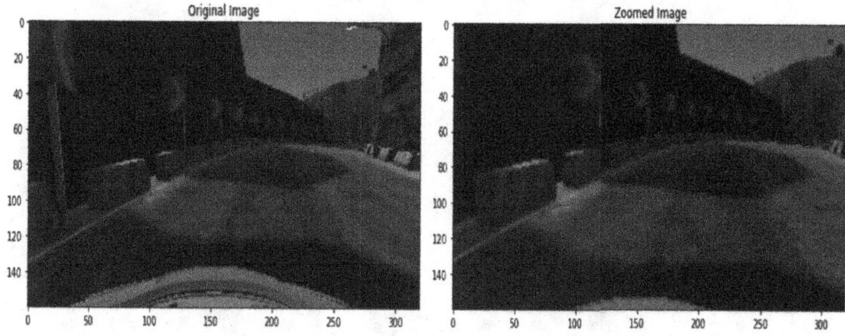

Fig. 5. Zoomed image

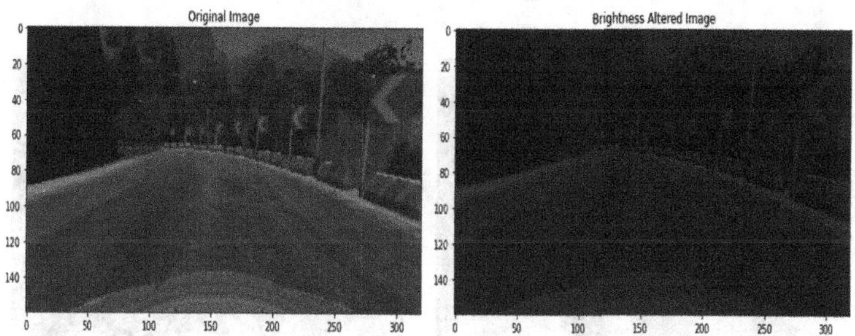

Fig. 6. Brightness altered image

Horizontal Flipping. Sometimes when we collect data, the data may be skewed to left side (or right side), i.e. if the track that we trained contained more no. of left turns compared to the no. of right turns, our model will always predict a left steering angle. Where as in real life tracks have an equal no. of left and right turns. To solve this problem, we randomly select some tracks and flip it horizontally and negating it's corresponding steering angle. This helped in making the dataset to contain nearly equal counts for left and right steering angles. Figure 8 shows the flipped image.

4.6 Pre-processing

The height of the image is reduced to bring focus on the track thereby ignoring the landscapes surrounding the track. The color images(RGB) are converted to YUV(Y-Brightness and UV - color) encoding pattern. Gaussian Blur of size 3 by 3 was applied to the image. Images were resized to the shape 200 by 66. Normalization of the images are done (Fig. 9).

4.7 Training

The recorded data is splitted into x_train and y_train. Figure 12 shows the splitted data, x-axis represents the steering angle, y-axis represents the count of

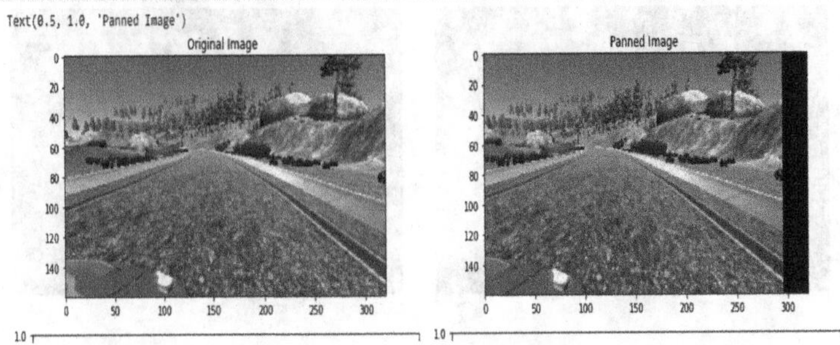

Fig. 7. Panned image

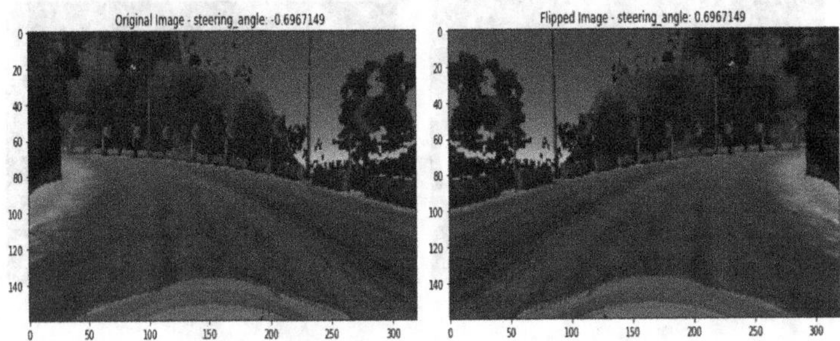

Fig. 8. Flipped image

images for each steering angle. Blue and red plot shows the histogram distribution for training and testing data respectively. x_train contains the images of the track and y_train contains the steering angle of the car.

A convolutional neural network model, is built and 80% of the collected dataset is used for training remaining 20% is used for testing. The weights of the network are adjusted by back propagation to minimize the mean-squared error between the predicted steering angle and the desired steering command of the human driver. Figure 13 shows the network architecture, The network architecture contains nine layers of which there are five convolution layers, three fully connected layers and a normalization layer. The image from the simulator is pre-processed and is converted into YUV planes and is passed to the network.

First layer of the network is normalization layer which performs normalization of the input image. Feature extraction is done by the convolution layers. 2×2 stride convolution and 5×5 kernel are used in the first three convolution layers and the last two convolution layers consist of a non-strided convolution and a 3×3 kernel. The convolution layers are designed to perform feature extraction, and are chosen through a series of experiments that vary layer configurations. We then use strided convolutions in the first three convolution layers with a 2×2 stride and a 5×5 kernel, and a non-strided convolution with a 3×3 kernel size in the last two convolution layers.

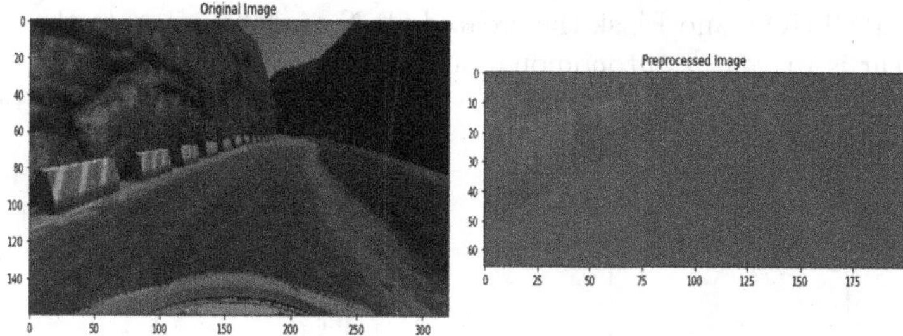

Fig. 9. Pre-processed image

The five convolution layers are shown in Fig. 13. The three fully connected layers which are designed to act as controller for steering, outputs the steering angle. To avoid over-fitting problem, we need a large amount of data to train on, so using data augmentation technique the batch generator creates large amount of data on the fly i.e. only during training after this the training begins. The Rectified Linear Unit-ReLU activation function-R(z) = max(0, z) was used during the initial stages of building and testing the model, however ReLU was not a good choice for this problem because ReLU function returns zero for values less than zero but our steering angles consist of both positive and negative values. So if a neuron gets an input of negative number it will return a value of zero, so the gradient at this point is zero and the weight of this neuron will never be changed because the back propogation uses the gradient value to change the weight values of the neurons. This phenomenon is called as dead ReLU. Due to this the neuron will always receive a value of zero and will always feed forward the value of zero and there is no learning. Sigmoid function can't be used as it would create vanishing gradient problem as our network is complex. So we chose Exponential Linear Unit-ELU activation function which is similar to ReLU in positive region but in negative region it returns the negative number. So unlike ReLU, ELU has a non-zero gradient value in the negative region, which means that it can always recover and fix it's weight parameters to decrease it's error i.e. it is always capable of learning and contributing to the model, unlike ReLU which can essentially die. Figures 10 and 11 shows the ELU, ReLU and Sigmoid functions. Based on the accuracy, the CNN model is modified by changing the no. of neurons, by adding dropout layers, changing the learning rate, data augmentation etc. to improve the accuracy.

Using PYTHON and Flask the created CNN model is given to the simulator and the car is driven in autonomous mode in the selected track. A speed limit is set to the car, the speed of the car increases till that limit and begins to gradually slow down after that.

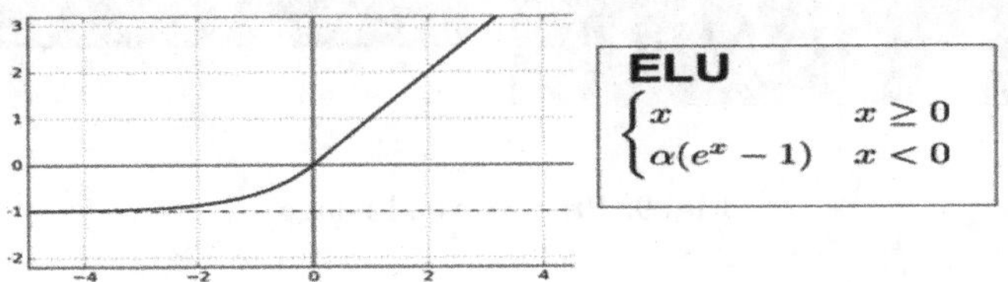

Fig. 10. ELU function

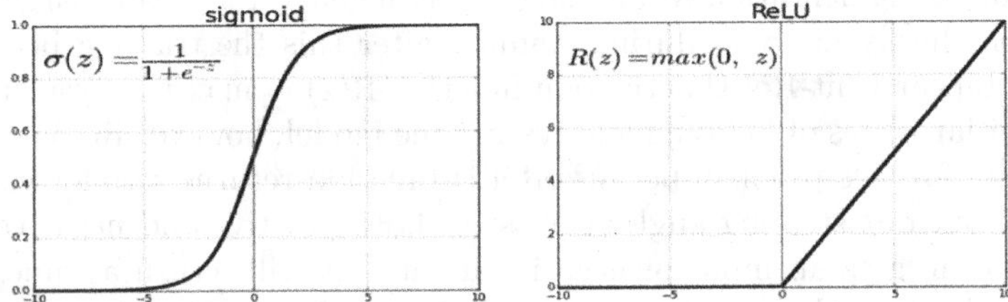

Fig. 11. ReLU and sigmoid functions

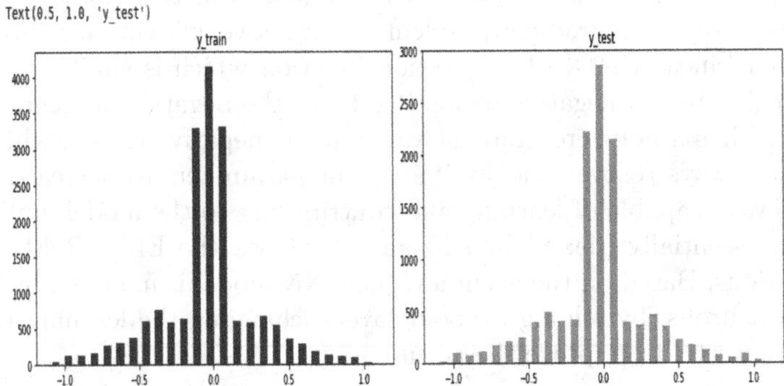

Fig. 12. Histogram distribution of steering angles after train-test split (Color figure online)

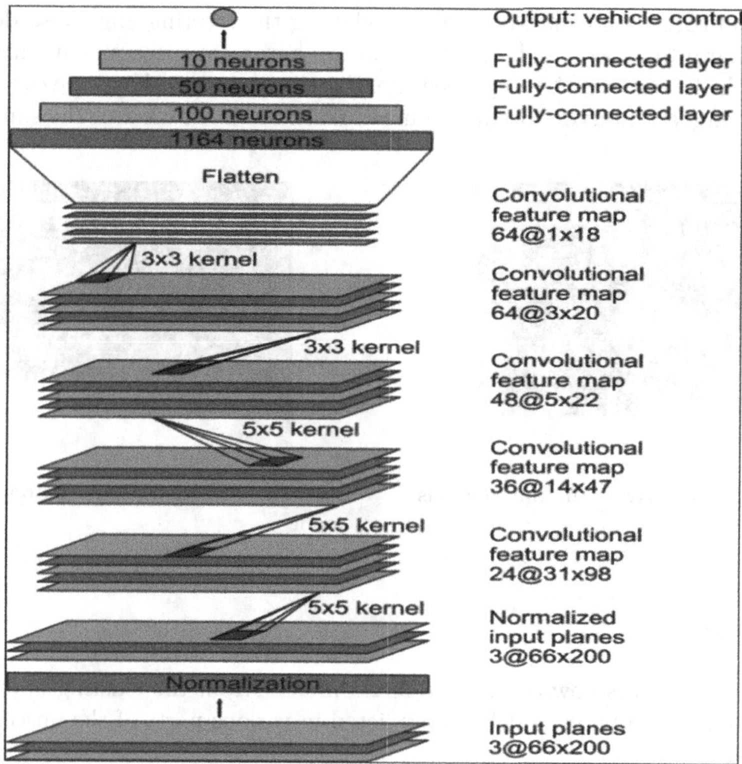

Fig. 13. Architecture

5 Testing

The built model is used in a python application which uses socketio to connect to the udacity simulator (server) by acting as a client. The Udacity simulator in autonomous mode acts as a server. In terminal the python driver file is run after loading the model. Inside the simulator, autonomous mode is selected and Track-2 - the unseen track is chosen. Unseen track is the one which the car has never seen before while training. The simulator sends the track images to the client (python application), which uses the built model to predict the steering angle for the car at that point of the track. The client code returns the steering angle to the simulator. To avoid the car going very fast, a speed_limit variable is used to control the throttle of the car. Response time is the sum of, time to send the track image to ML model, time for ML model to predict the steering angle for that point of track, time to send back the steering angle to the simulator. Here sending back steering angle takes very less time compared to other two factors. It takes a lot of time to send an image from simulator to model, but however since the model is available in local machine we can decrease this time by using it on a machine with decent hardware specs like atleast 8 GB ram and quad cores. And the ML model predicting the steering angle also depends on the hardware specs, so by using the above hardware specs we can altogether reduce the latency i.e. the response time. Figures 14 and 15 shows the car driving without human intervention in an unseen track i.e. in Track-2 of the simulator.

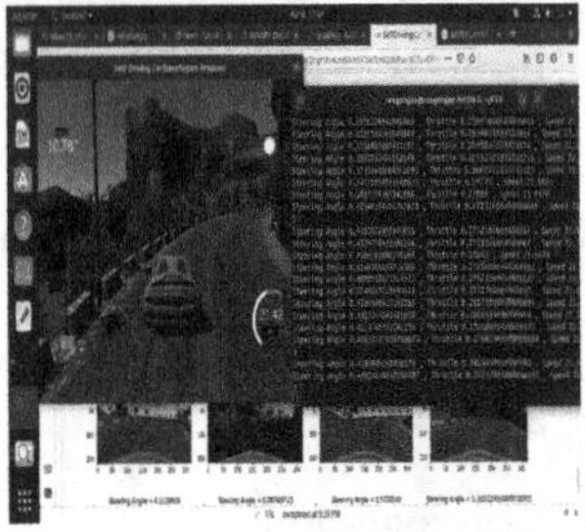

Fig. 14. Car driving in autonomous mode

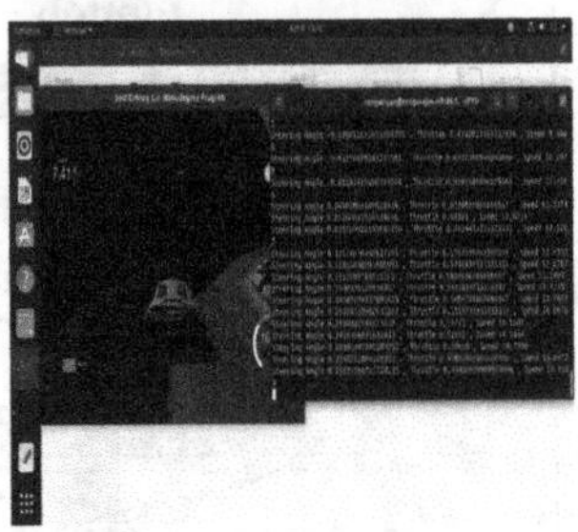

Fig. 15. Car driving in autonomous mode

6 Results

This section shows how our approach is different from the existing approaches and how well the built model has predicted in various parts of the unseen track (Track-2).

Our approach though it uses the same augmentation techniques as with the existing approaches mentioned in the literature survey, how we have used it matters. The existing approaches use all the augmentation techniques at once during data augmentation, whereas in our approach we apply the 4 augmentation techniques (zooming, panning, flipping images and changing brightness) randomly, we select an image at random from the training dataset and then we generate a random number between 0 and 1, if the value is greater than 0.5 we apply zooming technique to it, or else we don't apply zooming to that image, and again we repeat the same for other augmentation techniques. So a particular image chosen for augmentation may be applied with all the 4 augmentation techniques or 3 or 2 or 1 or even none. This approach produces a dataset with increased randomness in the images compared to the existing approaches. Also, we have used ELU activation function which drastically improved the performance in the unseen track i.e. Track-2.

Images below on the left column represent the true value of steering angle (TSA) for that point in the track.

Images on the right column represent the predicted value of steering angle (PSA) for that point in the track.

6.1 Left Curved Roads

See Figs. 16, 17, 18 and 19.

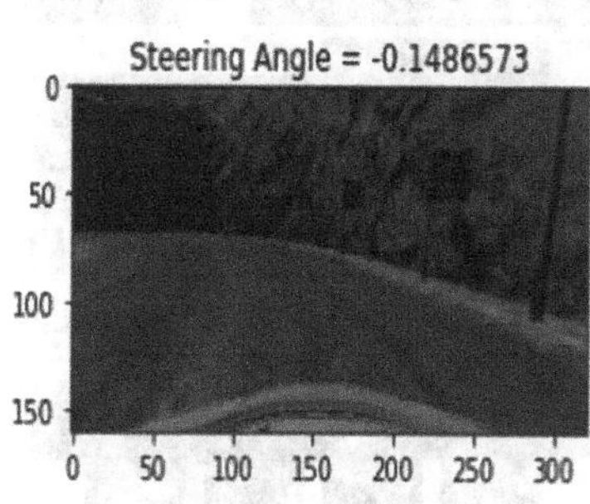

Fig. 16. True SA = −0.148

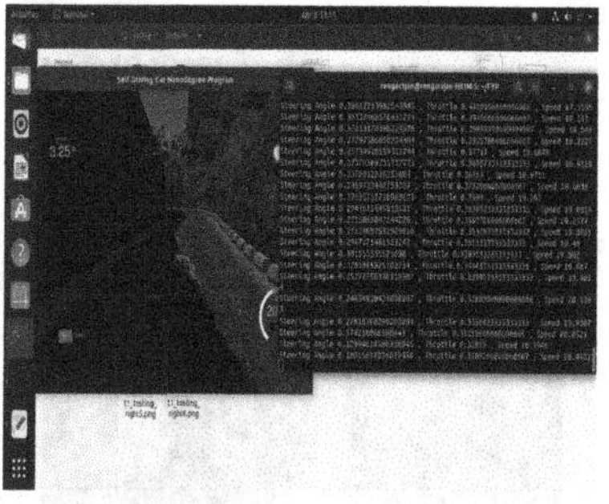

Fig. 17. Predicted SA = −0.106

Fig. 18. True SA = −0.238

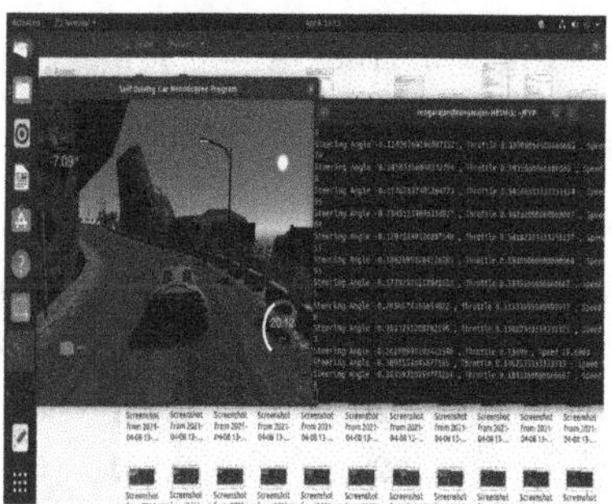

Fig. 19. Predicted SA = −0.283

6.2 Right Curved Roads

See Figs. 20, 21, 22 and 23.

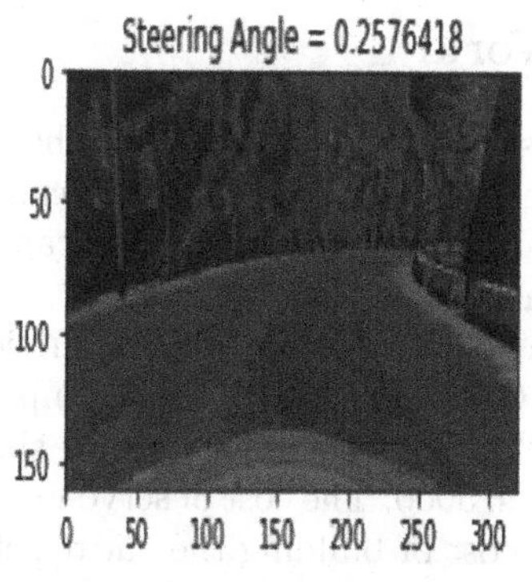

Fig. 20. True SA = 0.257

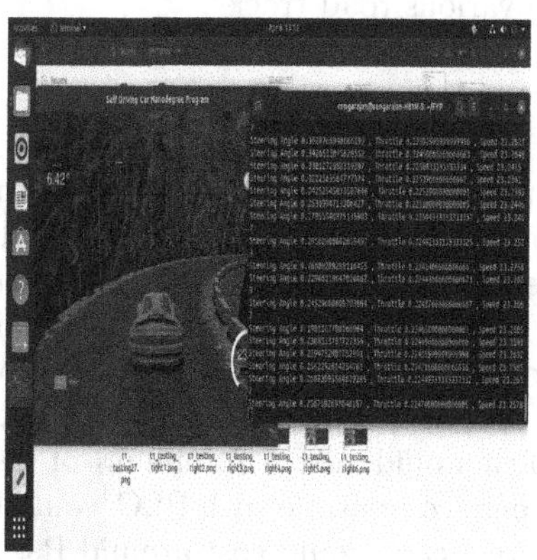

Fig. 21. Predicted SA = 0.256

Fig. 22. True SA = 0.381

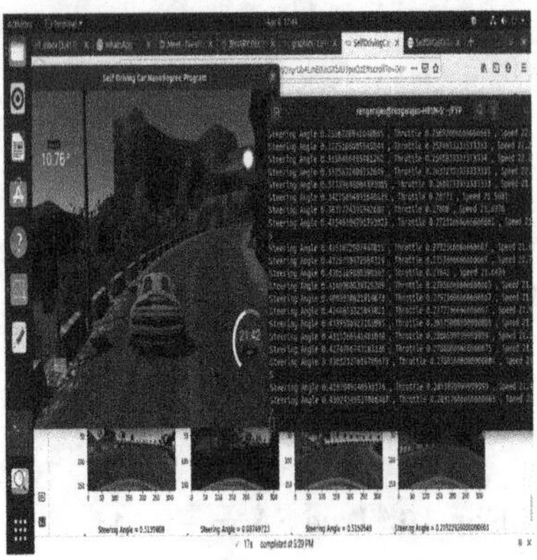

Fig. 23. Predicted SA = 0.430

S. No	Figure No	TSA	PSA	$\|PSA - TSA\|$	$\|PSA - TSA\|^2$
1	16,17	−0.148	−0.106	0.042	0.00176
2	18,19	−0.238	−0.283	−0.045	0.00202
3	20,21	0.257	0.256	−0.001	1.0000e−06
4	22,23	0.381	0.430	0.049	0.002401

$$\text{MSE(Mean Squared Error)} = \sum_{i=1}^{4} \|PSA - TSA\|^2/4 = 0.00154$$
$$\text{RMSE(Root Mean Squared Error)} = \sqrt{\sum_{i=1}^{4} \|PSA - TSA\|^2/4} = 0.03934$$

The table above shows the difference between True Steering Angle (TSA) and Predicted Steering Angle (PSA) i.e. $\|PSA - TSA\|$, $\|PSA - TSA\|^2$, for the various road tracks.

7 Scope of Deployment in Real World

Since this research focused on working in a constrained environment, in the real world it could be used in places like industries where unmanned cars can be used for transporting goods. The minimum hardware requirement is a camera to capture the track images, servo/induction motors to drive the car based on predicted steering angle and a computer to run the model and give instructions to the car. We can use a Programmable Logic Controller (PLC) as a computer which would cost a minimum of Rs. 20000. The cost of a good quality single camera compatible with PLC would be around Rs. 5000. The cost of servo motors for real cars would cost around Rs. 20000. The cost of building the entire setup would be around Rs. 20000. So the total cost to deploy this work with minimum hardware configurations in a constrained environment in the real world would be around Rs. 65000.

8 Conclusions and Future Work

This research started with capturing images of the tracks, using computer vision [4,6] OpenCV techniques to add shadows to tracks, zooming of tracks, etc. Initially the model performed well only on the already seen track and failed to perform well on new unseen tracks. So, many models were built by changing the parameters like the number of neurons or the activation function so that the model was able to generalize road conditions and achieve the similar performance on different tracks. The spatial features were obtained by using CNN [5]. In this research we used only the data obtained from the simulator, future works can be carried out by combining simulator data with the real world data and already many experimental configurations are being carried out in the field of autonomous cars. The models used in this research were built sequentially using Keras, future works can be done by trying parallel network layers for learning the specific track behaviour which can lead to an increase in performance. In this research the simulated environment didn't consist of traffic environment, multiple lanes, obstacles or other cars along the track, when these are placed on the tracks they would make it more closer to a real world environment and a challenge for the self-driving cars.

References

1. Bojarski, M., et al.: End to end learning for self-driving cars. arXiv preprint arXiv:1604.07316 (2016)
2. Khan, M.A.: Making A Virtual Self-Driving Car, Published on 1 April 2017. https://muddassirahmed.medium.com/making-a-virtual-self-driving-car-2d81f3f539e8
3. Fridman, L., et al.: MIT autonomous vehicle technology study: large-scale deep learning based analysis of driver behavior and interaction with automation. arXiv preprint arXiv:1711.06976 (2017)
4. Dai, J., et al.: Deformable convolutional networks. In: Proceedings of the IEEE International Conference on Computer Vision, pp. 764–773 (2017)
5. Jmour, N., Zayen, S., Abdelkrim, A.: Convolutional neural networks for image classification. In: 2018 International Conference on Advanced Systems and Electric Technologies (ICASET), pp. 397–402. IEEE (2018)
6. Badrinarayanan, V., Galasso, F., Cipolla, R.: Label propagation in video sequences. In: 2010 IEEE Conference on Computer Vision and Pattern Recognition (CVPR), pp. 3265–3272. IEEE (2010)
7. Naoki, Introduction to Udacity Self-Driving Car Simulator, Published on 25 February 2017. https://naokishibuya.medium.com/introduction-to-udacity-self-driving-car-simulator-4d78198d301d
8. Falk, A., Granqvist, D.: Combining deep learning with traditional algorithms in autonomous cars (2017)
9. Babhulkar, A.: Self-driving car using udacity's car simulator environment and trained by deep neural networks (2019)

Author Index